Phonetics, Phonology, and Cognition

OXFORD STUDIES IN THEORETICAL LINGUISTICS

General editors
David Adger, Queen Mary College London; Hagit Borer, University of Southern California

Advisory editors
Stephen Anderson, Yale University; Gennaro Chierchia, University of Milan; Rose-Marie Dechaine, University of British Columbia; Elan Dresher, University of Toronto; James Higginbotham, University of Southern California; Pat Keating, University of California, Los Angeles; Ruth Kempson, King's College, University of London; James McCloskey, University of California, Santa Cruz; Gillian Ramchand, University of Tromsø; Maria-Luisa Zubizarreta, University of Southern California

Published

1 The Syntax of Silence
Sluicing, Islands, and the Theory of Ellipsis
by Jason Merchant

2 Questions and Answers in Embedded Contexts
by Utpal Lahiri

3 Phonetics, Phonology, and Cognition
edited by Jacques Durand and Bernard Laks

4 At the Syntax-Pragmatics Interface
Concept Formation and Verbal Underspecification in Dynamic Syntax
by Lutz Marten

5 The Unaccusativity Puzzle
Explorations of the Syntax-Lexicon Interface
edited by Artemis Alexiadou, Elena Anagnostopoulou, and Martin Everaert

6 Beyond Morphology
Interface Conditions on Word Formation
by Peter Ackema and Ad Neeleman

7 The Logic of Conventional Implicatures
by Christopher Potts

8 Paradigms of Phonological Theory
edited by Laura Downing, T. Alan Hall, and Renate Raffelsiefen

9 The Verbal Complex in Romance
by Paola Monachesi

In preparation

Aspects of the Theory of Clitics
Stephen Anderson

Stratal Optimality Theory
Synchronic and Diachronic Applications
Ricardo Bermúdez Otero

The Syntax of Aspect
Edited by Nomi Erteschik-Shir and Tova Rapoport

Tense, Mood, and Aspect
edited by Alessandra Giorgi, James Higginbotham,and Fabio Pianesi

The Ecology of English Noun-Noun Compounding
by Ray Jackendoff

A Natural History of Infixation
by Alan Chi Lun Yu

The Oxford Handbook of Linguistic Interfaces
edited by Gillian Ramchand and Charles Reiss
[*published in association with the series*]

Phonetics, Phonology, and Cognition

edited by
JACQUES DURAND
and
BERNARD LAKS

OXFORD
UNIVERSITY PRESS

*This book has been printed digitally and produced in a standard specification
in order to ensure its continuing availability*

OXFORD

UNIVERSITY PRESS

Great Clarendon Street, Oxford OX2 6DP

Oxford University Press is a department of the University of Oxford.
It furthers the University's objective of excellence in research, scholarship,
and education by publishing world-wide in

Oxford New York

Auckland Bangkok Buenos Aires Cape Town Chennai
Dar es Salaam Delhi Hong Kong Istanbul Karachi Kolkata
Kuala Lumpur Madrid Melbourne Mexico City Mumbai Nairobi
São Paulo Shanghai Taipei Tokyo Toronto

Oxford is a registered trade mark of Oxford University Press
in the UK and in certain other countries

Published in the United States
by Oxford University Press Inc., New York

ISBN 0-19-829984-2

Antony Rowe Ltd., Eastbourne

Contents

Oxford Studies in Theoretical Linguistics

General Preface

The theoretical focus of this series is on the interfaces between subcomponents of the human grammatical system and the closely related area of the interfaces between the different subdisciplines of linguistics. The notion of 'interface' has become central in grammatical theory (for instance, in Chomsky's recent Minimalist Program) and in linguistic practice: work on the interfaces between syntax and semantics, syntax and morphology, phonology and phonetics etc. has led to a deeper understanding of particular linguistic phenomena and of the architecture of the linguistic component of the mind/brain.

The series will cover interfaces between core components of grammar, including syntax/morphology, syntax/semantics, syntax/phonology, syntax/pragmatics, morphology/phonology, phonology/phonetics, phonetics/speech processing, semantics/pragmatics, intonation/discourse structure as well as issues in the way that the systems of grammar involving these interface areas are acquired and deployed in use (including language acquisition, language dysfunction, and language processing). It will demonstrate, we hope, that a proper understanding of particular linguistic phenomena, languages, language groups, or inter-language variation all require reference to interfaces. The series is open to work by linguists of all theoretical persuasions and schools of thought. A main requirement is that authors should write so as to understood by colleagues in related subfields of linguistics and by scholars in cognate disciplines.

Jacques Durand and Bernard Laks and the authors they have assembled here address the question of what kinds of cognitive status should be imputed to phonological representations and how these representations are implemented phonetically. The chapters consider these questions from a variety of perspectives, bringing to bear arguments from classical universal-grammar based analyses, statistical and inferential approaches, and neurobiology. The initial chapter by the editors sets the scene for the debate which is developed in the rest of the book.

David Adger
Hagit Borer

Contributors

Christian Abry obtained a Doctorat d'État in Linguistics from the University Stendhal, Grenoble (France) in 1997, where he is Professor of Experimental Phonetics, Head of Linguistics, and leader of the Articulatory Modelling team at the Institute of Speech Communication (ICP) (CNRS UMR 5009). His current interests are speech control research in production, perception and decision, from the articulatory to the narrative organizations.

Renée Béland is a professor in the speech pathology department at Université de Montréal, and a researcher at the Centre de recherche of the Institut universitaire de Gériatrie de Montréal. She is currently in charge of multidisciplinary research projects focusing on the role of phonology in developmental and acquired dyslexia.

Louis-Jean Boë is an engineer, has a Ph. D. degree in electronics, and is also a phonetician. He is a researcher at the Institute of Speech Communication (ICP) at the University of Grenoble and a member of its board of directors. His main interests lie in sound structures in relationship with ontogenesis and phylogenesis, the history of the speech sciences and the deontological problems of forensic applications of phonetics.

Joaquim Brandao de Carvalho is a Senior Lecturer in Linguistics at the University René Descartes (Paris 5). After publishing widely on the evolution of the syllable in Ibero-Romance, his research has focused on the notion of markedness in phonology. This has led him to make original proposals on the nature and identity of phonological primitives and on the internal structure of segments.

Wiebke Brockhaus, Senior Lecturer in German Linguistics at the University of Manchester, has published mainly on aspects of the phonology of German and on the application of phonological theory to language engineering. She is the author of *Final Devoicing in the Phonology of German* (1995, Niemeyer).

Marie-Agnès Cathiard has a Doctorate in Cognitive Psychology from the University of Grenoble II (1994). She is 'Maître de Conférences' in Phonetics at Stendhal (Grenoble III) and a researcher at the Institute of Speech Communication (UMR CNRS 5009, Grenoble) on the multimodal integration of speech, with a special interest to perceptuo-motor interaction.

John Coleman is the author of *Phonological Representations* (CUP, 1998) and co-author of *Acoustics of American English Speech* (Springer-Verlag, 1993). He worked on speech technology at the universities of Hull and York before going to AT&T Bell Laboratories. Since 1993, he has been Director of Oxford University Phonetics Laboratory.

Jean-François Démonet, MD, PhD, is a neurologist and neuropsychologist working as Director of Research in a laboratory of INSERM in Toulouse (France). His work is devoted to neuropsychological and neuroimaging studies (PET, fMRI, and ERPs) of language functions and dysfunctions in normal subjects and patients suffering from aphasia, developmental dyslexias, and dementias.

Emmanuel Dupoux is Director of the Laboratoire de Sciences Cognitives et Psycholinguistique in Paris. His areas of expertise include psycholinguistics, speech processing in monolinguals and bilinguals, and the biological bases of language. He is specifically interested in the role of phonology in spoken word recognition and early language acquisition.

Jacques Durand is Professor of Linguistics in the English Department of the University of Toulouse-Le Mirail and a member there of the CNRS team,

Equipe de Recherche en Syntaxe et Sémantique, where he leads the phonology section. He is the author and editor of several books on phonology, including *Generative and Non-Linear Phonology* (1990), *Frontiers of Phonology* (1995, with F. Katamba) and *Current Trends in Phonology* (1996, with B. Laks).

Ludovic Ferrand is a researcher at the Laboratoire de Psychologie Expéri-mentale, CNRS and Université René Descartes, Paris. He completed his Ph.D. at the Ecole des Hautes Etudes en Sciences Sociales in Paris, and was a post-doctoral fellow at the University of Birmingham. His research interests lie in psycholinguistics.

John Goldsmith is the Edward Carson Waller Distinguished Service Professor of Linguistics at the University of Chicago, where he has been since 1984. He received his Ph.D. from MIT in 1976 for a dissertation entitled Autosegmental Phonology. He is the author of *Autosegmental and Metrical Phonology* (1990), co-author of *Ideology and Linguistic Theory* (1996) and *The Chicago Guide to Your Academic Career* (2001), and editor of the *Handbook of Phonological Theory* (Blackwell, 1995).

Michael Ingleby is Reader in Applied Mathematics at the University of Huddersfield. His interests are in general pattern recognition and artificial intelligence, and include improving the speaker-independence of automatic speech recognisers. With King Abdulaziz University, Jeddah, he is working on a recogniser for modern standard Arabic that incorporates knowledge of the phonology of that language. Within an EU funded consortium headed by the Dutch police, he also works on recognition of earprints for forensic purposes.

Rafael Laboissière got his PhD degree at INPG, France, in 1992. He is currently a CNRS researcher and worked at the Institut de la Communication Parlée, Grenoble. Since September 2001 he is with the Max-Planck Institut für Psychologische Forschung, Munich, Germany. His research interests includes biomechanics and neurophysiological modelling of motor control, and acoustical/articulatory relationships in speech.

Bernard Laks is Professor of Linguistics at the University of Paris X and the Director there of the CNRS team *Modèles, Dynamiques, Corpus*. He is the author of *Langage et cognition* (1996) and *Phonologie accentuelle* (1997). He has edited a number of books on phonology, including *Current Trends in Phonology* (1996, with J. Durand). His recent work has been in the area of language from a connectionist perspective.

Jean-Luc Nespoulous is Professor of Neuropsycholinguistics at the University of Toulouse-Le Mirail (Department of Language Sciences). He is Director of the Laboratoire Jacques-Lordat: Centre Interdisciplinaire des Sciences du langage et de la Cognition (E.A 1941) and of the Institut des Sciences du Cerveau de Toulouse (I.F.R No96.FR 2254). Over the past 30 years, he has constantly been involved in research programs on language disturbances in aphasia.

Carole Paradis is Professor at Laval University, supervising a multidisciplinary research project on phonological constraints, namely in loanwords. She developed the theory of constraints and repair strategies, expounded in an influential article in *The Linguistic Review* in 1988. She also edited *The Special Status of Coronals* with J.-F. Prunet (Academic Press, 1991) and *Constraint-Based Theories* with D. LaCharité (*Canadian Journal of Linguistics*, 1993).

Sharon Peperkamp is an assistant professor at the University of Paris 8, and an associated researcher at the Laboratoire de Sciences Cognitives et Psycholinguistique. Her research concerns the early development of linguistic knowledge and its consequences for adult speech processing. Specifically, she investigates the bootstrapping of phonological categories and rules during the first year of life.

Jean-Luc Schwartz received his Ph.D. in psychoacoustics from the Institut de la Communication Parlée (ICP), Grenoble, France, in 1981. He obtained a Doctorat d'État in the field of auditory modelling and vowel perception in 1987. Since 1983, he has been employed by the Centre National de la Recherche Scientifique, and leads the Speech Perception Group at ICP. His main areas of research involve auditory modelling, psychoacoustics, speech perception, auditory front-ends for speech recognition, bimodal integration in speech perception and source separation, perceptuo-motor interactions, and speech robotics.

Juan Segui is Director of the Laboratoire de Psychologie Expérimentale, CNRS and Université René Descartes (Paris). He is also Research Director at the Centre National de la Recherche Scientifique and has published extensively in psycholinguistics. He completed his Ph.D. at Université René Descartes in Paris. His research interests include speech perception and production, and visual word recognition.

Muriel Stefanuto is a speech therapist at the Medical and University Centre Daniel Douady, Grenoble, for language rehabilitation of brain injured people. She is also a research assistant in Experimental Psycholinguistics at Geneva University. Her interests and publications lie in aphasiology and neuropsychology in relation to phonological universal trends in the world's languages (research performed at the Institute for Speech Communication, CNRS, INPG-Stendhal, in Grenoble).

Guillaume Thierry received a PhD in Cognitive Neuropsychology from the University of Toulouse Le Mirail, France. He has been a lecturer in Psychology at the University of Wales, Bangor since September 2000. Dr Thierry's primary interest lies in the characterisation of language comprehension processes using Event-Related Potentials and functional imaging. He has been testing current models of word comprehension by studying phonological processing, grammatical processing and semantic categorization.

Anne Vilain completed a doctorate in Phonetics of the University of Grenoble in 2000. She has been 'Maître de Conférences' in Experimental Phonetics at the University of Grenoble since 2001. Her research at the Institut de la Communication Parlée at Grenoble (UMR CNR 5009) focuses on the control of speech production and coarticulation.

Introduction

Jacques Durand and Bernard Laks

As the title indicates, *Phonetics, Phonology, and Cognition* addresses the central question of the cognitive status of phonological representations and their relationship with phonetic implementations. We are aware that the term 'cognition' has become fashionable and has been bandied about in an irresponsible way in much linguistic and other theorizing over the last few decades. Our choice of theme, however, implies a real commitment to the view that phonology is a subsystem (not necessarily modular) of the mind/brain. This has become a standard position since the advent of the generative paradigm but the issue of implementation has often been neglected, indeed often relegated to a subordinate position from an epistemological point of view. But current research allows a much more precise and detailed examination of both cognitive and biological systems involved in speech. The fine-grained analysis of articulatory and acoustic events in phonetics has made it possible to sharpen our answers to questions such as the type of control required for the implementation of articulatory events (low-level vs. high-level strategies) and the nature of the loop existing between auditory and articulatory mechanisms. These are questions which have been at the core of work in psycho- and neurolinguistics: learning strategies and devices, the nature of innate knowledge, the possible modularity of language and its relationship with other abilities (e.g. vision), the role of inferential mechanisms, and so on. We are also in the fortunate position of being able to examine some of these ideas through the more or less direct study of the brain, and neuroscience does not have to rely solely on the post-mortem dissection of speech-impaired patients. The whole story told in the eleven chapters of this book is therefore a story of links between approaches to the mental and physical representation of sound systems and an attempt to break down some of the boundaries which have led to the emergence of various disciplines traditionally seen as sharply separated. Historically, these boundaries were no doubt justified and have often proved useful, but today converging advances in various disciplines are leading to a questioning of these classical divisions (divisions which we, as editors, see as counter-productive, as argued in Chapter 1). If phonology is important for us, it is not in the sense of a necessarily fully autonomous discipline with its own unique methodology, but as a field of enquiry which allows the integration of phonetics and cognition because, Janus-like, it looks both at the realization of representations in physical structures and at the way the sound structure of languages is linked to their internal form (morphological, syntactic, semantic, and pragmatic) and their mental coding.

Like some other recent contributions in the field (such as the work done within Laboratory Phonology), this book stresses the need for cooperation between closely related disciplines. *Phonetics, Phonology, and Cognition* offers a challenging selection of chapters by specialists in areas ranging from phonetics to neurology. To be more specific, the contributors come from the fields of phonology, experimental phonetics, acoustics, psychology, psycholinguistics, neurology, neurolinguistics, and neurophysiology. They have all published extensively in their respective disciplines and have an international reputation. Even more remarkable than their scientific standing is the willingness of the contributors to this book to transcend traditional boundaries and think provocatively about the relationship between disciplines, levels, and modes of analysis. It is the belief of the editors that this collection constitutes a unique cross-disciplinary book in the area of language and cognition.

The book opens with an introductory chapter by Jacques Durand and Bernard Laks, 'Phonology, Phonetics, and Cognition', in which the authors examine some of the historical links between these various domains of enquiry and discuss current debates in the field. Chapter 1, therefore, while putting forward a number of theses, provides a backdrop for many of the later chapters.

In Chapter 2, 'What Are Phonological Syllables Made of? The Voice/Length Symmetry', Joaquim Brandão de Carvalho deals in a detailed way with syllable structure—an issue which is central to most of the articles in this book. In all phonological models of syllable structure, 'sonority', and in particular one of its main correlates—voice(lessness)—are intrinsic properties of segments, as opposed for example to length, which also plays a major role in syllable structure, and was shown to be a prosodic effect by autosegmental phonology, by appealing to the notion of skeletal positions and the Obligatory Contour Principle. This has particular importance today, since the segmental nature of sonority may naturally be viewed as evidence for 'output-based' and non-representational approaches to the syllable.

The basic claim of Joaquim Brandão de Carvalho's article is that voice, and more generally all features associated with 'voice onset time' (VOT)—voice, voicelessness, and aspiration (henceforth VOT-values)—are not segmental features. Rather, VOT-values and length contrasts are to be assigned similar representations. It is proposed that phonological words are characterized by two parallel curves which follow from the association with the skeleton of two autonomous and opposed tiers: the O-tier, where 'onsets' are the roots of consonants, is assumed to stand for (articulatory) 'tension'; the N-tier, where 'nuclei' are the roots of vowels, represents (perceptual) 'sonority'. VOT-values and length contrasts are, as it were, contextual allophones of such abstract invariants which arise through autosegmental spreading. The representation of VOT-values and length in terms of O/N interactions is shown by Carvalho to provide a simple and straightforward solution to a set of six independent phonological problems. Beyond its explanatory power, the hypothesis of O/N interactions is important on cognitive grounds. By denying any symbolic status to aspiration and voice, one can no doubt reduce the number of segmental primitives. But more importantly, by assuming that both VOT-values and length contrasts are segmental effects of onset and nucleus weight, defined as the number of slots which onsets and nuclei are associated with, the author establishes a representational basis for the syllable: 'syllables' exist wherever VOT and/or length contrasts may emerge. This runs counter to the claims of output-based approaches, where syllables are constructed from smaller units. By contrast, the present theory may be argued to lend phonological support to other approaches such as MacNeilage's distinction between *frame* and *content*, whose neurological implications are examined in Chapter 9 by Abry, Stefanuto, Vilain and Laboissière.

In Chapter 3, 'Tone in Mituku: How a Floating Tone Nailed down an Intermediate Level', John Goldsmith studies the tonal system of Mituku, a tone language of the Bantu family, and considers the relationship between constraints and phonological representations. He argues that a well-known constraint, the restriction of a maximum of one tone per vowel, is operative in Mituku, but that its domain is restricted to a particular level in the grammar, and he further argues that this level is an intermediate phonological level, neither the underlying representation nor the surface representation. This example is argued by Goldsmith to illustrate the fact that constraint-based phonologies must not be committed to including only surface-level constraints, nor be committed entirely to non-derivational accounts. His conclusions lead him to some speculations on the possible neural basis for phonological knowledge and processes within the brain, an issue on which Goldsmith has made challenging proposals in other work discussed by Durand and Laks in Chapter 1.

Of course, the formalization of phonological entities and generalizations included here and in the classical phonological literature may well be mistaken. This is the view taken by John Coleman in Chapter 4: 'Phonetic Representations in the Mental Lexicon'. Coleman argues that (i) our mental representations of the form of words are essentially phonetic, rather than symbolic-phonological; (ii) phonological competence includes and makes use of statistical properties of the time-course of phonetic representations; and (iii) a combination of phonetic, statistical, and semantic knowledge is sufficient to explain many aspects of phonological structure. Since generative grammar claims to be concerned with real linguistic knowledge, generative phonologists might regard the mental existence of phonological representations as pretty incontrovertible. Yet in this chapter, the author argues that there is almost no material evidence of abstract phonological representations and units of the kind set out in mainstream works from almost all quarters. Rather, it is more probable in his view that the mental lexicon is populated by many kinds of detailed, variable, redundancy-rich phonetic representations, auditory, articulatory, and visual.

Coleman's critical position is, of course, not uncontroversial and not all chapters in this book reach the same conclusions. In Chapter 5, 'Phonological Primes: Cues and Acoustic Signatures', Michael Ingleby and Wiebke Brockhaus test and defend the 'elements' of Government Phonology in the context of speech analysis and synthesis. Brockhaus and Ingleby have two broad aims which require them to pay particular attention to the acoustic patterns with which individual primes are associated. First, they are seeking to learn more about the physics of the speech channel by establishing what kind of invariant patterns constitute the physical interpretations of certain phonological primes. Secondly, on a more applied level, they are interested in the ways in which cognitive entities as manifested in the physics of the speech channel can underpin the design of voice-driven computer software. At present, such programs tend to perform to an acceptable level of accuracy only in speaker-dependent mode, i.e. after having been trained for one user. To achieve true speaker independence, fundamental changes in the basic approach to automatic speech recognition will be required, and the insights gained in their work may have an important role to play in this. Ingleby and Brockhaus view primes as cognitive entities which provide a link between mental processes and acoustic patterns in the speech signal. They use Government Phonology as an exemplar because its primes are small in number and have been claimed to be phonetically interpretable in isolation (unlike traditional binary features). This assumption greatly facilitates the task of identifying the acoustic patterns characteristic of a particular prime. They demonstrate how such identification can be achieved, using a suitable set of relative cues providing the necessary speaker independence. Apart from enabling them to detect the presence of certain primes, these cues also give a good indication of how the phonological construct of headedness may be reflected acoustically.

Work in psycholinguistics and neurolinguistics over several decades has also tried to probe the psychological reality of phonological constructs and mechanisms. All the remaining chapters of our book deal with this issue in different but related ways. Chapter 6 by Ludovic Ferrand and Juan Segui deals with 'The Role of the Syllable in Speech Perception and Production'. The first part presents an overview of the syllable's role in speech perception, an area which Segui has studied extensively for a number of years in pioneering psycholinguistic work (in particular in collaboration with Jacques Mehler). The authors conclude that English listeners organize speech into syllables, as in other languages such as French, Spanish, Catalan, and Portuguese, but possibly at a comparatively later stage. The second part presents recent data on the syllable's role in speech production in the context of explicit psycholinguistic models and provides a possible answer for the (apparently) divergent treatment of the syllable across languages.

In 'Fossil Markers of Language Development: Phonological "Deafnesses" in Adult Speech Processing' (Chapter 7), Emmanuel Dupoux and Sharon Peperkamp deal with the acquisition of phonological and phonetic knowledge. The sound pattern of the language(s) we have heard as infants affects the way in which we perceive linguistic sounds as adults. Typically, some foreign sounds are very difficult to perceive accurately, even after extensive training. For instance, French subjects find it very difficult to distinguish foreign words that only vary in the position of the main stress. In this chapter, the authors propose to explore this effect across different languages and use it to understand the processes that govern early language acquisition. They propose to test the hypothesis that early language acquisition begins by using only regularities that infants can observe in the surface stream of speech (the Bottom-up Hypothesis), and compare it with the hypothesis that they use all possible sources of information, including lexical information (the Interactive Hypothesis). They set up a research paradigm using the stress system, since it allows one to evaluate the various options at hand within a single test procedure. They distinguish four types of stress systems corresponding to four possible sources of information that infants could use in order to determine whether stress is important or not in their language. They show that the two hypotheses make contrastive predictions as to the pattern of stress perception of adults in these four types of languages. They conclude that cross-linguistic research of adults' speech perception, when coupled with detailed linguistic analysis, can be brought to bear on important issues of language acquisition.

The syllable also plays a central role in the contribution by Carole Paradis and Renée Béland: 'Syllabic Constraints and Constraint Conflicts in Loan-word Adaptations, Aphasic Speech, and Children's Errors' (Chapter 8). This time, the discussion concerns the acquisition of language by children and language-impaired adults. In previous work, Béland and Paradis (1997) showed that the errors which affect the syllabic structure in aphasic speech are strikingly similar to syllabic adaptations in loanwords. The syllabic errors produced by a French-speaking patient suffering from Primary Progressive Aphasia (PPA) were compared to syllabic adaptations of French borrowings in Fula, Kinyarwanda, and Moroccan Arabic. Six marked syllabic contexts were tested: word-initial empty onset, branching onset, simple coda, branching coda, diphthong (branching nucleus), and hiatus. The results indicated that the pattern of errors in the aphasic patient and the syllabic adaptations in French borrowings obeyed two principles of the Theory of Constraints and Repair Strategies (TCRS), i.e. the Preservation and the Tolerance Threshold Principles (Paradis and LaCharité 1997). In the present study, they first verify the results reported in Béland and Paradis (1997) with a second PPA case, whose errors are studied in Paradis et al. (2001), and measure a factor which is frequently influential but which was not investigated in the first study, the word-length effect. Second, they extend the analysis to children's errors in order to show more conclusively that syllabic errors are not random but triggered by universally conditioned syllabic constraints that commonly apply in native and nativized words of natural languages. In a sense, they follow the steps of Jakobson's seminal work in relating children's errors to paraphasias. They examine two populations of pre-school children, normal children and children suffering from Phonological Awareness Disabilities (PAD). The results indicate that the syllabic errors of children are triggered by the same syllabic constraints as those which apply in loanword adaptations and paraphasias (the error rate is significantly lower in CV than in marked syllabic structure), and that the error rate in the form of segment deletion (as opposed to segment insertion) is higher in children than in PPA patients, and higher in PAD children than in normal children. The difference in the rate of segment deletion, which is clearly higher in both children's and aphasics' syllabic errors than in syllabic adaptations of loanwords, is attributed to two factors: (*a*) the tolerance threshold of children and aphasics is lower than that of normal adults, and (*b*) aphasics and children, and especially PAD children, have metrical limitations (i.e. a limit on word length) that normal adult subjects (including borrowers) do not have.

The chapter by Paradis and Béland is complemented by two contributions which deal specifically with the neural encoding of phonology. Chapter 9 by Christian Abry, Muriel Stefanuto, Anne Vilain, and Rafael Laboissière is entitled 'What Can the Utterance "Tan, Tan" of Broca's Patient Leborgne Tell Us about the Hypothesis of an Emergent "Babble-Syllable" Downloaded by SMA?' The authors start from the observation that nobody seems to have asked why Broca's first patient uttered repetitively the sequence 'tan, tan'. For those who did not forget that Broca's Tan, like Alajouanine's Titi-Titi, was not alone in just uttering one 'monosyllable', it is necessary to establish which speech mechanisms could account for this component. In the view defended by these authors—i.e. MacNeilage's *frame/content* theory—basic phonological units, whether they are syllables, phonemes, or features, are by-products and not primes. All these units are the result of the development in the child of two main control components. As in many other types of behaviour, the speech signal is biocybernetically a compound of a carrier control, on proximal effectors, and a carried control, on distal end-effectors. Starting from the sparse degrees of freedom of jaw waggles in babbling, the carried articulators, the tongue and the lower lip, produce contacts, labial [baba] or coronal [dada], depending on the baby's anatomy and current on-line, state-to-state, presetting behaviours. Then, for these carried articulators, independence from the jaw will emerge, giving rise to *content,* among which are phonological segments. The neural control of the basic skills for *frames* is still at issue. In addition to babbling, MacNeilage has gathered data on cortical stimulation and irritative lesions in support of the supplementary motor area (SMA), a cortical area producing repetitive phenomena when stimulated. Abry et al. in their chapter offer a fascinating discussion of various experimental results which appear to challenge MacNeilage's point of view. They maintain the hypothesis that CV recurring utterances can be controlled in the non-lateral left hemisphere but clarify the distinctive roles which may be played by different regions of the left hemisphere.

The next chapter is the result of collaborative work in psycholinguistics and neurophysiology. In 'Towards Imaging the Neural Correlates of Language Functions' (Chapter 10), Jean-François Démonet, Guillaume Thierry, and Jean-Luc Nespoulous show how recent imaging techniques, in particular Positron Emission Tomography and Event Related Potentials, can help our understanding of the connection between language and brain structures. In previous Positron Emission Tomography (PET) studies, the authors compared brain activations elicited by either phonological or lexical semantic monitoring tasks and described differential distributions of increases in regional cerebral blood flow over cerebral hemispheres. They found that phonological processes induced activations near the left sylvian fissure while lexical semantic tasks elicited a widely distributed pattern of activation involving association cortical areas of the temporal, parietal, and frontal lobes in both hemispheres. As PET provides only averaged data on brain regions activated over one minute, the same paradigm was used to further explore these language-specific neural correlates in terms of space and time resolution. Multi-channel Event Related Potentials using Neuroscan©️ were used to explore in the time domain the neural counterparts of these monitoring tasks that both involved sequential processing of cues and targets versus distractors. In general, the combination of imaging techniques providing spatial resolution on the one hand and temporal resolution on the other proves a powerful way to improve our knowledge of the spatiotemporal dynamics of large-scale neural ensembles that subserve language functions. The authors' data evidenced (at least) two interconnected subsystems: one of them, associated with phonological processing, is spatially distributed around the left sylvian fissure and operates in a sequential mode; the other, related to lexical semantic processing, is more widely distributed throughout the entire brain, and operates in a parallel mode.

Finally, in the last chapter of the book, 'Phonology in a Theory of Perception-for-Action Control', Jean-Luc Schwartz, Christian Abry, Louis-Jean Boë, and Marie Cathiard attempt to present an integrated framework in which it is the relationships between perception, action control, and phonology which are at the core of the study, rather than perception, action, or phonology independently of each other. Considering that speech production involves stereotyped syllabic gestures (a 'rhythmer') and learnable segmental specifications through the acquirable control of timing and targets (a 'modeller'), a theory of speech perception must, in their view, be elaborated in this context. Such a theory should tell us how listeners might track the vocalizations of their speaking partners, in order perhaps to understand them, but at least certainly to imitate and learn: in other words, how perception enables listeners to specify the control of their future actions as speakers. Alternatively this theory should also tell us how the perceptual representations of speech gestures transform, deform, and shape the speaker's gestures in the listener's mind, and hence provide templates which in return also help to specify the control of the speaking partner's own actions. Finally, this theory should be able to show how the choice of speech units inside the phonological system may be constrained and patterned by the inherent limitations and intrinsic properties of the speech perception system—and its indissociable companion, the speech production system.

In summary, Schwartz et al. defend an approach centred on the co-structuring of the perception and action systems in relation to phonology which is clearly different from a 'pure' perceptual approach but also from a 'motor theory' in which perception is nothing but a mirror of action, in the claim of a 'direct link' between sounds and gestures. Rather, it is focused on multimodal percepts regularized by motor constraints; or speech gestures shaped by multimodal processing. This chapter, in its valuable attempt to present an integrated view of speech production and perception, seems to us to provide a fitting conclusion to the whole volume.

ACKNOWLEDGEMENTS

Most of the chapters included here were first presented at the conference *Current Trends in Phonology II* which we organized at Royaumont in June 1998 with the help of an organizing committee made up of Wiebke Brockhaus (Manchester), Marc Klein (Paris VIII), Jean-Luc Nespoulous (Toulouse-Le Mirail), Marc Plénat (CNRS, Toulouse-Le Mirail), and Nigel Vincent (Manchester). We must also acknowledge the support of the members of the scientific committee: Christian Abry (Grenoble), Ernesto D'Andrade Pardal (Lisbon), Hans Basbøll (Odense), Geert Booij (Amsterdam), John Goldsmith (Chicago), Daniel Hirst (Aix-Marseille 1), Harry van der Hulst (Leiden), Jean Lowenstamm (Paris VII), Chantal Lyche (Oslo), Carole Paradis (Laval), Jean-François Prunet (UQAM), Peter Siptar (Budapest), Richard Wiese (Marburg), and Moira Yip (Irvine, California). The local organization was possible thanks to the work of Sally Durand and the following team from Paris X: Marianne Desmets, Antonio Balvet, Philippe Gréa, and Atanas Tchobanov.

We received the financial support of a number of organizations, and in particular the Universities of Chicago, Manchester, Marburg, Paris VIII, Paris X, Salford, Toulouse-Le Mirail, as well as the French Ministry for Education and Research and the CNRS. We would like to express our deep gratitude to all these colleagues and organizations. Without them, the conference and offshoots like this volume would not have been possible.

A number of people have directly contributed to the preparation of the manuscript. Without the help of Inès Brulard, Philip Carr, Sarah Dobson, Marianne Durand, Jackie Pritchard, Gabor Turcsan, and particularly Abderrahim Meqqori, this volume would not have seen the light of day. John Davey, commissioning editor at OUP, must also be thanked for his support and immense editorial patience.

I

Phonology, Phonetics, and Cognition

Jacques Durand and Bernard Laks

PRELIMINARY REMARKS

Phonetics and phonology have emerged as independent disciplines during the twentieth century. For somebody who does not know the field of language studies, the existence of two disciplines which are so similar and yet so different, both dedicated to the study of sounds, is rather strange. At least two types of explanation are possible for this state of affairs: one consists in invoking the accidental juxtaposition of historical persons and events, the other in invoking substantive issues and research programmes. As far as the separation of phonetics and phonology is concerned, both types of

Martin Atkinson, Marianne Durand, Chantal Lyche, and Élisabeth Delais-Roussarie have helped us in the preparation of the article. If somebody should be singled out, however, it is Philip Carr, who always had time to help us sharpen our ideas about the complex interrelationship between phonology, phonetics, and cognition. Although our views are partially divergent, his own work in collaboration with Noel Burton-Roberts (Burton-Roberts and Carr 1996, 1997, Burton-Roberts, 2000, Carr 2000) provides an important and challenging approach to the subject. The reader will find an essential complement to this volume in Burton-Roberts, Carr, and Docherty (2000). Their introductory chapter provides a scholarly and insightful discussion of the issues broached here.

explanation seem to be of some importance and are often difficult to disentangle. Undeniably, some major figures and schools have shaped the field in ways that were not necessarily predictable (except in a *post hoc* manner). Simultaneously, the success of various research programmes on both sides of the new divide has led to entrenched positions. But the rise of cognitive issues has forced specialists in phonology and in the phonetic sciences to converge in spite of differences often claimed as irreducible. The temptations of autonomy and hegemony may have been historically understandable but now prevent each of these disciplines from playing a vital role in the emergence of an integrated theory of linguistic sound structure. We will attempt to support this claim by examining in turn the separation of phonetics and phonology at the beginning of the twentieth century (section 1.1), the rise of autonomous phonology (section 1.2), the cognitive reorientation taken by phonology from Jakobson to the present day (section 1.3), the parallel developments in phonetics (section 1.4), and the possibility of a new synthesis (section 1.5). While epistemological breaks can and do occur, we have emphasized throughout the deep continuities within phonology and phonetics. This should not be surprising. If linguistics is a science, the objects, methods and results of successive generations of researchers should be (at least partially) cumulative.[1]

I.I. PHONOLOGY AND PHONETICS: THE PARTING OF THE WAYS

As is well known, until the 1920s, phonology and phonetics did not constitute independent disciplines and the vocabulary used to refer to subaspects of the field was itself in considerable flux. The roots of the modern separation between phonology and phonetics can be traced back to the rise of synchronic linguistics and, more specifically, to the emergence of the concept of *phoneme* (or distinctive sound unit) and the correlative concept of *allophone* (realization or variant of phoneme). Clearly, the assumption that the sounds of speech might be analysable into separate, successive units of the size of the phoneme is hardly new, since all alphabetic writing systems can be argued to rest on a kind of 'phonemic intuition'. And, at many times in history, grammarians have anticipated some of the concepts and procedures which are taken to characterize modern phonology. The work of Indian

[1] On this point, see Durand and Laks (1996*b*), Goldsmith and Laks (2000*a*, 2000*b*), Laks (1997*b*). For exemplification, see Durand and Laks (2000), Durand and Lyche (2000).

scholars like Pāṇini in the Vedic tradition readily springs to mind in this context (cf. Allen 1953, Pinault 1989: 304–13). Nearer our own time one can think of the so-called 'First Grammarian', the unknown Icelandic author of the twelfth century who in the *First Grammatical Treatise* put forward a writing scheme for his language explicitly based on contrastiveness and economy of symbols (or 'underspecification' in a more recent terminology). As Robins (1990: 83) notes about the First Grammarian: 'In addition to his advanced phonological theory, his discovery and demonstration procedures were quite modern. Phonemic distinctions were ascertained by controlled variation of a single segment in a constant frame along such ordered series of words as sár, sǫr, sér, sór, sør, súr, sýr and they were illustrated by sets of minimally different pairs of words whose difference in meaning depended on the difference of a single letter (one phoneme).' Moreover, although many traditional grammarians spoke about the pronunciation of letters, it is clear that they were not as naive about the nature of sounds as has been claimed in many introductions to linguistics.[2] In classical antiquity, the term *littera* has a dual meaning: it stands for a graphical symbol and an element of voice. But this ambiguous value of *littera* did not necessarily entail that grammarians then and later were confused about the difference between these two interpretations. A particularly good example is provided by the Port-Royal grammar, Arnauld and Lancelot's *Grammaire générale et raisonnée* (1660), where one chapter (I. 1) is devoted to the 'Letters as sounds' and another (I. 5) to the 'Letters considered as characters'. Nor did this mean that letters were taken as primary and sounds as secondary. In the Port-Royal grammar, it is stated unequivocally, well before Saussure's *Cours*, that men first expressed their thoughts in spoken words and then converted these into written symbols. Indeed, as noted by Chomsky (1968: 18), language for Arnauld and Lancelot was 'that marvellous invention by which we construct from twenty-five or thirty sounds an infinity of expressions, which, having no resemblance in themselves to what takes place in our minds, still enable to let others know the secret of what we conceive and of all the various mental activities that we carry out'. Nor was advanced work in sound description impeded by the use of the term 'littera' to refer to the sounds of a language as shown by various classical treatises such as Hellwag's *De formatione loquelae* (1781).[3]

---

[2] Thanks to the publication of a number of recent encyclopedias and histories of linguistics, we are today in a better position to assess past works on language than during the heyday of classical structuralism: see e.g. Auroux (1989, 1992, 2000).

[3] In fact, in Hellwag's work, 'littera' is a unit of sound, which is opposed to 'character' or 'figura', a unit of writing. See the 1991 French edition of Hellwag (1781).

Towards the end of the nineteenth century, however, the foundations began to be laid for the establishment of a clear conceptual opposition between phonemes and their allophonic realizations. It is worth pointing out in this connection that the term 'phoneme' (or more precisely 'phonème', which was first coined by the Frenchman Dufriche-Desgenettes) did not originally have its modern sense of 'distinctive sound unit'. For Dufriche-Desgenettes it is simply equivalent to the German 'Sprachlaut' and, in the writings of contemporaries such as Saussure, it simply referred to a segment of speech, a phonetic unit (cf. Anderson 1985: 38 *et passim*). In fact, Saussure called 'phonology' what would now be called 'phonetics' and the same terminology was adopted by other major sound specialists such as Grammont.[4] It was the Polish linguist Jan Baudoin de Courtenay who, while isolated in Kazan in central Russia, first used 'phoneme' in its modern sense and it is interesting to note that his definition, as we emphasize in section 1.2, was what would now be called 'cognitive'.

The distinction made by Sweet between a 'broad' and a 'narrow' transcription is often interpreted as a clear forerunner of the distinction between phonological and phonetic levels of representation. Indeed, the new *Handbook of the International Phonetic Association* (1999: 28) tells us: 'A connected text represented in terms of phonemes is known as a "phonemic transcription", or, almost equivalently, a "broad transcription". The term "broad" sometimes carries the extra implication that, as far as possible, unmodified letters of the Roman alphabet have been used . . . The term narrow transcription most commonly implies a transcription which contains details of the realisation of phonemes.' It should, however, be realized that the contrast between two types of transcription, which has existed within the IPA tradition ever since the second part of the nineteenth century, did not mean that the opposition between two levels of representation played exactly the same role as it did later. In fact, some of the earlier members of the IPA considered that the real, scientific transcription was the narrow one and that broad transcriptions were purely for convenience. Paul Passy, the founding

---

[4] Note that in his *Mémoire* Saussure also used 'phonème' to refer to the *etymological* sound which is the starting point of a family of sound units. As is well known, Saussure's terminology and positions are difficult to establish from the available sources. A full exegesis is beyond the scope of this chapter, but, for additional information, see Bouquet (1997) and the *Troisième cours de linguistique générale* (1910–11) established from Émile Constantin's notes by Komatsu and Harris (Saussure 1993). In any case, as appropriately stressed by Anderson (1985: 56 *et passim*), the work of Baudoin and his student Kruszewski (the so-called Kazan school) presented a view of phonology which was probably more original and better articulated than that of Saussure. If one starts looking for precursors for the 'phonemic' principle, the list is likely to be a very long one as noted earlier in our text. For further discussion of these issues, see Laks (1997*b*).

father of the IPA, felt that he had to defend the distinctiveness principle and warn phoneticians against the danger of cluttering transcriptions with all sorts of arbitrary phonetic details: 'Too many signs have already been invented for varieties of sounds which have no distinctive function. This is a fatal habit which will lead us astray—as there is no reason to stop—and which will ultimately render phonetic texts illegible. *Only significant differences must be transcribed in a text*—this is a golden rule that should never be broken' (quoted in Jones 1957, our translation).

Daniel Jones, in his 1957 history of the term 'phoneme', confirms that, when he became the first teacher of phonetics at University College London, he had not yet appreciated the full importance of the concept of phoneme:

The word 'phoneme' in the sense attributed to it by Baudoin de Courtenay was first brought to my notice by L. Ščerba (one of his pupils) in 1911, who referred to the concept in his pamphlet *Court exposé de la prononciation russe* published by the IPA in that year. About two years later the theory was explained to me more fully by another of Baudoin de Courtenay's pupils, Tytus Benni of Warsaw. The immense import-ance of the theory then became very clear to me, especially in its relation to the construction of phonetic transcriptions, to the devising of alphabets for languages hitherto unwritten or unsuitably written, and in general to the practical teaching of foreign spoken languages. Consequently by about 1915 the theory began to find a regular place in the teaching given in the Department of Phonetics at University College.

Interestingly, and perhaps not surprisingly given the central role he assigned to transcriptions, Daniel Jones himself continued to be committed to a purely instrumental view of phonemes since for him they were just convenient abbreviations for sets of similar sounds: a phoneme is nothing but a family of speech sounds (Jones 1950: 6). But, if we stress here the emergence of the concept of phoneme, in opposition to its allophones, it is not as a convenient fictitious unit but because it was to constitute the cornerstone of the new 'structuralist' approach to language launched by the Prague School in the 1920s under the leadership of Trubetzkoy and Jakobson, not to mention the fact that it also played a central role in the North American descriptive tradition at roughly the same time. Among the tenets of the Prague movement was the idea that phonology should explicate the way significant sound differences allow for the differentiation of forms and thus emancipate 'phonetic studies from the obsession with masses of detail in which they were effectively mired as instrumental techniques of observation were refined' (Anderson 1985: 88). In this context, it may be worth remembering that, in 1928, in preparation for the First International Congress of Linguists, a set of general questions on the nature of linguistics and its methodology was devised by the organizers. To the question 'Quelles sont les méthodes les mieux appropriées à un exposé complet et pratique d'une langue quelconque?' (What are the most appropriate methods for a complete and practical account of a given language?), Jakobson prepared a set of answers (also signed by Trubetzkoy and Karcevskij) which defended a radical reorientation of linguistic research and was enthusiastically supported by many of the participants. These answers, which became known as the Prague theses, were based on phonology (seen as quite distinct from phonetics) and took the network of phonemes of each language as central. The programme which was advocated comprised the following questions among others: What are the distinctive elements within each sound system? What recurrent features or 'correlations' can be found within such systems? What laws govern such 'correlations' across languages? Indeed, phonology, with its insistence on the fact that the object of linguistics should be the distinctive role played by phonemes and the abstract nature of their organization rather than their detailed acoustic or articulatory specifications, provided a *principium divisionis*. It allowed Trubetzkoy to distinguish those who are 'with us' and those who are not (private correspondence between Trubetzkoy and Jakobson; cited in Anderson 1985: 88).

In the United States, the difference between two levels of representation offered by sound structure and summarized as the 'emic'–'etic' distinction was equally taken as a model of linguistic research. No doubt, various researchers had different views of what phonemes were about but most of them shared the phonemic approach as a frame of reference. It is not an accident that Hockett opened *The State of the Art* (1968: 9) with the following retrospective:

Very roughly, the first part of the twentieth century saw the following major theoretical developments in our field of inquiry: (1) the confluence, with all appropriate turbulence, of the two relatively independent nineteenth century traditions, the historical-comparative and the philosophical descriptive, the practical descriptivism of missionaries and anthropologists coming in as an important tributary. (2) Serious efforts by Saussure, Sapir, and especially Bloomfield, not only to integrate the positive findings of these traditions into a single discipline but, even more, to establish that discipline with the proper degree of autonomy from other branches. (3) *The discovery and development of the phonemic principle.* (4) *Attempts, particularly during the last decade of the half-century, to put the rest of descriptive analysis ('grammar' other than phonology) on as exact and reliable a footing as we thought had been achieved for phonemics.* (our emphasis, J.D./B.L.)[5]

---

[5] For further discussion of the structuralists, cf. Hymes and Fought (1981), Matthews (1993). In the French context, Dosse (1991, 1993) is invaluable. With respect to phonology, Fischer-Jørgensen (1975) remains one of the essential sources.

1.2. AUTONOMOUS PHONOLOGY

In itself, the emergence of phonology as separate from phonetics did not imply that these two disciplines should be completely separate. But the birth of phonology coincided with the emergence of linguistics as a distinct, autonomous branch of study in the Saussurean mould. Indeed, it could be said that phonology provided the best exemplification of the 'langue'–'parole' dichotomy, phonemes belonging to 'langue' and allophones to 'parole'. This was interpreted by some linguists as entailing a sharp separation, indeed an abyss, between linguistic form and the material substance in which it is realized. As is well known, the Danish linguist Louis Hjelmslev (1899–1965) provided the most extreme example of such a position within the framework known as *glossematics*.

In his *Prolegomena to a Theory of Language* (1953), Hjelmslev advocated a view of linguistics as seeking to establish the *immanent* structure of language in strict independence of extra-linguistic phenomena (e.g. physical, psychological, logical, or sociological). In his words, 'The long supremacy of conventional phonetics has . . . had the effect of restricting the linguists' conception of even a "natural" language in a way that is demonstrably unempirical, i.e. inappropriate because non-exhaustive.' Following the analogy used by Saussure of language as a chess game which does not depend on the shape of the chessmen,[6] Hjelmslev saw linguistic structure as independent of the material substance in which it is actualized: thus, Hjelmslev went so far as to claim that if two consonants were systematically interchanged in the phonology of a language (e.g. /t/ and /m/ in standard German), the result would still be the same system. Even more radically, he argued that the very same linguistic system can be realized by sounds, orthography, Morse code, flag signals, or any other substance which is available. In so doing, Hjelmslev confuses two separate issues. The language faculty is indeed not inevitably linked to a particular realizational medium: while sound systems emerge naturally barring accidents, human beings can spontaneously acquire other systems such as a sign language. It does not follow that these systems should be studied in a way which treats the

---

[6] Recall the following quotes from Saussure's *Cours*: 'Language is a system that has its own arrangement. Comparison with chess will bring out the point . . . If I use ivory chessmen instead of wooden ones, the change has no effect on the system; but if I decrease or increase the number of chessmen, this change has profound effects on the "grammar" of the game' and later 'Take a knight, for instance. By itself is it an element in the game? Certainly not, for by its material make-up—outside its square and other conditions of the game—it means nothing to the player; it becomes a real, concrete element only when endowed with value and wedded to it' (Saussure, *Course in General Linguistics*, tr. W. Baskin 1959: 22–3, 110).

expression side as lying outside the scope of linguistics.[7] Nor does it seem correct to assume that there is an abstract representational system for the expression plane of languages which has the very same structure whether it is realized in, say, speech or writing. Even when a relatively close correspondence exists between speech and writing in given languages, the differences are quite striking. Take, as a simple example, the fact that in English /p, t, k/ are the only phonemes allowable after /s/ in triconsonantal word-initial clusters (*splice, strain, scrape*, etc.).[8] Phonologists who do not exclude reference to phonetic properties have long stressed that this was not an accident and that the elements in the relevant set /p t k/ were united by common features (be they 'voiceless plosives' or [-sonorant, -continuant, -voiced], or statistically based acoustic features as in Coleman's chapter, this volume). This set recurs in other contexts in the sound system of English and many other languages: it is for instance the group of segments which can be aspirated in stressed syllable initial position in English. Now, in the triconsonantal initial clusters of the spelling system of English, the letter ⟨s⟩ can be followed by ⟨c, h, p, t⟩ as in *screw, shrew, splice, strain*. While we do not doubt that letters too can be analysed in terms of distinctive graphic features, we are not aware of any natural property which brings together the set of second elements in such clusters. The generalizations to be captured with respect to these examples cannot therefore be of the same type with respect to speech and writing.[9]

The position of Hjelmslev was no doubt extreme. Nevertheless, it was historically part and parcel of a position which occasionally debased or downgraded phonetics and reduced it to a mere ancillary role. We have seen above that the Prague School programme was partially based on such an assumption. But the Prague School was by no means isolated. Bloomfield states: 'the physiologic and acoustic description of acts of speech belongs to other sciences than our own' (1926: 154). Even Pike, whose experience and status as a phonetician can hardly be doubted, said, 'Phonetics gathers raw material. Phonemics cooks it.' The metaphors varied but, as emphasized by Abercrombie (1991: 12), there was a phase during which the people who practised this art came to be regarded as 'the hewers of wood and drawers of water—indispensable, perhaps, but essential menial'.

This trend of regarding phonology as substance-free has had many followers over the ages and has remained a basic tenet of various schools. Hagège (1985: 171–2), a disciple of Martinet, says:

---

[7] This issue is taken up again in section 1.3.3.1.

[8] Leaving rare learned examples like /sfr/ in *sphragistics*.

[9] On the status of writing within a theory of language, see Durand (2000*a*).

Thus, whereas the natural sciences create for themselves the concepts and the categories they need to describe and explain the phenomena of the physical world, linguistics, which, in this respect, is similar to other human sciences, finds these categories and these concepts already constituted within languages. An illustration of this can be found in the opposition established by structuralist linguists between phonetics and phonology. Phonetics is similar to the natural sciences in so far as its object is to establish, on articulatory or acoustic bases, the categories of sounds which can be produced by the vocal apparatus (from the lips to the larynx). Phonology, on the other hand, has for its object, within a given language, the study of phonemes, i.e. the classes of sounds already constituted within this language. (our translation, J.D./B.L.)

Such statements explain to a large extent why phoneticians, rightly convinced that the study of linguistic sound structure could not afford to neglect the physical embodiment of whatever mental acts underlie speech communication, were often tempted to reclaim the whole field for their own approach.

1.3. FROM PHONOLOGY TO COGNITION

1.3.1. From Baudoin de Courtenay to Jakobson

While the emergence of phonology often led to a sharp separation between phonology and phonetics, on the one hand, and phonology and cognition, on the other, it should be remembered that psychological preoccupations have not been as absent from the work of phonologists as is often claimed. Thus, the originator of the term 'phoneme' in its modern sense, Baudoin de Courtenay, defended an approach which was very different from the instrumental and empiricist use of the concept of phoneme made by phoneticians like Jones. For Baudoin de Courtenay, phonemes were psychophonetic entities representing intentions and to be differentiated from the concrete objects studied by physiology or acoustics. To quote his definition:

'Phoneme' (Greek φωνή, φώνημα 'voice') is a linguistic term: a living psychological phonetic unit. So long as we are dealing with speech or hearing, which are fleeting actions, the term 'sound' is sufficient as it refers to the most simple phonatory or pronunciation unit which creates a single acoustico-phonetic impression. But if we move to the level of real language, a level which only exists in a continuous way in the mind, only as a world of representations, the notion of *sound* is not sufficient and we need another term for the psychological equivalent of sound. This is the term 'phoneme'. (our translation, J.D./B.L.; Baudoin de Courtenay 1963: i. 351)

Saussure's own work presents a very real tension between the sociological dimension and the psychological one, but the latter cannot be discarded as a mere addendum to the former. While the idea of language ('langue') as a common treasure is central to Saussure's thought, so is the description of the sign as a mental construct, the linking of a 'signified' with a 'signifier' which is an 'acoustic image'. As has now become clear, the psychological aspect of Saussure's work has been underemphasized both by Bally and Séchehaye as editors of the *Cours* and by later interpreters, or worse still, simply rejected as mistaken.[10] To take just one example, the French historian of linguistics Mounin (a disciple of Martinet) asks, 'What does Saussurean psychologism consist in?' His critical answer runs as follows:

First of all, in the self-confidence with which, like virtually all of his contemporaries, Saussure is a 'mentalist' (in Bloomfield's terminology), that is, assured by philosophy and introspection of knowing what goes on in the brain when man is thinking. He thus explains the facts of language by the facts of thought which are taken for granted. For instance, he assumes that 'the linguistic sign unites not a thing and a name but a concept and an acoustic image' (p. 98), therefore by means of two notions which the linguist has no handle on and understands far less than language. 'A given concept, he says, triggers in the brain a corresponding acoustic image' (p. 28). That is why he also states that 'in the last resort, everything is psychological in language' (p. 21) and that 'the linguistic sign is therefore a psychological entity' (p. 99). (our translation, J.D./B.L.; Mounin 1968: 25)

In North America, a psychological conception of phonological representations was central to Sapir's work.[11] To take one quote from many similar ones, 'Back of the purely objective system of sounds that is peculiar to a language and which can be arrived at only by a painstaking phonetic analysis, there is a more restricted "inner" or "ideal" system which perhaps equally unconscious to the naive speaker, can far more readily be brought to his consciousness as a finished pattern, a psychological mechanism' (Sapir 1921: 55).

The position of many of the 'structuralist' linguists, like Trubetzkoy, regarding cognitive issues is not always clear-cut and in many cases deserves to be reassessed. Did they reject a psychological analysis of the phoneme, when they did, because they did not believe in the relevance of such an approach, or because the concepts provided by psychology at the time did not seem fully adequate for a proper analysis of language, or, again, because they

---

[10] Bouquet (1997) corrects many of these questionable interpretations.

[11] In particular, Sapir (1933). For this reason, generative phonologists have seen their work as an extension of Sapir's work in important respects: cf. Chomsky and Halle (1968: 76, 349). For detailed discussion, see McCawley (1967).

wanted to remain neutral on issues of cognition? Bloomfield's own position in this respect is rather interesting. He first of all adopted the mentalistic approach to the psychology of language advocated by Wundt (Bloomfield 1914). Later, in 'A set of postulates for the science of language', Bloomfield (1926) offers a framework explicitly modelled on Weiss's behaviouristic paradigm for psychology, an approach he was to maintain in his subsequent work and particularly in *Language* (1933). While Chomsky's famous critique of Skinner's *Verbal Behavior* (1959) definitively demonstrated the fundamental weaknesses of classical behaviourism, Bloomfield's own approach has to be evaluated in the context of the time.

First of all, 'mentalism' was taken by Bloomfield to be a philosophical position which asserted a radical difference between mind and matter: 'The mentalistic theory, which is by far the older, and still prevails both in the popular view and among men of science, supposes that the variability of human conduct is due to the interference of some non-physical factor, a *spirit* or *will* or *mind* (Greek *psyche*, hence the term *psychology*) that is present in every human being. This spirit, according to the mentalistic view, is entirely different from material things and accordingly follows some other kind of causation or perhaps none at all' (Bloomfield 1933: 32). The numerous linguists who speak nowadays of language as a faculty of the mind/brain or stress that speakers are 'embodied' illocutionary agents would presumably not disagree with Bloomfield's distaste for radical dualism. Secondly, Bloomfield was rejecting a form of free-wheeling introspectionism which he saw as threatening the discipline, as illustrated for him by Paul's *Principles*, where statements about language are accompanied 'with a paraphrase in terms of mental processes which the speakers are supposed to have undergone' (1933: 17).[12] In fact, Bloomfield saw much of the psychological paraphrasing which took place in the study of language as based on western philosophical concepts and grammatical categories and he believed this was likely to inhibit the exploration of other language families. Thirdly, in some of his writings, Bloomfield also stated that linguistics could and should remain neutral as far as psychology was concerned (cf. Bloomfield 1926: 153). As he put it: 'the postulational method saves discussion, because it limits our statements to a defined terminology; in particular, it cuts us off from psychological disputes' (1926: 153 ff.) and 'Recall the difficulties and obscurities in the writings of Humboldt and Steinthal, and the psychological dispute of Paul, Wundt, Delbrueck. From our point of view, the last named was wrong in denying the

---

[12] In turn, of course, Paul's own work has to be understood as a reaction to the mystical belief of grammarians like Grimm in a Hegelian *Sprachgeist* which existed above and beyond individual speakers. Cf. Lightfoot (1999: 35–6).

value of descriptive data, but right in saying that *it is indifferent what system of psychology a linguist believes in*' (our emphasis, J.D./B.L.).

Not surprisingly Bloomfield's legacy in North America was a complex one. The post-Bloomfieldians were not as homogeneous as is often assumed, nor did they avoid being pulled in different directions like their own master. Much of the work done by the post-Bloomfieldians is better described as a form of descriptivism than a defence of behaviourism. When linguists after Bloomfield defended a 'hocus-pocus' approach, in contrast with 'God's Truth', they were indicating that they were more concerned with making progress in the description of languages of the world than with getting bogged down in debates about the mind that they saw as possibly sterile for their practical work. There had been for a long time in North America a point of view which could be summarized by the slogan: 'Leave psychology to the psychologists'! As noted by Lightfoot, this demarcation was already clearly advocated by William Dwight Whitney in the nineteenth century:

The human capacity to which the production of language is most directly due is, as has been seen, the power of intelligently, and not by blind instinct alone, adapting means to ends. This is by no means a unitary capacity; on the contrary, it is a highly composite and intricate one. But it does not belong to the linguistic student to unravel and explain . . . it falls, rather, to the student of the human mind and its powers, to the psychologist. So with all the mental capacities involved in language. (1875: 303, quoted in Lightfoot, 1999: 36)

It would of course be an overgeneralization to assert that the post-Bloomfieldians were never interested in the psychological status of their descriptions. If this were so, the following assertion by Hockett (1948: 279–80) would be incomprehensible:

The analytical process thus parallels what goes on in the nervous system of a language learner, particularly, perhaps, that of a child learning his first language. . . . The essential difference between the process in the child and the procedure of the linguist is this: the linguist has to make his analysis overtly, in communicable form, in the shape of a set of statements which can be understood by any properly trained person, who in turn can predict utterances not yet observed with the same degree of accuracy as can the original analyst. The child's 'analysis' consists on the other hand, of a mass of varying synaptic potentials in his central nervous system. The child in time comes to *behave* the language; the linguist must come to *state* it. (emphasis in the original, J.D./B.L.)

Nevertheless, it is also true that a number of post-Bloomfieldians were extremely militant in their anti-psychologism. Joos, as editor of *the* reference work of the 1950s, *Readings in Linguistics*, was to attack Sapir's students in no uncertain terms:

If their wits happen to be dimmer . . . their blunders may betray the essential irresponsibility of what has been called Sapir's 'method'. We welcome the insight of his genius, which allowed no scrap of evidence to escape at least subconscious weighing; where it is possible to check up, we normally find him right; thus we seem captious when we point out that he also said many things which are essentially uncheckable ('invulnerable') and thus not science. (Joos 1963: 25)

If there was a real turning point in phonology with respect to cognition, it was provided by Jakobson, and particularly by his theory of distinctive features. At the core of Jakobson's approach was a desire to understand the sound patterns of language within a model of communication, hence the idea that one had to start from the brain and the encoding stage of a message and move thereafter from articulation (via acoustics) to audition, and the decoding of the message by the listener. True enough, Jakobson did not provide a complete model of these stages. His prime contribution, in association with other researchers like Fant and Halle, was in the area of distinctive features. By rejecting the Saussurean assumption that the phonological system of each language imposes arbitrary distinctions on an undifferentiated speech tract and acoustic continuum, he forced phonology to renew its connections with phonetic substance and its mental representation. As is well known, for Jakobson, the distinctive features are universal (part of the human predisposition for language), they are binary (an assumption linked to hypotheses about communication and the brain), and they must have correlates in terms of both articulation and audition even though the latter takes precedence in his eyes.[13] Another aspect of Jakobson's work was his openness to data of all types. His speculations concerning language acquisition and breakdown provide the prime example of the difference between 'internal' and 'external' phonological evidence. While this dichotomy is untenable if conceived literally and mechanically, it offers a useful distinction between the data provided by the analysis of synchronic phonological systems, on the one hand, and the data provided, for example, by language acquisition or loss, experimental phonetics, psycholinguistics, and neurolinguistics. For Jakobson, the work of phonologists had to be properly cross- and interdisciplinary and involve links with specialists in other areas, as exemplified by the chapters in this volume. In many respects, however, Jakobson's approach remained programmatic and constrained by quite classical assumptions about language and its structure. In particular, in terms of the oscillation between 'rules' (or processes) and 'representations' which allows an interesting explanation of the historical

---

[13] For a discussion of this point and extensions, see Durand (2000*b*).

evolution of phonology (cf. Anderson 1985), he is definitely on the side of representations.

1.3.2. The Sound Pattern of English

The publication of *The Sound Pattern of English* (*SPE* hereafter) by Chomsky and Halle in 1968 is generally acknowledged as constituting a watershed in the history of modern phonology. It is customary in presenting developments in phonology to stress the profound formal changes which have taken place between, for example, structuralist models and classical generative phonology and between the latter and current non-linear models. But, in our view, a closer look at the history of our discipline shows much more continuity in depth.

To start with, the break away from previous phonemic approaches which is emphasized in early generative work (cf. e.g. Chomsky 1964, Postal 1968: 29–31) was not as radical as it may have appeared at the time. Within structural phonology, the system of phonemes was simultaneously the basis for description and explanation, as well as the target and source of synchronic and diachronic processes. And, as far as the contrast between units and processes is concerned, the former were privileged by the structuralists at the expense of the latter. On the other hand, in the wake of Jakobson's seminal work on distinctive features, generative phonologists were to stress the relevance of subphonemic units and of processes affecting them. But the divergence is less radical than it may seem. The phoneme was in fact not as defunct as appeared at first sight. For a start, in *SPE*, distinctive features were locked within unidimensional matrices which corresponded rather closely to phonemes. Secondly, in most early generative work, the representations which were the output of the phonological component were strangely similar to classical phonemic representations, even if the notion of a phonemic *level* was strongly rejected. In principle, Chomsky and Halle acknowledged the necessity of formulating all rules—including classical allophonic rules—characterizing the sound system of a language, but in practice they did not carry this out.[14] Indeed some influential generative phonologists such as Schane (1971) were quick to argue explicitly that the notion of phoneme remained central to generative work. Today most generative textbooks use

[14] See, for example, their remarks on p. 65 of *The Sound Pattern of English* where they refer in footnote 5 to Sledd (1966) 'for a discussion of very detailed phonetic rules for a Southeastern American dialect, within a general framework of the sort that we are discussing here'. Our feeling is that Sledd (1966) does not really offer a very detailed specification of low-level phonetic rules.

the term phoneme without even mentioning the acrimonious debates that took place around this concept during the 1960s.

But even if we leave the phoneme aside, it is clear that Chomsky and Halle did not reinvent the field of phonology.[15] At various points of *The Sound Pattern of English (SPE)*, they are at pains to point out that their approach is by no means new but owes a great deal to the pioneering work of Sapir and Bloomfield among others (see pp. 18 n. and 76 n.). And their debt to the post-Bloomfieldians can hardly be underestimated, since it is generally agreed today that one of the basic deficiencies of the *SPE* model was its linear architecture, the idea already mentioned that phonological units (whether phonemes or boundaries) are like beads on a string—a vision very close to classical phonemics. Finally, and crucially, the range of problems that they dealt with was largely handed down by tradition. To limit ourselves to one example: in the first twenty-seven pages (pp. 330–57) of their chapter 8 'Principles of phonology', they make crucial use of data and analyses associated with Grimm and Verner (pp. 340–2), Joos (pp. 342–3), Sapir (p. 344–50), Thurneysen (p. 352), Trubetzkoy (pp. 352–3), Bloomfield (via Menomini p. 356), Meinhof (p. 356), and Speiser (p. 357).

From a formal point of view, the 'process' approach (deriving surface forms from underlying forms through transformations) had already been used by Bloomfield in his 'Menomini Morphophonemics' and the *SPE* rule format, although much better articulated, can in essence be argued to go back to the rules of the neogrammarians (X → Y/in some phonetic context). Post-Bloomfieldians like Hockett had insightfully explored the difference between an 'item and arrangement' description and an 'item and process' approach. The importance of mathematical tools for linguistic work was well understood and well exemplified by Hockett's detailed excursus on 'Language, Mathematics and Linguistics' (1965). And the work of Zellig Harris provided one of the best illustrations of a transformational approach to language. What was however novel in *SPE* was the simultaneous commitment to universalism and cognition.[16] Whereas previous approaches saw

---

[15] For different points of view on the history of Chomskyan generative grammar, see Newmeyer (1986); Goldsmith and Huck (1995); Harris (1995). Encrevé (2000) offers a detailed criticism of the way Chomsky and Halle see their own relationship to the Bloomfieldian tradition.

[16] Setting aside the personal dimension to the disputes which divided American linguists, it was the general Chomskyan *Weltanschauung* (innatism, universalism, realism, etc.) and not the techniques that led Hockett (1965) to declare: 'Chomsky's outlook—not merely on language but also on mathematics, perhaps on everything—is so radically different from Bloomfield's and from my own that there is, at present, no available frame of reference external to both within which they can be compared . . . let the record show that I reject that [Chomsky's] frame of reference in almost every detail.' Interestingly, he immediately adds: 'The preceding

themselves as primarily descriptive and aimed at providing inventories of structures (which could converge on universal tendencies), *SPE* starts from the assumption central to Chomskyan generative grammar that the aim of linguistic theory is to establish a Universal Grammar (UG). UG will therefore provide all the formal operations and substantive units which underlie natural languages. A further assumption is that UG is made up of components (later called modules) which are interrelated but to a large extent self-contained. Thus, in the case of the phonological module, UG will specify the universal set of distinctive features from which each language draws a particular subset, it will define the way linguistically significant general-izations should be formalized (hence the stress on rule format and notational conventions), what their interrelationship is (extrinsic ordering), how many levels of representation are countenanced (two in *SPE*: phonological and phonetic), and so on. The link with cognition is seen as direct: UG is part of the innate language faculty which, barring accidents, characterizes human beings. It accounts for the ease, rapidity and uniformity of language acquisition. Thus, from the point of view of *SPE*, children will, for instance, know tacitly that the noises they hear are decomposable into segments, that these segments must be composed of distinctive features belonging to the universal inventory (and not to be rediscovered *ad hoc*), and that the distance between their phonetic percepts and stored forms is attributable to the fact that the phonological component specifies two levels of representation related by transformations.

While Chomsky and Halle repeatedly emphasize that what they put forward in *SPE* with respect to English is a competence model, they do believe that their general approach is highly relevant both for a performance model and for a model of language acquisition. The following long quotation leaves no doubt in this respect:

We might suppose, on the basis of what has been suggested so far, that a correct description of the perceptual process would be something like this. The hearer makes use of certain cues and certain expectations to determine the syntactic structure and semantic content of an utterance. Given a hypothesis as to its syntactic structure—in particular its surface structure—he uses the phonological principles that he controls to determine a phonetic shape. The hypothesis will then be accepted if it is not too radically at variance with the acoustic material, where the range of permitted discrepancy may vary widely with conditions and many individual factors. Given

declaration affects in no way my indebtedness to the transformationalists for the many specific points and procedures I have found it profitable to incorporate in my own thinking, as attested repeatedly in the present essay.' (This is part of a note added in proof 20 Aug. 1965 to Hockett's note 3, p. 156).

acceptance of such a hypothesis, what the hearer 'hears' is what is internally generated by the rules. That is, he will 'hear' the phonetic shape determined by the postulated syntactic structure and the internalised rules.

Among the internalised rules are some that are particular to the language in question and thus must have been learned; there are others that simply play a role in setting the conditions of linguistic experience. In the present case, it would be reasonable to suggest that the Compound and Nuclear Stress Rules are learned, while the principle of the transformational cycle, being well beyond the bounds of any conceivable method of 'learning', is one of the conditions, intrinsic to the language-acquisition system, that determines the form of the language acquired. If this assumption is correct, we would expect the principle of the transformational cycle to be a linguistic universal, that is, to be consistent with the empirical facts for all human languages, the Compound and Nuclear Stress Rules, on the other hand, might be in part language-specific. (1968: 24–5)

It should furthermore be pointed out that what made the strong link with psychology possible and provoked the epistemological break with the post-Bloomfieldians was Chomsky's commitment to realism. Whereas many linguists had adhered to a form of conventionalism or instrumentalism, Chomsky assumes that the constructs and entities in the theories he developed are real features of the world (more precisely the mind since he has always rejected an externalist point of view). This assumption, while arguably implicit in earlier work, becomes central in *Aspects of the Theory of Syntax* where the reader is warned that the term 'grammar' will be used with systematic ambiguity to refer either to the linguist's theory or to the system internalized by speaker-hearers. The realist stance is a major component of Chomskyan generative grammar and has been consistently maintained since the 1960s, as shown in sample quotations like the following: 'A naturalistic approach to linguistic and mental aspects of the world seeks to construct intelligible explanatory theories, taking as "real" what we are led to posit in this quest, and hoping for eventual unification with the "core" natural sciences: unification not necessarily reduction' (Chomsky 2000: 106). If one adopts this point of view, linguistics becomes not only a branch of cognitive psychology but arguably the major way of exploring the language faculty. As the following quote from Chomsky demonstrates, there is no more reason to ascribe reality to the constructs pursued in the laboratory than there is to those that are the subject of the linguist's investigation:

To take another case, the discovery of perceptual displacement of clicks to phrase boundaries is, for now, more of a discovery about the validity of the experiment than about phrase boundaries. The reason is that evidence of other sorts about phrase boundaries—sometimes called 'linguistic' rather than 'psychological' evidence (a highly misleading terminology)—is considerably more compelling and embedded in a much richer explanatory structure. If click experiments were found to be sufficiently reliable in identifying the entities posited in C-R [computational-representational] theories, and if their theoretical frameworks were deepened, one might rely on them in cases where 'linguistic evidence' is indecisive; possibly more as inquiry progresses. (2000: 25)

1.3.3. Post-*SPE* phonology

Post-*SPE* phonology is quite difficult to characterize, all the more so as we do not have the required historical distance to assess dispassionately a number of directions taken in the field. Moreover, when researchers have proposed alternatives to *SPE* assumptions, they have not always appreciated the full implications of the innovations they were putting forward. A non-trivial problem is the plethora of names which have multiplied since the 1960s and which can cover very different types of activity ranging from specific models to very general research programmes. A very incomplete and partly arbitrary list (in alphabetical order) of the types of phonology would include: articulatory phonology, autosegmental phonology, CV phonology, computational phonology, declarative phonology, dependency phonology, government phonology, harmonic phonology, laboratory phonology, lexical phonology, metrical phonology, natural phonology, natural generative phonology, non-linear phonology, radical CV phonology, tridimensional phonology. In parallel with this, we also find approaches such as moraic theory, optimality theory, theory of constraints and repair strategies, under-specification theory, and so on. We will discuss a number of these approaches under three headings: work within UG, other work, the connectionist challenge.

1.3.3.1. *Approaches within UG*

It is important to realize that most of the frameworks listed above have not necessarily represented separate paradigms but have often been models of phonology differing from each other only with respect to a few assumptions. For instance, theory A might assume binary features, rule ordering, and one level of derivation, while theory B assumes binary features, no rule ordering, and two levels of derivation, and theory C assumes monovalent features, no rule ordering, and two levels of derivation. In contradistinction to theories A, B, and C, theory D might assume that there are both binary and monovalent features but no rules at all. Many of the frameworks which have emerged are characterizable in relation to *SPE* and, indeed, some textbooks published in the 1990s have simply called themselves 'generative phonology' or 'phono-logy in generative grammar' to emphasize the continuity of a tradition within which they saw various developments.[17] One crucial aspect in which *SPE* reshaped the field is that the goal of specifying the nature of phonology within UG became a leitmotiv for researchers, even when they disagreed fairly sharply as to what the content of UG might be.

At the core of *SPE* is a commitment to a symbolic approach based on discrete mathematics and automata theory. While a number of the types of phonology listed above have remained within this paradigm, important shifts of emphasis have taken place. A good account of post-*SPE* phonology can be obtained by looking at the evolution of the field in terms of the relative weight attributed to rules and representations, a debate that stretches a long way back in the field as convincingly demonstrated by Anderson's (1985) historical account. The contribution of *SPE* was mainly in the area of rules (in the technical sense of local transformations) as a way of capturing various generalizations including invariance at the lexical level. Transformational rules made possible the positing of unique underlying forms for morphemes, even in cases where suppletive statements might have seemed warranted. These unique underlying forms were seen as quite resistant to historical change and as potentially shared by many dialects of the same language. For a number of years around the publication of *SPE* and in the decade that followed, much work was devoted to the issue of rule ordering and abstractness. This work was seen by many as having obvious implications for cognition. For instance, those working in Natural Generative Phonology (Vennemann 1973, Hooper 1976*b*) as well as others (Koutsoudas, Sanders, and Noll 1974) aimed at constructing a more realistic account of the human mind faculty by doing away with extrinsic ('stipulated') rule ordering. At some point the debate about rule ordering was felt to be counterproductive, all the more so as many of the proposed reanalyses remained very close to the standard *SPE* framework. Nevertheless, the discussions that took place around the excessive power of *SPE* (often compared with a Turing machine) had a lasting influence. Many later frameworks were constructed with the explicit aim of doing away with destructive operations (e.g. 'declarative phonology', Scobbie, Coleman, and Bird 1996, and various types of 'underspecification theory', Archangeli 1984, Anderson and Durand 1988).

Just as radical as the rejection of extrinsic rule ordering was the battle for naturalness. While the notational conventions of *SPE* and its metric of simplicity did allow an intuitively satisfying formalization of many processes,

---

[17] Cf. Kenstowicz (1994), Roca (1994).

it also failed in some fundamental respects. As Chomsky and Halle themselves acknowledged (1968: 400):

The entire discussion of English in this book suffers from a fundamental theoretical inadequacy. Although we do not know how to remedy it fully, we feel that the outlines of a solution can be checked, at least in part. The problem is that our approach to features, to rules, and to evaluation has been overly formal. Suppose, for example, that we were systematically to interchange features or to replace [αF] by [$-\alpha$F] (where $\alpha = +$, and F is a feature). There is nothing in our account of linguistic theory to indicate that the result would be a description that violates certain principles governing human languages.

The solution sketched by Chomksy and Halle was the use of markedness conventions but these, in actual fact, remained external to the notation. As a result, in many different ways, phonologists began to look for ways of capturing 'naturalness' more directly within their descriptions.[18] One striking example was the work of Stampe (1973), who advocates a theory of phonology based on natural processes (e.g. nasalize a vowel followed by a nasal consonant in the same syllable). All these natural processes are available to a child and the learning of a language takes place, so to speak, by forgetting. Adult systems can be seen as the result of inhibiting, downgrading, or restricting natural processes (an approach not so dissimilar to optimality theory discussed below). It can however be seen that, in so far as natural processes reflect general production and perception strategies, they do not sit happily within the UG paradigm if the latter is assumed to include factors not reducible to communication. This is an issue to which we return at various points below.

Another way of capturing naturalness was via representations. Phonological representations in *SPE* were quite austere. *SPE* has occasionally been compared to Russell and Whitehead's *Principia Mathematica*, since Chomsky and Halle attempted to reconstruct phonology on the basis of a few primitives and operations. In so doing, *SPE* discarded many concepts which had been explored by earlier phoneticians and phonologists (e.g. the syllable, 'long components', or 'prosodies'). During this phase, there emerged a number of frameworks (e.g. autosegmental phonology, tridimensional phonology, metrical phonology, dependency phonology, and then feature geometries) which put forward radical revisions of standard representations by appealing to the *SPE* idea that the notation must reflect the difference between accidental facts and linguistically significant generalizations.[19] One of the results now taken for granted by many phonologists is multilinearity

---

[18] See the essays in Bruck, Fox, and Lagaly (1974) and Dinnsen (1980).

[19] Among the influential collections of articles, a special place should be reserved for van der Hulst and Smith (1982, 1988).

(the idea that representations are organized along tiers that do not coincide) and the existence of suprasegmental constituents such as the syllable.[20] Indeed, the syllable is pivotal to this book as demonstrated by most of the chapters in this volume.[21] The syllable is seen by some of the contributors as the fundamental unit from which segments and subsegmental features emerge ontogenetically and which provides the link between a physically driven system and higher-level units.

In recent years, descriptions have again focused on rules. This assertion may seem surprising in view of the fact that many current models claim to dispense with rules altogether (and in fact one famous book edited by Goldsmith (1993*b*) is entitled *The Last Phonological Rule*). The use of the term 'rule' in this context must however be clarified. Until comparatively recently, successive Chomskyan generative grammars have included two types of mechanisms, both referred to as rules historically. The first of these have been 'constituency rules' ('phrase structure rules' in syntax) and the second, transformational rules. For a very long time now, constituency rules (e.g. S → NP VP, or Syllable → Onset Rhyme, Rhyme → Nucleus (Coda)) have not been construed in procedural rewriting terms (e.g. replace the symbol Syllable by the symbols Onset and Rhyme). Rather, constituency rules are regarded as well-formedness conditions or, in a more fashionable terminology, 'constraints'. By and large, current models have not questioned the need for such descriptive devices. What, on the other hand, has been rejected by many phonologists is the use of transformational rules, which were at the core of the *SPE* approach (although one will find a spirited defence in Bromberger and Halle 1989, 1997, 2000).

There is no doubt that the use of constraints and their interrelationships has provided the central development of the last ten years. Within this development, a number of models have been in competition[22] such as the Theory of Constraints and Repair Strategies (Paradis 1988*a*, Paradis and Prunet 2000, this volume), Declarative Phonology (Coleman 1995, 1998*a*), and Optimality Theory.[23] These various models show many

---

[20] For early post-*SPE* work on the syllable, see Fudge (1969), Hooper (1972), Vennemann (1972), Anderson and Jones (1974), and Kahn (1976). For a recent, encyclopedic treatment, see van der Hulst and Ritter (1999).

[21] See in particular the chapters by Abry, Stefanuto, Vilain, and Laboissière; Carvalho; Dupoux and Peperkamp; Paradis and Béland; Segui and Ferrand.

[22] For comparisons and debates, see Durand and Laks (1996*a*), Roca (1997).

[23] See Prince and Smolensky (1993) and McCarthy and Prince (1993) for the two founding texts. For advanced expository discussions and further references, see Archangeli and Langendoen (1997) and Kager (1999). For an interesting application to English, see Hammond (1999).

family resemblances but also differ along a series of different dimensions. Thus, in Optimality Theory, constraints cannot construct, destroy or trigger any processes. Their role is merely to select an output form. Moreover, constraints can be violated. In Declarative Phonology, constraints cannot be violated and act as constructive processes which together define the well-formedness of output forms. In the Theory of Constraints and Repair Strategies, as in Declarative Phonology, constraints determine the validity of output forms but they can be violated, in which case they can trigger constructive or destructive processes as repair strategies. While a detailed comparison of these models would be useful, it is however the cognitive implications of post-*SPE* work which will preoccupy us here.

Many of the frameworks which have emerged since *SPE*, while formally very different from that model, have pursued the basic goals of Chomskyan generative grammar. For instance, Government Phonology as defended by Kaye, Lowenstamm, and Vergnaud (and extended by the work of Harris and Lindsey 1995, Ingleby and Brockhaus, this volume) sees work on sound structure as contributing to UG. As the following quotation shows, this approach is consonant with the Principles and Parameters approach adopted by Chomsky in syntax since the 1980s:

Our programme incorporates the view that phonology is to be regarded as a system of universal principles defining the class of human phonological systems. These principles underdetermine the class of human phonological systems. A complete phonological system consists, then, of these principles along with sets of parameter-values. Taken together, the principles and language-specific parameter settings give a complete characterisation of the phonological component. In this model, a phonological system contains no rule component.

Similarly, when launching Optimality Theory in 1993, Prince and Smolensky asserted:

The basic idea we will explore is that Universal Grammar consists largely of a set of constraints on representational well-formedness, out of which individual grammars are constructed. Departing from the usual view, we do not assume that the constraints in a grammar are mutually consistent, each true of the observable surface or of some level of representation. On the contrary: we assert that the constraints operating in a particular language are highly conflicting and make sharply contrary claims about the well-formedness of most representations. The grammar consists of the constraints together with a general means of resolving their conflict. We argue further that this conception is an essential prerequisite for a substantive theory of UG. (1993: 2)

Despite appearances, it is quite difficult to assess what stance researchers who work within the UG paradigm take vis-à-vis the status of the phonological module within the mind/brain. For ease of description and to lighten the debate, we will divide generative linguists into religious groups.[24] The main groups within the UG church vis-à-vis this part of the faith are the disbelievers, the agnostics, and the faithful. There are also dissenters whose position is either critical or ambivalent. Finally, there are (as ever) other churches that we briefly examine later.

Disbelievers are rare animals. To work within Chomskyan UG but deny totally its usual psychological/biological interpretation is to live dangerously. One extreme example is that of the French linguist Milner (1982: 302–17). While accepting the realist and universalist stance of Chomskyan generative grammar, he denies the validity of a number of its basic tenets including the following (his definition E): 'The generative linguist considers the principles which determine the class of possible grammars as a genetically determined property of the human species.' He claims that definition E is neither logically necessary nor descriptive of a factual situation. He argues that logical necessity cannot be invoked here since other hypotheses can be envisaged: e.g. one might consider that 'the universal principles which constrain possible grammars are not different in essence from the incest prohibition which constrains the class of possible human societies and which cannot be reasonably interpreted as a type of information which is part of the genetic code of our species' (our translation; Milner 1982: 317). As to the factual claim, it is demonstrably false since, as Milner says provocatively, 'there is at least one generative linguist, namely myself, who rejects (E)'. The agnostics are more widespread and provide the least challenging position from an epistemological point of view. While leaving open the question of how a grammar is instantiated in the brain, they use the concepts and hypotheses of UG as heuristic tools for describing and exploring the languages of the world. One common fate of agnostic generativists over time is to become descriptivists or to turn into formalists. The formalist orientation will be taken by those who believe that the classical goals of generative grammar are more important than the psychological dimension: i.e. the function of the grammar is to provide a fully explicit (mathematical) representation of the differences between the well-formed and the ill-formed strings of a given language. In syntax, various unification models could be taken as possible examples of this position. Within the field of sound structure, Declarative Phonology can be argued to adopt a similar position. Coleman (1995, 1998a), for instance, provides a particularly trenchant

---

[24] It is important to realize that no value judgement is being passed here. In terms of this terminology, Durand (1990, 1995) is a 'faithful' while Laks (1996b) is a 'dissenter'. The same person may belong to several categories as time unfolds and occasionally at the same time in different publications. Such contradictions are not usually fatal!

example of such an approach. He argues that post-*SPE* phonologies have failed in their attempt to restrict the excessive power inherent in the *SPE* approach.

> Inspired by the success of non-transformational, non-derivational syntactic theories (such as Lexical Functional Grammar and Generalized Phrase Structure Grammar) in challenging, matching and improving on transformational, derivational syntactic theory, a number of phonologists (including myself) are examining the applicability of non-derivational grammar formalisms to the phonological domain. The strategy offered by non-derivational phonology to the problem of excessive power is to drop the notion of derivation from the characterization of the surface forms of words. All rules R that alter representations in a way that gives rise to derivations, so that applying rule R before some other rule R′ brings about a different result from applying R after R′, are to be prohibited. Such a grammar attempts to characterise the set of surface forms of utterances directly, not via representation-altering rules from lexical entries which differ from the surface. (Coleman 1995: 335)

The faithful, as far as phonology is concerned, form a complex set. There are those who, under a realist stance, take it as axiomatic that phonology is part of UG and that phonological descriptions mirror the competence system internalized by speakers. They hope that other approaches (e.g. psychological experiments) will help as we progressively sharpen our CR (computational-representational) theories but they reject the notion that psycholinguistics or neurolinguistics has any special status in helping to validate our theoretical constructs.[25] Let's call this group 'contemplative'.[26] There are also faithful, we shall call them 'working', who actually attempt to validate their CR theories by leaving the traditional field of phonological description in search of 'external' evidence and would, if they are consistent, accept that such evidence could invalidate a description that seems satisfying on theoretical

---

[25] Recall the quote by Chomsky at the end of 1.3.2.

[26] Within this group some even go so far as to claim that, although much remains to be learned, the competence model of the linguist is equivalent to a performance model. A recent example is provided by Bromberger and Halle (2000: 35) who assert: 'Some people may object to our way of looking at phonology on the grounds that it construes phonology as about performance not competence. If they mean that we view phonology as about processes in real time responsible for the occurrence of tokens, they are right about our view. . . . Some will object that we have loaded phonology with unwarranted assumptions. Do speakers REALLY [emphasis in the original, J.D./B.L.] retrieve morphemes from their memory, invoke rules, go through all these labours when speaking? We think they do. In fact we would like to know more about how they do it. We may be mistaken. Time will tell. But intuition will not. Clearly speakers are not aware of performing such actions. But then we perform actions like zombies (to borrow a phrase from Ned Block). That is how we learn language, recognize faces and solve most of our problems.' As far as we are aware, most phonologists are much more prudent about the 'realization' or 'implementation' issue.

grounds. One interesting example of this approach is provided by Paradis and Prunet (this volume). But the main reason we stated that the 'faithful' do not form a homogeneous set is that, setting aside the question of how the phonology can be integrated into a performance system, one can also believe in UG but deny that phonology is strictly part of the innate language faculty.

To understand, at least partially, the debate about phonology and UG, it is useful to realize the very real shift which has taken place in linguistics since the 1960s with respect to the externalization of language or, to use current terminology, with the status of the interface systems which are accessed by the language faculty. Until the 1960s, linguists adopted wholeheartedly the idea that the use of the vocal-auditory channel was a defining property of natural languages. This was the position typically adopted in structuralist introductions to language[27] and it was taken over in most frameworks, including generative-transformational grammar which posited three components as part of UG: semantics, syntax, and phonology (Chomsky 1965, Chomsky and Halle 1968). Until relatively recently, sign languages were not mentioned or, when they were, they were treated as systems parasitic upon speech, echoing Bloomfield's position in *Language* (1933: 39–40):

Some communities have a *gesture language* which upon occasion they use instead of speech. Such gesture languages have been observed among the lower class Neapolitans, among Trappist monks (who have made a vow of silence), among the Indians of our western plains (where tribes of different language met in commerce and war), and among groups of deaf-mutes. . . . It seems certain that these gesture languages are merely developments of ordinary language and that any and all complicated or not immediately intelligible gestures are based on the conventions of ordinary speech . . . Whatever may be the origin of the two, gesture has so long played a secondary role under the dominance of language that it has lost all trace of independent character. Tales about peoples whose language is so defective that it has to be eked out by gesture, are pure myths. (1933: 39–40)

If Bloomfield was right to criticize the idea of primitive languages based solely on gestures (and, one assumes, inarticulate cries!), it is now generally recognized that the sign languages used by deaf people have the same semiotic potential as spoken languages. In fact, some recent textbooks in English (which are good indicators of which direction the field has taken) have attempted to integrate sign languages to their overview of language (Jackendoff 1993, Fromkin and Rodman 1998). On the basis of this

---

[27] Cf. e.g. Martinet's definition of language (1960: 20) as 'an instrument of communication through which human experience can be analysed, differently in each community, in units made up of a semantic content and a phonic expression, i.e. the monemes' (our translation, J.D./B.L.).

argument and others, a number of linguists have questioned or severed the connection between the language faculty and speech. Thus John Lyons (1991: 7) points out:

On present evidence, this [i.e. the idea that the association between language and speech is innately determined, J.D./B.L.] would be a hasty conclusion to draw. In my view, it is quite possible that the language-faculty and the predisposition to vocalise are biologically independent and contingently associated in speech.

And Chomsky himself has adopted an unequivocal stance on this point:

Though highly specialised, the language faculty is not tied to specific sensory modalities, contrary to what was assumed long ago. Thus, the sign language of the deaf is structurally much like spoken language, and the course of acquisition is very similar. Large-scale sensory deficit seems to have limited effect on language acquisition. Blind children acquire language as the sighted do, even colour terms and words for visual experience like 'see' and 'look'. There are people who have achieved close to normal linguistic competence with no sensory input beyond what can be gained by placing one's hands on another person's face and throat. The analytic mechanisms of the language faculty seem to be triggered in much the same ways whether the input is auditory, visual, even tactual, and seem to be localised in the same brain areas. (1995: 16)

This whole issue is obviously highly relevant for phonology and its place within UG, on the one hand, and the nature of phonological representations within the mind/brain, on the other. Some phonologists have taken the position that phonology is not part of UG at all (Burton-Roberts and Carr 1996, 1997, Burton-Roberts 2000, Carr 2000). One simple argument given by these linguists to defend their position is that the constraints posited in most models of phonology (including optimality theory) are rooted in a range of physiological, perceptual, and general cognitive capacities which must by definition fall outside of UG. This does not mean that sound systems cannot be studied scientifically but it means that they will have properties different from those one finds in the abstract syntax that UG seeks to characterize. Others such as Durand (1995) consider that phonology is part of UG. The reasoning rests (*a*) on the 'structural analogy' between phono-logical, morphological, and syntactic representations, (*b*) on the classical idea that the essence of UG is to offer a *relational* system linking semantic representations/computations and a 'signology'. Saussurean signs represent the language faculty at its most basic except that they need to be enriched with a syntactic part. Since the predisposition to vocalize is universal and severely constrained by species-specific mechanisms and as a result of evolution, it is naturally accessed by the language faculty. (We are describing human beings not Martians!) In human beings suffering from a speech/hearing impairment, it cannot be excluded that the abstract features/properties specified for phonology are recoded into an interface with a different medium.[28] Harry van der Hulst (1993, 2000) advocates a somewhat different position: phonology is part of UG but is concerned with the specification of something more abstract than standard phonological features, i.e. a system which underlies both speech and sign language.

This constellation of positions is extremely difficult to disentangle but many of the researchers working within the UG paradigm share the belief that a symbolic metalanguage is a good way of specifying the nature of the language faculty. Just as crucially, they often share what has been aptly called by Lindblom (1995: 464) the 'view from syntax'. In brief, the claim about sound structure (for those who include it within UG) is that, once everything linked to the use of language (production, perception, memory, social factors, etc.) is accounted for, there will remain a large core of phenomena which belong to 'Language *per se*' or the innate language faculty. This faculty 'is not reducible to features of other kinds' and therefore 'ought to occupy the central concern of linguists if they wish to arrive at an adequate conception of the essential and special nature of human Language' (Anderson 1981: 495). As we shall see in the rest of this chapter, strong challenges to this assumption have appeared both within phonology and within phonetics.

1.3.3.2. *Other approaches*

While a number of traditional models pursued their existence after the publication of *SPE* (e.g. Martinet's functionalist approach in France), it became increasingly difficult for phonologists not to situate themselves either in relation to *SPE* or in reaction to some post-*SPE* models symbiotically related to *SPE*. The main thrust of 'dissident' approaches has probably been a renewed emphasis on phonetic and general cognitive factors as opposed to the formal approach of *SPE*. As ever, there have been exceptions. A notable one is the work of James Foley (1977, 1979, *inter alia*), who adopts a point of view similar to Hjelmslev's in that phonology is seen as totally abstract,[29] a science of relations rather than objects, the latter (phonetic units) being epiphenomena resulting from other fundamental notions such as relative position on abstract strength scales. This hypothesis and the analyses offered by Foley are not without their appeal, but his model, if cut off from either

---

[28] This point of view is quite different from that of Burton-Roberts and Carr and compatible with that defended by Carstairs-McCarthy (1999) who traces all asymmetric relations in language (head/complement, topic/comment, predicate/argument) to the C/V split within syllables. Extending this idea, all syntax is derivable from phonology/phonetics!

[29] Foley goes so far as to call the *SPE* approach 'transformational phonetics'.

cognition or phonetic substance, can be shown to be impossible to falsify (cf. Coates 1979, Durand 1982). It seems to us that it is precisely the opposite point of view which has been dominant among the 'dissidents'.

For a number of researchers, the notion of explanatory adequacy in phonology cannot be theory internal but must rest on phonetic facts (auditory or physiological explanations) and on the nature of human communication with the constraints it imposes on signs. No more than a flavour of this type of approach can be given here. To take one example, Dressler (1981: 116 *et passim*) states that 'basic teleologies (or "functions") are assigned to each language component'. Thus, the purpose of segmental phonology lies in 'the double teleology of making language perceivable and pronounceable'. The function of natural phonological processes (e.g. the palatalization of velar consonants before [j, i, e]) is to aid or even constrain pronounceability or perceptibility by the structural change it imposes between input and output. Since this teleology can be served only by phonetic facts, the various criteria of phoneticity (plausibility, regularity, generality, phonologicalness of domains of application, etc.) can be combined as means to the same ends. More generally, following the philosopher Peirce, Dressler asserts that the more iconic a sign, the more natural it is. From this a number of consequences follow: for instance, an intrinsic allophone is favoured over a different phoneme as the output of a phonological rule. Properties which are part of UG in a generative approach and assumed to be not strictly explicable in functional terms are derived here from the semiotic nature of communication. Thus, the fact that transparency is preferred to opacity in phonological systems (cf. Kiparsky 1973) is not mysterious but the simple reflection of iconicity in language.

Another interesting type of approach refusing to sever phonology from actual performance has been that of Articulatory Phonology (Browman and Goldstein 1986, 1992). Instead of operating with classical distinctive features, Articulatory Phonology models *events* through the position of 'gestures' organized in 'tiers' within their respective subsystems in a 'gestural score'. The subsystems are the main components of speech production: i.e. the velic, glottal, and oral subsystems. The oral subsystem, to take just one example, is itself further divided into three tiers involving different coordinative structures: i.e. those controlling lip, tongue tip, and tongue body constrictions. One of the advantages of Articulatory Phonology, through the use of gestures, is the proximity of its constructs to phonetic realizations which are typically continuous and not discrete. By allowing gestures to overlap, blend, and mask one another, Articulatory Phonology offers a concrete approach, but also demonstrates that patterns of physiological activity are only indirectly reflected in the speech signal. The need for a more concrete link with observable speech processes is indeed a strand which has been accelerating over the last decade. Thus, Coleman (this volume), after working for many years within Declarative Phonology, now advocates the abandonment of symbolic-phonological representations in favour of the hypothesis that our mental representations of the form of words are essentially phonetic. More specifically, a combination of phonetic, statistical, and semantic knowledge is sufficient in his view to explain many aspects of phonological structure. In so far as researchers, like Coleman, reject the dual view of sound structure (the idea of a phonetic component dealing with the gradient bolted onto a phonological component dealing with the discrete) and wish to devise models which directly account for performance, they must integrate facts from a variety of disciplines and be ready to abandon the sharp opposition between phonology and phonetics which has characterized the field in the past. This is precisely what has taken place with the movement known as Laboratory Phonology.

Laboratory Phonology is not a specific model with shared assumptions about a theory of language. Rather, it is a research strategy based on the cooperation of people who do not necessarily agree about phonological theory, but who believe in the need to strengthen the scientific foundations of phonology through improved methodology, explicit modelling, and cumulative results. In the words of Pierrehumbert, Beckman, and Ladd (2000: 274):

Laboratory phonologists are scientists who use laboratory methods to discover and explain the sound structure of human languages. Their philosophical stance is generally that of researchers in the mature sciences, such as biology and physics. Specifically, most laboratory phonologists have abandoned the doctrine of dualism. They view language as a phenomenon of nature, albeit a particularly complex one. Language as a cognitive system imputed to individuals is thus to be explained in terms of general facts about the physical world (such as the fact that the resonances of an acoustic tube are determined by its shape; in terms of specific capabilities of the human species that arose through evolution).

As will be obvious from the above, Laboratory Phonology is definitely not a specific model within assumptions about phonological/phonetic primitives, the nature of phonological generalizations, and the way various levels of linguistic representations are interfaced. It is a reaction to the nature of formalism defended in *SPE* and indirectly in many of the models which appeared in its wake. We saw earlier that Chomsky and Halle reacted to the limitations of the 'overly formal' route taken in their analysis of English by introducing a new type of notational device (markedness conventions). Much post-*SPE* work in phonology has been devoted to devising notations able to mirror linguistically significant generalizations. Laboratory Phonologists do not deny the usefulness of this work. They question the assumption that work in phonology can proceed without paying attention to the nature of phonetic events and realistic models of phonetic performance. They question the modular decomposition of phonology and phonetics in which one module (phonology) is categorical and free of the gradient cumulative effects which are assumed to characterize the phonetic module uniquely (Pierrehumbert, Beckman, and Ladd 1996: 540). In a word, they defend an approach which breaks away from what they see as a traditional way of working (field work with informants and intuitions about sound structure) in favour of a more experimental, multidisciplinary paradigm.[30]

Laboratory Phonology offers a healthy position which is seen by some as a threat but which we are sympathetic to, as will be obvious from the selection of chapters in this book. It seems to us that the 'realist' position assumed in much Chomskyan work is open to discussion not necessarily in the letter but in the spirit with which it is applied. When we set up an account of any aspect of phonological structure, we agree with Chomsky that we do so in the hope of reaching 'truth' in that domain. In the absence of alternative accounts, the analysis proposed has to stand as 'true' and therefore in principle ascribable to the grammar internalized by speakers. But, the degree of idealization in phonological work, as in the rest of linguistics, is very high. Idealization is unavoidable and an essential component of any scientific work. It is customary in theoretical linguistics to quote approvingly work in the physical sciences to show that this is the only way to proceed. We fully understand this position. For instance, to study velocity in physics, scientists initially ignored friction. But, it should also be noted that at a later stage the scientist will reintroduce friction and such moves often lead to radical re-evaluations of previous assumptions or formalizations. Moreover, at various points in the history of science, it has not been the lack of mathematical sophistication which has impeded progress but the lack of experimentation. By this we do not mean one crucial experiment[31] but the cycles of conjectures and refutations involving different types of methodologies and technological innovations which have characterized modern science. We are well aware of the dangers of a naive empiricist approach, as examples can readily be found of famous scientists correcting empirical observations on the basis of

---

[30] Examples of this kind of work have been provided in the *Papers in Laboratory Phonology*, see Kingston and Beckman (1990), Docherty and Ladd (1992), Keating (1994), Connell and Arvaniti (1995), Broe and Pierrehumbert (2000).

[31] Thus, doubt has been expressed as to whether Galileo did perform the famous Leaning Tower experiment, see Boas (1970: 208). Boas notes the mathematical sophistication of some of the accounts of motion in the 17th century such as the Merton Rule, after the Oxford college, which gave a geometric account of accelerated motion.

their bold hypotheses. For instance, on several occasions, Newton asked Flamsteed, the first Astronomer Royal, to correct his 'data' since they clashed with his own theory and this led to a bitter personal controversy between the two men. As Lakatos (1970: 131) put it, 'One can understand the constant humiliation and slowly increasing fury of this great observer, having his data criticized and improved by a man who, on his own confession, made no observations himself.' But classical astronomy, although it has often been seen as a model for linguistic research, is not the only example one can follow. If one moves to physics, one may wonder how the idea that 'Nature abhors a vacuum' could ever have been falsified without Torricelli tubes and the kinds of experiments performed by Pascal at Clermont-Ferrand and the Puy-de-Dôme (cf. Pascal 1663).[32] Such a point of view will not yield a grand theory quickly but, for the practitioners of Laboratory Phonology, will contribute to the emergence of much more realistic and comprehensive models of speech production and perception in a biological perspective. What it entails however is a rejection of a strong divide between phonology and phonetics.

1.3.3.3. *The connectionist challenge*

In the last two decades, the greatest challenge to the cognitive approach adopted in the Chomskyan tradition (referred to as 'classical cognitivism' from now on) has arguably come from what is often referred to as 'connectionism' (Rumelhart, McClelland, et al. 1986; Elman et al. 1996). Classical cognitivism is seen by connectionists as narrowly linked to a classical approach to computation based on the division of labour between a central processor and static memory, and a digitalization of logical processes. This von Neumann architecture characterizes digital computers and finds a typical interpretation within Artificial Intelligence. Connectionism has different roots but central to its approach is the notion of analogical computation.[33] In this approach founded on an explicit neuronal metaphor, computation is basically energetic and dynamic. The analogical coding consists in implementing the problem to be solved in the form of energies which affect processing units which are simple but strongly interconnected: formal neurones. A neural network forms a kind of computational lattice within which possibly antagonistic energies will circulate. Ever since the seminal work of McCulloch and Pitts (1943), it has been known that the energetic

[32] On the new experimentalism in the philosophy of science, see Chalmers (1999: ch. 13) and the references therein.

[33] Contrary to what is often asserted, parallel or neuronal architectures are not a recent innovation. See for instance von Neumann (1992), who offers an explicit comparison of modes of coding (analogical/digital) and architectures (parallel/serial).

stabilization of these networks, sometimes referred to as their dynamic relaxation, allows for the analogical simulation of the calculation of logical functions and has thus been claimed to offer a first approximation to mental operations. Since the new impetus which was given to these studies in the 1980s, connectionist approaches have known extensive developments in all areas of computational and cognitive modelling. Rumelhart, McClelland et al. (1986) offer a synthesis of possible connectionist approaches to vision, reasoning, calculation, and above all language processes which, from the very beginning, have been the linchpin of cognitive modelling. In particular, they present fascinating results in the learning of irregular English verbs, the modelling of semantico-pragmatic scenarios, and the recognition of spoken words.[34] In phonology an original approach in the form of Dynamic Linear Models (DLMs) has been developed by Goldsmith and Larson.[35] DLMs are not classical connectionist models capable of implementing any function but networks specifically dedicated to phonology. Within this framework, Laks (1995, 1996a, 1996b, 1997b) has shown how a unilayered perceptron with bilateral inhibition such as the one represented in Fig. 1.1 is able to model accentual patterns in a wide variety of languages or to model French syllabification.[36]

In this network made up of six formal neurones (K1 . . . K6), the synaptic connectivity is bilateral (α1 . . . α6, β1 . . . β6). At time To, inputs are introduced in the form of quanta of activation for each formal neurone (a(K1)To . . . A(K6)To). The rule of dynamic relaxation for the network which leads to its stabilization at T via energy propagation through its synapses, is fixed as follows:

$$a(k_i)^{t''} = a(k_i)^{t^0} + \alpha_i \left(a(k_{i-1})^{t^{n-1}} \right) + \beta_i \left(a(k_{i+1})^{t^{n-1}} \right)$$

In connectionist approaches, a formal neurone is in fact defined as an extremely simple processor able to receive and transmit energy through its synaptic connections. The updating of the energy level of a neurone is a

[34] For an overview of this general approach, see Bechtel and Abrahamsen (1993). The first connectionist analyses of various morphological features of English were clearly limited and gave rise to criticisms by various linguists and psycholinguists (e.g. Prasada and Pinker 1993, and the references therein). For revisions of the connectionist treatments, see MacWhinney et al. (1989), MacWhinney and Leinbach (1991), Marchman (1993), Ling (1994), Ping and MacWhinney (1996).

[35] Cf. Goldsmith (1991, 1992, 1993a, 1993b, 1994), Goldsmith and Larson (1991).

[36] A unilayered perceptron is a simple neuromimetic structure made up of interconnected logical processors (formal neurones). The architecture is non-hierarchical (unilayered) and the connections are inhibitory. Within a level, connectivity is complete (bilateral). The network presented in the text is taken from Laks (1995). Whereas for Goldsmith α and β are fixed for the whole network, they are variables in Laks's approach.

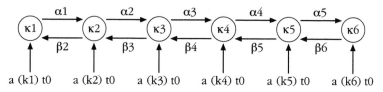

FIG. 1.1. Unilayered perceptron.

function of its inputs/outputs as well as that of its parameters of connectivity. What is usually called the 'semantics of the network', that is, its ability to deal with specific problems, is completely determined by its architecture and its synaptic weights. Connectivity and weights can be progressively adapted so that the network's answer (i.e. its final state) may fit a predefined target more closely. Thus the learning process exhibits some of the properties usually considered as typical of intelligent learning: spontaneous classification and generalization, systematization, and the drawing of inferences. A network such as the one presented in Fig. 1.1 therefore implements a dynamic computation which is algebraic but not algorithmic. No rule, no rewriting symbolic rule, no predefined explicit process applies to the calculus which is strictly non-symbolic. In this cognitive approach, processes and mental states are coded and implemented without recourse to the rich symbolic lexicon linguists are familiar with (constituent, syllable, nucleus, stress) and without recourse to a more or less complex syntax based on that lexicon.[37] The difference between this approach and AI, and indeed all linguistic models that use a symbolic architecture, is obvious: in neuromimetic (connectionist) approaches there are no explicit symbolic representations, and calculations do not proceed through logico-syntactic manipulations. It can of course be objected that the initial coding and the external inputs reflect a representation of the problem to be dealt with, but this representation is totally or partially (according to the model) *distributed* throughout the network. No formal neurone can represent alone an element or a subpart of the representation. Rather, the representation is a function of the network as a whole.

   The type of holistic approach just described has been analysed by Smolensky (1988) as *subsymbolic*. It offers a precise hypothesis as to the functioning of the mind/brain. According to this hypothesis, there is no autonomy of the mind with respect to its physiological substratum and it is seen as axiomatic that cognition takes place within dynamic systems and not within numerical computers. This is claimed to be more in agreement with the findings of neurobiology, in particular with the idea that the human brain

---

[37] For an analysis of the central role played by syntax in classical cognitivism, cf. Fodor and Pylyshyn (1987).

is defined less by the characteristics of individual neurones than by the extraordinary complexity of its architecture, the parallelism of its operations, and the vast interconnectivity of its components. This is why connectionism is often presented as a neuromimetic approach, not because the architectures it develops are necessarily fully realistic but because the principles it adopts mirror basic properties of the brain. Connectionism thus sees itself as strongly physicalist and profoundly different from the Chomskyan approach. The most advanced properties of the human mind *emerge* directly from the extraordinary complexity of the human brain. In this strictly ascending empiricist approach, there is no need for the postulation of innate functions. It is sufficient to postulate a genetic conditioning of neuronal structures. Only the physical level is truly causal.

On the basis of the notions of synaptic connectivity and synaptic plasticity, connectionism has developed a whole gamut of tools and techniques for exploring the notion of learning. Unlike Chomskyan innatism, it is claimed that learning is essentially conditioned by the repeated restructurings and reactions of an organism in response to external data plus the initial states whenever there is evidence for specialization of the brain in a particular domain (as seems plausible for phonology and phonetics). These reactions are accompanied by a continuous evaluation of the performances of the network through a process of feedback or retroactive evaluation. There is undeniably a similarity with classical behaviourism. Nevertheless, this neobehaviourism tries to integrate data collected during the last decades in psycholinguistics and does not exclude prespecification (at least in the version which seems to us defensible).

Connectionist models come in many different varieties. The most extreme varieties have often been referred to as 'eliminationist connectionist models'. Among the tenets of these approaches is the idea that the basic analytic concepts of generative and most other linguistic theories are simple artefacts which can and should be eliminated in some sense and that the dynamic numerical computations embodied in neural nets should replace all symbolic approaches. There is however a problem in adopting such a strong stance. Connectionism is neither quantitatively nor qualitatively fully realistic from a neurobiological point of view. First, the current techniques of dynamic calculations and the size, complexity, and architecture of the networks effectively manipulable are vastly inferior to the capacities of the human brain. Secondly, our knowledge of neural architectures, synaptic processes, and more generally of the neurophysiology and neurochemistry of the brain is still in its infancy, despite the very real progress which has been achieved (see Démonet et al., this volume). Thirdly, while one might disagree with the particular modular view advocated by Chomsky, and in particular the 'radical autonomy' of syntax, it is difficult to deny that there are psycholinguistic examples (e.g. dissociations) which support specialization or a form of modularity in the present state of knowledge.[38] Finally, in the systemic approaches which connectionism takes as a point of departure, the quantitative complexity factors are in fact functional qualitative factors. It is often such factors which lead systems to diverge. From this angle, and in terms of complexity and therefore also of functional properties, neural networks and neuromimetic networks are within orders of magnitude which are not fully comparable. Indeed, it cannot be excluded that the typical properties of each of them might be substantially modified as sizes increase.

Our own view is that the best way to proceed is to see connectionism as allowing us to explore functional and cognitive processes in what is, in our current state of knowledge, a plausible framework from the point of view of neurobiology.[39] Thus, the neuromimetic metaphor is only a first approximation. We do not see connectionism as a realist model (except by fiat) but as an interesting way of simulating a number of higher cognitive processes (whether linguistic or not) such as reasoning, drawing inferences, or categorizing. The position taken by Laks (1996*a*) is that connectionism offers an intermediate level of modelling. This level seems interesting from the point of view of cognition. The reason is that, if the physical and neuronal level is ultimately the *causal* level, it is not (partially for the complexity reasons raised above) analysable or penetrable as such. This has always posed severe problems for strictly physicalist approaches. To solve them, a better strategy is to analyse neurophysiological causality and cognitive processes in general at two levels: on the one hand, the level of the concrete implementation of these processes which is solely neurophysical and, on the other hand, the description, analysis, and understanding of these same processes which are, whether we like it or not, constructed on the basis of a symbolic and discursive vocabulary and belong therefore to a quite distinct symbolic level.

1.4. PHONETICS:
AN ALTERNATIVE PARADIGM?

As was stressed earlier on, phonetics until the twentieth century was not an autonomous discipline separate from the study of language.[40] Even if we

---

[38] Cf. Yamada (1990), Gopnik and Crago (1991), Smith and Tsimpli (1995).

[39] For a recent attempt to devise a biologically credible model of language, see Lamb (1998).

[40] For a thorough assessment of the historical relationship between phonology and phonetics from the perspective of a speech specialist, cf. Boë (1997).

insisted on reinterpreting past works in terms of present-day distinctions (a questionable approach), the emergence of phonetics would be seen to coincide with the beginning of the 'grammaticalization of language' in the terminology of the historian of linguistics Sylvain Auroux. But it is in the nineteenth century that phonetics reaches a form close to the modern one. First of all, it provides a tool for the description and notation of the sounds found in the languages of the world. It is not an accident if Bell's (1867) book *Visible Speech* is subtitled: *the science of universal alphabetics, or self-interpreting physiological letters for the printing and writing of all languages*. It also permits a more thorough description of the dialects of each language and, fundamentally in the century which saw the birth of Darwinism, it offers a scientific account of the evolution of sounds. In the European tradition, phonetics was the discipline which allowed the Neogrammarians to break loose from orthography and build a theoretical picture of the evolution of Indo-European. In North America, phonetics provided the indispensable foundation for describing the native Amerindian languages which presented anthropologists, linguists, and missionaries with sounds usually outside the ambit of what Benjamin Lee Whorf called SAE (Standard Average European). In addition, for many centuries, the study of sounds has had an applied dimension which should not be underestimated.

One salient example of the applied role of phonetics is that of the International Phonetic Association, which from the beginning set itself very practical aims beside the description of the sound patterns of the world's languages: e.g. giving tools for devising or improving orthographic systems and helping to develop an aural-oral approach to language teaching. This practical approach has been maintained since the creation of this body in 1886 as is evident from the publication of the recent *Handbook of the International Phonetic Association* (1999). To limit ourselves to Great Britain in the twentieth century, the IPA has been linked to a rich descriptive tradition with phoneticians like Daniel Jones, then students of his such as Gimson and Abercrombie, who, in turn, trained numerous distinguished phoneticians. Their work has been in the form of advanced manuals of general phonetics (Catford 1977, Laver 1994, Ladefoged and Maddieson 1996), dictionaries (Jones 1917, Wells 1990, Roach and Hartman 1997) and pedagogical overviews of the pronunciation of various languages (e.g. for English, Jones 1956, Gimson 1962, Cruttenden 1994, Roach 2000). Because of its diverse aims, this particular strand has often steered a middle path between linguistics on the one hand and speech science on the other. A more cognitive and technical orientation has however been taken in the application of phonetics to language pathology. To help deal with a wide range of problems such as the delayed onset of language acquisition, aphasia, or teaching the hard-of-hearing,[41] speech specialists have inevitably looked at both ends of the communication chain: the coding of language in the brain on the one hand and its concrete embodiment in speech patterns on the other. Such work has strongly contributed to the constitution of a multi-disciplinary programme, that of the phonetic sciences.

If one speaks of the phonetic sciences (in the plural form), it is because progress in this field of enquiry has benefited from various scientific advances in physiology, acoustics, electronics, and computing which have built on the theoretical and practical knowledge accumulated over several centuries. The groundbreaking work of physicists like Fourier and Helmholtz has made the modern developments in speech acoustics possible, in particular the theory of resonators. In the twentieth century, the development of the sound spectrograph and the combined use of techniques such as X-ray photography, then cineradiography, and more recently MRI (Magnetic Resonance Imaging)[42] have fulfilled the dream of 'visible speech' which had eluded the nineteenth century (except via the use of symbols). But it should not be thought that phoneticians have been passive recipients of knowledge developed in other fields. For a start, many past scholars such as Helmholtz (1867) were authentic phoneticians whose aims were indeed to explore linguistic sounds and who combined physiology and acoustics in their approach. In the twentieth century, this interdisciplinary work has been continued by specialists like Chiba and Kajiyama (1941), Fant (1960), Flanagan (1972), and their inheritors.[43] The birth of the phonetics laboratory took place approximately a hundred years ago and already the experimental work of specialists like Rousselot had recourse to an impressive array of techniques and machines. In its wake, modern phonetics has seen the development of essential research tools such as electro-palatography or electromyography (EMG).

Progress in phonetics during the twentieth century has been so rapid and so successful that the old dream of talking machines has been reawakened. Cordemoy's *Discours physique de la parole* (1668) was by no means putting forward a new idea when he envisaged this possibility. It is also interesting to note that the success of Vaucanson in building famous machines like his 'flautist' and his 'digesting duck' (exhibited in Paris in 1738) led some well-known contemporaries to press him to build a 'talking automaton' ('automate parlant'). As La Mettrie (1751) observed:

[41] It should however be noted that the teaching of the deaf was linked to an emphasis on 'oralism' which was questionable in the repressive form it often took. For sensitive discussions of this question, see Sacks (1989), Rée (1999).

[42] See Démonet et al. (this vol.) for the use of some of these techniques in neurolinguistics.

[43] e.g. Stevens (1999) and the references therein.

If Vaucanson needed more talent to make his Flautist than his Duck, he should have endeavoured even more to devise a Talker: a machine which cannot be considered as impossible, especially in the hands of this new Prometheus. (our translation, J.D./B.L.)[44]

Until the recent decades, however, the possibility of high-quality speech synthesis of whole utterances has not been possible and speech analysis continues to pose serious, if not insuperable, problems to specialists. One facetious version of the difficulties faced by engineers in these areas blamed the continued presence of linguists within research projects. Allegedly, every time a linguist was sacked the performance of the systems would undergo a dramatic increase! This phase was often the result of a mismatch between, on the one hand, the unrealistic hopes of engineers and their lack of appreciation of the complexity of language, and, on the other hand, the refusal by linguists to descend to the materiality of speech. At the present time, the position of many researchers in speech synthesis and analysis seems much less polarized and the need for high-level linguistic knowledge is taken for granted in a number of approaches.[45]

As can be seen from the many disciplines mentioned so far, one obvious problem is whether phonetics has a core around which research is organized. Ladefoged (1988), reflecting on the fact that communication engineering, physical acoustics, psychology, anatomy, physiology, linguistics, computer science, and poetry are part of the lives of phoneticians, ended up saying: 'we are phoneticians, we the people who come to phonetic congresses, and know something about some of these diverse disciplines. None of us can know enough about all of them, which is why being a complete phonetician is an impossible task. *But every four years we can get together and pool our knowledge. This is phonetics*' (our italics, J.D./B.L.).[46] But, as noted by Lindblom, while there is a sociological dimension to phonetics and while phoneticians have to learn from other disciplines, it is possible to define a research programme for phonetics. It could be defined thus:

Phoneticians seek facts and insights about how speech is produced, perceived and acquired. And about how the world's sound patterns are related to the on-line phenomena of speaking, listening and learning. (Lindblom 1995: 462)

This view of phonetics seems to us pretty close to a consensus view of the subject. The way a number of phoneticians have interpreted this programme

---

[44] Quoted in Boë (1997: 18) who offers a worthwhile discussion of this question and further references.

[45] See, *inter alia*, the essays in Sagisaka, Campbell, and Higuchi (1997), Botinis (to appear).

[46] Quoted in Lindblom (1995: 462).

and seen it as quite different from a linguistic approach is that it emphasizes 'substance' as opposed to abstract form which is meant to be the trademark of the phonologist. Many speech specialists reject what they consider a Saussurean dogma: i.e. that 'Language' has logical priority over 'speech'. This 'substance-oriented' approach is often seen as providing a new framework for the study of language in its biological context (Liljencrants and Lindblom 1972; Lindblom 1986; Boë *et al.* 2000; Schwartz et al., this volume). The description of sound systems should be based on non-phonological principles, whether listener-oriented (perceptual contrast and stability) or speaker-oriented (articulatory contrast and stability). While this is to some extent similar to some of the 'natural' approaches mentioned in 1.3.3.2 (e.g. Dressler 1981), the difference is that most of the linguistic concepts of the former are replaced here by hard constraints imposed by the physics and physiology of speech.[47] Because modern phonetics sees itself as dealing with the whole speech chain (from the coding of messages in the brain to utterances and back), it is at the same time cognitive and grounded in physiology and physics. It could be argued, and some distinguished phoneticians have taken that position, that such an approach makes phonology redundant.

It seems to us that this conclusion would be totally unwarranted. First of all, many of the hypotheses made about the 'physiological' dimension are themselves dependent on the work of phonologists. Lindblom's definition above mentions the world's 'sound patterns'. These 'sound patterns' are however not acoustic facts. They are, more often than not, the result of painstaking analyses by phonologists of the languages of the world. Indeed, notions such as 'opposition' and 'complementary distribution' or 'phonotactic constraint' which lie at the root of many of the databases currently used by experimental phoneticians are built on the 'phonemic' insight of early twentieth-century phonology. Secondly, when one defines principles such as perceptual or articulatory contrast as non-phonological, it is purely a matter of definition. The perception and production of contrasts can no doubt be tested in the laboratory but the basic concept of contrast cannot be divorced from its linguistic function. Thirdly, and this is a problem faced by speech synthesis/analysis, at some point hypotheses have to be made with respect to mentally represented structures. At this point, if one wants breadth of coverage (e.g. to deal with an open-ended lexicon and therefore include derivational processes and take into account the fact that language allows the construction of an indefinitely large number of utterances) it is difficult to ignore linguistics and its classical offshoot 'phonology'. One of the

---

[47] See Schwartz et al. (this vol.) who defend a dispersion-focalization theory of vowel production and perception.

long-standing insights of phonology (reasserted by the generative paradigm), has been that the sound systems of the world's languages are not made up of sounds qua sounds but rather show that the network of contrasts is embedded in a rich morpho-syntactic and semantic-pragmatic structure. Phonetics without phonology, and conversely phonology without phonetics, are perhaps possible but at what price?

1.5. A NEW SYNTHESIS?

After this survey of selected aspects of the evolution of phonology and phonetics, one question can be raised: since there are undeniable signs of convergence between these two disciplines, are they likely to merge in the near future? Sociologically, a rapid merger does not seem probable. At one extreme, the fact that many phonologists teach and do research in arts faculties places constraints on the type of work they will undertake. Their students usually pursue qualifications in subjects like general linguistics, foreign languages, and English (in English-speaking countries), and they will rarely be willing or able (in terms of time or competence) to follow a highly technical literature on physiology or acoustics. The research will often be carried out in an environment which is not as rich in sophisticated equipment as that of a science faculty. Moreover, the research areas will be expected to link up with the exploration of levels of linguistic structure (e.g. morphology, syntax, semantics) which might themselves be studied by colleagues in a mode which does not favour the integration of neurobiological or phonetic analyses. Lastly, much work of a descriptive nature still has to be carried out (e.g. field work on endangered languages) which by its very nature does not favour an instrumental approach in the phonetics laboratory. At the other extreme, phoneticians who work on speech synthesis within an industrial environment (e.g. a telecom group) may have little time to worry about the ontological nature of the entities they deal with, their significance for a theory of language, or even the psychological plausibility of the techniques employed to generate high-quality signals. In addition, the publications expected of these two types of researcher, the conferences they attend, the networks within which they operate, and the external and financial recognition they receive for their work will be among the factors that will continue to divide phonologists and phoneticians.[48] At the same time, it

---

[48] These 'external' factors are of course part of the history of the linguistic sciences, see e.g. Chevalier (2000). Recall the quote from Ladefoged in section 1.4: 'But every four years we can get together and pool our knowledge. This is phonetics.'

seems to us likely that at the cutting edge of research the boundaries will become more and more blurred. As our understanding of the neurophysiological basis of language production and perception progresses and as our theories of language become more sophisticated, a fully integrated approach may become possible. The stratal approach still assumed by many researchers (a phonetic module dealing with the gradient bolted onto a phonology module dealing with the discrete) may well prove untenable. In the meantime, we believe that the knowledge accumulated by phonologists of the interaction of sound systems with the morphology, syntax, semantics, and pragmatics of natural languages will continue to pose a challenge to purely 'substance-based' accounts if they restrict themselves to the 'biological hardware'. What seems to us to be a thing of the past (or if one prefers a 'degenerative' research programme in the sense of Lakatos 1970) is a strident call for two totally autonomous disciplines with sharply delineated boundaries and separate research methods.

2

What Are Phonological Syllables Made of? The Voice/Length Symmetry

Joaquim Brandão de Carvalho

2.1. INTRODUCTION

There are, in the phonetic and phonological literature since the beginning of
this century, two traditions according to whether syllables are viewed as
primitive or emerging objects (cf. Klein 1993). *Constituency*-based views of
the syllable have prevailed in most phonological frameworks, from Pike and
Pike's (1947) and Kuryłowicz's (1948) classical arborescences to Levin's
(1985) metrical model. According to such models, segmental features or
elements are licensed (cf. Goldsmith 1990: § 3.4) by hierarchically ordered
symbolic primes such as onsets, rhymes, nuclei, and codas (or their X-bar
counterparts). Little attention has been paid by modern phonological theory

This chapter is a revised version of a paper presented at the Inaugural Conference of the
GDR Phonologie of the CNRS, 'The Strong Position: Lenition and Fortition', held in Nice,
24–25 June 1999. I am grateful to Jacques Durand, Tobias Scheer, and Philippe Ségéral for
helpful comments. I am particularly indebted to Marc Klein, whose views on syllable structure
had a strong influence on the formalization proposed in this chapter.

to the second trend. In *curve*-based approaches to the syllable, from Jespersen (1904), van Ginneken (1907), and Saussure (1976) to dynamic computational networks (cf. e.g. Goldsmith 1993*a*), syllable structure is assumed to follow from segmental content, more accurately from segmental 'aperture' or 'sonority', hence the well-known 'sonority scales', or the assignment of sonority coefficients to segments. As a result, there are only segmental primitives in these models. In both approaches, however, sonority, and, in particular, one of its main correlates—voice(lessness)—are intrinsic properties of segments, as opposed, for example, to length, which also plays a major role in syllable stucture, and was shown to be a prosodic effect by autosegmental phonology, thanks to the notion of skeletal positions and the Obligatory Contour Principle (cf. Goldsmith 1976). This has particular importance today, since the segmental nature of sonority may naturally be viewed as evidence for 'output-based' and non-representational approaches to the syllable.

The basic claim in this chapter is precisely that voice, and, more generally, all features associated in articulatory phonetics with 'voice onset time' (VOT)—voice, voicelessness, and aspiration (henceforth VOT-values)—are *not* segmental features, just like length. It is proposed here that phonological words are characterized by two parallel curves which follow from the association with the skeleton of two autonomous and antinomic tiers: the onset-tier, which contains the roots of consonants, is supposed to stand for articulatory 'tension'; the nucleus-tier, which bears the roots of vowels, represents perceptual 'sonority'. Both VOT-values and length contrasts are 'allophones' of such abstract invariants: they result from the varying weight of tension and sonority, i.e. from the number of slots onsets and nuclei are associated with. Hence, VOT and length are to be seen as intrinsic, or rather, constitutive properties of syllables: 'syllables' exist wherever VOT and/or length contrasts may emerge. Hence, also, in so far as VOT and length imply specific phonological units such as onsets and nuclei, representational approaches to the syllable are still necessary.[1]

---

[1] The question of whether the primitives required for VOT and length are ultimately *symbolic* units or not is a different point. In what follows, notions like 'onsets' and 'nuclei' are represented much as in current phonological works. It should be noted, however, that the present chapter is partly based in Carvalho's (1998) Boolean theory of segmental and syllabic units, where primitives lack any intrinsic content; rather, phonological content emerges from Boolean operations (cf. n. 5). Though this theory inspires most notions that will be presented below (ON and NO interactions, different markedness values for one element, ON symmetry in unmarked syllables, etc.), an attempt was made here to formulate the mathematical apparatus that underlies Carvalho's (1998) model into current autosegmental terminology.

The chapter is organized as follows. In section 2.2, VOT-values are shown to exhibit structural and functional properties which differentiate them from other phonological primes, but make them similar to length (section 2.2.1). In order to explain these facts, which are not naturally accounted for by current phonological theories, it is argued that VOT-values and length contrasts are to be assigned a similar representation: just as length follows from the spreading of a given 'melody' to two skeletal slots, so do aspiration and voice emerge from the association of one phonological object with two slots (section 2.2.2). In section 2.3, it is claimed that the spreading objects are onsets and nuclei, in such a way that both VOT and length contrasts result from ON and NO interactions respectively. This is shown in section 2.4 to lead to a model of syllabic structure where 'CV' is the only syllable type, i.e. where neither V- nor CVC-syllables (as in *cap*, *cap-tive*) are allowed at a phonological level; unlike Lowenstamm's (1996) similar thesis, however, it implies branching onsets and nuclei in terms of O/N interactions. As will be seen, syllable markedness naturally follows from such interactions. Empirical evidence for the present approach is adduced in section 2.5: we shall see how it provides a natural account of: (*a*) compensatory lengthening, (*b*) edge-specific phenomena like initial aspiration and final devoicing, (*c*) lenition processes and their relationship with lengthening. In section 2.6, we relate our conclusions to some of the positions defended in this volume.

2.2. THREE PROBLEMS WITH ASPIRATION AND VOICE

2.2.1

Three problems at least arise whenever aspiration and voice are viewed as primitive features or elements, as are, e.g., [±low], [±round], [±nasal], etc. or the elements A, U, N . . . in unarist theories. None of these problems is specific to laryngeal features; only laryngeal features, however, share the three points that will be discussed below.

2.2.1.1

In binarist frameworks that allow underspecification (e.g. Kiparsky 1982, Steriade 1987, Archangeli 1988), as well as in unarist theories (cf. Schane 1984, Kaye, Lowenstamm, and Vergnaud 1985, 1990, Anderson and Ewen 1987, Carvalho 1994), segments may be characterized by one and only one feature or element: for example, the 'primary' vowels /i/, /a/, and /u/ are currently described within unarist models as containing one element each, i.e. I, A, and U respectively; likewise, the velar nasal consonant that is often the only nasal occurring word-finally can be said to have only the [+nasal] feature (or the N-element), 'backness' being a default feature; finally, when /s/, and sometimes all fricatives, turn into [h] in coda position, the laryngeal consonant may be viewed as having only one element: its manner ('fricative') feature.

Now, it has never been reported that a consonant can be exhaustively characterized by its being 'voiced' under similar conditions. In sum, unlike presumably most segmental primes, voice(lessness) does not behave as an 'independent' feature: it necessarily presupposes the presence of other features or elements (typically place features) within the segment. This property of VOT-values is not naturally accounted for either by feature geometries (cf. Clements 1985, Sagey 1986, McCarthy 1988) or by other devices like 'charm' (cf. Kaye, Lowenstamm, and Vergnaud 1985, and note 4 below). In the first case, it is not clear why there should not be a process delinking all nodes except the one that dominates the VOT-values. Actually, a similar situation is attested when the place node is delinked, but the manner node is preserved, hence well-known processes like /p t k/ → [ʔ] or /f s χ/ → [h]. Now, the geometries proposed so far do not explain why features like voice(lessness), which share with [ʔ] and [h] a glottal basis, should not behave like manner features with respect to the place node. In this respect at least, feature geometries are not sufficiently constrained. Regarding the other concept which has been proposed in phonology in order to constrain the relationships between primes, that is, charm, nothing but their intrinsic content explains why L (= voice, low tone) and H (= voicelessness, high tone) form a natural class of elements among the set of unary primes.

2.2.1.2

Another functional problem concerning the VOT-values is provided by the well-known lenition processes. A historical change like the western Romance lenition, through which a /tt/ ~ /t/ contrast turns into a /t/ ~ /d/ opposition, is clearly problematic for any theory of segmental primitives. The difficulty is that a change like /tt/ ~ /t/ > /t/ ~ /d/ suggests that gemination and voice behave as the opposite poles of a strength scale. Now, though vocalic height may perhaps be formalized in such a way, Foley's (1977) claim that /tt/ ~ /t/ ~ /d/ show a gradient relationship is hardly acceptable for modern phonological theory: unlike voice, gemination is no longer viewed as primitive; it follows from the spreading of a given melody to two skeletal positions, which is supported by a large array of facts, from compensatory lengthening and syllable weight to evidence adduced by word games and lapsus. How, then, can a quantitative distinction like /tt/ ~ /t/ become a qualitative one such as /t/ ~ /d/? No satisfactory answer is given by the current systems of phonological primes, which assume the autosegmental representation of length, and the primitive status of voice and voicelessness.

2.2.1.3

Finally, there is a structural problem with VOT-values. Aspiration and/or voice contrasts are not, say, 'symmetric' features: they are universal among consonants; they are, however, highly marked among vowels, where voicelessness (or rather breathy voice) is extremely rare as a distinctive feature. This well-known fact (which, by the way, also concerns nasality) is not naturally accounted for by standard theories. For example, glottal features are assigned the same place in both consonant and vowel geometries, which is obviously misleading as to their role in either of these major classes. Hence, arbitrary licensing stipulations are required in order to account for this asymmetry. Even if these stipulations might be phonetically grounded, they remain formally arbitrary; they do not follow from any phonological theory.

2.2.2

These considerations suggest the three following hypotheses on the phonological nature of the VOT-values:

(1) *a.* There are no specific segmental primitives underlying VOT (cf. section 2.2.2.1);
   b. VOT-values result from autosegmental spreading (cf. section 2.2.2.2);
   c. VOT and length are contextual realizations of the same invariants (cf. section 2.2.2.3).

2.2.2.1

The dependent character of voice (cf. section 2.2.1.1) makes its behaviour similar to that of length: there is no 'voiced' consonant *tout court*; likewise, no system shows only one 'long' vowel or consonant, which could thus be viewed as having this unique distinctive feature. Now, length is not a primitive (cf. section 2.2.1.2). Therefore, voice is not a primitive either.

This amounts to saying that there is no specific voice feature. For the sake of generalization, the same will be assumed about the 'mirror image' of voice: aspiration. Thus, the fact that voice is never found without other features within a segment is no longer surprising: should these features be deleted, there would be nothing left!

2.2.2.2

Let us go on with the analogy between length and voice suggested by the strength scale /tt/ ~ /t/ ~ /d/ (cf. section 2.2.1.2): if gemination is an effect of autosegmental spreading, then voice is also the result of propagation. No particular problem, thus, arises from the lenition process mentioned in section 2.2.1.2, which now has a homogeneous basis: it is no longer the case that a quantitative distinction (/tt/ ~ /t/) turns into a qualitative one (/t/ ~ /d/); a quantitative contrast is replaced with another quantitative contrast.

On the other hand, if /tt/ ~ /t/ ~ /d/ functions as a strength scale, this is also the case of the /tʰ/ ~ /t/ ~ /d/-triplet: both aspiration and voice oppositions have always been interpreted as *fortis* ~ *lenis* contrasts. Hence, if voice results from spreading, so does aspiration.

As a result, the following problem arises: assuming that both voice and aspiration emerge from autosegmental spreading, what are the spreading objects involved here? This will be discussed in section 2.3.

2.2.2.3

Finally, if we continue to take seriously the analogy between length and VOT, we can observe that just as aspiration and voice are marked in word-final consonants, as if they implied a *following* nucleus, so is gemination in word-initial consonants, as if consonantal length presupposed a *preceding* nucleus. Hence, there is no particular problem again with the 'asymmetry' of the VOT-values (cf. section 2.2.1.3): there is, indeed, a symmetric relationship between VOT and length. Aspiration and voice are optimally associated with consonants because they are emerging properties of the onset, or rather, of the onset/nucleus sequence; likewise, gemination, and more generally length, are properties of the rhyme, or, more accurately, of the nucleus/onset sequence. In short, VOT and length are in complementary distribution: they occur in mirror contexts within the syllable. Assuming this complementarity, the following question arises: what are the invariants whose 'allophones' are VOT and length?

2.3. O/N AND N/O INTERACTIONS

2.3.1

To summarize the points discussed in sections 2.2.2.1–2, we assume that VOT and length emerge from the spreading of some objects which are not specific primes corresponding to aspiration and voice or to consonantal and vocalic length. What, then, are such objects? Given this parallelism between VOT and length, a first hypothesis would be that the spreading objects which are responsible for the VOT contrasts are the same as those involved in length. Within standard frameworks (slightly modified for the sake of simplicity), we have /atta/ or /aata/ according to whether the second slot of a branching rhyme is associated with the *root* of /t/ or that of /a/ (represented in (2) by *t* and *a* respectively):

(2) *a.* /atta/   *b.* /aata/

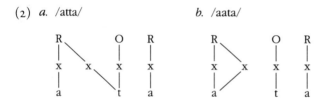

Similarly, thus, we should have /tʰa/ or /da/ according to whether the second slot of a branching onset is associated with the root of /t/ or that of /a/:

(3) *a.* /tʰa/   *b.* /da/

There is, however, at least one objection against this parallelism between length and VOT: as can be seen in (3), /tʰa/ and /da/ involve a complex onset. Indeed, if complex onsets were to be admitted in /tʰ, d/, what about /pl/, /tr/, etc.? While there are a number of reasons, like epenthesis and syncope processes, for assuming two skeletal slots for /pl/, /tr/, etc., and hence three slots for /pla/, /tra/, etc., the absence of similar reasons suggests that in the case of /tʰd/, these consonants involve only one position, and therefore that /tʰa/ and /da/ have only two slots. We must, then, seek another representation of VOT-values.

2.3.2

As was pointed out in section 2.2.2.2, /tʰ/ ~ /t/ ~ /d/ functions as a strength scale. What is interesting about this scale is that it involves two inversely proportional values, 'tension' (the *fortis* term) and 'sonority' (the *lenis* term), which are the very same concepts as those that have long been discussed, since Jespersen (1904), regarding the nature of the syllable. According to van Ginneken (1907), for example, the syllable is something like a vector spreading from a maximum of tension and a minimum of sonority to a maximum of sonority and a minimum of tension (for a detailed discussion of such matters, cf. Klein 1993). As a result, the syllable 'onset' is nothing but a tension peak with virtually null sonority, while the 'nucleus' is its mirror image: a sonority peak with minimal tension.

We shall return to van Ginneken's views in section 2.4. Let us just assume here that the 'tension' and 'sonority' mentioned by phonologists regarding consonantal scales are the same articulatory and perceptual objects as those recognized by earlier scholars within the syllable: 'tension', that is O, can thus be defined, in articulatory terms, as an open state of the glottis; 'sonority', i.e. N, is a closed state of the glottis. It follows that there is a natural solution to the problem of complex onsets in (3):

(4) Given an ON-sequence, VOT-values are properties that emerge:
   a. either from the spreading of the onset to the following N-position (aspiration),
   b. or from the spreading of the nucleus to the preceding O-position (voice).

As can be seen in (5), /tʰa/ and /da/ no longer involve complex clusters in the usual sense: O and N do branch in (5a) and (5b) respectively; yet, both syllables contain two positions, and only two positions. The resulting ambiassociation of one slot in (5a, b) naturally accounts for the principle of voice onset time: O-propagation to N in (5a) implies voice delayed release; inversely, N-propagation to O in (5b) stands for voice anticipation:

(5) ON interactions (provisional account):

   a. /tʰa/   *b.* /da/

2.3.3

Assuming both (5*a*, *b*) and the complementarity hypothesis between VOT and length, we must then revise the case of the complex rhymes in (2), i.e. /atta/ and /aata/. Given the ON interactions in (5), the present theory necessarily allows for the NO interactions in (6):

(6) NO interactions (provisional account):

    a. /att/   *b.* /aat/

An important observation must be made here. Actually, (6*a*) and (6*b*) do not necessarily involve length, (6*a*) underlies certain types of i.e. vowel + coda sequences, and not only gemination; (6*b*) underlies complex nuclei, i.e. both long vowels and heavy diphthongs. Either case depends on the segmental material associated: e.g., in a geminate, only O spreads to the preceding nucleus; in the case of homorganic nasal codas, however, additional segmental content is associated with the nucleus. Likewise, (5*a*), which stands for aspirates, may represent affricates as well, if segmental elements also spread to the nucleic position. In sum, each configuration in (5, 6) is supposed to license a given set of segmental strings.

2.3.4

We can now answer the question asked in section 2.2.2.3: what are the phonological invariants underlying the different realizations of ON and NO interactions? The claim that VOT and length are formally equivalent, i.e. mere symmetric reflexes of each other, rests on the existence of two time-based ternary scales which characterize O-N and N-O transitions, i.e. 'onsets' and 'rhymes' respectively. As was assumed in section 2.3.2 for ON interactions, both scales will be seen to result from the relative weight of 'tension' (=O) and 'sonority' (=N):

(7) *a.* ON-scale: /t^{h}a/ ~ /ta/ ~ /da/
    b. NO-scale: /att/ ~ /at/ ~ /aat/
    c. O-weight: 2   1   0
       N-weight: 0   1   2

The terms usually said to be 'strong' are those where tension prevails, that is, where O is associated with two slots like in (5*a*, 6*a*), and thus has maximal weight: aspirated onsets and closed rhymes with minimal duration of the nucleus (*coupe ferme*). 'Weak' terms show maximal weight of sonority, that is, association of N with two slots, as in voiced onsets and open rhymes with maximal duration of the nucleus. The scales in (7*a*, *b*) are often mixed: hence the well-known /atta/ ~ /ata/ ~ /ada/-triplet shown by lenition processes (cf. section 2.2.1.2).

Let us consider the table in (8), which summarizes contextual realizations of tension and sonority, with association of two C and V segments with one slot each (cf. section 2.3.3):

(8)

	'Onset' (ON interaction) VOT	'Rhyme' (NO interaction) Length
'Tension' (O-spreading)	Laryngeal aperture (aspiration)	Supralaryngeal closure (C-gemination)
'Sonority' (N-spreading)	Laryngeal closure (voicing)	Supralaryngeal aperture (V-lengthening)

As can be seen in (8), the difference between 'place' (laryngeal vs. supralaryngeal articulation) and 'manner' (aperture vs. closure) rests on the *directionality* of O/N-spreading: aspiration and gemination follow, respectively, from rightward and leftward propagation of O; conversely, voicing and vowel lengthening result from leftward and rightward spreading of N. Therefore, an interesting issue of the theory is that two major phonological contrasts (glottal/oral and open/closed) play an allophonic role, and differ from each other merely on temporal grounds, depending on the anticipated vs. delayed 'release' of O and N.[2]

---

[2] One might object that voice should not be assigned to leftward propagation of nuclei because some systems, like those of Semitic languages, are known to have (*a*) consonantal roots, which may contain voiced consonants, and (*b*) morphologically distinct syllabic templates, which are supposed to provide the voicing nuclei according to our theory. This objection (Scheer, personal communication) actually rests on the following hypothesis: if different morphemes can be distinguished within a word, then their phonological material cannot 'overlap'. Thereby, morphemes are assumed to be stocked separately at the lexical level. However, such a claim, which is inherited from early generative grammar, is hardly acceptable within modern 'no-rule' phonological theories. Widespread syncretisms like French *à* + *le* = /o/ clearly show that morpheme *signifiants* do overlap, since there is no *phonological* rule by which an underlying synchronic form such as */al/ turns into [o]. Rather, morpheme

2.4. TENSION AND SONORITY AS AUTOSEGMENTS

2.4.1

Given the structures assigned in (5, 6) to /tʰa, da/ and /att, aat/, it may be asked what /ta/ and /at/ are supposed to be. As is well known, voiceless non-aspirated obstruents and open light syllables are, on the one hand, the only universal types and, on the other hand, the middle terms of the strength scales /tʰa ∼ ta ∼ da/, /atta ∼ ata ∼ aata/, and /atta ∼ ata ∼ ada/. If we assume that /tʰa ∼ da/ and /att ∼ aat/ result from the ON and NO interactions in (5, 6), then there are two possible and opposite claims on the nature of /ta/ and /at/:

(9) *a.* /ta/ and /at/ follow from the absence of any O- and N-spreading;
    b. /ta/ and /at/ follow from the existence of both O- and N-spreading, which, as it were, annul each other.

According to (9*a*), /ta/ and /at/ would simply involve the current representations in (10), where neither O nor N is associated with more than one slot:

(10) *a.*   *b.*

This seems to be a reasonable assumption on markedness grounds: /ta/ and /at/ could then be said to be unmarked vis-à-vis /tʰa, da/ and /att, aat/ respectively, because they show non-branching onsets and nuclei; hence, they are universal, contrary to aspiration, voice, and length, and neutral in terms of strength, since they are neither 'too' strong nor 'too' weak.

Yet, we shall postulate that (10)-like representations are ill formed or, rather, incomplete and hence ambiguous. The representations in (10*a, b*), unlike the ones in (5, 6), clash with the well-known fact that syllables and

overlapping might bring crucial evidence for claiming that the actual lexical units are phonological *words* viewed as 'morphemic clusters'. Hence, returning to the Semitic facts, O/N-*elements* can 'belong' to both roots and templates; some ON and NO *interactions*, however, can be specific to templates (e.g. length), while others characterize roots (e.g. voice). Thereby, note, the same interaction can be 'radical' in one language, but 'templatic' in another one: cf., e.g., the status of voice in Arabic and Kikuyu, and aspiration in Mandarin and Classical Greek.

syllabification, i.e. what is quite appropriately called *enchaînement* in French, are not reducible to mere sequences of segments; they form a chain of rhythmic units, where C/V-coarticulation is a necessary consequence. There is, thus, a 'movement' from /t/ to /a/ in /ta/ that can be viewed as the core of the syllable; similarly, there is a movement from the first /a/ to /t/ in /ata/ that may be regarded as the unmarked rhyme. Now, it will be assumed that such movements do not follow from any general and 'late' phonetic-interpretative principle; they are, say, 'default versions' of those that trigger aspiration and voice. As constitutive properties of syllables and rhymes, these interactions should thus be embodied within phonological theory, where they should not be limited to the marked cases in (5, 6). However, they are not captured by (10), in which no interaction occurs between O and N. In this sense, (10*a*) and (10*b*) lack phonological naturalness.[3] They might be taken, at best, as lexical representations containing a morpheme boundary (/t + a/, /a + t/), before application of phonological rules (if any). We shall therefore defend the claim in (9*b*) instead of the one in (9*a*).

2.4.2

Let us assume, as we did in (5), that /t^{h}a/ ~ /da/ contrasts are based on O- versus N-spreading to the following or the preceding slot respectively. If O and N belong to the same autosegmental tier, then the No Line Crossing Principle (NLCP) disallows simultaneous propagation of O and N; in other words, there cannot be aspirated voiced consonants. Now, this is empirically false: some languages (in particular, many Indian languages) do have such a combination, which is often referred to as 'breathy voice' (cf. Ladefoged 1993: 139–47). That this is not a phonologically distinct state of the glottis, but indeed the 'sum' of aspiration and voice, is shown by the fact that all languages having /d̤^{ɦ}/ also have both /t^h/ (i.e. aspiration) and /d/ (i.e. voice),

---

[3] The problem with (10)-type notations perhaps needs further explanation. It may be worth stressing that the necessity of showing symbolically the connection between O and N does not rest on mere iconicity considerations. For example, one might refuse the notation

for a falling tone on the grounds that the actual fall is not explicitly represented. However, this comparison is not valid. The *concept* of the falling contour is, indeed, adequately, that is formally, accounted for by means of many-to-one association, more so than by purely iconic devices such as, say, H $_L$. On the contrary, the unitary character of the syllable does not follow from a pure sequence of symbols, such as O + N in a model like the present one, where constituency plays no role, i.e. where no σ-component is assumed.

though the converse is false. Hence, there is an implicational scale of laryngeal values where breathy voice functions as the most marked degree:

(11) Markedness:

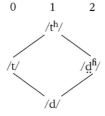

How, then, can breathy voice be accounted for in terms of O/N-spreading?

Assuming that aspiration and voice are due to O/N-propagation, it is clear that the possibility of both O- and N-spreading in /dʱa/ implies that onsets and nuclei belong to different autosegmental tiers. O and N would, thus, be segregated in the same way as consonants and vowels are separated within non-concatenative morphologies (cf. McCarthy 1979, 1981). Accordingly, syllable components will be assigned here to two distinct planes, which will be provisionally labelled the 'O-tier' and the 'N-tier', in such a way that aspiration and voice may combine without violation of NLCP:

(12) /dʱa/:

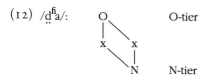

Furthermore, it will be assumed that O/N segregation is universal and not limited to 'breathy voice languages', which would be a circular thesis. The fact that only a few languages, which necessarily show both aspiration and voice as distinctive values, have breathy voice must be explained on different grounds.

2.4.3

It has been admitted so far that both /ta/ (cf. section 2.4.1) and /dʱa/ (cf. section 2.4.2) result from O- *and* N-propagation within the syllable, i.e. in an ON-sequence. Hence, both the unmarked and the most marked terms of the scale in (11) would be based on (12)-type representations. How, then, can /t/ and /dʱ/ be distinguished?

A second problem arises from the structure in (12): if O and N belong to different tiers, then any form of linearity within the syllable is ruled out. Indeed, it is no longer true that (12) is an 'ON-sequence', in the sense that neither O 'precedes' N, nor does N 'follow' O. As a result, odd structures like the ones in (13) cannot be formally disallowed by the theory:

(13) *a.* 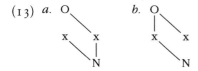 *b.*

Our point is that both problems—/t/ ~ /d͡ʰ/ distinction and ON-linearity—can be solved simultaneously: they are, indeed, different aspects of the same point. Given the multiplanar representation of syllable structure adopted here, the only way of introducing a linear relationship between the onset and the nucleus is to assume that there is, as it were, a nucleus in the O-tier, just as there is an onset in the N-tier. O/N-segregation should thus consist in two ON-tiers. In each tier, O and N have, say, different and specific values or, as we shall put it, different *markedness states*: in the 'O-tier', O has a marked value which contrasts with an unmarked value of N; conversely, in the 'N-tier', N is marked while O is unmarked.

Following on from Kaye, Lowenstamm, and Vergnaud's (1985) theory of charm, the O-tier could be said to bear a 'cold' nucleus whereas the N-tier bears a 'cold' onset. In the line of the charm hypothesis developed by Kaye, Lowenstamm, and Vergnaud (1990), this will be formalized by assigning a neutral value to these cold elements (N° and O°), while their marked counterparts will be characterized by negative (O^-) and positive (N^+) values according to consonantal and vocalic charm. The 'hot features' of O^- and N^+ are aspiration and voice respectively; they emerge as properties of the syllable onset whenever O^- and N^+ spread to two skeletal positions.[4] It

---

[4] According to Kaye, Lowenstamm, and Vergnaud (1985, 1990), *charm* is, from a 'technical' point of view, an intrinsic ternary property of phonological elements which conditions their combinatory faculties, two like-charmed elements repelling each other: as a somewhat simplified example, A is 'positively charmed' (A^+) versus I and U, which have neutral charm (I°, U°); hence, both combinations $A+I$ (=/e/) and $A+U$ (=/o/) are unmarked, while $I+U$ (=/y/) is marked, and requires additional conditions that will not be mentioned here. On conceptual grounds, positive charm is 'voweliness', i.e., as it were, all that would remain from vowels if non-vowel-specific content could be left aside; hence, negative charm characterizes specifically consonantal elements. Any element is a specified feature matrix. In any element combination, one element necessarily *governs* the other one: the features of the governed element are replaced with those of the governing element. Any element, except the 'cold element' (v°) by definition, has a 'hot feature', which is its dominant

follows from the assignment of two different values to each syllabic element O and N that /ta/ and /d̤ʰa/ can be distinguished in markedness terms:[5]

(14) ON interactions:

    a. /ta/ (voiceless)   *b.* /d̤ʰa/ (breathy voice)

    c. /tʰa/ (aspirated)   *d.* /da/ (voiced)

Let us assume the following definition of markedness of ON interactions: in a given ON-tier,

(15) ON interaction is unmarked if and only if the unmarked element spreads to more slots than the marked one (i.e., iff X°-weight $> Y^{\alpha}$-weight) within the ON-sequence.

feature: it is the only feature of governed elements that is not replaced with the corresponding feature of governing elements.

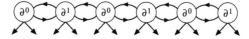

It follows from (15) that (14*a*) is an unmarked symmetry. Another issue is that the stronger the violation of this symmetry is, the more marked the resulting structures are: thus, the symmetric structure in (14*b*) is the most marked type, since all marked elements and only marked elements spread to two slots therein, while (14*c*) and (14*d*) are intermediate types. Indeed, as was shown in (11), (14*b*) implies both (14*a*) and (14*c, d*) in a given language, whereas either (14*c*) or (14*d*) presupposes (14*a*) only.

2.4.4

If O/N are autosegmental objects, then they must behave as such. Beyond the spreading faculty of O and N, three claims will be presented concerning their place within current autosegmental theory.

Our first claim is that the marked elements O^- and N^+ are the *roots* (cf. Clements 1985) of consonants and vowels respectively: all segmental elements are thus linked either to O^- or to N^+, hence two interesting issues. First, the C/V segregation postulated by McCarthy (1979, 1981) for non-concatenative morphologies is actually a universal effect of O/N coplanarity. Secondly, *empty* segments, i.e. segments lacking segmental material, can be defined as having empty and/or floating segmental roots:

(16) *a.* Empty onset: /(ʔ)V/   *b.* Empty nucleus: /C(ə)/

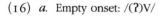

Empty segments are to be distinguished from null segments. *Null* segments are segments which lack skeletal position as in (17), and hence usually have no phonetic realization, or both marked and unmarked elements, and then have phonetic realization, as will be shown below in section 2.5.2.

(17) *a.* Null onset: /V/   *b.* Null nucleus: /C/

Null segments are marked by definition, because they necessarily violate the condition on syllable unmarkedness given in (15): indeed, O^0 and N^0 spread to only one slot in (17*a*) and (17*b*) respectively; they have, thus, the same weight as N^+ and O^-.

Our third claim concerns the conditions on O/N-spreading. It will be assumed that:

(18) *a.* Unmarked elements can be delinked by propagation of marked elements.

   b. Marked elements cannot be delinked by propagation of unmarked elements.

In other words, only marked elements (i.e. O^- and N^+) actually obey NLCP. The association of unmarked elements (O^0 and N^0) with skeletal slots occurs, so to speak, by default, whenever it is not disallowed by the spreading of marked elements.

2.4.5

Given all that was said in sections 2.4.2–3 about ON interactions, the symmetry postulated in section 2.2.2.3 between VOT and length entails the following NO-counterparts to (14*a–d*):

(19) NO interactions:

   a. /at/ (short nucleus)   *b.* /aatt/ (long nucleus + coda)

   c. /aat/ (long nucleus)   *d.* /att/ (short nucleus + coda)

The same markedness considerations as those formulated for (14) can apply here: (19*a*) is an unmarked symmetry since all unmarked elements and only unmarked elements spread to two slots; the structure in (19*b*) is the most marked type of rhyme since all marked elements and only marked elements spread to two slots; (19*c*) and (19*d*) are intermediate types of rhyme as to their markedness degree. Indeed, as is well known, any language having (19*b*) also has both (19*a*) and (19*c, d*), whereas either (19*c*) or (19*d*) implies (19*a*) only.

2.4.6

By 'coda' in (19*b, d*), we mean strongly constrained segments like those found in Romance languages, where only a small set of consonants is allowed in syllable-final position. There is no 'coda' in a cluster which lacks phonotactic constraints, or violates the normal phonotactic patterns of a given language. For example, in Arabic, almost all consonants can combine in a CC-cluster, so that, for any C_iC_j-string, there is a well-formed C_jC_i-cluster; here, CC is to be analysed as an ONO-sequence in which the nucleus is null. The same can be said about the consonant clusters of Spanish and Portuguese words like *ritmo, captar, ignorar*, etc., which are not 'normal' clusters in the language since plosives (except /d/ in Spanish) cannot occur in syllable-final position.

This distinction between free and constrained consonant clusters is, in sum, the same as the one that is currently made in the case of vowel clusters: free VV-clusters are, as is well known, disyllabic hiatuses, i.e. NON-sequences with a null onset in our account; constrained VV-clusters are always monosyllabic diphthongs, i.e. (19*c*)-type structures.

The question of how a given CC (or VV) cluster is to be interpreted cannot be fully discussed here: cf. Angoujard (1997) for a similar distinction. The basic idea is that, if two consonants are *phonologically* adjacent, then interactions necessarily occur between them, just as between onsets and nuclei, as was seen above, and cause phonotactic restrictions. This is the case of the 'coda + onset' sequences in (19*d*). It should be noted in particular that, if (19*d*) implies strong phonotactic constraints, then it necessarily underlies geminates and homorganic NC-clusters, which represent the highest degree of phonotactic restriction.[6] On the contrary, if there are no such constraints between two contiguous consonants, these are to be viewed

[6] Furthermore, it should be noted that, if geminate clusters are viewed as simply resulting from NO interactions, without involving additional positions, then their well-known integrity (cf. Kenstowicz and Pyle 1973) is more naturally explained than if they implied two slots, as in current frameworks, or even three slots, as in Lowenstamm's (1996) model: indeed, there is no skeletal motivation for epenthesis in the present approach.

not as phonologically adjacent, but as two onsets separated by a null nucleus: indeed, ONO-sequences do not normally exhibit phonotactic restrictions.

Note that 'free' CC-clusters often show agreement in voice; typically, this is the only phonotactic constraint occurring in both types of CC-clusters. Now, voice assimilation in non-constrained clusters provides empirical evidence for the representation of voice proposed here. It naturally follows from the (de)linking of N^+ in [ə] ~ Ø alternations (cf. (16)), and from the assumption that unmarked elements are not sensitive to NLCP (cf. (18)), that the /k/ of French *paquebot*, for example, can be voiced by the last nucleus:

(20) French [paⱪbo]:

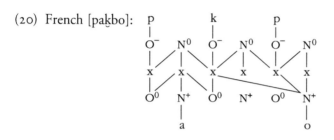

2.4.7

The important point here is the phonological value conveyed by both ON-tiers. Charm or, better, markedness coefficients are, in (14) and (19), mere symbols for capturing the constitutive properties of syllables, which were referred to as 'tension' and 'sonority' (cf. section 2.3.4). The fact that O^- and N^+ operate in parallel and autonomous tiers with respect to the skeleton means that: (*a*) tension and sonority *are* parallel and autonomous aspects; (*b*) the interface of both aspects is time. In the ON-interval, O^--spreading stands for a significant peak of tension, which may be defined, in articulatory terms, as the assignment of some length to laryngeal aperture, hence noise from an acoustic point of view; N^+-spreading represents a peak of sonority, which is a significant duration of laryngeal closure, by which the whole CV-sequence is voiced. Likewise, in the NO-interval, O^--spreading represents a peak of tension, which is a 'long' period of supralaryngeal closure; N^+-spreading stands for a peak of sonority, which is a significant duration of supralaryngeal aperture. Hence, syllables and rhymes follow from curves defined by the varying weight of their constitutive properties, 'weight' being the number of skeletal slots associated with O^- and N^+ (cf. section 2.3.4); in other words, syllables and rhymes emerge from the weight of either of the ON-tiers:

(21)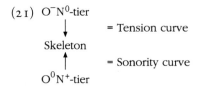

This is an attempt to formalize Klein's (1993) views on the nature of syllables as the 'interface between production and reception'. The cognitive scope of the markedness values assumed here will not be fully discussed in the present chapter. Let us only say that the idea of O^-/N^+ interaction via the skeleton might ultimately be based, as is claimed by Klein, on the necessary integration within the syllable of the articulatory and acoustic-perceptual 'controls' of speech. Actually, syllables are nothing but the integration of both control types: the former, which is mainly related to the consonantal domain, is represented here by the O^-N°-tier; the latter, in which vowels play the most important role, corresponds to the $O^\circ N^+$-tier. Thus, it follows from the structures in (14) and (19) that the markedness of syllables and rhymes depends on the equilibrium of both cognitive planes; unmarkedness (e.g. /ta/ vs. /t^{h}a/ and /da/, /at/ vs. /att/ and /aat/) implies a perfect balance between the weight of articulatory control and the weight of perceptual control.

2.5. EMPIRICAL EVIDENCE

2.5.1

It follows from section 2.4.6 that there are no underlying CC- or VV-sequences at the syllabic level. On the one hand, as seen above, surface VV-clusters correspond either to (19c)-type NO-structures or to dissyllabic ONON-sequences, the second onset being null. Similarly, on the other hand, there is no 'coda' viewed as a phonological primitive: surface CVC-CV-strings may be represented either by disyllabic (ONON) or by trisyllabic (ONONON) sequences, the second nucleus of the latter being null. Finally, complex onsets, which will not be discussed here, imply two slots attached to one O-element, as in current frameworks. Hence, ON is the only underlying syllable type here. In this respect, our proposal resembles Lowenstamm's (1996) 'CV-theory'. It differs from it, however, by assuming autosegmental interactions between O and N. Thus, unlike Lowenstamm's model, which excludes branching components, O and N necessarily branch, as was shown in (14, 19).

2.5.1.1

It would be interesting here to give an example of how a branching CV-model of syllable structure is likely to preserve a remarkable advantage of Lowenstamm's non-branching CV-theory over standard frameworks, where the coda is a primitive concept. As is well known, coda deletion may trigger compensatory lengthening of the preceding vowel. This is currently accounted for as in (22) by 'coda theories':

(22) Middle French *teste* [tɛstə] > Early Modern French *tête* [tɛːtə]

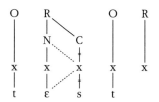

However, (22) implies a somewhat complex and redundant mechanism: it involves delinking of *both* C and /s/, as well as spreading of *both* N and /ɛ/. Secondly, (22) does not naturally explain why there is no compensatory lengthening whenever an intervocalic *onset* is deleted: cf., e.g., */ˈgenesos/ > Early Ancient Greek /ˈgeneos/, and not */ˈgeneːos/. Indeed, why shouldn't O be delinked like C in (22), which would allow N-spreading? Note that the same problems arise from an X-bar theory of syllable (cf. Levin 1985), where both syllable elements and segmental features are affected by the lengthening process.

These problems are easily solved by Lowenstamm's (1996) theory, where /ɛ/, and only /ɛ/, automatically spreads to the empty nucleus in (23*a*) if /s/, and only /s/, is delinked:

(23) *a.*

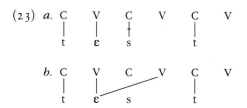

b.

It follows that compensatory lengthening is impossible if an intervocalic /s/ is deleted, since there is no empty nucleus available by definition:

(24)

```
C   V   C   V   C   V . . .
|   |   |   |   †   |
g   e   n   e   s   o
```

Thus, Lowenstamm's account has both descriptive and explanatory power: (*a*) it avoids complexity, since only segmental elements are affected by delinking and spreading; (*b*) it naturally explains why compensatory lengthening is restricted to cases of 'coda' loss.

2.5.1.2

Now, these advantages are preserved within the branching 'CV-theory' adopted here. While lengthening in *feste* > *fête* involves replacement of O⁻- with N⁺-spreading, i.e. vowel root propagation, as is shown in (25*a*), onset deletion would imply a structure, like the one in (25*b*), with no slot available for N⁺-spreading:

(25) *a.*

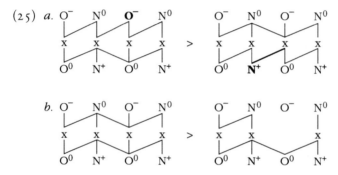

Thus, compensatory lengthening brings crucial evidence for both CV-models, as opposed to coda-frameworks. Interestingly, however, lengthening is prevented by a full nucleus in (24), but by a null onset in (25*b*). This divergence between Lowenstamm's (1996) theory and ours clearly illustrates our thesis that surface 'onsets' and 'codas' are intrinsically different objects (under the conditions exposed in section 2.4.6): the so-called coda is nothing but the effect of interactions between NO-elements; only the 'onset' implies a skeletal slot of its own.

2.5.2

Let us now consider two examples of data that only the present theory is able to account for in a natural and straightforward way. The first concerns two facts that are typical of word edges: initial aspiration and final devoicing.

2.5.2.1

One problem arises from aspiration: why is it that /h/ is so often restricted to word-initial position throughout world languages? This is typically the case in English and most Germanic languages: cf. the well-known 'complementary distribution' of /h/ and /ŋ/. Likewise, Classical Greek has /h/ in initial and only in initial position. Though many languages have /h/ in all positions available to consonants, two points must be emphasized: (*a*) even in these cases, /h/ is more frequently found in initial position: cf., e.g., Classical Latin; (*b*) we do not know of languages having /h/ everywhere but word-initially.[7]

A similar problem arises from devoicing: regardless of clear cases of assimilation triggered by consonant clusters, why is it so often restricted to word-final position in the world languages? Many languages have only voiceless final obstruents; many languages have both voiced and voiceless final obstruents; almost no language shows only voiced obstruents in word-final position, Somali being the sole exception we know of.

A second problem arises from both initial aspiration and final devoicing. As is well known, many languages lack /h/ *tout court*, even word-initially; all languages, however, have /#CV-/ (where /C/ stands for a full or an empty (/ʔ/) onset), and most have /#V-/. Likewise, many languages lack closed, i.e. (C)VC-syllables; hence, both voiceless and voiced obstruents are absent therein in final position. It follows that there are two parallel implicational scales which characterize both word edges:

(26) Markedness: 0   1   2
    a.   /#ta-/ < /#a-/ < /#ʰa-/
    b.   /-a#/   < **/-at#/** < /-ad#/

We have, then, to explain: (*a*) why aspiration and devoicing are typically found in initial and final contexts; (*b*) why they have a different markedness status in their typical contexts, as is shown in (26), where initial aspiration appears as more marked than final devoicing.

2.5.2.2

In the present model, both problems are given a simple and straightforward solution by assuming that all marked terms of (26) imply null segments, as is shown in (27):

---

[7] We shall not take into account the case of languages where a change has occurred of the form /s/ > [h] in coda position, and which lack /h/ elsewhere (e.g. *rioplatense* Spanish). Though this point would need further discussion that is not possible in this chapter, let us say that, according to the principles which underlie the present theory, the same can be said about languages without aspirated consonants in general. There is no necessary one-to-one correspondence between surface segments and their phonological representations. Hence, it is not the case that all *h*-sounds have to be assigned the same phonological structure: more accurately, the mentioned Spanish [h] is a 'normal', i.e. non-empty, segment, which contains an A-element (cf. Carvalho and Klein 1996, Carvalho 1998, Scheer 1998).

(27)   *a.* /#a-/   *b.* /-t#/   *c.* /#ʰa-/   *d.* /-d#/

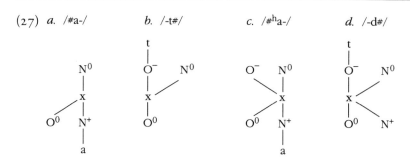

As was seen in section 2.4.4, (27*a–d*) are marked by definition: null segments *necessarily* imply violation of the condition on syllable unmarkedness in (15). However, the violation of (15) is even stronger in (27*c, d*), where it occurs in *both* ON-tiers, than in (27*a, b*), which show only one marked ON interaction; hence, (27*c, d*) are more marked than (27*a, b*). Thereby, the present theory provides a simple and unitary account of the implicational scale in (26).[8]

Furthermore, the reason why aspiration and devoicing are edge-specific phenomena also follows from the same markedness definition given in (15). It is clear that, while its violation by (27*a–d*) is restricted to the sole ON-sequence in initial and final position respectively, word-internal null segments would imply a violation of (15) in *both* ON- and NO-sequences, that is, on both sides of the null segment: cf. the null nucleus of Fr. *paquebot* in (20), with leftward and rightward spreading of N^o, but no symmetric propagation of both flanking O^o's. Likewise, many languages have /#V-/-words, with initial null onsets, but avoid hiatuses (via gliding, for example), which involve intervocalic null onsets. Restricting null segments to word edges is, thus, a natural way of restricting violation of the condition on syllable unmarkedness.

2.5.3

The facts invoked in section 2.5.2 provide us with empirical evidence for the O/N symmetry within the syllable. Let us now consider some facts

---

[8] For the same reason, /aːt/ is marked vis-à-vis /at/: in the following structure, indeed,

$$N^0 \quad\quad O^- \quad\quad N^0$$
$$| \quad\quad\quad | \quad\quad\quad |$$
$$x \quad\quad\quad x$$
$$| \quad\quad\quad |$$
$$N^+ \quad\quad O^0 \quad\quad N^+$$

both $O^- N^o$ and $N^+ O^o$ interactions are marked (O^o-weight < N^+-weight); hence the well-known closed syllable shortening.

supporting the ON/NO symmetry within the word, which is the second mirror relationship postulated in the present theory. Perhaps the clearest examples of this second symmetry are provided by well-known lenition processes, like those attested in the evolution from Latin to western Romance languages.

2.5.3.1

As was seen in section 2.2.2.2, the phonological interpretation of voice assumed here allows a homogeneous representation of the well-known 'chain' /tt/ > /t/ > /d/: voicing is no longer formally different from gemination, since both result from leftward spreading of N and O respectively. This does not provide, however, an explanation for the following question: why is it that voicing appears as a particularly typical process in intervocalic position, and only in intervocalic position (cf. Ségéral and Scheer 1999)? There is, indeed, a problem here, which can be summarized as follows.

If voicing results from simple N^+-spreading to the preceding onset, as was assumed above, and as is supported by final devoicing (cf. section 2.5.2), when there is no vowel at the right, then nothing in the theory explains why /t/ > /d/ should not occur word-initially and after coda as well, that is, in what is often called the 'strong position'; indeed, strong position typically prevents voicing: cf. Lat. *lacu* > Sp. *lago*, *ripa* > *riba*, *rota* > *rueda* vs. *campu* > *campo*, *porta* > *puerta*.

If voicing (and not length) resulted from simple N^+-spreading to the *following* onset, contrary to our hypothesis, but as is suggested by the absence of voicing in strong position, i.e. wherever there is no vowel at the left, then nothing in the theory would explain why /t/ > /d/ does not occur in coda position, which is confirmed at least by final devoicing.

The problem, thus, lies in the formalization of the well-known triggering context of voicing: the assumed 'unilateral' definition of voice cannot account for voicing as a process, which implies voiced segments on either side of the consonant; it seems that voicing processes suppose a double interaction: in both NO- and ON-intervals.

2.5.3.2

It follows from section 2.4 that any non-empty segment is characterized by an 'X°/X^α polarization' ($\alpha = +$ or $-$): a non-empty onset results from the association of an O^--element with an O°-element *via* the skeleton; a non-empty nucleus results from the association of an N^+-element with an N°-element:

(28) /ttattta/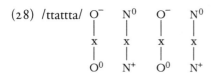

Empty segments (cf. section 2.4.4) reveal a markedness principle governing polarization: marked elements (O^- and N^+) can be absent, as in (16); unmarked elements (O° and N°), however, are always present.

On the other hand, we saw that all unmarked elements and only unmarked elements spread to more than one skeletal position in the unmarked *enchaînement*:

(29) /tata/

Hence, still assuming that voice is the leftward spreading of N^+, intervocalic voicing can be accounted for by claiming that N^+-propagation to a given slot *depends* on the rightward association of the preceding unmarked N° with this slot. As in empty segments, the converse is false, as is shown in (29): if N° is linked to a given slot, it is not necessarily the case that the following marked N^+ is also associated with it. More generally, thus, we shall admit the principle in (30) on the basis of the markedness considerations underlying the representation of segments:

(30) Polarization principle:
      If X_i^α spreads to a given slot, then $X_{i\pm1}^\circ$ is also associated with this slot.

As a result, intervocalic voicing is an 'N°/N^+ polarization' of the onset; hence, intervocalic voiced onsets undergo both O- and N-polarizations:

(31) /tada/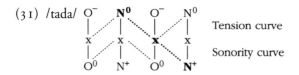

It follows from (30) that voicing is impossible in strong position, that is, wherever N° cannot spread to the right, either because there is no N° at all, as is the case word-initially, or because N°-spreading is disallowed by NLCP since O^- spreads to the left, as is the case after coda (cf. section 2.4.4):

(32) /tatta/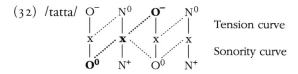

2.5.3.3

We are now able to provide a homogeneous *and* natural account of /tt/ > /t/ > /d/-chains. As is represented in (33), /tt/ ~ /t/ > /t/ ~ /d/ consists in the replacement of contrasts based on tension polarization with oppositions based on sonority polarization. The fact that /t/, and not /tt/, undergoes voicing is simply due to NLCP.[9]

(33) Western Romance lenition:

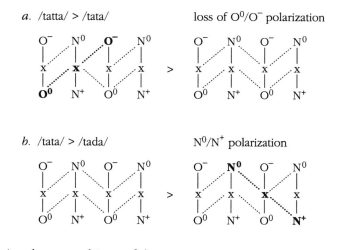

a. /tatta/ > /tata/   loss of O^0/O^- polarization

b. /tata/ > /tada/ N^0/N^+ polarization

Another natural issue of the representations in (33) is that voicing is only one possible 'strategy' among others that are likely to be adopted by speakers in order to eliminate gemination. Thus, sonorants show the change in (33*a*) and the one in (34) in Northern Gallo-Romance (*langue d'oïl*), hence, e.g., Lat. *annu* > Proto-Oïl */'anu/ (> Fr. *an*) vs. *manu* > */'maːnu/ (> *main*) (cf. Haudricourt and Juilland 1970: § 2):

[9] Actually, (30) functions as a categorical *principle* in so far as processes are concerned: thus, changes such as /tt/ > /dd/ are expected to be impossible. However, regarding structural patterns, e.g. voice rather than voicing, (30) behaves much like a violable *constraint*: languages do have voiced geminate obstruents, which are, of course, allowed by the theory; yet it should be noted that languages having voiceless geminates may lack their voiced counterparts, while the converse seems to be impossible.

(34) /tata/ > /taːta/

$$O^- \quad N^0 \quad O^- \quad N^0 \qquad\qquad O^- \quad N^0 \quad O^- \quad \mathbf{N^0}$$
$$| \qquad | \qquad | \qquad | \qquad\qquad\qquad | \qquad | \qquad | \qquad |$$
$$x \quad\quad x \quad\quad x \quad\quad x \quad > \quad x \quad\quad x \quad\quad \mathbf{x} \quad\quad x$$
$$| \qquad | \qquad | \qquad | \qquad\qquad\qquad | \qquad | \qquad | \qquad |$$
$$O^0 \quad N^+ \quad O^0 \quad N^+ \qquad\qquad O^0 \quad \mathbf{N^+} \quad O^0 \quad N^+$$

As can be seen, (33*b*) and (34) differ solely in terms of 'axis' of sonority polarization. Thereby, voicing and lengthening may be shown to be formally equivalent lenition strategies. Only the present theory is able to capture this functional equivalence.[10]

2.6. CONCLUSION

The representation proposed in this chapter for VOT-values and length has been shown to provide a straightforward account of seven facts at least.

The three problems mentioned in section 2.2 are given a simple and natural solution. The definition of both VOT and length in terms of O/N-propagation enables us to explain: (*a*) why no segment can contain the sole 'feature' [voiced] or [aspirated]; (*b*) why gemination and voice behave as the poles of the same strength scale; (*c*) why voice contrasts are much more frequent among consonants than among vowels.

In addition, our proposals explain the four facts discussed in section 2.5. First, the theory shows why compensatory lengthening is impossible before a vowel. Secondly, it reveals and accounts for the relationship between two 'edge-specific' marked phenomena: initial aspiration and final voicing. Thirdly, it explains why voicing normally takes place in intervocalic position, and fails to occur either word-initially or after coda. Fourthly, it shows that voicing and lengthening are alternative lenition strategies.

Finally, beyond its explanatory power, the hypothesis of O/N interactions has two theoretical issues that are worth being outlined. First, concerning the phonological models of the syllable, the present approach to syllabic structure preserves, as was seen in section 2.5.1, a crucial advantage of Lowenstamm's (1996) CV-theory over current frameworks, but avoids its main weakness: the multiplication of empty categories it entails.

Secondly, and still more importantly on cognitive grounds, by denying any symbolic status to aspiration and voice, we are led to reduce the number of

---

[10] A last issue of the present account is that final devoicing (cf. section 2.5.2) is not to be viewed either as a fortition or as a lenition process: devoicing (without gemination) is the 'neutral' that is expected whenever both fortition and lenition fail to occur.

segmental primitives; by assuming that both VOT-values and length contrasts are segmental effects of onset and nucleus weight, defined as articulatory tension versus perceptual sonority, we are assigning a representational basis to syllables. As was observed in section 2.1, this runs counter to the claims of output-based approaches, where syllables emerge from smaller units; in this respect, our proposals are clearly opposite to non-representational views such as those defended by Coleman (this volume). *A contrario*, the present theory is likely to lend phonological support to quite independently grounded ideas, since based on brain studies, like MacNeilage's (1998) distinction between *frame* and *content*. In particular, to quote Ziegler, Kilian, and Deger (1997: 1205; *apud* Abry et al., this volume), the above assumed autonomy of syllabic structure, i.e. of VOT/length, vis-à-vis segmental material proper (cf. section 2.3.3) is consonant with 'the idea that speech production branches into "metrical" and "segmental spellout" processes, and that syllabic frames are conceptually separable from their phonemic content'.

3

Tone in Mituku: How a Floating Tone Nailed down an Intermediate Level

John Goldsmith

3.1. INTRODUCTION

This chapter presents some straightforward facts from the tonal system of a Bantu language, Mituku, described by Stappers (1973). The interest of the facts lies in the way they help clarify notions about constraints and certain kinds of representation-based generalizations. As we shall see, there is a simple principle at work to which we can appeal in order to explain why in a small number of cases—and only in these cases—a contour tone can appear on a single vowel. The contour-toned vowels in question are among those where the vowel can be shown to be the surface manifestation of two distinct vowels at deeper level (indeed, the two vowels are from distinct morphemes). Mituku, we will say, displays the *no more than one tone per vowel* (*1 TperV*) restriction. It is, of course, an utter banality in the world of tonal systems to find a restriction on tone to the effect that no more than one tone may appear per mora (or short vowel), and indeed it is that banality that reassures us that we have the right generalization here. But the *1 TperV* generalization does not hold for Mituku on the surface, and there is no plausible way that the restriction can be revised or rewritten so as to make it a surface restriction or constraint—and still do its job correctly in Mituku.

The picture that appears to be appropriate for Mituku is one that explicitly recognizes three levels of phonological representation, minimally: a phonetic representation, an underlying representation, and, mediating between these two, a level of representation whose existence is known to us primarily through the constraints that can be expressed there and only—or preferentially—there. Most theories of phonology of this century have incorporated some version of this picture, which can be restated thus: the relationship between outer form—phonetics—and the underlying representation of the morpheme is the composition of two components, as in Fig 3.1, where I have used very neutral terminology to describe both the representations (underlying, intermediate, surface) and the ways in which representations at these levels are related (sectors 1 and 2).

Now, optimality theory (Prince and Smolensky to appear, and elsewhere) has left the door open to more than one interpretation. It can be interpreted as a general computational scheme which can be used to model the input–output relations of components as in (1), and on that view, one could compose any number of sets of such OT devices; on that interpretation, optimality theory makes no claim about its output being in any sense a surface representation as understood by linguists; it could, in the terminology of Fig. 3.1, be an account of how 'sectors' work. On other interpretations (more theoretically ambitious interpretations), optimality theory replaces the compositional character of alternative approaches, and the consequences for our understanding of phonology are considerably more wide-reaching. (Consequences of a principle being wide-reaching are not grounds for firmer belief in that principle, needless to say.) The analysis of Fig. 3.1 would be ruled out on that interpretation. The evidence discussed in this chapter weighs in favour of the first, less ambitious interpretation, and against the second, as the reader will see.

3.2. SOME BASIC FACTS ABOUT MITUKU

The basic facts to bear in mind about Mituku are the following, several of which are already offered by Stappers:

1. On the surface, a syllable will bear one of four identifiable tones: High, Low, Falling, or Rising; in addition, between two Highs (or a High and a

F IG. 3.1. Phonology with an intermediate level.

Falling tone), downstep (also known as tone slip) can occur. Downstep is well known to students of tone languages; its phonetic manifestation is a lowering by about a whole step (in the ordinary musical sense of the term) of the pitch of a High tone, and all subsequent High tones in the phrase.[1] We will see shortly that the downstep is the result of a floating Low tone, a state of affairs frequently found among African languages. It is not hard to show that the Falling tone is the result of the concatenation of a High tone and a Low tone, and that the Rising tone is the result of the concatenation of a Low tone and a High tone.

2. Under some conditions, vowels may appear in hiatus, that is, following one another directly without intervening consonants. In such cases, the vowels appear in separate syllables. Under other conditions (which will be the ones that interest us in this chapter), sequences of vowels merge to form a single syllable, including the case where the second vowel is the Tense Marker of the verb.

When a surface syllable is the realization of two separate vowels (which means in Mituku that the vowels are from separate morphemes), the vowel that is realized cannot be phonetically distinguished from a vowel which is the realization of a single underlying vowel—or to put the matter more simply: there is no surface vowel length contrast (and there is no underlying vowel length contrast either, a separate matter), regardless of the source and composition of the surface vowel in question. This is the first of the two important facts about Mituku tone to bear in mind.

The second important fact is this: a contour tone (i.e. Rising or Falling tone) may appear on a vowel if and only if that vowel is the realization of two underlying vowels (or vowel positions, to make the same point in slightly different terms). And the floating Low tone which concerns us in this chapter obeys this principle absolutely: it will associate with a vowel (or vowel position) if and only if such a vowel position is available and accessible, and will otherwise not be associated to any vowel. But the level at which this behaviour can be thus expressed and thus understood is not the surface level: it is an intermediate level of representation which contains information (such as syllable length) which is not represented on the surface.

The Mituku verb has a morphological structure which is similar to that described for many Eastern Bantu languages. Reduced to the simplest

[1] See Clements (1979), for example, for further discussion of downstep.

elements that concern us (and ignoring certain complexities that are amply described by Stappers, and which do not bear on our interests), we may say that a finite verb begins with a Subject Marker (SM), which is followed by a Tense Marker (TM), an optional Object Marker (OM), the verb radical, an optional sequence of derivational suffixes, and a Final vowel (FV), which marks tense and mood.

The infinitive differs from the finite verb by having neither Subject Marker nor Tense Marker, and in their stead has a nominal prefix (*ku-*).

From a tonal point of view, each of the groups of morphemes just listed other than the derivational suffixes may display behaviour that shows that it is underlyingly specified for tone. That is, some morphemes in each of these groups consistently display the same tone in all environments (High or Low tone), and we would naturally interpret this as the realization of that morpheme's underlying tonal specification. And a High/Low contrast is found within each morphological class, which is to say that our decision to mark the morphemes tonally underlyingly cannot be replaced by a decision to assign tones by rule. Verb radicals (to take the simplest example) divide into two classes, those which are consistently High in all contexts (and thus are High underlyingly), and those which are Low in most or all contexts. Object Markers are likewise divided into two groups, those which are consistently Low in tone, and those which are consistently High.

This brief discussion does leave open the possibility that the High versus Low contrast in Mituku could be viewed as a contrast between vowels linked to a High tone and vowels linked to no tone, a High/o contrast, as has been argued for in a range of languages.[2] We will see that in some cases, the evidence in Mituku clearly resolves the ambiguity between these two ways to analyse a surface High/Low contrast, and when the data disambiguates the analysis, it always points in the direction of a High/Low contrast rather than a High/∅ contrast.

3.3. THE ISSUE: THE NUMBER OF LEVELS IN PHONOLOGICAL THEORY

The prime interest of the material discussed in this chapter derives from the fact that it demands an analysis with three levels of representation, because there is a level of representation distinct from both the underlying and the

[2] See, for example, Stevick (1969), McCawley (1970), Goldsmith (1984*b*), Pulleyblank (1986), and many other sources too numerous to mention.

surface phonological levels at which a simple phonological constraint must be stated. This constraint is a familiar one: a vowel may be associated with at most one tone; or, putting the same matter slightly differently, a toneless vowel (but only a toneless vowel) will associate with a floating (i.e. a vowelless) tone at this derived phonological level. We will be at pains to make clear that the level at which this generalization must be stated is not the underlying level (for the constraint is operative on a representation which is the *output* of a phonological rule) nor the surface (for on the surface, there is no indication that a vowel is long or bimoraic, though only the vowels which were bimoraic at a deeper level are candidates for associating with two tones on the surface).

3.4. THE TONE OF THE INFINITIVE

The tone of the infinitive is largely a direct expression of the underlying tonal specifications. The examples in (1)–(2) illustrate that the verb radical bears its own underlying tone, either High or Low, and in the infinitive it is followed by a suffixal High tone which associates with all following extensions.[3] The raised exclamation point marks tonal downstep, which we return to below.

(1) Infinitive, Low radical
  a. No Object Marker (OM)

   'faire tournoyer'...

  b. Low-toned OM

  c. High-toned OM

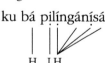

---

[3] Following standard Bantu notation, vowels with a dot underneath indicate vowels higher (or tenser) than their counterparts without the underdot.

(2) Infinitive, High radical

   a. No OM

      ku kúlúmánísá

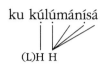

      (L)H H

      'rassembler (des gens)'

   b. Low-toned OM

      ku mu kúlúmánísá

      L(L)H H

   c. High-toned OM

      ku ba! kúlúmánísá

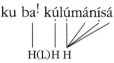

      H(L)H H

Object Markers, whose presence or absence is determined by syntactic considerations, are specified underlyingly as either High or Low, and retain that tonal specification in all contexts, as we see illustrated in (*b, c*) in both (1) and (2).

In the case of the High-toned radical (2*a, b, c*), a floating Low tone is specified as preceding the High-toned radical. This is the Low tone which is the focus of the discussion of this chapter, and it appears before all High-toned radicals, though not before Low-toned radicals. In the cases illustrated in (2), there is only one place where the floating Low tone could be phonetically perceptible, and that is in case (2*c*), where it appears floating between two High tones. In this case, the Low tone creates a downstep—that is, the pitch of the second High is lowered by about a whole musical step, the same degree of lowering that it would display if a fully realized Low tone had appeared before it. This tonal effect is indicated by a raised exclamation point.

3.5. THE HISTORICAL PAST

The historical past is marked in Mituku by a Tense Marker of the form *-a-* with no associated tone. In the next section we will compare this Tense Marker to that of the optative, which is similarly composed of a

Tense Marker *-a-*, but this time associated with a High tone. (Many of the most volatile and interesting Tense Markers from a tonal point of view have the segmental form *-a-*; see Goldsmith 1984*a* for a discussion of this.)

The first half of the relevant data is presented in (3), where we see the tonal behaviour of Low-toned verb radicals, with Low (*a, b, c: tu-*) and High (*d, e, f: ba-*) toned Subject Markers, and each with no Object Markers, with a Low-toned Object Marker (here, *-mu-*), and a High-toned Object Marker (*-ba-* and *-tu-*). *Underlying* forms are given in the first column, with surface forms on the right. In each case the essential difference between the underlying forms and the surface form is that the vowel of the Subject Marker and the vowel of the Tense Marker have merged to form a single syllable. That merged syllable surfaces with a level tone, however, either Low or High, depending on the tone of the Subject Marker. As we shall see below, there are other cases where the merger of the Subject Marker and an *-a-* Tense Marker (from a different tense, however) gives rise to a syllable with a contour tone (High–Low [Falling] or Low–High [Rising]). In light of this behaviour which we shall encounter in the next section, we can tentatively (but correctly) draw the conclusion that the Tense Marker of the historical past is itself toneless underlyingly. Hence it contributes no tone(s) to the syllable formed when it merges with the preceding Subject Marker. Forms with High-toned verbs are given in (4). (All the verbal forms in (3) and (4) are followed by the word *múno* in Stappers 1973.)

(3) Historical past, Low-toned verb

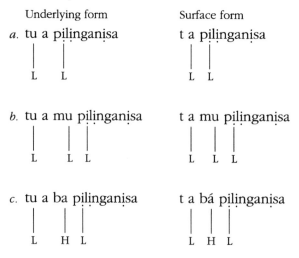

d. ba a pilinganisa   b á pilinganisa

    H   L   H   L

e. ba a mu pilinganisa   b á mu pilinganisa

    H   L   L   H   L   L

f. ba a tu pilinganisa   b á tú pilinganisa

    H   H   L   H   H L

(4) Historical past, High-toned verb

    Underlying form   Surface form

a. tu a kulumanisa   t a kúlumanisa

    L (L) H   L (L) H

b. tu a mu kulumanisa   t a mu kúlumanisa

    L   L(L)H   L   L(L)H

c. tu a ba kulumanisa   t a bá! kúlumanisa

    L   H(L) H   L   H(L) H

d. ba a kulumanisa   b â kúlumanisa

    H   (L)H   H L   H

e. ba a mu kulumanisa   b á mu kúlumanisa

    H   L(L) H   H   L(L) H

f. ba a tu kulumanisa   b á tú! kúlumanisa

    H   H(L) H   H   H(L)H

The forms in (4) show us two critically important aspects of Mituku tone. First, they illustrate in (4c, f) the presence of a floating Low tone that is realized as a downstep in front of a High-toned radical, although that downstep is phonetically perceptible only when a High-toned syllable immediately precedes, for in Mituku, as in most languages with downstep, the difference between a High tone and a downstepped High tone is phonetically perceptible only immediately after a High tone. Secondly, and more importantly, we find in the right-hand version of (4d) a Falling tone on the surface syllable *bâ*, the syllable which is the merger of the Subject Marker *bá-* and the Tense Marker *-a-*. This is the first instance that we have seen of a contour tone, and it illustrates the generalization that a contour tone can appear on a syllable in Mituku only if the syllable is derived from a bimoraic representation at a deeper level (which means, in fact, that the syllable is bimorphemic). And where does the Low tone come from, the second half of the Falling tone? It is not particularly difficult to see that this Low tone is the same Low tone that in examples (4c, f) created the downstep; here, however, the Low is phonetically manifested. The Low, that is, is a Low that ultimately comes from the High-toned radical (note that there is no parallel Low tone at play in the parallel cases in (3), the cases constructed from a Low-toned radical). That floating Low tone associates with the *-a-* of the Tense Marker precisely because the Tense Marker is a toneless vowel.

We thus find an association is created between the (toneless) Tense Marker *-a-* and the (vowelless) L tone. The examples in (4e) and (4f) show that this added association line appears only when its addition would not cross an already present association line.

We may summarize our conclusions so far in this way: at a certain level of representation (and we must dig a bit deeper to be clearer on precisely what that means), the representations in Mituku appear to undergo a rule that adds an association line between any toneless vowel and any vowelless tone, with the understanding that such a rule cannot create an association line crossing another association line. Put slightly differently, we can say that (at that certain level of representation) there is a strong pressure (due, if you prefer, to a highly ranked constraint) for all vowels to be associated with at least one tone, and for all tones to be associated with at least one vowel; but that pressure (or constraint) is not as highly ranked as the generalization that an association line in underlying representations may not be crossed by another association line. Rather than get bogged down in a formulation any more precise than this—committing us to either a rule-based or a constraint-based formalization—let us merely note that there are quite a few variations on each style of description, and that the situation we are looking at in Mituku is simple, and not difficult to state in the vernacular of several theories.

While we are not yet in a position to settle definitively at what level our generalization is to be stated, we can already note this: the generalization cannot be stated on the surface, since the association site for the floating Low (which is the vowel position, or the mora, of the Tense Marker -*a*-) is not distinct from that of the Subject Marker on the surface. Put another way, there is no representational difference *on the surface* between a short vowel derived from a short vowel, and a short vowel derived from a long vowel. Hence the rule(s) or constraint(s) involved must address a level of representation deeper than the surface. (We will see in our discussion of the optative tense that this level cannot be the underlying level, either, but rather must be a derived level of representation.)

3.6. THE OPTATIVE TENSE MARKER -*á*-

The optative tense in Mituku is formed, like the historical past, from a Tense Marker of the form -*a*-. In the optative, however, the Tense Marker is clearly associated with an underlying High tone. Consider the data in (5) and (6), which we will explore case by case.

In (5*a*), the Rising tone on the first syllable of the surface form shows us immediately that we are dealing with a Tense Marker with a High tone (it has here combined with a Low-toned Subject Marker to create a Rising tone). In this respect the optative Tense Marker is minimally different from the historical past Tense Marker, though as we shall see shortly, there are cases where the optative Tense Marker loses its High tone, and it then behaves just like the historical past's Tense Marker (this happens clearly in cases (5*c*) and (6*a, c*); there are other cases where the rules that we will posit delete the Tense Marker's H tone, but where this has no perceptible result, and in those cases I have not indicated the effect of the H-tone deletion).[4]

Of the six forms in (5*a–f*), only (5*c*) requires the application of any tonal rule to derive the surface form. In (5*c*), however, we see no trace of the Rising tone on the first syllable that the other parallel cases display. (5*c*) requires the postulation of a rule of Rising Tone Absorption,[5] a widespread rule among the Bantu languages. This rule is formalized in (7).

---

[4] This may create some confusion, in that I give some surface forms in which Meeussen's Rule's effect is not shown: cases where a single syllable bears a sequence of two High tones, as in (5*d, e, f*), for example. The reader should understand that these double High sequences are (according to our analysis) actually simplified to a single High tone.

[5] The term *absorption* for this phenomenon is due to Hyman and Schuh (1974).

(5) Optative tense, Low-toned verb

Underlying forms   Surface forms

a. tu a pilinganisa   t ă pilinganisa

L H   L

LH L

b. tu a mu pilinganisa   t ă mu pilinganisa

L H   L L

L H L   L

c. tu a ba pilinganisa   t a bá pilinganisa

L H H L

L H L

d. ba a pilinganisa   b á pilinganisa

H H L

HH L

e. ba a mu pilinganisa   b á mu pilinganisa

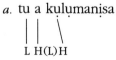
H H   L L

HH L L

f. ba a tu pilinganisa   b á tú pilinganisa

H H H L

HHH L

(6) Optative tense, High-toned verbs

Underlying forms   Surface forms

a. tu a kulumanisa   t a kúlumanisa

L H(L)H   L (L) H

b. tu a mu kulumanisa   t ă mu kúlumanisa

L H   L(L)H   L H L(L)H

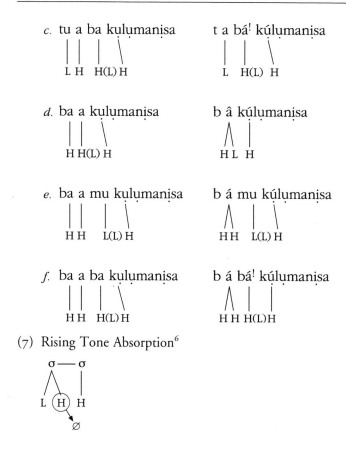

c. tu a ba kulumanisa

L H H(L) H

t a bá¹ kulumanisa

L H(L) H

d. ba a kulumanisa

H H(L) H

b â kulumanisa

H L H

e. ba a mu kulumanisa

H H L(L) H

b á mu kulumanisa

H H L(L) H

f. ba a ba kulumanisa

H H H(L) H

b á bá¹ kulumanisa

H H H(L)H

(7) Rising Tone Absorption[6]

σ —— σ

L (H) H

∅

---

[6] There is an important point lurking in the details of the formalization of this rule; the point remains regardless of whether one conceives of the generalization as a rule or as a representational constraint. The point is this: for the rule to come into effect, the *syllable* with the Rising tone and the *syllable* with the High tone must be adjacent. However, paradoxical as it may sound, the *tones* comprising the Rising tone and the High tone need not be adjacent: they may be separated by the floating Low tone. Thus it appears we must specify on which tier adjacency is required, and the requirement is adjacency on the syllable tier.

There has been much discussion in the tonal literature regarding just this question, though posed slightly differently. The effects of what is known as Meeussen's Rule in Bantu tone studies (Goldsmith 1984*b*, *c*) operate to lower or delete a High tone following a High tone, and in most (though not all) languages this restriction is interpreted as requiring that the tones be associated with successive syllables. In at least one case, the two tones need not be associated with successive vowels. In Goldsmith (1987) I suggested that the widespread Eastern Bantu pattern (specific to certain tenses) by which a High tone appears on the second mora of a Low-toned stem, and on the Final vowel of High-toned stems, could best be understood as the effects of Meeussen's Rule applying between the stem-tone and the second-mora High tone (no longer distance effect there) and also between the second-mora High tone and the Final Vowel High tone; the latter case would in general be a long-distance Meeussen's Rule effect. If this is correct, then we have further cases where adjacency must be parameterized to select, or

The final cases which interest us are those in (6), formed with a High-toned verb and thus possessed of a floating Low tone on the analysis which we are exploring. In cases (6*a*) and (6*c*), the High tone of the Tense Marker is deleted by the rule of Rising Tone Absorption.

In (6*a*), though not in (6*c*), the Floating L tone can (and thus will) associate with the now-toneless vowel position of the Tense Marker. Since this is merged with the Low-toned vowel of the Subject Marker, however, the effect of the 'docking' of the Low tone is imperceptible. In (6*c*), the Floating Low tone cannot associate because it would have to cross the association line of the intervening Object Marker.

We turn now to the last three cases in (6), cases *d*, *e*, and *f*, where a High-toned stem is formed with a High-toned Subject Marker. In all three cases, we have a High-toned Subject Marker merged with a High-toned Tense Marker, followed by one of three possibilities: a floating Low (case *d*); an associated Low (case *e*); or an associated High (case *f*). If no rules were to apply, we would expect to find a High on the first syllable in all three cases (formed from joining of the Subject Marker High and the Tense Marker High). However, we find a High tone on this first syllable only in cases *e* and *f*; in case *d*, we find a Falling tone, clearly the result of the docking of the floating Low to the vocalic position of the Tense Marker. If the Tense Marker is free to associate with the floating Low in this context, though, there must be a rule which deletes the Tense Marker's High tone. This, we suggest, is an intrasyllabic version of Meeussen's Rule, formalized in (8).

(8) Intrasyllabic Meeussen's Rule

This rule will delete the High tone of the optative tense in all three cases in (6*d*, *e*, *f*), though its effects will be masked in cases (*e*, *f*), for the result remains phonetically unchanged in those two cases. In (6*d*), however, the effect of Meeussen's Rule is to free the vocalic position of the Tense Marker so that it may now associate with the floating Low tone of the High-toned stem. (Note that this rule will also apply in an imperceptible fashion in (5*d*, *e*, *f*), though I have not marked its effects in the surface forms.)

---

not to select, adjacency on one tier or another. There is material enough to fill a book on this subject, and the interested reader may consult Archangeli and Pulleyblank (1994: esp. ch. 1), Odden (1994), and many other studies.

The reader must bear in mind that each of the thirty forms which we have looked at refers not simply to itself, but to each of an indefinite number of forms made up of morphemes with the same underlying tones: each is a point in the tonal paradigm of verbs, and stands for a limitless number of verbs. In that sense, the 'single' case in (6*a*), for example, represents not just one word in the Mituku vocabulary, but an unbounded set of cases, and fully one sixth of all verbs in the optative tense.

3.7. WHEN DOES THE FLOATING TONE ASSOCIATE?

It is now time to pull together the threads of this analysis. Three facts have emerged:

Point 1. There are no bimoraic representations of vowels on the surface: that is, there are no long vowels (on the surface).

Point 2. The floating Low tone associates with a vowel position if and only if there is a toneless vowel with which it can associate without crossing an association line.

Point 3. The toneless vowel with which the floating tone associates may be either underlyingly toneless (the case of the Tense Marker of the Historic Past) or it may be made toneless by rule (either by Rising Tone Absorption or by Meeussen's Rule).

When does the floating tone association described in point 2 occur, or at what representation? Point 1 establishes that it cannot even be described using a surface representation, and point 3 establishes that it cannot be described using an underlying representation. The conclusion is inescapable that the generalization stated in point 2 must 'occur' on—or be stated with respect to—an intermediate level of representation. Most phonological theories have well-defined levels of this sort, whether it be called the phonemic level, the output of (a stratum of) the lexical phonology, W-level representation, or some other term.

Only theories with no more than one or two levels of phonological representation will founder on such facts, theories such as Koskenniemi's two-level model (embodied, for example, in the PC-Kimmo system) or, more recently, one interpretation of optimality theory, as we noted earlier.

I do not think that the structure of the data offered here is in any way particularly unusual, and it should be borne in mind that the nub of the argument is not that the relationship between the underlying and the surface can be, or should be, decomposed into two or more composed operations, with one feeding the other. The argument is that there is a simple constraint which governs where and when the floating tone will associate, but the level at which this simple constraint ('associate a floating tone to a toneless vowel so long as this involves no crossing of association lines') operates is an intermediate level of representation, neither the underlying nor the surface representation.

3.8. A SPECULATIVE NOTE

I would like to speculate briefly on the likely origin of the *1 tone per vowel* constraint. I believe that the biological substratum that underlies much autosegmental structure, as well as the relations between the rows on a metrical grid, is the phase-locking of biological oscillators, an area that has been the centre of considerable attention by scientists interested in both the neuroanatomy and functioning of the central nervous system.[7] It is a banality to observe that rhythm is important in languages; metrical phonology is indeed based on the interacting and intersecting rhythms of syllabicity and stress. But what are the consequences for linguistics of taking this seriously? Rhythmicity, both in neural organization and in overt behaviour, is the result of neural oscillators passing regularly through repeated cycles of activation, and the most important (and well-studied) properties of collections of such neural oscillators is their strong attraction to phase-locking (especially at 1 : 1 ratio, but also at 2 : 1 and other rational ratios).

In early work on autosegmental phonology, it was often said (correctly, no doubt) that the function of association lines was to indicate the co-registration, in abstract or concrete time, of elements on the autosegmental tiers they linked. We can today, I think, ask for a more concrete explanation of that phonological metaphor. An action which unrolls in time, such as a sequence of segments or moras, requires a timekeeper (often referred to as a *Zeitgeber* in the literature; see the references cited in note 7) which completes one cycle with each unit of the action.

In work that has grown out of the network models developed with Larson,[8] I have been exploring ways of modelling the dynamics of accent systems.

---

[7] Glass and Mackey (1988) is the classic reference, but work in this area has burgeoned over the last ten years with the development of non-linear dynamics. Work of Haken (1987), and following him, Kelso (1995), is particularly relevant. An overview of mathematical modelling in this area is given in Ermentrout (1994).

[8] See, for example, Goldsmith (1993*b*, 1994) and Larson (1992).

Each row of a metrical grid is modelled by an oscillator with a basic (or *natural*) frequency (the frequency at which it would oscillate if not coupled or driven by external forces), and these oscillators are coupled to one another by links of varying strengths. Under a wide variety of settings, as noted in the neural network literature (see again note 7), attractor states are those where the oscillators are in phase-lock: that is, the peak of a relatively low-frequency oscillator consistently coincides with the peak of a relatively high-frequency oscillator. While this modelling is most easily interpretable in the case of rhythmic metrical systems, it is tempting to view the timing tier in a phonological model (or simply, in this case, the mora tier) as a relatively high-frequency *Zeitgeber*; the circumstances under which two tones could be associated with one mora would be those in which the oscillator associated with the tonal tier reached a frequency twice that of the mora. But the natural frequency of the tonal tier is normally lower than that of the moraic tier, and a probabilistic argument can be made that a two-to-one alignment of tones to moras would arise only under relatively rare conditions. If this line of attack proves useful and valid, it suggests that both formal and functional explanations may be grounded in dynamical explanations.

4

Phonetic Representations in the Mental Lexicon

John Coleman

4.1. INTRODUCTION

In this chapter I shall argue that (i) our mental representations of the form of words are essentially phonetic, rather than symbolic-phonological; (ii) phonological competence includes and makes use of statistical properties of the time-course of phonetic representations; and (iii) a combination of phonetic, statistical, and semantic knowledge is sufficient to explain many aspects of phonological structure. Since generative grammar claims to be concerned with real linguistic knowledge, generative phonologists might regard the mental existence of phonological representations as pretty incontrovertible. Many psychologists of language too, though rarely so concerned with the kind of relatively abstract relations that phonologists focus on, are happy to speak of phonemes, syllables, and the phonological lexicon (see e.g. Dell 1986, Ellis and Young 1988, Cutler and Norris 1988, Fear, Cutler, and Butterfield 1995). It would be odd to deny the reality of such things. Yet in this chapter I shall argue that there is almost no material evidence for abstract phonological representations and units of the kind set out in mainstream works from almost all quarters, including the phonological frameworks described by Kenstowicz (1994), Goldsmith

(1990), Kaye (1989), Prince and Smolensky (1993), and even Coleman (1998*a*). Rather, it is more probable that the mental lexicon is populated by many kinds of detailed, variable, redundancy-rich phonetic representations, auditory, articulatory, and visual. The position I set out is not especially original: to a large extent I shall simply present a collection of arguments in support of the 'episodic' view of lexical representations set out by Pisoni, Goldinger, Mullenix, Johnson, and co-workers (see their papers in Johnson and Mullenix 1997).

Central to this discussion is the following question: if we entertain the existence of non-abstract, superficial phonetic representations (such as articulatory and auditory representations), are there *any* phonological phenomena which cannot be described or formulated using phonetic representations, and which *require* us also to employ more abstract, phonological representations? To an extent, I shall adopt a deliberately (i.e. provocatively) sceptical stance in order to highlight the dearth of evidence for our 'convenient fictions'. Along the way, I shall adopt a rule: theory-internal philosophical argumentation alone is not sufficient. If we wish to speak of knowledge, we require that the usual yardstick of scientific scrutiny be employed: experiments that a priori offer the possibility of more than one outcome, reflecting distinct hypotheses, and as a result of their outcome point to a particular view as being more likely to be right and another as more likely to be wrong. In short, the study of grammar must rest on good science, not on philosophy.

In section 4.2, I review studies that offer some reasons to believe in syllables, feet, parts of syllables, and possibly features (but probably not phonemes). I discuss some recent psychological studies that provide some direct evidence for rich, detailed, and redundant phonological representations. I also raise alternative accounts of knowledge of these categories that come from statistical models of language learning and processing. In section 4.3, I argue that certain facts regarding sociolinguistic variation, gradual phonetic change, and child language acquisition are problematic for parsimony of representation. Finally, in section 4.4, I conclude by sketching an alternative account, in which the assumption of parsimony is given no hearing.

4.2. REVIEW OF SOME EVIDENCE FOR PHONOLOGICAL UNITS

In this section I shall review some of the evidence for phonological units of various kinds. But just because certain kinds of unit exist does not mean that they have the form proposed for them in generative phonology. We shall see that in most cases there are other views of the nature of phonological knowledge than the letters and lines that fill the pages of phonology textbooks.

4.2.1. Syllables

Among the many theoretical arguments for the necessity of recognizing a non-phonetic, structural level of representation for syllables one comes from the observation that in some words there is a mismatch between the number of syllables in a word and the number of sonority peaks. In words and phrases such as 'buying' /baɪɪŋ/, 'payee' /peɪiː/, and 'the eel' /ðiiːl/, two syllable nuclei are adjacent to one another. Consequently, a diphthong or triphthong is made, with a single sonority peak (Fig. 4.1*a*).

Contrariwise, in other words consisting of a single syllable, there may be more than one sonority peak. For example, in 'spray', the initial /s/ is more open than the /p/ which follows it, and is thus a sonority peak, as well as the diphthong /eɪ/ of the second syllable (Fig. 4.1*b*). The sonority profile of this word is little different from that of the two-syllable word 'osprey'. In some dialect pronunciations, the presence of epenthetic vowels may yield apparently disyllabic pronunciations of words which in other dialects are monosyllabic. (I like to call such words 'sesquisyllabic'.) For example, the North-East British English (Tyneside, or 'Geordie') pronunciation of 'milk' and 'film' as [mɪlək] and [fɪləm] leads us to consider whether to regard them as lexical disyllables (like 'bullock', in which case Tynesiders may have quite different lexical representations of these words from other speakers), or disyllabic pronunciations of lexical monosyllables. A similar example is afforded by the fairly widespread American pronunciation (and occasional non-RP British pronunciation too, according to Wells 1990) of passives in -*n* as [ən] in e.g. 'known' [noʊən]. Are these disyllabic, like 'Owen' or 'bitten', or monosyllabic, but with diphthong 'breaking', like 'file' [faɪəl], 'sail' [seɪəl], etc. Or are the latter disyllabic too?

Faced with these difficulties, employing two separate levels of representation, phonological vs. phonetic, can help. For example, we could propose that any or all of [mɪlək], [fɪləm], [noʊən], [faɪəl], and [seɪəl] are phonetically disyllabic realizations of the phonological (i.e. lexical) monosyllables /mɪlk/, /fɪlm/, /noʊn/, /faɪl/, and /seɪl/. That works, but is it true? Unfortunately, I know of no experimental studies of this question.

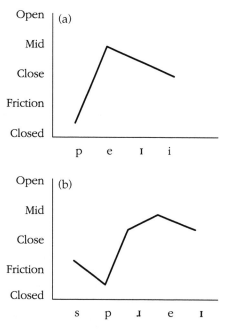

F IG. 4.1. Sonority is not a reliable guide to syllabification. In Fig. 4.1*a* the syllabic word 'payee' has a single sonority peak. In Fig. 4.1*b* the monosyllabic word 'spray' has two sonority peaks.

Now let us think the unthinkable, and consider what these examples look like in a world without autonomous, symbolic phonology. [mɪlək], [fɪləm], [noʊən], [faɪəl], and [seɪəl] are phonetically disyllabic. In their articulation, they each have two peaks of vocal tract opening. Since speakers know how to articulate, we can say that a speaker saying [fɪləm] knows to open their mouth twice. As a result of these vocal tract openings, the resulting acoustic signal has two amplitude maxima. A speaker of the same dialect is accustomed to hearing [fɪləm] in tokens of the word 'film'. A speaker of another dialect, who is used to hearing [fɪlm] and who has not heard [fɪləm], may initially be puzzled by the Tyneside pronunciation. Since they do not normally hear [fɪləm] for 'film', they must make an interpretation of what they hear. If speech perception were entirely a bottom-up process (i.e. such that phonetic decoding is followed in turn by phonological decoding, morphological decoding, lexical access, syntactic decoding, and semantic interpretation), we would expect that they might initially interpret [fɪləm] as 'fill 'em', which would then give rise to problems of syntactic and semantic processing. But we know that in speech perception, syntactic and semantic processing can guide lexical access and the process of phonological decoding (Tyler and Marslen-Wilson 1977, Shillcock 1990, Nicol 1996). So although [fɪləm] is not a perfect match for their expectation [fɪlm], syntactic constraints, the referential context, and every speaker's knowledge that sometimes other people pronounce things a little differently from themselves conspire to force the interpretation of [fɪləm] as a variant pronunciation of [fɪlm].

With 'buying' [baɪɪŋ], 'payee' [peɪi], and 'the eel' [ðiil], each syllable is also transparently a morpheme. Although morpheme boundaries do not always coincide with syllable boundaries, the location of morpheme/ syllable boundaries in this case can be determined by the speaker-hearer from the fall in transition probabilities between successive consonants and vowels (for convenience, I take [aɪ] as a single unit here), because [baɪ] and [ɪŋ], being morphemes and syllables, occur more frequently than [aɪɪ]:

(1) p(#b) = 0.0076   Bi-phoneme probability decreases from here
     p(baɪ) = 0.0004 ↓
     p(aɪɪ) = 0.0003 to here (syllable and morpheme boundary), and then
                      rises
     p(ɪŋ) = 0.014   ↓
     p(ŋ#) = 0.011   to here.

As another example, 'antidisestablishmentarianism' contains about as many syllables and morphemes as you could find in an English word. Table 4.1 shows that, again, high bi-phoneme probabilities are associated with common within-syllable constituents (rhymes, CVs, and onset and coda consonant clusters), whereas low bi-phoneme probabilities relate to syllable and/or morpheme boundaries.

The statistical identification of syllable boundaries can be improved a little if the bi-phoneme frequencies are normalized for the frequency of their constituent phonemes, to take account of the fact that in the above example, for instance, /tɪ/ has a high bi-phoneme frequency in part simply because both /t/ and /ɪ/ are high-frequency phonemes. Similarly, /iə/ has a low frequency in part because /i/ has a relatively low frequency. In Table 4.2, normalized bi-phoneme frequency

$$n = \frac{\text{bi-phoneme frequency}}{\text{phoneme 1 probability} \times \text{phoneme 2 probability}}.$$

Note that normalized frequency differs from unnormalized frequency in having local maxima at the end of the first syllable, /nt/, the first mora of the third syllable, /dɪ/, the onset of the sixth syllable /bl/, and the cluster /nt/ at the end of the morpheme /mənt/, and local minima at the boundary of the third and fourth syllables, /ɪs/.

TABLE 4.1. Syllable and morpheme boundaries are correlated with bi-phoneme frequency

Bi-phoneme	Frequency (ppm)	Comments
#a	2412	Local minimum at word edge.
an	4367	
nt	8437	
tɪ	13446	Local maximum at very common CV combination.
ɪd	5743	Local minimum at end of syllable.
dɪ	7937	
ɪs	9110	
sɛ	2212	Local minimum at end of frequent morpheme /dɪs/.
ɛs	2641	
st	12857	Local maximum at start of new syllable; a very frequent cluster.
ta	1310	
ab	750	Local minimum at end of syllable.
bl	3682	
lɪ	12562	Local maximum at very common CV combination (often a morpheme).
ɪʃ	1928	
ʃm	98	Local minimum at end of syllable; not a syllable constituent.
mə	4330	
ən	10438	Local maximum at a common VC combination (often a rhyme, sometimes a morpheme).
nt	8437	
tɛə	148	Local minimum.
ɛər	773	
ri	3335	Local maximum at common CV combination.
iə	258	Local minimum at syllable boundary (hiatus).
ən	10438	Local maximum at rhyme; end of morpheme.
nɪ	4820	Local minimum.
ɪz	7898	Local maximum at rhyme.
zə	1241	Local minimum at syllable boundary. Also, /z/ is rare.
əm	3572	Local maximum at rhyme.
m#	2104	Local minimum at end of syllable and word.

The reason that bi-phoneme frequency is a good (albeit imperfect) guide to syllable constituency is simply that pairs of phonemes occur more frequently within constituents than across constituent boundaries. The final consonant or vowel of one syllable and the initial consonant or vowel

TABLE 4.2. Syllable boundaries correlated with normalized bi-phoneme frequency *n*

	Bi-phoneme frequency (ppm)	Phoneme 1 probability	Phoneme 2 probability	*n*	Unnormalized frequency profile	Normalized frequency profile
#a	2412	0.224	0.018	0.6	Min	Min
an	4367	0.018	0.05	4.9		
nt	8437	0.05	0.021	8.0		Max
tɪ	13446	0.021	0.083	7.7	Max	
ɪd	5743	0.083	0.034	2.0	Min	Min
dɪ	7937	0.034	0.083	2.8		Max
ɪs	9110	0.083	0.054	2.0	Max	Min
sɛ	2212	0.054	0.018	2.3	Min	
ɛs	2641	0.018	0.054	2.7		
st	12857	0.054	0.021	11.3	Max	Max
ta	1310	0.021	0.018	3.5		
ab	750	0.018	0.017	2.5	Min	Min
bl	3682	0.017	0.043	5.0		Max
lɪ	12562	0.043	0.083	3.5	Max	
ɪʃ	1928	0.083	0.01	2.3		
ʃm	98	0.01	0.023	0.4	Min	Min
mə	4330	0.023	0.05	3.8		
ən	10438	0.05	0.05	4.2	Max	
nt	8437	0.05	0.021	8.0		Max
tɛə	148	0.021	0.015	0.5	Min	Min
ɛər	773	0.015	0.037	1.4		
ri	3335	0.037	0.01	9.0	Max	Max
iə	258	0.01	0.05	0.5	Min	Min
ən	10438	0.05	0.05	4.2	Max	Max
nɪ	4820	0.05	0.083	1.2	Min	Min
ɪz	7898	0.083	0.031	3.1	Max	Max
zə	1241	0.031	0.05	0.8	Min	Min
əm	3572	0.05	0.023	3.1	Max	Max
m#	2104	0.023	0.224	0.4	Min	Min

of the following syllable may be almost any pair of phonemes, because syllables are relatively independent, whereas the range of pairs of consonants that may form an onset or coda, or the range of CV and VC pairs that may form a mora or rhyme are also restricted to a subset of the full set of possible combinations of all vowels and consonants. Thus, in the 190 most frequent bi-phonemes (out of a total 1,412 types) in Mitton (1992), (a machine-readable version of the *Oxford Advanced Learners' Dictionary*), only three (1.6

per cent) are not syllable constituents of some kind, namely /ʃn/ (47th most frequent, 4106 ppm), /tl/ (130th most frequent, 1543 ppm), and /dl/ (169th most frequent, 1174 ppm). These are all a combination of the final consonant of one syllable and the first consonant of the next. Among the 190 least frequent bi-phonemes, on the other hand, 177 (62 per cent) are undebatable cross-syllable consonant clusters or vowel–vowel hiatuses.

These statistical regularities are not just epiphenomena without cognitive relevance. To the contrary, much recent developmental research highlights the importance of statistical properties of language for the language learner. For example, Jusczyk, Luce, and Charles-Luce (1994) show that 9-month-old children are attuned to the phoneme transition probabilities of their ambient language, using this information to respond with greater attentiveness to stimuli that exhibit the statistical phonotactics of their own language than to another language. Contrary to the Chomskyan description of language as being a poor stimulus for language learning and his concomitant sniffiness about statistical approaches to grammar (see e.g. Chomsky 1957: 15–16, where his misunderstanding of statistical language models is evident), the thrust of current research shows that statistical regularities are a rich vein of information for the baby acquiring language, permitting a much more data-oriented approach to language acquisition than the more speculative 'top-down' proposals of models such as parameter-setting learning (Dresher and Kaye 1990). For example, Jusczyk and Aslin (1995) show that babies are sensitive to the contrast between strong and weak syllables and the probabilities of transitions between these two kinds of syllables several months before they begin to be sensitive to bi-phoneme probabilities. In a landmark paper, Saffran, Aslin, and Newport (1996) show that 8-month-olds can segment a continuous stream of spoken syllables into word-like units after only two minutes of listening experience. Aslin, Saffran and Newport (1998) demonstrate that the mechanism by which the babies perform this feat is by using the relatively low phoneme transition probabilities found at syllable junctures. This body of results largely confirms Brent and Cartwright's computational proposals as to the mechanism children might use in learning word divisions, words, and their internal structure (Brent and Cartwright 1996).

Evidence for knowledge of phonotactic statistics in adults, and the relevance of phonotactic statistics to phonological competence, is provided in several recent studies in which subjects rated the acceptability (or 'wordlikeness') of various kinds of nonsense words (Coleman and Pierrehumbert 1997, Pierrehumbert, Hay, and Beckman MS, Frisch, Large, and Pisoni 2000, Vitevich et al. 1997, Vitevich and Luce 1998). These studies establish that the acceptability of non-words is closely related to their likelihood, i.e. it is based on the frequency of the parts of the non-word that are attested in the lexicon. The statistical character is so strong that, as Coleman and Pierrehumbert (1997) showed, nonsense words containing a patently ill-formed substring, according to standard generative phonology (such as 'mrupation'), may actually be rated as more acceptable than nonsense words containing no ill-formed parts (such as 'spletisark'), because the relatively high frequency of the well-formed parts may be sufficient to outweigh the low frequency (i.e. zero) of the ill-formed part, and may even be sufficient to make the word more acceptable than a word made entirely from attested, but low-frequency, parts.

In a follow-up study, Pierrehumbert, Hay, and Beckman (MS) showed that people are sensitive to the probability of the phonological *parse* of a sequence of phonemes. They coerced subjects to analyse the exact same spoken sequence of nonsense syllables in two different ways, by using different priming sentences, e.g. either (2a) or (b).

(2) *a.* This is a zam, and this is a plirshdom. A plirshdom for a zam is a zam-plirshdom.
   b. This is a zamp, and this is a lirshdom. A lirshdom for a zamp is a zamp-lirshdom.

Subjects were then required to rate the acceptability of the pseudo-compound (in this example, 'zamplirshdom'). In both cases, however, exactly the same recording of the nonsense word was presented to the subjects, so that there was nothing about the pronunciation of the word that could signal the different parses of the made-up compound word. Similarly, 'zam', 'zamp', 'lirshdom', and 'plirshdom' were simply cut out of and copied from 'zamplirshdom'. But because (in this case) /p/ has a different frequency of occurrence when it occurs in word-final and word-initial positions, and coda /m/ and /mp/ and onset /l/ and /pl/ have different frequencies too, the two parses of 'zamplirshdom' have different probabilities. Pierrehumbert, Hay, and Beckman found that the subjects rated the acceptability of 'zamplirshdom' etc. differently according to the different parse probabilities appropriate to each priming environment.

There is abundant additional psycholinguistic evidence for syllables. For example, Levelt and Wheeldon (1994) found that words ending in a high-frequency syllable are named faster than words ending in a low-frequency syllable, an effect that is independent of and additive to the influence of word frequency on naming latency, and independent of syllable complexity. They interpret these results as evidence for a mental syllabary. Cutler and Norris (1988) and Fear, Cutler, and Butterfield (1995) show the importance of syllable weight contrasts in speech production and in word segmentation. Eimas (1999) has shown that infants demonstrate sensitivity to syllables before the earliest signs of segmental awareness can be detected. Additional, related evidence for syllables is discussed in section 4.2.3.

4.2.2. Feet

Phonologists have proposed the existence of metrical feet in order to explain patterns of stress assignment. In languages where stress placement always occurs at a particular position in the word, such as the first, last, second, or second from last syllable, the foot is clearly a dispensable construct. In order to demonstrate the psychological reality of feet, we could show that they are called into play in assigning stress to novel words in non-obvious places. For example, if subjects judge the correct position for main stress placement in 'antenuant' to be on the second syllable, we could explain that even though there are neighbouring syllables that are metrically heavier (note that /an/ is closed, /nju/ contains a diphthong, and /ənt/ ends in a consonant cluster), we can correctly predict stress placement by saying that it falls on the first syllable of the last foot. Because the last syllable is extrametrical, the final syllable cannot form a foot by itself. Because the diphthong /ju/ is short, the penultimate syllable cannot be a foot, and because feet may not be more than two syllables long, stress may not fall any further back than the antepenultimate syllable: it has to fall on /tɛ/, even though it is a light syllable.
QED

Despite the great simplicity and power of such an explanation, do we need symbolic foot structures in our picture of the mental reality of language? The evidence is not strong, as there are two other models that may explain stress patterns.

First, Larson (1992), working in a connectionist framework, notes that in order to model the syntagmatic alternation between strong and weak syllables found in sequences of binary feet, it is sufficient to postulate excitatory and inhibitory connections between adjacent syllables in the storage of words, such that some syllables (which we might refer to as 'strong', though they need not be explicitly classified as such in the model) inhibit their neighbours. That is, they make their neighbours weak. The other syllables excite their neighbours, i.e. make them strong. The net result of these interactions is a tendency for the strength of a sequence of syllables to alternate between highly excited (strong) and highly inhibited (weak). For languages with initial stress, the left edge of the word can be set to excite the first syllable, making it strong, which in turn inhibits the next syllable, making it weak, and so on. In a language with penultimate stress, the end of the word can be set to inhibit its predecessor, the last syllable, thus making it weak. To capture the effects of heavy syllables and extrametrical syllables, in more complex systems, Larson shows that it suffices to allow certain syllables to be intrinsically highly activated or inhibited. His model makes no reference to feet, but it nevertheless has simple mechanisms that give rise to alternations of prominence and related metrical phenomena. I do not mean to nail my colours to Larson's model (though I'll count myself as an ally), in particular: I mention it here as evidence that the foot construct is not unassailable, and that in fact there exists an interesting alternative account that has so far been mostly ignored by mainstream phonologists.

A second alternative account of stress placement in neologisms is sometimes called 'analogy' (e.g. Coker, Church, and Liberman 1990, Dedina and Nusbaum 1991). In this approach, words are stored in their surface phonemic form, including stress and surface vowel qualities. (Orthography is usually stored too, as the method is used for grapheme–phoneme conversion, but that does not concern us here.) Novel words may be generated out of parts of stored words, and heard novel words may be perhaps partly understood if their parts may be understood by reference to parts of known words. The pronunciation of orthographic neologisms may be inferred from the sum of the pronunciation of the attested parts. In each case, where more than one analysis is available, the lexical statistics of occurring words may be invoked to determine which of several decompositions of a neologism is the most plausible.

To see how this approach to analogy works, consider 'antenuant', /antɛnjʊənt/, again. The beginning of this neologism has only two familiar lexical neighbours, 'antenna', /anˈtɛnə/ and 'antennae' /anˈtɛni/: in both cases, main stress is on the syllable /tɛ/. The ending of this word, /ʊənt/ occurs in very few surface forms (likewise for /ənt/). /antɛnjʊənt/ is not a very plausible neologism. However, it has several lexical neighbours, some with penultimate stress (3*a*), others with antepenultimate stress (3*b*):

(3) *a.* Penultimate stress
          pursuant   /pəˈsjʊənt/
          truant   /ˈtrʊənt/
          fluent   /ˈflʊənt/
    b. Antepenultimate stress
          effluent   /ˈɛflʊənt/
          constituent   /kənˈstɪtjʊənt/
          congruent   /ˈkɒŋgrʊənt/
          confluent   /ˈkɒnflʊənt/
          affluent   /ˈaflʊənt/

In other words, the lexicon suggests two alternative stressings of words ending in /ʊənt/. Antepenultimate stress mostly occurs in words of three or more syllables, and penultimate stress generally in disyllables, except for 'pursuant'. The morphological make-up of the words is not much help either, as the last morpheme is /ənt/ in each case. It is not sufficient to consider the independent probability of penultimate and ante-penultimate stress: the probability of penultimate stress, estimated over the entire dictionary, is about 0.5, and the probability of antepenultimate stress is about 0.23. By this criterion alone, we expect 'antenuant' to receive penultimate stress, but that does not seem correct. Nor is it adequate merely to consider the stress patterns of words ending in /ʊənt/, for then we would say that since 5 (the number of words in 3*b*) is greater than 3 (as in 3*a*), antepenultimate stress is more likely. That computation ignores the different likelihoods of different stress assignments to the initial substring 'anten-'.

We can determine which is most likely in the neologism by considering the observed likelihoods of all attested syllables at each attested place in metrical structure, as well as the likelihood of all aspects of metrical structure. We could then use these data to calculate the probability of all the possible stressings of 'antenuant'. In that way, we can determine which metrical structure, and thus which pattern of stress assignment, is the most likely.

The probabilistic context-free grammar rules in (4) are taken from a complete probabilistic metrical grammar of English described at greater length in Coleman (2000). In these rules, PrWd = 'prosodic word', Σ = 'foot', σ = 'syllable', s = 'strong' (i.e. stressed), w = 'weak', i = 'initial', m = 'medial', and f = 'final'. (The last three features were found useful in earlier work, reported in Coleman and Pierrehumbert 1997 and Frisch, Large, and Pisoni 2000, for discriminating between the different distributions of different syllable constituents at different positions in the word.) Because the range of rule and substring probabilities observed in the dictionary is great, including both very frequent and very infrequent items, I express the likelihood of each rule as a log probability. This has the additional computational advantage that the overall probability of a parse, i.e. the product of the rule probabilities, can be calculated by simply *adding* the log probabilities used in the grammar. The log probabilities are negative because the probabilities are all fractions, less than 1. Rules with negative log probabilities nearer to 0 are thus more likely than rules with the same left-hand side and a larger negative log probability. Thus, (4*a*) is more likely than (4*b*).

(4) *a.* PrWd $\rightarrow \sigma_{wi} \Sigma_{sf}$, $\quad \log_{10} p \approx -0.71$
  b. PrWd $\rightarrow \Sigma_{wi} \Sigma_{sf}$, $\quad \log_{10} p \approx -1.03$
  (. . . other prosodic word rules)
  c. $\Sigma_{wi} \rightarrow \sigma_{si} \sigma_{wm}$, $\quad \log_{10} p \approx -0.15$
  d. $\Sigma_{sf} \rightarrow \sigma_{sm} \sigma_{wf}$, $\quad \log_{10} p \approx -0.32$
  e. $\Sigma_{sf} \rightarrow \sigma_{sm} \sigma_{wm} \sigma_{wf}$, $\quad \log_{10} p \approx -0.65$
  (. . . other foot rules)
  f. $\sigma_{wi} \rightarrow$ [an], $\quad \log_{10} p \approx -2.43$
  g. $\sigma_{si} \rightarrow$ [an], $\quad \log_{10} p \approx -2.27$
  h. $\sigma_{wm} \rightarrow$ [tɛn], $\quad \log_{10} p \approx -3.48$
  i. $\sigma_{sm} \rightarrow$ [tɛn], $\quad \log_{10} p \approx -2.46$
  j. $\sigma_{wm} \rightarrow$ [jʊ], $\quad \log_{10} p \approx -2.94$
  k. $\sigma_{sm} \rightarrow$ [jʊ], $\quad \log_{10} p \approx -3.60$
  l. $\sigma_{wf} \rightarrow$ [ənt], $\quad \log_{10} p \approx -3.11$
  (. . . many other syllable rules, including rules for within-syllable structure)

Because there are many more types of syllable than types of foot and prosodic word, metrical rule probabilities are generally greater than syllable probabilities, and hence the overall probability of a parse depends more on its metrical structure than on the syllables within it. For example, consider two of the several possible parses of 'antenuant' in Fig. 4.2.

The log probability of the suprasyllabic structure in Fig. 4.2*a* is about -1.5, compared with -1.36 for Fig. 4.2*b*. The log probabilities of the first three syllables differ in the two cases, because of the different metrical context in which each syllable occurs. Consequently, the sum of log syllable probabilities is -12.46 in Fig. 4.2*a*, versus -10.94. The total log probability of the parses is -13.96 in Fig. 4.2*a* and -12.3 in Fig. 4.2*b*. By each criterion, Fig. 4.2*b* is a more likely metrical parse than Fig. 4.2*a*, so that the more likely stress pattern for 'antenuant' is /anˈtɛnjʊənt/, not /ˌantɛnˈjʊənt/.

As an estimate of the 'value added' by using probabilistic rules, the complete grammar partially listed in (4) and its non-probabilistic counterpart were both employed to assign stresses to 3,943 entries with initial capital letters from the Mitton (1992) dictionary. These items comprise mostly personal and place names, together with some abbreviations; a high proportion of them are monomorphemic, and thus give few cues from affixation as to whether they should be stressed in the Latinate manner (as in the Japanese-like name 'Yamazota'), or in the Germanic manner (as in 'Schnitzenbausel'). This test is among the hardest that any theory of stress assignment faces. The non-probabilistic grammar assigned stress correctly to 67 per cent of the test words, whereas when its rules were augmented by probabilities, as in (4), the success rate rose to 75 per cent correct. The grammars are currently being tested by comparing their success rates in stress assignment to the remainder of the dictionary. A complete presentation of this work is in preparation.

4.2.3. Onsets, rhymes, moras

There is now a large body of psycholinguistic results demonstrating the cognitive reality of the syllable (see e.g. Segui and Ferrand, this volume) and some of its parts, especially onsets. Pierrehumbert and Nair (1995) describe concept generalization ('word-game') experiments which concur with those of Treiman (1983) in establishing the accessibility of a division of the syllable between the initial consonant sequence and the vowel. Pierrehumbert and Nair argue for moraic representation on the grounds that it is more parsimonious. But no one has yet conducted a word-game experiment that would explicitly test the salience of the boundary between the two moras.[1] In the moraic theory, all kinds of heavy rhymes, i.e. long vowels, diphthongs, and closed rhymes, are given the same representation. In other words, the second part of a long vowel or a diphthong is attributed to the same syllable position as a consonant following a short vowel. If mora theory is correct, we would expect subjects who are trained to insert a consonant and vowel (e.g. /ta/) between a vowel and a consonant (i.e. to form /pɒtat/ from /pɒt/, and /pɪtak/ from /pɪk/) to split long vowels and diphthongs too, thus forming /butau/ from /buu/, /fitai/ from /fii/, /petaɪ/ from /peɪ/, etc.

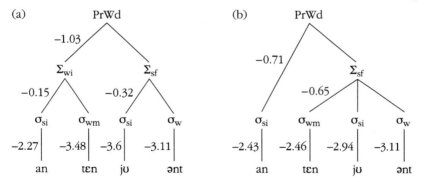

FIG. 4.2. Probabilistic parse trees for two candidate assignments of stress to the neologism 'antenuant'. Tree (*a*), that of 'àntenúant', has a lower probability than tree (*b*), that of 'anténuant'.

[1] This statement was true when this paper was written. Since then one of my M.Phil. students, James Henderson, has conducted such a study. In that experiment, subjects were very reluctant to divide diphthongs into two moras.

(Alternatively, we might expect diphthongs and VCs to be splittable, but long vowels might not be, because of their 'geminate integrity'.) By contrast, if the more traditional view of syllable structure in which a rhyme is divided into a (vocalic) nucleus and a (consonantal) coda is correct, subjects trained to infix /ta/ between a vowel and a consonant will be expected not to split a long vowel, and probably not to split a diphthong. We do not yet know what the outcome of this experiment will be.

There is already good evidence for the mental reality of onsets and rhymes, however. Meyer (1991) describes a series of experiments in which subjects first learned a series of three or five stimulus–response word pairs. Then, written stimuli were presented on a computer screen, and the subjects required to speak the appropriately paired response word as quickly as possibly. The speed of their responses and any errors were recorded and analysed. When the five stimulus–response word pairs were related in meaning, responses were faster when the words had the same onset, but not the same rhyme. Meyer argues from this and another aspect of the study that in the speech production process, onsets are encoded before rhymes. The relevance of that study in this context, however, is that evidence for the mental reality of onsets and rhymes was obtained.

It is not clear from Meyer's study that the observed effect relates to the onsets of all syllables (and not just word-initial syllable onsets, or 'word onsets'). Shattuck-Huffnagel (1987) argues from speech error data that word onsets have a special status as the locus of slips of the tongue involving consonants. Word onsets are also phonotactically important, as many languages allow word onsets to differ from within-word syllable onsets. For example, word onsets may be empty where elsewhere they must always or usually be filled. In stress-initial words (i.e. the majority of English words), word onsets are the only part of the word that is not relevant to the poetic rhyme-class of the word. For example, 'heather', 'leather', and 'weather' are rhymes in /-ɛðə/ which differ by word onset.

4.2.4. Phonemes

The usual arguments for the reality of phonemes need little spelling out here. There is the invention of alphabetic writing, and its continued utility in the development of new orthographies, for instance. (If alphabetic writing draws upon the mental reality of phonemes, however, it is surprising that it was only invented once. In contrast, moraic, syllabic, and logographic scripts have been independently invented by several cultures.) The very existence of alphabetic writing is a confounding factor here: if we ask an alphabetic literate 'how many sounds are there in *pat*', care must be taken to ensure that the answer three arises solely from phonological intuition and not from English spelling. If phonemes are real, why do many students have difficulty at first in determining how many phonemes there are in orthographic 'x', 'ng', 'ch'? Can even a professional phonologist considering the alternation *feel* vs. *feeling* be confident as to whether 'eel' has two phonemes /il/ or three /iəl/, without the security of a fairly fully worked-out phonemic analysis? Are diphthongs and affricates one phoneme or two? And given the independent existence of /h/ in most phonemic analyses of English, should we analyse aspirated stops as /ph/, /th/, and /kh/? The phoneme hypothesis countenances all these possibilities as equally workable, which is fine for the practicalities of alphabet-making but unfortunate from a scientific perspective.

Then there is Sapir's testimony about the informants who insisted on the presence of a sound in a word where none was to be heard, but where phonological alternations provided evidence for an underlying 'latent' phoneme in the speaker's lexical representation (see e.g. Kenstowicz 1994: 2–5 for a recapitulation). But how much weight should we give to an anecdote, against which we can balance a body of scientific research that demonstrates that certain aspects of phonological competence, far from being part of the human genetic inheritance, are strongly affected by learning to read? Phonemic awareness, in particular, is much more advanced in alphabetic literates than in illiterates and non-alphabetic literates (Morais 1985, 1993, Morais et al. 1979). That is, alphabetic literates can segment words into phonemes, and delete or add phonemes to a nonsense word, whereas illiterates from the same sociocultural background had much poorer performance on such experimental tasks.[2] On the other hand, the level of usual spoken language abilities (e.g. speaking, aural comprehension, etc.) is similar in literates and illiterates, suggesting that the awareness of phonemes is sharpened by learning to read an alphabetic script, or even that people get on fine without phonemes, and do not 'acquire' them other than by learning to read. Although we do not yet know which of these positions is correct, we know enough to be cautious of experiments purporting to demonstrate the mental reality of phonemes in literate subjects. In my view, it is a poor bet for

[2] The tension between Sapir's observations and Morais's results should not be exaggerated. On the one hand, Sapir's argument can be seen as more relevant to the question of underlying forms (or surface–surface correspondences) rather than to the existence of the phoneme in particular. On the other hand, Morais's demonstration of a difference in the degree of phonemic awareness between alphabetic literates and others does not necessarily imply that others are completely *lacking* in phonemic awareness, evidence for which can be discerned in infants (Eimas 1999).

phonological theory to make too much of a theoretical proposal for which there is little evidence from illiterates or those literate in non-alphabetic scripts. The importance of Morais's studies has been recently strengthened by Castro-Caldas et al. (1998), a brain activation study using PET. In that study, literate and illiterate subjects repeated words and pseudo-words while their brain activity was recorded. Statistical comparison of the brain activity associated with contrasting groups of subjects and tasks showed that during repetition of real words, the two groups performed similarly. Illiterate subjects had more difficulty repeating pseudo-words correctly, however, and their brain activation patterns were different from those of literate subjects, confirming that literacy has an impact on spoken language competence.

Several studies of the brain activation during phoneme monitoring tasks (i.e. listening for auditorily presented words containing or beginning or ending with a specified phoneme, presented in different phonetic environments) have found a specific site of activation in a perisylvian area, the anterior part of Broca's area, adjacent to and just in front of a part of primary motor cortex where movements of the face and organs of speech are initiated (Zatorre et al. 1996, Mummery et al. 1996, Démonet et al., this volume). (A homologous area in monkeys is implicated in their production of vocalizations, according to Passingham 1993: 247.) This site of activation is interesting because in nearly two decades of neuroimaging research it has been found to be rather difficult to elicit activity in Broca's area in single-word tasks, especially in perceptual tasks. In contrast, all manner of word perception and production tasks usually elicit activation of extensive cortical regions in and around the primary auditory cortex (including auditory association cortex), even when no speech is presented to the subjects (e.g. Paulesu, Frith, and Frackowiak 1993, Calvert et al. 1997), which led me to argue in Coleman (1998*b*) that auditory representations are central to word production as well as recognition, whereas articulatory representations are employed only in speech production, not the long-term storage of words. Whether the arguments presented in that paper are correct or not, it seems clear that (*a*) phoneme monitoring, almost alone of perceptual tasks, seems to require an articulatory encoding of word forms, and that (*b*) the activation site found in the phoneme monitoring task is not evidently employed in many lexical tasks, which suggests that it is not particularly relevant to lexical representation. Coincidentally, the phonemes employed in the monitoring experiments cited here happened to be consonants, which are known to have a complex articulatory encoding, due to their coarticulation with neighbouring vowels. It is possible that the activation in the articulatory system found in those experiments reflects some kind of processing to disentangle the consonant articulation, in the manner proposed by advocates of the motor theories of speech perception (e.g. Liberman et al. 1967, Liberman and Mattingly 1985). A monitoring experiment employing a vowel might cast further light on this issue, the prediction being that vowel monitoring might *not* invoke the articulatory system, if, for instance, the proposal of Ladefoged (1989) that vowels are classified on the basis of acoustic properties, or that of Fiez et al. (1995), that perception of rapidly changing consonant transitions, but not steady-state vowels, employs a left frontal region, are correct. It is quite clear, however, that the perisylvian site implicated in phoneme monitoring tasks does not furnish evidence of phonemes in *lexical* representations: the ERP results presented in Démonet, Thierry, and Nespoulous (this volume) show that the activation of this area in phoneme monitoring comes much later than the normal course of lexical access, suggesting that mentally decomposing a nonsense word into constituent vowels and consonants is a quite different (and slower) task from the competence needed to access a lexical entry on the basis of an auditory input and then find the associated meaning. As Démonet et al. express it:

the phonological task was performed in a sequential, step-by-step, parsing mode. This sequential processing is much slower than the probabilistic, non-exhaustive way of processing lexically valid items in the semantic task.

Now that phonological theory generally recognizes a variety of supra-segmental but subsyllabic units, a number of consequent epistemological questions arise. How can evidence for phonemes be distinguished from evidence for other phonological units, e.g. syllable onset, syllable coda, and word onset? Since there is good evidence for the latter, we have less reason to believe in the existence of the former. It would be hard to distinguish evidence that might seem to support the psychological reality of /t/, for instance, from an alternative explanation in which only 'onset-t' or 'coda-t' (on equal terms with 'onset-st' or 'coda-nt', perhaps) are the relevant explanatory units. Evidence for English /h/, likewise, will generally only be evidence for 'onset-h', and evidence for English /ŋ/, likewise, only provide evidence for 'coda-ŋ'. The fact that there are different distributional possibilities at different places in structure led Firth (e.g. 1948), by the same reasoning, to deny the relevance of a monosystemic list of phonemes to the phonology of a language and to emphasize the system of alternative possibilities at each structural position. In any discussion of phoneme theory, the interrelationship between units and places in structure still remains to be addressed.

Prototype theory (Kuhl 1992) claims to show the mental representation of phonemic categories (with language-specific realizations that are tuned from a very early age) with evidence of a 'perceptual magnet effect'. According to this account, there are points in the vowel space of each language which are the best exemplars of each vowel category, with a 'fuzzy' region around each prototype of less typical exemplars. In other words, the division of the vowel space into phonologically contrastive categories is not a carve-up along well-defined boundaries: instead, the *centres* of each category are well defined, but the boundaries between them are unclear. (For this reason, for example, English speakers may find it difficult to judge whether an acoustic stimulus that might be transcribed [bet] is an instance of /bɪt/ or /bɛt/.) Prototype theory is interesting as it rests on data that seems to show the categorization of vowels in two dimensions at the same time (and thus does not suffer from the weakness of standard one-dimensional categorical perception experiments discussed in the next section). However, it differs little from the identification of vowel phonemes from statistical clustering of points in a phonetic space (Fig. 4.3), and consequently adds to the general proposal that phonological categories can be built upon statistical generalizations over detailed phonetic representations.

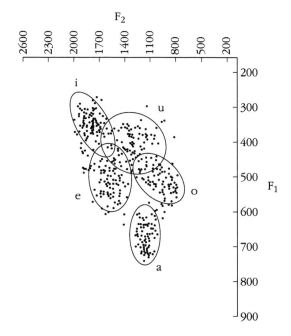

FIG. 4.3. Phonological categories (in this case vowels) as clusters of tokens in a physical space. First and second formant frequencies of individual tokens of five Japanese vowels in spoken prose by a single speaker are shown in this scatterplot. Radii of the ellipses are drawn at two standard deviations from the mean of each cluster along the two principal components.

Source: Keating and Huffman (1984: 202). Reproduced by permission of S. Karger AG, Basle.

4.2.5. Features

Halle (1997*a*) argues that the selection of the /s/ allomorph of the English genitive suffix -s in the form 'Bach's' constitutes evidence for a feature, and for the primacy of featural representations over e.g. classical phonemic representations. For most words, the two rules in (5) work equally well:

(5) *a.* (Phonemic version)
> If the last phoneme of the word is a member of the set {/p/, /t/, /k/, /tʃ/, /f/, /θ/}, the genitive allomorph is /s/.

b. (Featural version)
> If the last segment of the word bears the features [+consonantal, −vocalic, −sonorant, −voice] (and if also [+continuant, +coronal] then [−strident]), the genitive allomorph is [+consonantal, −vocalic, −sonorant, +continuant, +coronal, +strident, −voice].

(5*b*) is hardly less complex than (5*a*), and it is hard to see why the arbitrary list of six phonemes in (5*a*) is any more objectionable than the arbitrary list of seven feature values mentioned in the antecedent of (5*b*). Both rules correctly account for the genitives ending in /p/, /t/, /k/, /tʃ/, /f/, and /θ/, but Halle astutely notes that (5*b*) has an advantage over (5*a*) when loanwords ending in voiceless phonemes other than those in this list are considered. The German name 'Bach' is just such a case, as it ends in the voiceless velar fricative [x]. Since [x] is not mentioned in the list of phonemes in rule (5*a*), that formulation does not tell us how to pronounce the genitive 'Bach's'. But as [x] bears the features [+consonantal, −vocalic, −sonorant, −voice], the genitive allomorph is correctly predicted to be /s/, despite the fact that [x] is not usually recognized as a phoneme of English. Rule (5*b*) works correctly in this case, and thus furnishes strong evidence for featural representations, and some additional problems for phoneme theory.

However, this case also provides an argument against abstract phonological representations because, rather than working with a predefined set of units, the correct formulation of the rule refers crucially to a set of phonetic properties. Rule (5*b*) might equally well be expressed more directly in terms of articulatory plans or even acoustic properties, e.g. (6). (6*a* is just a rather wordy restatement of rule 5*b*.)

(6) *a.* (Articulatory version)
> If at the end of the word there is an obstruction within the vocal tract, but the vocal cords are not vibrating (and if furthermore there is a

critical constriction between the tongue tip and the alveolar ridge, but the teeth are covered so that any turbulence is generated along the walls of the vocal tract rather than at the teeth), the genitive is formed by a critical constriction between the tongue tip and the alveolar ridge with the teeth uncovered so that turbulence is caused at the teeth, the vocal cords continuing not to vibrate.

b. (Acoustic version)

If at the end of the word there is an interval of relatively low amplitude, either silence or with aperiodic excitation, and if in the latter case higher frequencies predominate in the spectrum and the lower limit of the frequency distribution is relatively high, but with comparatively low amplitude relative to other aperiodic intervals and a stronger resonant structure), the genitive is formed by aperiodic excitation with higher frequencies predominating in the spectrum, the lower limit of the frequency distribution being relatively high, comparatively high amplitude and a weak or indiscernible resonant structure.

(6*a*) and (*b*) merely paraphrase (5*b*) into phonetic terminology, demonstrating that Halle's argument against phonemes turns out to be indistinguishable from claims for concrete phonetic representations. That is, the success of (5*b*) is due to the fact that it is divorced from a pre-established inventory of phonemes, as in (5*a*). It does support distinctive feature theory, but it also supports almost any non-phonemic theory of representation based on phonetic parameters.

From another direction, evidence of categorical perception in e.g. acquisition studies (Eimas et al. 1971) supports the idea of distinctive features. These studies are often erroneously cited as evidence for phonemes, which they are not, as only a single acoustic dimension is usually tested in these studies (e.g. Voice Onset Time). Although categorical perception of several such dimensions has been established, there are few if any studies in which all the dimensions of a phoneme are manipulated and shown to be perceived categorically. The sum total of studies of single dimensions lends a little support to phoneme theory, but more clearly provides substantial evidence for the psychological reality of independent dimensions of contrast.

In a typical case, categorical perception (Repp 1983) is shown to occur when subjects' responses to a linear continuum follow a non-linear (logistic) function, as in Figure 4.4*a*. The linear continuum is divided into two categories at the point at which subjects distinguish between the two categories with a performance no better than chance. Half the responses at

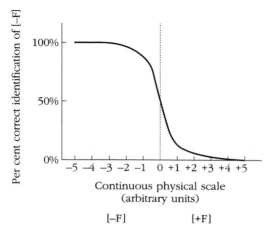

(*a*) Categorical perception is characterized by a non-linear classification function, which divides a continuous physical scale into two distinct regions. Close to the category boundary, subjects' classification ability is poor, with discrimination close to chance. Away from the category boundary, subjects are very insensitive to large physical differences.

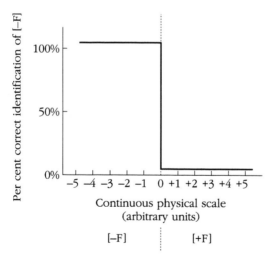

(*b*) If categorization by humans were perfect, classification would be characterized by a step-function, as here, instead of the somewhat less sharp function found in (*a*).

FIG. 4.4

this point on the scale place it in one category, and half in the other category. Either side of the category boundary, however, the accuracy of subjects' judgements as to category membership improves rapidly, so that a small distance either side of the category boundary subjects can discriminate between the categories extremely well. But as with all real cognitive abilities, people's categorization ability, though good, falls a little short of the perfect model of categorization supposed in phonological theory, illustrated in Fig. 4.4*b*.

I can think of two ways of interpreting the phonological relevance of the fact that the model shown in Fig. 4.4*b* is not quite exhibited in the actual behaviour typified by Fig. 4.4*a*. According to one view, we could invoke the competence/performance dichotomy, and declare that Fig. 4.4*b* is a competence model, but that performance, represented by Fig. 4.4*a*, is a defective realization of the underlying competence. If we ask further where the competence shown in Fig. 4.4*b* resides, however, this line of argument becomes difficult to sustain. It is implausible to suggest that Fig. 4.4*b* is a realistic model of any mental representation, as the logistic model of categorization proposed to explain behavioural data also applies very well to computational and physiological models of neural function. Fig. 4.4*b* seems at best to be a convenient fiction, or a philosophical, non-cognitive, idealization.

We are left with the alternative of rejecting the idealization of Fig. 4.4*b* completely, and taking Fig. 4.4*b* as a model not just of categorization performance, but also of human competence at categorization. The plain fact is that we are very competent at categorizing certain continuous domains in regions that are away from the category boundary, but we are rather incompetent at categorizing stimuli that are right on the category boundary. Phonological categories are a little 'fuzzy'. Frisch (1996) shows how the use of the logistic function can be extended from categorization and word discrimination to other aspects of phonological cognition, especially the encoding of phonotactic constraints and the analysis of speech errors.

Näätänen et al. (1997) presents evidence for the neurological encoding of phonemes in auditory cortex. The analytical approach employed in that paper employs the usual model of categorical perception. However, a cautious reading, while conceding that it offers evidence for featural distinctions, must reject its claim for the demonstration of phonemic encoding *per se*, because as with categorical perception studies, only a single acoustic dimension (F_2) was tested.

These studies support a view of phonological categories in which distinctions use representations that employ two dimensions, one a continuous physical scale, the other a continuous probability scale (e.g. per cent correct identification). With this necessary formalism, additional discrete symbols are superfluous.

4.3. EVIDENCE FROM OTHER AREAS OF LINGUISTICS

4.3.1. Effect of word frequency

In a series of works (e.g. Hooper 1976*a*, 1981, Bybee 1996), Bybee [Hooper] has articulated a theory of gradual sound change in terms of the accretion of gradual changes to stored phonetic representations, conditioned by the frequency of use of individual lexical items. For example, in considering the lenition of /s/ to [h] and zero in Dominican Spanish, Bybee (2000) notes (citing Terrell 1986) that the more conservative form, [s], is retained inside phrases that are so frequent as to be conceivably stored as single units, akin to words. Examples include plural definite articles e.g. *las otras* 'the others', *las únicas* 'the only'; the phrases *más o menos* 'more or less', *es igual* 'it's the same'; and a handful of other very frequent phrases. Similarly, in English, the historical development /sj/ > /ʃ/, the outcome of which is evident word-internally in e.g. *face, facial; race, racial,* etc. is also found across word boundaries in frequent phrases (e.g. *miss you, kiss your father*) but not in infrequent phrases (e.g. *miss Eunice, takes United Airlines*). John Local (personal communication) cites a similar example, the (otherwise rare) assimilation of a bilabial nasal to a following alveolar stop in some high frequency words, such as *sometimes* (i.e. [(sʌntaɪmz]) and *timetable* (i.e. [(taɪnteɪbḷ]) and the cliticized auxiliary verb in *I'm gonna* [aɪygana] (see also Ogden 1999).

4.3.2. Preservation of phonetic detail

A further argument comes from the evolution of stress systems. Bybee et al. (1998), following Hyman (1977) to a large extent, observes that in languages with demarcative stress, if weak syllables are lost, for any reason, we would expect the location of stress to be transferred to another syllable. If stress placement in such languages were really simply a matter of counting off the syllables from one end, as Metrical Phonology proposes, we predict that loss of syllables in relevant cases would result in a change in the location of stress.

This is not what happens, however. Instead, stress tends to remain in its original place, making determination of the stressed syllable less predictable. For example, in Latinate words in English (in which stress placement is sensitive to the distinction between heavy and light syllables and is bounded to the final three syllables of the word), we expect adjectives ending in the disyllabic suffix *-ian* to have stress on the antepenultimate syllable, as in

'Albanian', 'Argentinian', 'Brazilian', etc. Where an alveolar or post-alveolar obstruent precedes the suffix, however, palatalization of the obstruent with concomitant loss of [i] is found, as in 'Alsatian' (-[ʃən]), 'Christian' (-[tʃən]), and 'Georgian' (-[dʒən]). Note that despite the loss of [i], and with it the reduction of the syllable count by one, these forms retain stress on the 'underlying' antepenultimate syllable, thus 'Alsátian', not 'Álsatian'. In generative phonology these data are normally taken as evidence that the rules of stress assignment and i-deletion apply in a counterbleeding order, i.e. stress assignment applies first, i-deletion later. However, if lexical representations are detailed phonetic representations, stress will be stored even where it is completely predictable. If sound changes take place that obscure the predictability of stress placement, since it is the full phonetic form of a word that is stored, stressed syllables will continue to be heard and spoken as stressed, and thus opaque stress placements will tend to endure. As a general illustration of this, note that words of Germanic origin in English still have stem-initial stress and words of Latinate origin still show the complex pattern of quantity-sensitive stress in the final foot, despite the passage of over 900 years since the Norman Conquest brought these two vocabularies together, in which time English has undergone extensive loss of final unstressed syllables and numerous segmental changes. A more striking example of the stability of the stress system over an extensive period of time is provided by Russian and Lithuanian, which, according to Halle (1997*b*), largely continue to show the accentuation of stems of the Proto-Indo-European parent language. When stress placement principles *do* change over time, we sometimes find striking evidence for the continuation of phonetic forms appropriate to the older pattern of stress placement. For example, stressed syllables in Welsh are shorter, quieter, and lower in pitch than unstressed syllables, according to Williams (1982). The explanation for this unusual state of affairs, according to Williams, is that until the late eleventh century those syllables were unstressed. They still continue to bear their former 'weak' phonetic characteristics, though a variety of phonological evidence points to their now being stressed. Additional evidence may perhaps be adduced from Welsh English, in which stressed vowels are also often short and bear low pitch accents. This makes little sense under a cross-linguistically uniform rule-based account of the phonetic interpretation of stress (or even a more mechanistic account such as that offered by Ladefoged 1993: 249–50). However, it makes perfect sense if phonological representations are phonetic memories, as the syllables in question perpetuate their old forms even if the new stress reckoning now counts them as unstressed.

4.3.3. Incomplete neutralization

The robust preservation of sub-phonemic phonetic differences under incomplete neutralization and near merger presents further evidence for phonetic representations in some cases. The existence of incomplete neutralization in the grammar of a single speaker presents no great problem for frameworks that combine symbolic lexical representations with continuous phonetic representations, such as those proposed by Mohanan (1986: 154–81), Pierrehumbert and Beckman (1988: ch. 7), and Coleman (1992): all that is required is for two distinct symbols to regularly map onto two points that are very close together in the phonetic continuum. If these two points are otherwise usually found as variants of a single phoneme, we have a case of incomplete neutralization. Arguably, final devoicing in German provides an example.

Incomplete neutralization presents a problem for theories of phonological representation in terms of discrete, contrastive categories in cases where a subsequent generation learns and maintains the fine phonetic distinction between the two forms though they do not have them as separate categories. Peng (2000) argues that Mandarin Tone 3 sandhi presents just such a case. In separate experiments on the production and perception of the high rising sandhi realization of Tone 3 and the similar if not identical lexical Tone 2, she demonstrated that native speakers of Mandarin do not perceive Tone 2 and the high rising realization of Tone 3 as distinct, even though there is a small (*c.*3Hz) but statistically significant difference in the fundamental frequency of the two tonal contours. In view of the fact that the two contours have been described in numerous grammars and phonological descriptions of Mandarin as identical for at least fifty years (cf. Chao 1948), Peng concludes that recent generations of Mandarin speakers must hear, learn, and reproduce a fine phonetic distinction between Tone 2 and sandhi Tone 3 words that in adulthood they do not categorize as distinct. I infer that the mental representations of Tone 2 and sandhi Tone 3 words are phonetically distinct, for they have been kept distinct in production for so long. The failure of native speakers to perceive them as distinct reflects not a collapsing of the two tonal patterns in their lexical storage, but a limitation of their categorization abilities under adverse discrimination conditions.

4.3.4. Sociolinguistic variation

Sociolinguists have argued for some time that knowledge of the social relevance of small phonetic differences in the realizations of phonological categories is a form of knowledge that grammars should model. In general, however, this has not led them to propose phonetically rich lexical phonetic representations. Instead, the 'Labovian' variable rule formalism (Labov 1972, Cedergren and Sankoff 1974, Rand and Sankoff 1988), as with standard probabilistic phrase-structure grammars (Suppes 1972), maps discrete linguistic symbols—those of standard grammatical descriptions—in environments expressed using discrete symbols onto a selection of discrete, socially meaningful, symbolic realizations. Only the rule *weight* is a continuous variable: all other aspects of the rules and representations are discrete symbols.

Pierrehumbert (1994) observes that there is a problem with reconciling generalization across similar environments with the different statistical distributions found in each instance of an environment. The example she gives is of glottalization of word-final /t/ and /p/ in consonant clusters in American English compounds and phrases such as 'oatmeal', 'grant money', 'outlook', 'tape-measure', and 'stopwatch'. She found that the likelihood of glottalization depends on the environment:

(7) Environment   Observed glottalization probability

t/—m	0.96
t/—w	0.96
t/—l	0.83
All /t/s	0.92
p/—m	0.5
p/—w	0.12
p/—l	0
All /p/s	0.21

Pierrehumbert observes that the general form of the Labovian rule of glottalization before sonorant consonants, (8), overgenerates, whereas the empirically more accurate set of rules in (9) miss the generalization—a linguistic Catch 22! The addition of data relating to other consonant clusters would only exacerbate this problem. (In the rules which follow, angle brackets mark symbols whose occurrence is variable, with probabilities written above the arrow.)

(8)
$$
\begin{bmatrix} -\text{sonorant} \\ -\text{continuant} \\ -\text{voice} \end{bmatrix} \xrightarrow{p} \langle +\text{constricted glottis} \rangle / \underline{\hspace{1em}} \begin{bmatrix} +\text{sonorant} \\ +\text{consonantal} \end{bmatrix}
$$

$$(9)\ a.\ \begin{bmatrix} -\text{sonorant} \\ +\text{coronal} \\ -\text{continuant} \\ -\text{voice} \end{bmatrix} \xrightarrow{0.96} \langle +\text{c.g.} \rangle - \begin{bmatrix} +\text{sonorant} \\ +\text{consonantal} \\ +\text{labial} \end{bmatrix} \quad \text{i.e. } t/-\{m, w\}$$

$$b.\ \begin{bmatrix} -\text{sonorant} \\ +\text{coronal} \\ -\text{continuant} \\ -\text{voice} \end{bmatrix} \xrightarrow{0.83} \langle +\text{c.g.} \rangle - \begin{bmatrix} +\text{sonorant} \\ +\text{consonantal} \\ +\text{lateral} \end{bmatrix} \quad \text{i.e. } t/-l$$

$$c.\ \begin{bmatrix} -\text{sonorant} \\ +\text{labial} \\ -\text{continuant} \\ -\text{voice} \end{bmatrix} \xrightarrow{0.5} \langle +\text{c.g.} \rangle - \begin{bmatrix} +\text{sonorant} \\ +\text{consonantal} \\ +\text{labial} \\ +\text{nasal} \end{bmatrix} \quad \text{i.e. } p/-m$$

$$d.\ \begin{bmatrix} -\text{sonorant} \\ +\text{labial} \\ -\text{continuant} \\ -\text{voice} \end{bmatrix} \xrightarrow{0.12} \langle +\text{c.g.} \rangle - \begin{bmatrix} +\text{sonorant} \\ +\text{consonantal} \\ +\text{labial} \\ -\text{nasal} \end{bmatrix} \quad \text{i.e. } p/-w$$

A solution to this problem must be able to associate different probabilities with more and less specific contexts at the same time. This can be done by setting up a hierarchy (a lattice, in fact) of more and less specific contexts, associating a probability with each node in the lattice, as in Fig. 4.5.

By means such as these, it becomes possible to begin to model the relationship between variability and specific structural configurations, instead of attempting to spirit it away.

4.3.5. Evidence from speech perception and production studies

Evidence from some speech perception and production studies also suggests that speaker-hearers are aware of much finer phonetic differences than phonological theory has a place for. For example, Kelly and Local (1986) observed fine variations in all the vowels and consonants up to several syllables away from an /l/ vs. /r/ contrast in English sentences such as 'Terry'll be about tomorrow' vs. 'Telly'll be about tomorrow' (all the emphasized part of the sentences). In experimental studies of particular

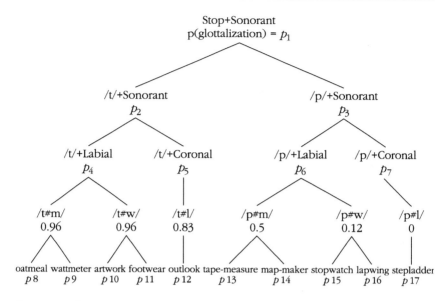

F I G. 4.5. A lattice structure can be used to model the glottalization probabilities of a large variety of distinct contexts. Unlike a simple list, however, generalizations over contexts are also encoded in the lattice structure. For example, glottalization is generally more likely in p + Sonorant clusters than t + Sonorant clusters, though within each of those classes there are many specific patterns.

aspects of Kelly and Local's claim West (1999) showed that when stretches of speech around the /l/ or /r/ are replaced by noise, the small remote variations are sufficient to allow subjects to determine (in a forced choice) whether the excised word contained /l/ or /r/. This shows that, under the appropriate circumstances, hearers may employ so-called redundant features to resolve a contrast. Though the possibility of doing so has been anticipated since the beginning of feature theory (Jakobson, Fant, and Halle 1952: 8), the phonetic details at work in this case seem to be much more subtle than is usually recognized by feature theory.

There is now an extensive literature on the perception of speaker identity suggesting that non-contrastive, speaker-specific details of spoken words are stored together with the usual phonological information. For example, Goldinger (1997) describes an experiment in which listeners identified 300 spoken words presented in noise during study sessions. In later test sessions, they repeated the same identification task, and their recognition accuracy in the study and test sessions was compared. In both sessions, subjects heard words spoken by two, six, or ten different voices, and the time-lag between study and test sessions was five minutes, one day, or one week. The results show that subjects identified words more accurately when they were spoken by a (hitherto unfamiliar) speaker whom they had heard before, even a week previously, than when they were spoken by an unfamiliar speaker. This and numerous convergent studies (see Johnson and Mullenix 1997) shows that people have very acute auditory memories of words, in which details of the voice quality of those whom we hear are stored together with the linguistic information.

Phonetic detail and its relationship to word frequency is implicated in speech production too. R. Wright (MS) shows that vowel qualities are slightly more centralized in the production of perceptually 'hard' words (those of lower frequency and/or more lexical neighbours) than in equally familiar 'easy' words (those of higher frequency and/or fewer lexical neighbours), tying small details in production to lexical frequency. When subjects read word lists aloud, C. Wright (1979) found that lower-frequency words were spoken more slowly and with longer pauses between words than higher-frequency words, suggesting that less frequent articulatory patterns take longer to prepare and execute. Theoretical phonologists addressing these results might be inclined to attribute them to 'performance effects' (i.e. of lexical recall and articulatory 'spell-out' of more or less practised items), but that line of defence suffers from two weaknesses. First, it does not address the perceptual effects of voice familiarity mentioned in the preceding paragraph. Second, it neglects the fact that the 'hard' words in Wright's study, though relatively low in frequency, are not obscure or articulatorily difficult: they are all familiar CVC monosyllables, such as 'pat', 'white', 'fade', 'bead', and 'cot'. Taking these studies together, it is difficult to escape the conclusion that very specific pronunciation details, such as speaker-specific detail, and word frequency, are encoded in the lexicon.

4.4. AN ALTERNATIVE PROPOSAL

We are faced with overwhelming evidence that knowledge of word forms includes (i) knowledge of fine phonetic details not normally reckoned among the inventory of features, (ii) knowledge of word frequencies, and frequencies of parts of words, and (iii) knowledge of the statistical patterns of phonetic variation and its correlations with linguistic and non-linguistic factors, such as structural context, word frequency, communicative situation, social identity, and other factors. Where these kinds of knowledge have been discussed before, they have usually been regarded as outside the bounds of grammar, presumably because mainstream phonological theory finds itself incapable of talking about them: generative phonology lacks any settled phonetic representation at a level of detail finer than distinctive features and timing slots of a size in the order of a segment (half a segment is usually the smallest interval considered). Neither is there any formal mechanism (apart from Labovian rules) for describing variation other than equiprobable 'optional rules', or a limited range of possibilities for different rule orderings (or different rankings of constraints, in Optimality Theory). Consequently, knowledge of fine phonetic details is deputed to a vaguely delineated 'postlexical component', or hoped to follow from the biomechanics of the articulatory system. Knowledge of word frequencies is relegated to 'perform-ance', denied a place in grammar, and thus out of bounds to linguists. Knowledge of variation, too, is treated as an 'interface issue' of no relevance to grammar, for phoneticians or sociolinguists to deal with, if they wish. The study of these kinds of knowledge is tolerated by phonologists, as long as they do not upset the apple-cart of abstractions.

Knowledge of phonetic details, phonological statistics and all kinds of subtle phonetic variation is better explained in a new conception of lexical representations based on the following ideas:

1. Word forms are stored as memories of psychophysical (auditory and articulatory) experience (not abstract structures of distinctive features).
2. Phonological constituents are statistical regularities over those psychophysical spaces.
3. Some phonological abilities follow from the manner of storage (e.g. the discrimination of contrastive words); other phonological properties must be computed on-line (e.g. phoneme monitoring).

Such a neo-empiricist view of the lexicon has been essayed by several researchers in recent years, in particular by those interested in connectionist modelling.

Let us attempt to sketch a cognitively realistic theory of phonology from the 'bottom up', and see how far the state of our current understanding takes us. The child's experience of the sound of words is laid down by repeated exposure in long-term auditory memory. The main areas activated by the immediate process of hearing are in primary auditory cortex, a relatively circumscribed portion of the superior temporal gyri, in both left and right hemispheres. Activations in this region by speech and non-speech sounds are tonotopically organized, that is, different frequency components in the speech map onto anatomically distinct parts of this region (Romani et al. 1982, Lauter et al. 1985, Howard et al. 1996, Phillips et al. 1997). Some phonetic details are lost at this level of representation, however. For example,

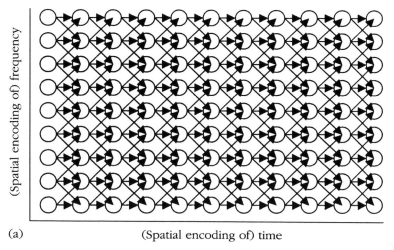

(a)   (Spatial encoding of) time

(*a*) A two dimensional array of neuron-like elements linked together by excitatory and inhibitory connections can be used to model a two-dimensional psychophysical space, such as (sampled) time vs. frequency (quantized to a finite set of frequency bands).

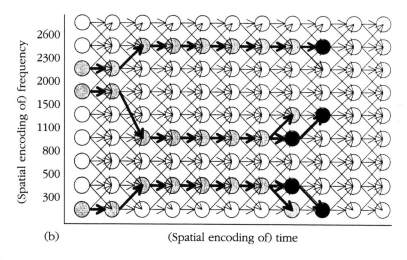

(b)   (Spatial encoding of) time

(*b*) In such a network, the changing pattern of formant frequencies that unfold in time during the auditory perception of a word (in this case, 'cart') gives rise to an evolving pattern of activation of elements (grey shading). But duration differences between different tokens of the same word yield possibly unwanted differences in the sequence of activated nodes. For example, the nodes shaded black will be activated in a token of 'cart' containing a longer vowel.

FIG. 4.6

VOT differences less than 20 ms are probably not differentiated at this level, whereas even fine differences over 20 ms are (Phillips et al. 1995). The exact nature of the spatial and temporal organization of neural responses to auditory stimuli is still not understood, but it is clear that for primary auditory cortex, at least, it is sensible to talk about representations in some psychoacoustic space. We are reasonably confident that auditory correlates of F_1 and (some aspects) of VOT are represented here. An illustrative example of a two-dimensional acoustic space is given in Fig. 4.6a. We are familiar with the use of such graphs to show static details such as the placement of vowels (or rather their mid-point measurements) in a general vowel space, as in Fig. 4.3. If we wish to postulate some neural hardware for such a representation, an array of neural elements or regions can be proposed, each activated most strongly by a specific frequency component. Linking these elements to one another by inhibitory connections will tune each one more sharply to a specific combination of frequencies. (Rather than a single such tonotopic map, in fact, there appear to be numerous ones in primary auditory cortex. This is one way of adding a further dimension to the two that are provided most easily by a flat surface.) Each time a neural element responds to a specific combination of frequencies, its propensity to fire again (not immediately, but on another occasion) is reinforced, as also may be its inhibitory effect on other elements. In this way, through repeated exposure to the recurrent acoustic characteristics of the ambient language, a neural network may be attuned to very specific acoustic properties of the ambient language.

Some sort of representation of time is needed, so that diphthongs, consonant–vowel transitions, and other sequences of speech events can be encoded. Representing time in space as in Fig. 4.6a is possible, though perhaps implausible, as it would mean that a word spoken at different speech rates will yield different activation patterns (Fig. 4.6b). A partial solution to variations in local speech rate is offered by a state-space representation such as that in Fig. 4.7a, but this method of generalization over slightly different timings of an utterance will be problematic where durational differences are in fact semantically contrastive. Auditory representations alone are not sufficient for encoding phonological knowledge. In order to encode the semantically contrastive function of differences between the sounds of different words, the auditory space must be associated with semantic spaces (illustrated in Fig. 4.7b). The phonetic space may be quasi-continuous, but in places it is effectively carved up by virtue of these associations to discrete semantic categories.

Beckman and Pierrehumbert (MS) argue that the evidence of phonetic and semantic interactions in lexical access tasks (such as confusions and priming

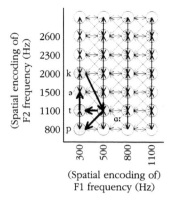

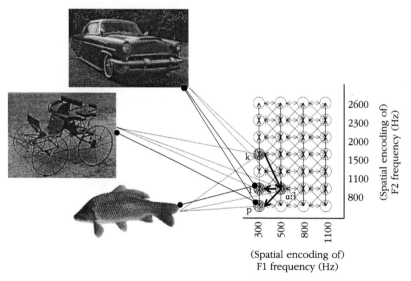

(a) In a network without a spatial encoding of time (a state-space network), durationally distinct tokens of the same word will be mapped onto the same (or similar) excitation trajectories through the space, whereas different words may give rise to different excitation trajectories. In this example, 'carter' and 'carp' share the same path through the space to begin with, but the later parts of their paths diverge.

(b) A difference in form alone is not sufficient to constitute a lexical difference: formal elements must be associated with representations of meaning. In this example, the nodes labelled [k] and [ɑː] have connections to semantic representations for 'car', 'cart', and 'carp'. The later nodes of these word-form trajectories, where the forms diverge, are associated with distinct semantic representations. The separation of form–meaning connections means that the difference in form is a phonological contrast. The formal locus of the contrast is toward the end of the two words. Excitatory connections between phonetics and semantics are shown by dotted lines, and inhibitory connections by solid lines.

FIG. 4.7

effects) shows that the association between phonetic and semantic representations requires an intermediate layer of neural structure, which they regard as the locus of phonological representations. As well as associations between auditory and semantic representations, it is fairly obvious that a cognitive model of phonology probably also needs associations between auditory and articulatory representations, semantic and articulatory, auditory and visual-orthographic, etc. Rather than seeking for a single kind of word-form representation, we are not surprised by the wealth of evidence for a variety of many different kinds of modality-specific representations, and various paths of association between them.

5

Phonological Primes:
Cues and Acoustic Signatures

Michael Ingleby and Wiebke Brockhaus

5.1. PRODUCTION VERSUS PERCEPTION
ASPECTS OF PHONOLOGICAL PRIMITIVES

Phonological primitives have several functions, the most important of which, most phonologists would probably agree, are the following:

(*a*) to represent the phonological segment inventories of the world's languages;
(*b*) to group these segments into natural classes;
(*c*) to capture both static distributional restrictions and dynamic phonological events.

These functions can be performed by a variety of primitive types, including binary features and unary (monovalent, privative) primes. Primitives can be defined with reference to articulatory parameters or acoustic properties. Both types of definition have been proposed in the phonological literature of the twentieth century, but there can be no doubt that mainstream generative phonology has been dominated by features with a clear articulatory bias. This emphasis was largely established by Chomsky and Halle (*SPE,* 1968), and it has been maintained in the vast majority of recent work (e.g. Halle 1995). Unary primes, recent challengers to binary features, have also been associated with articulatory labels (see e.g. Kaye, Lowenstamm, and Vergnaud 1985, Anderson and Ewen 1987). However, a small, but growing, number of researchers (especially Harris and Lindsey 1995) have argued that more attention should be paid to the acoustic manifestations of phonological primitives.

Stated baldly, the argument for increased acoustic emphasis is based on the truism that speech is communication. Speakers communicate with listeners by producing understandable acoustic effects, and listeners use these effects to make essential lexical distinctions. Indeed, this simple point was made before *SPE* by Jakobson, Fant, and Halle (1952), and has been raised more recently, by Anderson and Ewen (1987), for example. In reviewing the acoustic/auditory basis of distinctive features, Durand (1990) emphasizes that, in spite of articulatory labelling, these primitives occupy a neutral position between production and perception, reaffirming the view of Halle (1983) that distinctive features constitute the link between articulation and auditory sensation.

In this chapter we take up the notion of phonological primitive as a link or channel entity, and outline recent developments concerning the nature of the linkage. First, we discuss some characteristics of unary primes, selecting the elements of Government Phonology as exemplar. We make this selection because GP researchers have put forward strong claims regarding the autonomous interpretability of elements and the acoustic patterns associated with individual elements (e.g. Harris and Lindsey 1995). Then, secondly, we emphasize observational or physical aspects of the link itself, taking it as a physical medium or CHANNEL that can be observed with instruments—that is, with microphones and spectrographs eavesdropping on the communication between speaker and hearer. Although we are aware that GP elements are generally taken to be cognitive entities, the focus of the present chapter is on aspects of their physical interpretation, which is not intended to challenge their cognitive status, but simply focuses more sharply on the facet of physical events associated with cognitive units.

Our broad aims are twofold. At a basic research level, we are concerned with questions about what kind of invariant patterns in the speech channel can be attributed to primes. Such questions bear on the 'physics' of the speech channel, and we are interested in where primes fit into this. At a more applied level, we are concerned with questions about how the physics of the channel can underpin the engineering of voice-driven computer software. Over the last few years, voice-driven software has become a market commodity through heavy investment in the development of voice-to-text systems capable of recognizing over 30,000 words. These systems are trained to a single speaker's voice and subsequently provide accurate access to a single-language lexicon. They open the way to a new generation of language-engineering products whose conception will call for a greater understanding of the speech channel.

New products that can recognize the speech of speakers on which they have not been trained, or can recognize the speech of a speaker whose habits of articulation are evolving dynamically during second language learning or speech therapy, are only very slowly beginning to appear on the market (e.g. the AURALOG *TaLk to me* package). The future of voice input in language engineering rather depends on being able to characterize speech sounds to better support such demanding types of input, and this calls for more sophisticated, language-engineering-friendly ways of representing the invariant aspects of patterns embedded within the speech channel. We hope that our discussion of acoustic signatures of primes is moving towards this knowledge representation ideal.

The idea that phonological primitives are abstracted away from production and perception to constitute a separate classificatory dimension of speech patterns is clearly stated for the feature-based tradition in Durand (1990: 61–71). In the unary prime tradition, the idea has taken a different form, borrowed from cognitive psychology (see, for example, Kaye 1989). Primes are taken to be cognitive entities that mediate the processes of articulation and colour the perception of speech sounds. Nevertheless, the labelling of unary primes has remained largely articulatory. To the extent that forming speech intentions and using speech sounds to access a listener's mental lexicon are cognitive processes, it is difficult to argue against a cognitive dimension of phonological primitives—they *must* figure in the 'mentalese' associated with speech processing. The position that we adopt differs, however, from the purely cognitive in two significant respects. First, we are not concerned exclusively with lexical contrasts: we consider wider distinctions that do not refer to a specific language or lexicon but rather point to what patterns are physically present in the speech channel. Secondly, we seek to describe patterns in the speech channel using CUES that are expressible in terms of the acoustics of the channel. Obviously, the cues should relate to the types of excitation, e.g. periodic glottal pulsing, random shedding of vortices at a constriction site, abrupt release of pressure after an interruption of airflow. Cues should also relate to the formant resonances of the channel, and these depend on the current shape and size of a speaker's vocal tract. In physical terms, the time-based signal in the speech channel is a convolution of a time-varying excitation and the causal response of an air column. In terms of the Fourier transforms used to display frequency distributions via a spectrogram, the frequency-based signal in the speech channel is the product of an excitation spectrum and a frequency response that shows broad peaks around formant frequencies. There is, of course, a long history behind cues to speech intention in acoustic phonetics. The historical emphasis has been segmental rather than subsegmental, but that is not counter to our present purpose. Putting aside his preoccupations with a 'motor theory of speech perception' which few researchers have been willing to accept entirely, Liberman (1966) has been very active in researching sets of cues which can be 'painted' into a spectrogram to produce a required response in a listener. The general tenor of this type of work can be summarized as follows (Liberman and Mattingly 1985, for example):

(*a*) there are multiple rather than single cues to the phonetic class of a segment;
(*b*) if some cues are painted out, listeners can still classify a segment accurately using other cues;
(*c*) certain segments, such as plosives, cast cues before them and after them, into the trajectories of formants in neighbouring vowels, for example;
(*d*) cues are qualitatively similar for different speakers and contexts, but exhibit much quantitative variation.

Focusing on subsegmental material, Blumstein and Stevens (1981) have linked distinctive features to 'invariant' cues embedded in the data of the speech channel, and more recently a similar linkage of GP elements to cues has been mooted by Harris and Lindsey (1995). The strength of linkage of GP elements to the speech channel has been variously called 'the stand-alone phonetic interpretability of elements', 'their realisational autonomy', and 'their autonomous interpretability' (see Lindsey and Harris 1990, Harris and Lindsey 1993, 1995). Harris and Lindsey (1995) assume that all elements are pronounceable in isolation, a view which is not fully compatible with the segmental representations proposed by a range of researchers (e.g. Jensen 1994, Szigetvári 1994, Rennison 1995). Nevertheless, it is generally accepted that elements can exist in different degrees of combination with other elements, those of lowest degree representing the most autonomous interpretations of the elements concerned.

Views about the way elements combine to form expressions that represent segments, or, indeed, how many elements are needed to model the phonological processes attested in speech (and, of course, the segment inventories of natural languages) have varied as GP has developed. For illustrative purposes here, we posit the nine elements described in Table 5.1: in order of tabulation, four resonance elements (**I**, **U**, **A**, and **R**), three manner elements (**ʔ**, **h**, and **N**), and two source elements (**L** and **H**). The table includes phonetic interpretations of elements. In some cases, there is an interpretation corresponding to isolated occurrence of a single element in a segment. This is what we will refer to as SIMPLEX occurrence of an element. Examples include the resonance elements **I** and **U**, both of which are contained in isolation in the representations of the monophthongs [i], [ɪ], [u], and [ʊ], and the glides [j] and [w], respectively. However, we found it impossible to identify segments composed solely of one of **N**, **L**, or **H**. It seems that these elements always occur in combination with at least one other element. The elements **N**, **L**, and **H**, then, do not conform to the claim that all GP elements are autonomously interpretable. For reasons which will be discussed in detail in section 5.3, we take a particular interest in elements occurring in their purest form, that is, ideally in isolation or, where simplex occurrence is not attested, in MINIMAL combination with other elements, i.e. in combination with the smallest number of partners possible. Minimal combination in the case of **N**, for example, would involve one resonance element, with the compound expression made up of **N** and the resonance element representing a nasalized vowel. The compounding of **N** and, say, **A** would yield [ɑ̃], as in French *sans*.

GP, like other current phonological theories, requires audible material to be bound into a prosodic hierarchy through which this material receives the necessary licensing. For this to be possible in the case of elements, they need to be attached to skeletal positions. All skeletal positions are immediately dominated by a constituent node, and GP recognizes three constituents, namely O(nset), N(ucleus), and R(hyme) (see e.g. Harris 1994 or Brockhaus 1995 for further details). In other words, any given skeletal position could be described as being nuclear (if immediately dominated by N) or non-nuclear (if immediately dominated by either O or R). Whether an element is associated with a nuclear or a non-nuclear skeletal position has some bearing on how that element is interpreted.

Another factor influencing the interpretation of elements is the role which an individual element plays in an expression. Expressions may contain one predominant element, the so-called HEAD, while any other element(s) present in the expression would be labelled OPERATOR(s). However, it is possible for none of the elements to be marked as the head, in which case the expression is referred to as HEADLESS or EMPTY-HEADED. Even where an element occurs in isolation, i.e. in a simplex occurrence of an element, it is possible for the

TABLE 5.1. Interpretations of GP elements.

		Nuclear position	Non-nuclear position
I	**Head**	[i]—E f*ee*, G *Vieh*, F *fit*	N/A
	Operator	[ɪ]—E *mid*, G *mit*	[j]—E *yarn*, G *Jahr*, F *yeux*
U	**Head**	[u]—E *who'd*, G *Hut*, F *vous*	N/A
	Operator	[ʊ]—E *put*, G *Butter*	[w]—E *wean*, F *oui*
A	**Head**	[ɑ/a]—E *palm*, G *Kahn*, F *pâle*	N/A
	Operator	[ʌ/a]—E *hut*, G *hat*, F *patte*	present in rhotics, e.g. [ɹ], [ʁ], [ʀ̥], [ʀ] E *rod*, G *rot*, F *rôle*
R	**Head**	[ɜ]—E *bird*	N/A
	Operator	[ə]—E *abide*, G *bitte*, F *porte-clés*	[r]—E (General American) *bu*[r]*er*, *wa*[r]*er*
ʔ	**Head**	N/A	[ʔ]—E (London) *bu*[ʔ]*er*, *wa*[ʔ]*er*
	Operator	present in creaky vowels, e.g. JM [ja̰]	present in nasals, e.g. E *dim*, *din*, G *Ding*, F *digne*
h	**Head**	N/A	present in strident fricatives, e.g. E *see*, *she*, G *Sie*, *Schi*, F *si*, *chie*
	Operator	present in breathy vowels, e.g. JM [ja̤]	[h]—E *house*, G *Haus*
N	**Head**	N/A	present in nasals, e.g. E *dim*, *din*, G *Ding*, F *digne*
	Operator	present in nasalized vowels, e.g. F *plein*, *sans*, *bon*, *lundi*	N/A
L	**Head**	N/A	N/A
	Operator	present in low-toned resonants e.g. K t*ò* tòm *ír*	present in voiced obstruents, e.g. F *bis*, *dent*, *gare*, *vous*, *zut*, *je*
H	**Head**	N/A	N/A
	Operator	present in high-toned resonants, e.g. K t*ó* tòm *ír*	present in voiceless obstruents, e.g. E *pin*, *tin*, *kin*, *chin*, *fin*, *thin*, *sin*, *shin*

Note: E = English (RP, except where otherwise indicated), G = German, F = French, JM = Jalapa Mazatec (Ladefoged and Maddieson 1996: 317), K = Kikuyu (Goldsmith 1990: 12)

Source: Brockhaus et al. 1996.

relevant expression to be either HEADED or headless, because the element may or may not be marked as the head of the simplex expression. If not, the element is assumed to be playing the role of operator, and the expression would be considered headless. In what follows, heads are marked by surrounding full stops, so that a simplex headed nuclear expression composed of the resonance element **U** in isolation would appear as .U. [u], while the corresponding headless expression would be **U. _ .** [ʊ]. The minimal nuclear compound expression representing the vowel [ɑ̃] mentioned above, with **N** in the role of operator and **A** as head, would be written **N.Â.**

Table 5.1 reflects both this distinction and the one described in the previous paragraph, showing four possible STATES OF OCCURRENCE, even in the case of simplex expressions consisting of just one element. These four are occurrence as head in a nuclear position, head in a non-nuclear position, operator in a nuclear position, and operator in a non-nuclear position. Although the four states of occurrence exist in principle, Table 5.1 shows only two or three for any given element. This is so for one of two reasons: either we were unable to identify a segment which would have allowed us to fill an additional cell (e.g. in the case of **h**, there do not seem to be any attested segments which would require this element to be the head in a nuclear position) or we have deliberately placed restrictions on the functions individual elements are permitted to perform (i.e. resonance elements are prohibited from forming heads in non-nuclear positions).

To summarize, an element has four possible states of occurrence in the speech channel: as head of, or operator in, an expression, attached to either a nuclear or a non-nuclear position. This variety of states of occurrence of elements in GP expressions is of vital importance when searching for cues to the occurrence of primes in the speech channel.

Independently of these states of occurrence, we can further classify elements according to the 'size' of the expression which they help to form. As already outlined above, where an element occurs in isolation, we speak of simplex occurrence or a simplex state of combination of the element concerned. Examples of this include the resonance elements **I**, **U**, and **A** as they appear in Table 5.1. Minimal states of combination pertain where elements are not fully autonomous in their interpretability, but appear with the smallest number of partners possible, e.g. with just one resonance element in the case of the manner element **N** (as illustrated by [ɑ̃] above). Expressions of any other size, where elements compound more freely, would be termed COMPLEX.

If combinations of acoustic cues (such as those discussed by Harris and Lindsey 1995) are conceived metaphorically as signatures of primes, then the simplex states of occurrence are, according to the metaphor, the different strokes of the signature, while the minimal and complex states of occurrence correspond to the concurrent appearance of several strokes in the same part of the signature. Another metaphor that is widely used in pattern recognition is that of fingerprint. If simplex states of occurrence of primes are thought of as prints produced by one finger, corresponding fingers of a suspect's two hands are nuclear and non-nuclear simplicial states of occurrence, and prints in which one finger has partly overlaid another with some occlusion of detail correspond to minimal and complex occurrences. Such metaphors help to emphasize that the acoustic signatures of primes have to be built up piecewise from cues taken from the various states of occurrence that are phonetically interpretable.

5.2. CHARACTERISTIC ACOUSTIC PATTERNS OF PRIMES

Harris and Lindsey (1995) describe graphically some simple acoustic discriminators for the GP resonance elements **A** (an overlapping mAss of the resonant frequency response to glottal pulsing in the first two formants F_1 and F_2), **I** (an amplitude dIp in frequency response between formants F_1 and F_2), and **U** (a rUmp or fall in height of resonance peak from F_1 to F_2 to F_3). These graphic patterns are seen in spectrograms of vowels from a wide range of speakers, being interpretations of (typically nuclear) simplex states of occurrence for the corresponding elements. It is quite straightforward to convert the graphics into dimensionless numerical cues that vary little from speaker to speaker. If formant F_1 has the frequency $f(F_1)$ and amplitude $a(F_1)$, and so on for other formants, the ratio that measures relative WIDTH of the F_1–F_2 frequency response gap is cue $R_1 = [f(F_2) - f(F_1)]/[f(F_1) + f(F_2)]$. This width is small for a mAss pattern and large for a dIp pattern. By sampling in different contexts from many speakers, one can set a threshold for **A/I** discrimination that in practice turns out to be about 0.5. Similarly, with little variation between speakers, the sum of amplitude ratios that measures the FALL in frequency response at successive formant resonances is cue $R_2 = [a(F_1)/a(F_2)] + [a(F_2)/a(F_3)]$. This is high for a rUmp pattern, but low for either a mAss or a dIp pattern. The two cues R_1 and R_2 together implement a classificatory cue space for vowel quality, much like the familiar vowel quadrilateral of acoustic phonetics (e.g. Ladefoged 1982: 179). In practice, because the R_2 decision boundary tends to be context-dependent, one can achieve improved discrimination by using another cue, a dimensionless measure of the falling formant trajectory seen in the spectrograms of [u] but not of [ɑ] or [i]. If the segment-initial, mid-segment, and segment-final frequencies of a formant are denoted, respectively, $f(F_2)_{init}$, $f(F_2)_{mid}$, and $f(F_2)_{final}$, then a possible measure of trajectory slope is cue $R_3 = [f(F_2)_{init} - f(F_2)_{final}]/[f(F_2)_{mid}]$.

The effect of gathering cues like these from the speech of several speakers is shown in the typical scatterplot in Fig. 5.1, which represents five speakers' pronunciations of the vowels in *heed* (.**I**.), *heard* (.**R**.), *who'd* (.**U**.), *hard* (.**A**.) and *hoard* (**U.A.**), mostly uttered using an accent approximating RP. It is notable that there is clustering: different speakers articulating the same vowel

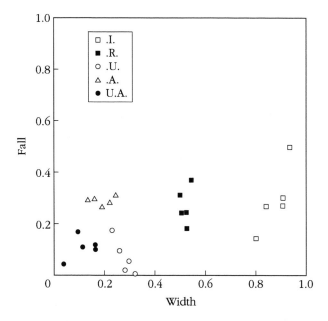

F I G. 5.1. Two-dimensional scatterplot of tense English monophthongs (five speakers).

does not result in cues at the same point of cue space, but the points derived from the same vowel sound do cluster together and can be separated from other points by appropriate decision boundaries. Strict invariance would imply that the same vowel from different speakers would map to the same point in cue space, but the evidence indicates only statistical invariance. One of the five vowels constitutes an interpretation of a complex nuclear state of occurrence, with the expression being composed of **U** (operator) and **A** (head). The location of the corresponding cluster illustrates a pattern that we have observed in a range of data. Complex clusters are typically located between simplex clusters, tending to be nearer to the cluster representing the head of the complex (**A** in Fig. 5.1) than to the cluster(s) representing operators in the complex (**U** in our example). Evidently, a cue space like the one illustrated for vowels provides both a statistical notion of invariant pattern in the speech channel, and a numerical correlative for the GP notion of head of an expression. Characterizing primes and expressions as clusters in a cue space thus gives us reasonable hope of providing pattern recognition support for the future or incipient language-engineering products described in section 5.1.

We have, in fact, prototyped a voice-input system based on cluster representations or signatures of phonological primes (Ingleby and Brockhaus 1998). The prototype is a crude one and does not have any of the corpus-derived statistical parsing capability of commercial single-speaker products. Its word recognition accuracy is highly speaker-independent, however, and it shows a promising degree of language independence. It was trained using five speakers of English (whose vowel utterances were used for Figs 5.1 and 5.5), three human and two synthetic—the latter, of course, having known formant and excitation models. The three humans were a male and a female RP speaker and a male Northern English speaker, while both synthetic speakers ('Venus', a female contralto, and 'Thor', a male baritone) approximated RP. Yet, when given speech from an unknown speaker pronouncing segments not attested in English (e.g. in German *ich* [ɪç] 'I', *müde* ['myːdə] 'tired', or French *tu* [ty] 'you', *mon* [mɔ̃] 'my'), the prototype voice-input system is able to locate these segments appropriately in a cue space like that exemplified above.

5.3. ADEQUACY OF CUES FOR DETECTION OF PRIMES

5.3.1. Introduction

Cue sets are not uniquely determined by the need to serve for the detection of primes, but a few adequacy requirements can be stated. In this section, we will focus on the following three, which we discuss one by one in the subsections below:

(*a*) cues must be relative quantities to favour speaker independence;
(*b*) cues must exhibit good multi-speaker clustering, with the ratio of within-class variance to between-class variance being small for well-separated clusters;
(*c*) cues must provide good statistical indication of phonological headedness.

5.3.2. Cues must be relative quantities

A first requirement is that cues must be relative quantities: dimensionless ratios or groups of physical quantities, such as ratios of formant frequencies, energy distribution ratios measuring the noise coloration of frication, etc. Unless this relativity requirement is imposed, there is little hope of building from cues a speaker-independent signature for each prime. Some examples of cue sets that have been used in experimental prototype systems for detecting primes are given in Chalfont (1997), Williams (1998), and Ingleby and Brockhaus (1998). Four types of cue that satisfy relativity requirements have been used in experimentation: the frame-based cue, the frame-differential cue, the knowledge-based cue, and the segment-based cue. The first two types are traditional in ASR research. The second two types are drawn from more basic knowledge of how phoneticians read spectrograms.

Frame-based cues are calculated from one Fourier transform window of a speech spectrogram—a frequency spectrum obtained from 256 successive digital samples of microphone output taken over about 10 ms. Similar cues carrying the same information in different form can be calculated using linear predictive coding (LPC) techniques—but for the sake of simplicity here we avoid all discussion of digital signal processing technicalities and use Fourier spectra in our illustrative examples. An example of a spectral frame from a vowel segment is shown in Fig. 5.2, and a frame for a fricative is shown in Fig. 5.3.

Typically, one could extract the formant amplitudes and frequencies from the data of Fig. 5.2 and hence calculate values for the cues R1–R3 introduced in section 5.2. Formant parameters, though, are not the only source of significant cues extractable from channel data. If the breathiness of a vowel segment were of interest—an indicator of element **h** in a nuclear position— one could remove the glottal excitation from a frame like that in Fig. 5.2, the remaining excitation being frication at constrictions. A rough way to estimate how much of the excitation is glottal pulsing is to average the peak heights

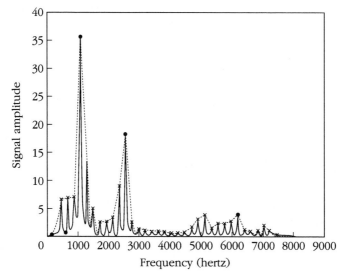

F I G. 5.2. Spectral frame showing a vowel segment.

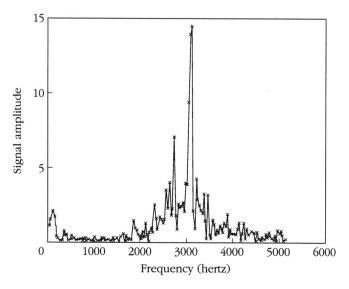

F IG. 5.3. Spectral frame showing a fricative segment.

and trough levels of the intensity striations over the whole frequency range and match these to the waveform of a periodic pulse representing glottal excitation. Signal processing engineers have a variety of more precise techniques for separating out parts of the speech signal due to glottal excitation, frication, and formant resonance, but we are not concerned to review such technical detail here.

The type of frame-based cue that indicates the presence of the element **h** in obstruents and vowels has to measure the 'triangular spikiness' of the spectrum in Fig. 5.3 compared to the smoother variation of amplitude with frequency in Fig. 5.2. If the amplitudes in three successive frequency bins f_i, f_{i+1}, and f_{i+2} of the spectrum are denoted $a(f_i)$, $a(f_{i+1})$, and $a(f_{i+2})$, then the quantity $[\,|a(f_{i+1}) - a(f_i)| + |a(f_{i+2}) - a(f_{i+1})|\,]$ is a measure of the length of the triangular path $a(f_i) \rightarrow a(f_{i+1}) \rightarrow a(f_{i+2})$, while the length of the direct path $a(f_i) \rightarrow a(f_{i+2})$ is measured by the quantity $[\,|a(f_{i+2}) - a(f_i)|\,]$. The dimensionless ratio R_4 of these quantities, averaged over all triples of successive frequency bins, is large for frames with frication and small for frames with mainly glottal excitation. Other frame-based cues indicative of frication noise in obstruents capitalize on the fact that frication excites higher frequencies than glottal pulsing. If the frequency range of a frame is divided into overlapping bands and the ratios of amplitude totals in different bands are calculated, then ratios of a high- to a low-frequency band can serve as an indicator of **h** head and **h** operator. In the investigations of Chalfont (1997) and Williams (1998), three bands were found useful, but by using more bands to measure noise coloration (also known as energy distribution) in fricatives, it is possible to get indications of resonance elements in non-nuclear positions, too. Much of the extensive work on Hidden Markov Models (HMMs) uses frame-based cues involving as many as a dozen frequency bands, however, and makes use of rates of change of these from frame to frame. For a fairly recent review of HMM work, see, for example, Young (1996).

There is, of course, a long history of automatic extraction of acoustic channel parameters relating to formants, glottal pitch, and frication noise from speech data. Automatic extraction is the basis of historical and current speech coder-decoder telephony. Flanagan and Rabiner (1973) comment on key early papers, and a more recent industry perspective on acoustic and articulatory parameter mapping of speech using modern artificial neural net pattern recognizer techniques is given, for example, by Rahim (1994). For present purposes, we suppose that any desired frame-based cue can be automatically extracted in real time.

Frame-differential cues are the differences between values of frame-based cues in successive frames, and are measures of rate of change. Like the coloration cues above, they too are used in HMM speech recognizers. The more basic importance of interframe differences derives from their role in automatic segmentation. With a few noise coloration cues, it is fairly easy to detect the manner elements of GP (see, for example, Chalfont 1997, Ingleby and Brockhaus 1998), and the corresponding frame-differentials peak where the manner class changes. In principle, pattern-recognition techniques that are trainable could be used to set decision thresholds on the height of peaks and use the thresholds subsequently to perform automatic manner class segmentation of new input. In practice, however, automatic segmentation tends to miss a few segment boundaries. For example, vowel-approximant boundaries (*caliper*, *coyote*, **aware**) and boundaries between sibilant and non-sibilant fricatives (*offset*, *bashful*) are a source of segmentation errors. It is possible to correct such omissions in a second pass over the data in a speech channel, but knowledge-based cues need to be invoked.

A typical knowledge-based cue is the relative time-duration of a segment—a difficult quantity to deal with because it complements pitch as an indicator of stress, and therefore varies prosodically. During speech communication, the duration scale of segments is varied dynamically by the speaker ('time-warping'). All the early and most of the more recent work on the practical development of speech recognition has been directed at obtaining, in one computational pass, a segmental view of patterns whose presence is obscured by time-warping. The two most widely researched one-pass approaches to duration dynamics are dynamic programming/dynamic time-warping (see, for example, Holmes 1988) and the more successful HMM approach (Young 1996). Here, however, we do not limit cue extraction and segmentation to one-pass algorithms. A fundamental reason for stepping outside the one-pass limitation is that important cues of the segmental type (Liberman and Mattingley 1985) can be extracted only *after* segmentation of the signal— because they involve ratios of signal amplitudes in mid-segment and segment-boundary frames. Also, a practical reason is that faster microprocessors and task-sharing, agent-based computing techniques now make multi-pass and concurrent-pass approaches possible. A simple notion of how a second pass at segmentation and a third pass at segment-based cue extraction fit together can be gained from the following.

Given a multi-speaker but language-specific, hand-segmented corpus, statistical parameters for the relative duration of segments by manner class can be extracted. There are very significant differences between the relative duration parameters of different languages. For example, English obstruents do not fall into separate groups for (true) geminates and non-geminates, but some obstruents of Italian certainly do. Our own measurements on a few of these indicate that Italian geminates have durations around 50 per cent greater than those of non-geminates. An extreme case of gemination contrast is found in Arabic *shadda* consonants. Here, our own measurements (carried out with the assistance of researchers in Jeddah) show that Arabic geminates have durations more than double those of non-geminates. Generally, once a knowledge base of relative durations has been constructed, this can be referred to when checking the automatic segmentation of new speech. If segments are assigned to manner class using frame-based cues, and a segment's duration is over-long (compared to that of the preceding segment of known manner class), then an additional segment boundary is to be found somewhere in the middle of the over-long segment, and a second pass at segmentation is needed to find it. In the second pass, the segment is divided into an initial group of frames and separate middle and final groups. The two outer groups can be assigned to separate manner classes using their frame-based cues. For example, the initial frames might indicate a vowel, while the final frames might exhibit somewhat reduced intensity, indicating an approximant. Then the two new manner classes' durations allow the segment to be split in proportion to their relative durations, thereby estimating the position of the additional segment boundary. With improved segmentation from the second pass, the way is then open to look at formant trajectory and other segment-based cues. Such cues are measures of temporal order in the acoustic signal over a longer interval than the 30 ms or so picked up by current HMM methods.

Formant trajectory cues—which depend on knowing which frames are segment-initial, segment-medial, and segment-final—are not necessarily concerned with the signature of what is present in the segment from which they are extracted. Plosive bursts often contain so little noise coloration that resonance element detection is indecisive. The formant trajectories of a following vowel supply the only reliably discriminating cues to the resonance elements present in the plosive segment. This segment-external type of cue is likely to be important in languages with more consonant contrasts than English—such as the pharyngeal contrasts which split the [s] and [ð] fricatives of Arabic into emphatic ([sˤ] and [ðˤ]) and non-emphatic variants.

5.3.3. Cues must exhibit good multi-speaker clustering

Having chosen cues which achieve some degree of speaker-independence through the relativity requirement, the adequacy of the choice of cues is to be decided on the basis of the statistical clustering properties of multi-speaker training or sample data. An example of good multi-speaker clustering is shown in the two-cue scatterplot of Fig. 5.1: cues from phonologically identical speech sounds (that is, the 'same' vowels produced by different speakers at various times) plot as points in multidimensional cue space and form compact clusters separated from the clusters derived from phonologically dissimilar sounds. Each point in such a scatterplot is located by the values of cues marked off along only two or three axes of the chosen plot, but in general a point or CUE VECTOR has many more components than are displayed. A well-formed set of clusters has a low value for the ratio of within-class to between-class variance, low enough that speaker-independent boundaries between clusters can be delineated. The systematic analysis of clumps or clusters in statistical populations has a long history and many practical uses in applications of pattern recognition, where it is variously known as mathematical taxonomy (Jardine and Sibson 1971), numerical taxonomy (e.g. Sneath and Sokal 1973), and cluster analysis (e.g. Everitt 1993).

One of the data visualization tools used in mathematical taxonomy to test for the presence of well-formed clusters in a set of sample data is the dendrogram. An example is shown in Fig. 5.4 for the vowel data of Fig. 5.1. It displays an automatically generated class hierarchy, with all the sample in one coarsest class on the left, and the finest singleton classes on the right. The latter are labelled as follows: MN1 = male Northern English speaker, VEN = synthetic female contralto, THO = synthetic male baritone, CEN = central location of the cluster, FRP = female RP speaker, MRP = male RP speaker. The horizontal axis of the dendrogram is a distance scale showing a threshold distance between clusters above which they are regarded as separated. The distances used in the software that generated the Fig. 5.4 dendrogram were calculated from the usual Euclidean straight-line distance between points in cue space. To make this into a distance separating clusters of points, a between-cluster average of point distances was used. The dendrogram shows that the simplex interpretations of resonance elements in nuclear positions—the leaves of the dendrogram—are in well-formed clusters on the same branch for all speakers.

Sampling and visual clustering experiments on chosen cues could confirm, using dendrograms, whether or not the choice separates the interpretations of minimal combinations of elements in their various states of occurrence into well-formed clusters. For the mathematically inclined researcher, there are more rigorous ways of testing well-formedness of clusters. One such is the so-called Wilks criterion (the ratio of determinant of within-class covariance to determinant of between-class covariance), whose statistical distribution for large samples from a population made up of several classes is known. The ratio is small for well-formed clusters, larger when clusters overlap, and decision thresholds can be obtained from statistical tables. We put aside such rigour in an exploratory chapter such as this, but commend it for closer investigation.

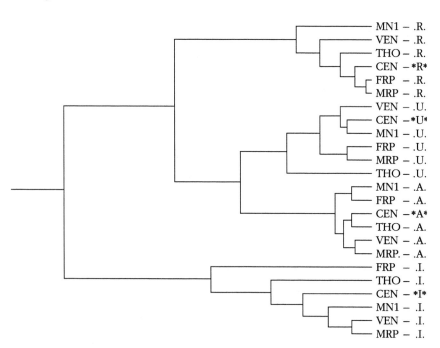

Fig. 5.4. Dendrogram of tense English monophthongs (five speakers).

5.3.4. Cues must provide good statistical indication of phonological headedness

A third requirement on cue sets is that they provide good statistical indications of headedness. Our discussion of states of occurrence of elements distinguishes between phonetic interpretations of elements as heads of expressions, and elements as operators, so indications of headedness relate to two clusters: a head cluster and an operator cluster. A point in cue space representing a new segment can be assigned to one or the other on the basis of a suitable inter-cluster distance. Two questions arise here: *what inter-cluster distances are suitable?* and *what is to be done about the fact that the new segment may be represented by a complex expression?* The answers depend on what sort of statistical distribution of cues occurs within a multi-speaker cluster.

There is a mathematically rigorous way to settle on a distribution by invoking theorems of multivariate statistics (the so-called central limit theorems). Such theorems refer to statistical quantities, which, in the present context, are cue vectors with many components. The tenor of central limit theorems is: if a statistical quantity (i.e. a cue vector with several components) is the sum of many contributions all of small variance, then the quantity has a multivariate normal distribution. This distribution is sometimes referred to as Gaussian distribution. Since our cues are calculated from 256 samples or more of a pressure waveform, it is reasonable to suppose that some kind of central limit theorem applies. We compromise scientific rigour only a little by taking both our head and operator clusters to be samples from a Gaussian population, though not both from the same population. Similar compromises are at the heart of HMM speech recognition.

A Gaussian distribution is characterized by a central location vector, and a dispersion matrix, both of which can be estimated from a sample (i.e. from members of the cluster). The vector mean x_0 of a sample $\{x_1, x_2 \dots x_j \dots\}$ of cue vectors estimates central location, and dispersion is estimated by the sample variance matrix

$$\mathbf{W}_{pq} = \Sigma_j (x_j - x_0)_p (x_j - x_0)_q$$

(in which indices p and q are components of cue vectors and the summation is over points in a cluster). Because clusters of widely different dispersion occur when clustering simplex interpretations of primes, a measure of distance from cluster centre in units of cluster dispersion is needed to normalize distance comparisons. If a new segment is represented by a cue vector x_{new}, then the normalized distance of this vector from the cluster is the quantity

$$d_M(x_{new}, x_0) = (x_{new} - x_0)^T \mathbf{W}^{-1} (x_{new} - x_0),$$

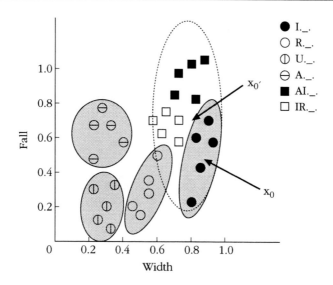

FIG. 5.5. Lax English monophthongs with the umbrae for **I. _ .**, **R. _ .**, **U. _ .**, and **A. _ .** appearing shaded, and the penumbra for **I. _ .** indicated by a dotted line (five speakers).

which is a quadratic function of the components of the cue vector determined by the matrix inverse of dispersion **W**, known in cluster analysis as the MAHALANOBIS DISTANCE. This distance measures how dissimilar the new cue vector is to those in the cluster centred at x_0. One can compute the distance of the new cue vector from both head and operator clusters and compare them: the closer cluster gives the more likely interpretation for the new cue vector. We conclude that the answer to the first question we asked above must be that the Mahalanobis distance is the most suitable inter-cluster distance.

The straightforward pattern-recognition criterion based on Mahalanobis distances deals with the case of a cue vector from a segment that is an interpretation of an element in a state of occurrence involving only minimal combination. It shades ellipsoidal regions of cue space around simplex clusters that serve as a signature for the existence of elements in purest form: segments whose cue vectors fall into the shadow belong to that cluster. In Fig. 5.5 some of these UMBRAL regions are shown schematically for lax vowels of English: they are shaded ellipses in the two-dimensional scatterplot, but represent ellipsoids in the larger space of cue vectors.

The situation for cue vectors from a complex segment is less straightforward. The other elements in the complex make the cue vector more dissimilar, pushing it out of the shaded umbra and into a PENUMBRAL region where other complexes are found. This penumbral region is a crucial part of the acoustic signature of an element, and before answering the second question above (about the manifestation of complex expressions in cue space) a more detailed notion of signature must be taken into consideration.

5.4. SIGNATURES AND QUADRATIC DISCRIMINANTS

Fig. 5.5 shows the distribution of cue vectors from vowel segments uttered by the same speakers as in Fig. 5.1, but in the new figure the vowels are lax rather than tense—as in the words *hid* (**I.**_.), *ahead* (**R.**_.), *hood* (**U.**_.), *hut* (**A.**_.), *head* (**IR.**_.), and *had* (**AI.**_.). The shaded ellipses represent the umbral regions where cue vectors from segments corresponding to simplex occurrences of resonance elements cluster. The cluster singled out for discussion corresponds to the expression **I.**_., has a central location at point x_0, and a within-cluster variance matrix **W**. Point x_0 is estimated as the centroid of sampled points from the given speakers, and variance **W** is the sample variance for the same sampled points. Around the shaded umbral ellipse, there is a larger ellipse with a dotted line boundary, and this represents the penumbral region for element **I** in its state of occurrence as operator in a nuclear expression.

If λ denotes the Mahalanobis distance of the boundary of the cluster from its centre (chosen, typically, to guarantee that 95 per cent of the cluster lies inside the boundary), then a point in the umbra satisfies the inequality

$$(x_{\text{umb}} - x_0)^{\text{T}} W^{-1} (x_{\text{umb}} - x_0) \leq \lambda$$

A similar inequality defining the interior of the penumbral ellipse is found by estimating from the cue vectors of all the segments, simplex and complex, a new central location $x_{0'}$ and a new within-cluster variance matrix W'. It is important to note that subsegmental representations figure in the selection of sample data used to estimate $x_{0'}$ and W'. Having estimated these, the region of cue space inside the penumbral ellipse is defined by the inequality

$$(x_{\text{penum}} - x_{0'})^{\text{T}} W'^{-1} (x_{\text{penum}} - x_{0'}) \leq \lambda$$

The region outside the umbral ellipsoid but inside this penumbral ellipsoid is the penumbra where segments containing nuclear operator occurrences of **I** in combination with other resonance elements fall. Both the inner and outer boundary of the penumbra are determined from training data designed to cover cases of occurrence of an element in both minimal and complex expressions. This kind of system training is needed to answer empirically questions about complex occurrences and indeed define the notion of acoustic signature *relative to a chosen set of cues*.

Collecting together the various parts of the definition of signature, relative to chosen cues and a choice of subsegmental representations, each element or prime has a signature made up of umbrae and penumbrae estimated from training data, centroids, and variances as above. There is an umbra and penumbra for each attested state of occurrence of the element (nuclear versus non-nuclear, head versus operator). The full signature is a union of these. A careful definition of signature such as this presages a way of investigating both cue sets for efficacy and subsegmental representations for the way they lead to successful acoustic pattern recognition. This could be the beginning of a physics contribution to the cognitive science of the speech channel, but only time will tell.

6

The Role of the Syllable in Speech Perception and Production

Juan Segui and Ludovic Ferrand

Over the past decade, as shown by the articles in this volume, the syllable has come to enjoy a privileged status as a critical unit in phonology both from a linguistic (e.g. Clements and Keyser 1983, Fudge 1969, Kaye 1989, Selkirk 1982) and a psycholinguistic (e.g. Cutler et al. 1986, Levelt and Wheeldon 1994, Mehler et al. 1981, Meyer 1990, Segui 1984, Segui, Dupoux, and Mehler 1990) perspective. In this chapter, we will argue that the syllable is a likely processing unit of speech perception and production in French whereas it might not be the case for English and Dutch.

6.1. AN OVERVIEW OF THE SYLLABLE'S ROLE IN SPEECH PERCEPTION

In a seminal study of speech perception, Mehler et al. (1981) demonstrated that French subjects responded faster in a monitoring task when the target corresponded to the first syllable of the stimulus word than when it corresponded to a longer or a shorter segment than the first syllable. Each target corresponded to a complete syllable in only one of the two words: PA was exactly the first syllable of the word PA.LACE[1] but less than the first syllable of the word PAL.MIER whereas PAL was exactly the first syllable of PAL.MIER but more than the first syllable of PA.LACE. Thus the target PA was detected faster in the word PA.LACE than in the word PAL.MIER, whereas the target PAL was detected faster in PAL.MIER than in PA.LACE. These results provide therefore evidence for the syllable as a fundamental unit of speech perception in French, with a prelexical level of stored syllables mediating between the speech input and the mental lexicon (see Segui 1984 and Segui, Dupoux, and Mehler 1990, for a review).

This syllable effect discovered twenty years ago by Mehler and colleagues is very robust with French listeners. It has been observed not only with French stimuli, but also with English and Japanese stimuli heard by French subjects (Cutler et al. 1983, 1986, Otake et al. 1993). The role of the syllable has been confirmed many times in French with a phoneme detection task (Dupoux and Mehler 1990, Dupoux 1993, Segui, Frauenfelder, and Mehler 1981), in the detection of illusory words (Kolinsky, Morais, and Cluytens 1995), with a word-stem completion task (Peretz, Lussier, and Béland 1996, 1998) and with the attentional allocation task (Pallier et al. 1993). A similar syllable effect has also been observed under certain conditions in Catalan (Sebastian-Gallés et al. 1992), Spanish (Bradley, Sanchez-Casas, and Garcia-Albea 1993, Pallier et al. 1993) and Portuguese (Morais et al. 1989).

In speech perception, units of segmentation have been shown to vary as a function of native language. Romance languages such as French, Spanish, Catalan, and Portuguese show positive evidence of the role of the syllable in the perception of spoken words. In contrast, Germanic languages such as English and Dutch have yielded different outcomes. Some syllable effects have been reported for Dutch by Zwitserlood et al. (1993), although other studies have failed to find such an effect (e.g. Cutler 1997). Direct analogues of Mehler et al.'s (1981) study failed to find a syllable effect in English (Cutler et al. 1986, Bradley, Sanchez-Casas, and Garcia-Albea 1993). However, Treiman and colleagues (Bruck, Treiman, and Caravolas 1995, Treiman and Danis 1988, Treiman et al. 1995, Treiman, Straub, and Levery 1994) have collected a wealth of data suggesting that the syllable is an important unit in English processing using a variety of experimental tasks such as word games, serial recall, and phoneme shift tasks. One possibility to reconcile the results of Treiman and colleagues (e.g. Bruck, Treiman, and Caravolas 1995) and those of Cutler et al. (1986) is to assume that syllabic structure is imposed late in speech processing in English. Using an induction

---

[1] Throughout the chapter we denote syllable structure using a dot (e.g. BAL.CONY).

variant of the phoneme monitoring task (Pallier et al. 1993) in which listeners monitored for phonemes in multisyllabic words that began with CVCCV-structure, Finney, Protopapas, and Eimas (1996) showed that English listeners used syllabic information during processing. Pitt, Smith, and Klein (1998) also used the same technique and obtained results that led them to conclude that English listeners organize speech into syllables, as in other languages such as French, Spanish, Catalan, and Portuguese, but possibly at a comparatively later stage.

6.2. AN OVERVIEW OF THE SYLLABLE'S ROLE IN SPEECH PRODUCTION

6.2.1. The masked priming technique as a tool for investigating speech production

Recently, Ferrand, Grainger, and Segui (1994) reported a series of word and picture naming experiments using a masked priming paradigm with primes exposures brief enough to prevent identification. This masked priming technique is illustrated in Fig. 6.1. Ferrand, Grainger, and Segui (1994) found chance-level performance when subjects were asked to judge whether the masked prime word was nominally the same as the target, suggesting that very little precise information about the prime was available for conscious identification. This absence of awareness was taken as clear evidence for the automaticity of the processes under study. Even in such impoverished prime presentation conditions, there is evidence that high-level representations are activated during prime processing and can subsequently affect word and picture naming. Under this masked priming technique, Ferrand, Grainger, and Segui (1994) examined the type of codes that are generated under masking conditions when prime stimuli are words or pronounceable strings of letters. In particular, they demonstrate that the prior presentation of the same word prime facilitated both picture and word naming independently of target frequency. Furthermore, similar effects were obtained using primes that were pseudohomophones or homophones of the picture and word targets (see Ferrand 1995, Ferrand, Segui, and Grainger 1995, Ferrand, Humphreys, and Segui 1998). Given that these results were obtained in conditions that prevent conscious identification (briefly presented forward and backward masked primes), they are consistent with recent evidence showing that phonological information about a written word becomes available rapidly and automatically (see Berent and Perfetti 1995, Ferrand

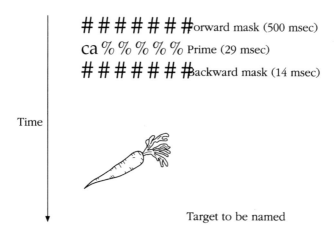

#orward mask (500 msec)
ca % % % % % Prime (29 msec)
#ackward mask (14 msec)

Time

Target to be named

FIG. 6.1. Sequence of events in the masked priming paradigm used in Ferrand, Segui, and Grainger's (1996) experiments. The subject's task was to name the target (either a word, or a picture) as quickly as possible.

Source: Adapted from Sevald, Dell, and Cole 1995.

and Grainger 1992, 1993, 1994, 1996, Grainger and Ferrand 1994, 1996, Lukatela and Turvey 1994, Perfetti and Bell 1991). It should be pointed out, however, that the stimuli used by Ferrand et al. (Ferrand, Grainger, and Segui 1994, Ferrand, Segui, and Grainger 1995, Ferrand, Humphreys, and Segui 1998) were only monosyllabic words compared to the bi- and trisyllabic words to be used in the experiments described below. In what follows, we examine more precisely the nature of the representations subserving the observed facilitation effects. In particular, we examine the possible role of sublexical phonological units, namely syllables, as functional units of speech production, an area that has received little attention as yet. This point is important given that in our previous pseudohomophone and homophone experiments we used only monosyllabic items making it impossible to distinguish between lexical and syllabic effects.

In a more recent study, Ferrand, Segui, and Grainger (1996) used the masked priming technique combined with the naming task (see Ferrand, Grainger, and Segui 1994) and applied Mehler et al.'s design to study the possible role of the syllable in speech production. The present study was designed to find out if the phonological codes that are generated from a masked prime are structured syllabically at some level in the information processing hierarchy. Note that French has a regular syllable structure and clear syllable boundaries, with minimal consonantal ambisyllabicity, especially between the first and second syllables of polysyllabic words. For example, for the French word BALADE there is a clear syllable boundary between BA- and -LADE. If syllables play a central role over and above phoneme units in speech production, then a facilitation should be observed when primes and targets share phonemes that constitute a syllable unit as opposed to when primes and targets share phonemes that do not constitute a syllable unit. Using the same type of stimuli, Mehler et al. (1981) found evidence for the syllable's role as a unit of speech perception. This is also what Ferrand et al. found for speech production: French subjects responded significantly faster in word, non-word, or picture naming tasks when a masked orthographic prime corresponded to the first syllable of the stimulus than when it corresponded to a longer or a shorter segment than the first syllable. The word BA.LADE was named faster when preceded by the prime BA than by BAL, whereas the word BAL.CON was named faster when preceded by the prime BAL than by BA. The same words that produced a syllable priming effect in the naming task did not produce a similar effect in the lexical decision task. The fact that very similar syllabic priming effects were observed in picture, word, and non-word naming but not in a lexical

TABLE 6.1. Mean latencies (ms) obtained in different conditions by Ferrand, Segui, and Grainger (1996)

	CV targets	CVC targets
Experiment 1A (bisyllabic word naming)		
CV primes	567	589
CVC primes	599	558
Experiment 1B (trisyllabic word naming)		
CV primes	608	626
CVC primes	632	604
Experiment 2 (bisyllabic non-word naming)		
CV primes	612	656
CVC primes	646	616
Experiment 3A (lexical decision task for words)		
CV primes	587	588
CVC primes	591	590
Experiment 3B (lexical decision task for non-words)		
CV primes	715	711
CVC primes	719	718
Experiment 4 (picture naming)		
CV primes	715	750
CVC primes	755	706

decision task strongly suggests that they are indeed located at the level of output phonology (articulatory encoding) where presumably the same processes are involved in naming these different types of targets. These results obtained in French are summarized in Table 6.1.

6.2.2. The case of English and Dutch

In a later report, Ferrand, Segui, and Humphreys (1997) extended these results to British English. The positioning of the syllable boundary in English is by no means clear-cut. In traditional treatments of English syllabification, a word such as TALCUM, in which the boundary between syllables is uncontroversial, would consist of two syllables, [TAL] and [CUM] (see Anderson and Jones 1974 for linguistic evidence and Derwing 1992 and Treiman and Zukowski 1990 for empirical evidence). This is due to the *legality principle* of syllabification (Hooper 1972, Pulgram 1970), which states that any consonants that begin a syllable within a word must be a legal onset. Likewise, any sequence of consonants that ends a syllable within a word must be a legal coda. For example, TALCUM cannot be broken before /l/ because /lk/ is not a legal English onset. Another clear case of syllabification in English occurs when the primary stress falls on the second syllable, as in BABOON. All phonological theories (see Treiman and Danis 1988) appear to agree that the boundary must fall between the first vowel and the medial consonant (giving BA.BOON).

However, contrary to French, English tends to have great variation in syllable weight and syllable boundaries in English are frequently unclear. In particular, English has many words with ambisyllabic consonants, which are treated as part of the first as well as the second syllable (Fallows 1981, Gussenhoven 1986, Kahn 1976, Treiman and Danis 1988). For instance, in the word BALANCE, in which the primary stress is on the initial syllable, the syllable boundary falls neither clearly before nor after the /l/, because this intervocalic consonant can be legal in both word-initial and word-final positions. For English, there is agreement to treat these intervocalic consonants as ambisyllabic (see, however, Selkirk 1982, who argued that the notion of ambisyllabicity is unnecessary). Phonologists represent the syllable structure of ambisyllabic English words such as BALANCE as [BA[L]ANCE], where the /l/ properly belongs to both first and second syllables (Anderson and Jones 1974, Bell and Hooper 1978). According to Cutler et al. (1986: 396), 'English . . . has extremely irregular syllable structure and frequently unclear syllable boundaries, particularly as a result of the widespread occurrence of ambisyllabicity in intervocalic consonants.

Ambisyllabic consonants between the first and the second syllable of polysyllabic words—as in *salad*—are especially common.'

In five experiments, Ferrand, Segui, and Humphreys (1997) provided compelling evidence in favour of the syllable's role in speech production in English (these results are summarized in Table 6.2). In their Experiment 1, they replicated the design of the French experiment by Ferrand, Segui, and Grainger (1996) including ambisyllabic word targets. For CVC-words with clear initial syllable boundaries (such as BALCONY), primes were more effective when they constituted the first syllable of the target than when they were only phonologically related (with CVC as opposed to CV primes). For target words with ambisyllabic consonants (such as BALANCE), there were no differences between the effects of CVC and CV primes. However, this could have been because neither prime type was effective or because both were effective. In another experiment, they failed to observe such syllable

TABLE 6.2. Mean latencies (ms) obtained in different conditions by Ferrand, Segui, and Humphreys (1997)

	CV[C] targets	CVC targets	CV targets
Experiment 1 (word naming)			
CV primes	546	549	
CVC primes	545	524	
Experiment 2 (lexical decision)			
CV primes	627	638	
CVC primes	628	640	
Experiment 3 (word naming with a neutral baseline)			
CVC primes		524	
CV primes		559	
Neutral		560	
Experiment 4 (word naming: ambisyllabicity)			
CVC primes	528		
CV primes	528		
Neutral primes	570		
Experiment 5 (word naming)			
CV primes			551
CVC primes			586
Neutral			590

priming effects in the lexical decision task (replicating Ferrand et al. 1996). In their Experiment 3, they tested the nature (facilitatory or inhibitory) of such syllable priming effects observed for CVC-words with clear initial syllable boundaries by introducing a neutral condition (composed of per cent signs: %%%%%%).

As shown in Table 6.2, naming latencies were consistently shorter in comparison with a neutral condition only when primes formed the first syllable of the target. However, it could have been that CVC primes were more effective than CV primes simply because of increased phonological and/or orthographic overlap, not because of their status as the target word's first syllable. In their Experiment 4, they tested the hypothesis that ambisyllabic words can be primed equally (or not) by their two possible initial syllables. The results (see Table 6.2) showed that the two possible initial syllables of ambisyllabic words facilitated word naming to the same extent in comparison with the neutral condition. In a final experiment, they tested the hypothesis that the syllable priming effect obtained in Experiments 1 and 3 was simply due to increased phonological and/or orthographic overlap. The results (see Table 6.2) demonstrated that the syllabic priming effect obtained for CV-words with clear initial syllable boundaries (such as DIVORCE) was not due to increased phonological and/or orthographic overlap, since CV primes were more effective than CVC primes. So, English speakers are clearly sensitive to the syllables of word targets to be named and this holds for the unambiguous as well as for the ambisyllabic words. However, a recent study conducted in American English by Schiller (1998*a*) failed to replicate the syllable effects observed by Ferrand, Segui, and Humphreys (1997).

Turning now to the Dutch language, Wheeldon and Levelt (1995) have also used a production variant of the classical syllable monitoring task in speech perception (Mehler et al. 1981). In Wheeldon and Levelt's (1995) production monitoring task, Dutch subjects (who had a good knowledge of English) were instructed to silently generate the Dutch translation of an auditorily presented English word and to monitor their production for a given syllable target. Wheeldon and Levelt replicated the syllable monitoring effect in Dutch: responses to targets were faster when they corresponded to the initial syllable of the carrier word (for example, /maag/ in the word MAAG.DEN) than when they did not (e.g. /maa/ in MAAG.DEN). According to these authors these results provide evidence that subjects base their responses on the generation of a syllabified phonological representation. However, in a recent study, Schiller (1998*b*) reported a series of experiments in Dutch using the same masking procedure and naming task as Ferrand, Segui, and Grainger (1996) but failed to replicate the syllable priming effect.

A possible reason for the absence of syllable priming effects might be that syllables are not involved in the visual word recognition of Dutch. A parallel can be drawn with findings in auditory word recognition where one finds syllable effects in languages like French, but not in languages like Dutch (Cutler et al. 1986). Cutler et al. (1986) argued that in French, with its clear syllable boundaries, the syllable is an important unit used for the segmentation of continuous speech (see also Segui, Dupoux, and Mehler 1990). In contrast with French, Dutch is a stress language, characterized by a stress rhythm, with large differences in syllable weight between strong and weak syllables. According to Cutler et al. (1986), stress-based procedures make the information from syllables superfluous. However, some syllable effects have been reported for Dutch by Zwitserlood et al. (1993); although other studies have failed to find such an effect (e.g. Cutler 1997). Differences between Dutch and French do not come as a surprise therefore, since the two languages belong to different language families, Germanic and Romance languages respectively.

The results obtained in French by Ferrand, Segui, and Grainger (1996) strongly suggest that the syllable is indeed a basic unit of speech production in French. However, there remains a discrepancy between the English results obtained by Ferrand, Segui, and Humphreys (1997) and those obtained by Schiller (1998a), and between the Dutch results obtained by Wheeldon and Levelt (1995) and those obtained by Schiller (1998b).

6.2.3. Are syllables chunks, schemas, or both?

One potential problem in Ferrand et al.'s (1996, 1997) experiments is that the syllabic frame and the segmental composition were confounded. Indeed, in the conditions where the prime and the target shared syllabic structure, they also shared segmental composition or phonological content (e.g. bal/BALCONY).

Theories of speech production hold two different views of the syllable (see Sevald, Dell, and Cole 1995, for a review). The first view is that syllables are *chunks* that specify their phonological content. Words are stored as strings of syllables and each syllable is represented by a symbol that indicates its sounds. The second view is that syllables are *schemas* (or frames) that specify an abstract structure independently of its phonological content (e.g. consonant-vowel-consonant). For instance, the chunk view holds that syllables like /sit/ and /bed/ are simply different chunks, because the sounds are different, but by the schema view they are similar because they share the same structure (a CVC-structure here).

Priming experiments conducted by Romani (1992), Meijer (1996), and Costa and Sebastian-Gallés (1998) have shown that the word's syllabic structure can be primed. Romani (1992) studied the effect of shared syllabic structure on naming, using an interference paradigm in which subjects prepared to repeat heard non-words. In a minority of cases, instead of the go signal to initiate repetition of the non-word, the subjects saw a word which they had to read aloud. The relation between the non-word prime and word target was manipulated. Reading latencies were faster when prime and target overlapped in syllabic structure and lexical features (such as 'margin-'kolpǝk) than when there was no overlap with respect to stress and syllabic structure (such as 'margin-es'keed). In another experiment, Romani tried to separate the contribution of syllabic structure and lexical stress using full structural overlap (such as in 'wisdom-'lerjǝt), only lexical stress overlap (such as in 'wisdom-'anlet), and no structural overlap (such as in 'wisdom-ga'pel), but no significant results were obtained. Unfortunately, several properties of the experimental design complicate the interpretation of these results. Romani used a reading paradigm and the priming results might have been influenced by the reading-specific orthography-phonology conversion processes. Furthermore, the second experiment failed to replicate the significant difference between full and no structural overlap. The problem might be methodological: the paradigm used might not be sensitive enough to replicate the results.

More recently, Meijer (1996) used the translation naming task, in which subjects translate aloud words presented visually in a foreign language (English) into their native language (Dutch). Meanwhile, primes were presented auditorily and the subject was told to ignore these words. The results showed that structural overlap led to facilitation in naming latencies. For instance, when primes shared the abstract syllabic structure with the target (e.g., 'bi.zon-'ZE.NUW in Dutch), the target was produced significantly faster compared to an unrelated priming condition (e.g. 'bor.stel-'ZE.NUW). Meijer (1996) replicated these results with mono-syllabic words. These results support the hypothesis that structural properties of the word are stored and retrieved independently from the phonemic content of the word.

Using an induction technique, Costa and Sebastian-Gallés (1998) showed that picture naming latencies were significantly faster when Spanish subjects had first read aloud words with the same syllabic structure than when these words did not share the syllabic structure with the picture target.

Sevald, Dell, and Cole (1995) also reported results that support the idea that the abstract structure of syllables is represented. In three experiments, speakers were asked to repeat pairs of phonological words as often as possible in a 4-second period. Speech rate was faster when both the structure and content of the first phonological word were repeated in the first syllable of the second one, compared to a condition in which all or most of the sounds were repeated but the structure was not. They demonstrated an advantage for repeating the initial structure (e.g. KEM TIL.FER), but this effect was the same for repeating both content and structure (e.g. TIL TIL.FER). This suggests that the benefit may be due to repeating abstract structure only, since there was no advantage for repeating both structure and content. The results support the view that syllable structure is separable from phonemic content and are consistent with a view of syllables as abstract schemas, not chunks.

In summary, the available evidence is compatible with the view that structural properties of the word are stored and retrieved independently from the phonemic content of the word. Therefore, the results of previous experiments (Ferrand, Segui, and Grainger 1996, Ferrand, Segui, and Humphreys 1997, Wheeldon and Levelt 1995) could be due either to the repetition of particular syllable strings or to the repetition of syllable structure. In other words, these results could support either the chunk view or the schema view of the syllable.

In a recent study, Ferrand and Segui (1998) tested whether the abstract syllabic structure (independently of the phonological content or segmental composition) plays a role as a unit in the construction of the phonological frame. In these experiments, the subject's task was to name words, non-words, and pictures as quickly as possible. The experimental conditions differed in terms of the type of relationship between the prime and the target. In Experiment 1, using the masked priming technique combined with picture naming (see Ferrand et al. 1996), bi- and trisyllabic target picture names were preceded by visual sequences that shared (e.g. dis%%%%%-CAR.TABLE, di%%%%%-CA.ROTTE) or did not share (e.g. di%%%%%-CAR.TABLE, dis%%%%%-CA.ROTTE) the abstract syllabic structure without the phonological content. Using exactly the same picture stimuli primed by visual sequences that corresponded or not to the full initial syllable (with its phonological content), Ferrand, Segui, and Grainger (1996) found evidence for a syllable priming effect. In Experiment 2, using a new technique called the induction technique, subjects had to perform two tasks. First, they had to read aloud a list of words or non-words (inductors) as fast as possible. At the end of each list, a picture (target) was presented on the screen and subjects had to name it as fast as possible.

Once again the experimental conditions differed in terms of the type of relationship between the set of inductors and the target: bi- and trisyllabic target picture names were preceded by visual sequences that shared (e.g. dis.cours-CAR.TABLE, di.vorce-CA.ROTTE) or did not share (e.g. di.vorce-CAR.TABLE, dis.cours-CA.ROTTE) the abstract syllabic structure without the phonological content. Experiment 2A used word inductors and Experiment 2B used non-word inductors.

The results (see Table 6.3) showed that the same picture stimuli that produced a syllabic priming effect in Ferrand, Segui, and Grainger (1996, Experiment 4) did not produce a similar effect when primes shared only the abstract syllabic structure without the phonological content. This null result provides support for the hypothesis that syllables are chunks rather than schemas. However, there is at least one major difference between our experiments and those of Sevald, Dell, and Cole (1995) that might be

TABLE 6.3. Mean naming latencies (ms) and per cent errors obtained by Ferrand and Segui (1998)

Picture targets	CV picture targets (e.g. ca.rotte)	CVC picture targets (e.g. car.table)	Mean
Experiment 1 (Masked priming)			
CV primes (e.g. di%%%%)	783 (15%)	791 (18.5%)	787
CVC primes (e.g. dis%%%%)	780 (16.5%)	785 (20%)	782.5
Mean	781.5	788	
Experiment 2A (Induction)			
CV word primes (e.g. di.vorce)	616 (9%)	671 (11%)	643.5
CVC word primes (e.g. dis.cours)	668 (12%)	621 (11%)	644.5
Mean	642	646	
Experiment 2B (Induction)			
CV non-word primes (e.g. fu.maste)	720 (13%)	755 (12%)	737.5
CVC non-word primes (e.g. fil.mor)	760 (12%)	719 (10%)	739.5
Mean	740	737	

responsible for this difference. It is the use of different methodologies: repeating aloud in the Sevald et al. study and a masked priming technique combined with naming here. Indeed, in the present experiment, a single prime was masked and did not involve overt production, while in experiments which yielded positive results, the primes were produced overtly and repeatedly either together (Sevald, Dell, and Cole 1995) or before the target (Costa 1995, 1997). Therefore, the condition that seems to be necessary to demonstrate effects of abstract syllable structure is the overt production of repeated primes.

In Experiment 2, we used a task more similar to those used by Sevald, Dell, and Cole (1995). Subjects had to perform two tasks. First, they had to read aloud a list of words or non-words (inductors) as fast as possible. At the end of each list, a picture (target) was presented on the screen and subjects had to name it as fast as possible. This induction technique (adapted from Costa and Sebastian-Gallés 1998) is based on the assumption that a sequence that repeats aspects of a plan should be easier to produce than one that requires the plan to be changed. We expected that subjects would have to plan the response and that they would benefit when aspects of the plan were repeated. Following Sevald and Dell (1994) and Sevald, Dell, and Cole (1995), a benefit for repeating some property of the utterance will be taken as evidence that this property is represented in speech planning. The induction technique was designed to confront subjects with a same initial syllabic structure using a repetition task. According to the *editing view of speech planning* (see Rosenbaum et al. 1986), a relevant structure in speech production can be retrieved faster if subjects can reuse it. If the syllabic structure is relevant as an abstract unit in speech production, its retrieval could be speeded up by reusing it through a repetition task.

When a target picture was preceded by a set of inductors that shared the same syllabic structure (without its phonological content) as the picture name's first syllable, naming latencies were faster when compared to the case in which inductors did not share the same syllabic structure with the first syllable of the picture's name. These results support the idea that the abstract structure of syllables is represented (Costa 1997, Costa and Sebastian-Gallés 1998, Meijer 1996, Sevald, Dell, and Cole 1995). The effect was entirely due to repeating abstract structure, since there was no phonological overlap. Indeed, in each experiment, subjects benefited by repeating the structure (independently of its phonological content) of an initial syllable in the next syllable of the sequence, thus confirming the results of Sevald, Dell, and Cole (1995).

A caveat to this explanation is the possibility that the effects are strategically induced by the present experimental technique. Subjects can discover a regularity in abstract syllabic structure: after having been presented with and pronounced five stimuli, words or non-words, that all start out with, for instance, a CVC-structure, the subjects might be prepared to pronounce yet a further CVC-syllable, the first syllable of the picture name, and not prepared to pronounce a syllable with a different structure. But this is unlikely for at least three reasons. First, in the debriefing, subjects were asked if they used a specific strategy to perform the task and none of them reported an ability to discern clearly the relationship between the (word and non-word) inductors and the picture targets. Second, the rhythm of presentation of the items was fast, making it difficult for the subjects to detect any regularity in the abstract syllabic structure. Third, Costa (1997) conducted similar experiments but added a neutral condition (composed of mixed CV- and CVC-structures). In four experiments, he found no evidence for an inhibition effect when subjects were not prepared to pronounce a syllable with a different structure (compared to the neutral condition). This suggests that it was not possible for the subjects to set up an expectancy of a particular syllable structure. Therefore, it seems unlikely that the present results are due to strategic anticipation effects.

The other interesting result is that this effect of syllabic structure was observed with word and non-word inductors. The processes used to produce pronounceable non-words may not be identical to normal retrieval, but the fact that the same effect is observed with both words and non-words suggests that the syllabic effects we have demonstrated are not lexical in nature. The results we report are the first instance we know of in which syllabic effects have been reliably found for both words and non-words. None of the previous reported experiments has yet provided data about the locus of the representation used in this task, that is, whether it is a lexical or non-lexical representation. To make the argument that the syllabic effects we have demonstrated are not lexical in nature, we showed that the syllabic effect still occurred with non-words that follow the phonotactic rules of the language, but have no lexical entry.

6.2.4. A mixed model of the syllable using both syllable frames and stored syllable chunks

The induction experiments provide evidence for an abstract syllabic effect in speech production in French, in contrast with the masked priming experiment which has argued against the existence of such an effect. One possible source of this difference in results is the task asked of the subject: in the masked priming technique combined with naming, subjects did not

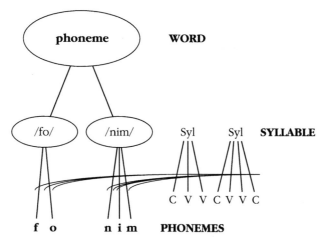

FIG. 6.2. A mixed model of the syllable.

pronounce the primes since they were heavily masked, whereas in the induction technique, subjects had to repeat aloud visual primes five times. Taking together the present results, the results obtained in French by Ferrand, Segui, and Grainger (1996), as well as the results obtained in English by Ferrand, Segui, and Humphreys (1997), the data support a mixed model of the syllable (Dell 1986, Levelt 1989, MacKay 1987), in which both frames and chunks are linked to words (see Fig. 6.2).

6.3. INTERLUDE: UNITS USED IN SPEECH PERCEPTION AND PRODUCTION

Research in languages with clear syllable boundaries such as French shows positive evidence for the listener's sensitivity to the syllable in speech perception (Kolinsky, Morais, and Cluytens 1995, Mehler et al. 1981, Pallier et al. 1993, Segui, Frauenfelder, and Mehler 1981, Segui, Dupoux, and Mehler 1990), whereas the results for English are less clear (Cutler 1993, Cutler et al. 1983, 1986). These results suggest that the syllable is probably not a universal unit of speech processing. Instead, Cutler (1993, 1997) and Otake et al. (1993) suggest that language rhythm determines the segmentation units most natural to native listeners. Thus, French has syllabic rhythm and French listeners use the syllable in segmentation, while English has stress rhythm and segmentation by English listeners is based on stress. In the case of Japanese which has a mora rhythm, Japanese listeners use the mora in segmentation.

The speech production results obtained in French by Ferrand et al. (1996) mirror those obtained in speech perception, suggesting a similarity between units involved in speech production and speech perception in French. Similarly, the mora (rather than the syllable) plays an important role in the perception (Otake et al. 1993) and production (Kubozono 1989) of Japanese (see Cutler 1995). It would therefore appear that spoken word recognition and production involve the same basic units (at least for French). In contrast with the results obtained by Ferrand, Segui, and Humphreys (1997) in speech production, several studies of speech perception have shown that syllables do not play a role in tasks in which native speakers of English monitor for fragments such as /bœ/ and /bœl/ (see Bradley, Sanchez-Casas, and Garcia-Albea 1993, Cutler et al. 1986). These results suggest that native speakers of English do not instantaneously use the syllable as an immediate segmentation unit. However, syllables may become important at later stages of processing. For instance, Bruck, Treiman, and Caravolas (1995) found evidence for a role of syllables in a non-word comparison task. In this task, subjects were asked to judge whether two successively presented non-words had sounds in common at the beginning, the middle, or at the end. For all three locations, judgements were faster when the non-words shared phonemes that constituted a syllable than when the non-words shared phonemes that constituted only part of a syllable. In an auditory lexical decision task, Corina (1992) found also significant priming for words that shared their complete first syllables. However, no priming was observed for words that shared the same number of initial phonemes but did not share their entire first syllables. Syllables also play a role in metalinguistic tasks (see e.g. Treiman and Danis 1988, Treiman and Zukowski 1990). Thus, research on speech perception has also shown that ambisyllabicity may undermine the role of syllabic units in English (e.g. Bradley, Sanchez-Casas, and Garcia-Albea 1993, Cutler et al. 1986, but see Bruck, Treiman, and Caravolas 1995, Finney, Protopapas, and Eimas 1996); it is interesting to see that this is not the case with speech production.

6.4. INTEGRATING SPEECH PERCEPTION AND SPEECH PRODUCTION: THE COARTICULATION PHENOMENON

Altmann (1997) proposed an interesting hypothesis to reconcile the results obtained on the differing role of the syllable in French and English. According to him, French sensitivity to syllabic structure is merely the consequence of the presence or absence of coarticulation. For instance, in a French word like BA.LANCE, there is little coarticulation of the /l/ on the preceding vowel; the /l/ falls in a different syllable. For the word BAL.CON, it falls on the same syllable and coarticulation on the vowel will occur. Therefore, when French speakers hear the sequence /bal/ from BAL.CON, they use the coarticulation on the vowel of the following consonant. They can thus eliminate from the search any words like BALANCE which would require the vowel to be free of coarticulation. On the other hand, in English, the /l/ in BALANCE belongs to both syllables, meaning that the vowels in both syllables will be coarticulated with the /l/. English speakers hearing the /bal/ of BAL.CONY would also be able to eliminate any words whose first syllable is not /bal/. However, they would not be able to eliminate words like BALANCE because both BALCONY and BALANCE are compatible with coarticulation of the /l/ on the preceding vowel. Where does this leave us?

Differences in syllabic structure between French and English are reflected in differences in coarticulation. Altmann (1997) suggests that speakers use the smallest coarticulation details to distinguish between alternative words in the mental lexicon. Because French words like BAL.CON and BA.LANCE can be distinguished on the basis of coarticulation details, whereas English words like BAL.CONY and BALANCE cannot, it suggests that both French and English use coarticulation information, but it helps much more in French than in English. Because speech that we hear and produce does not consist of sequences of simple, individually identifiable phonemes, it is not surprising to see that the syllable is considered to be the best candidate as a unit of articulation in French and in English. At the level of speech production the syllable captures the complex but harmonic cooperation of articulatory muscles which constitutes the rhythmical nature of speech.

7

Fossil Markers of Language Development: Phonological 'Deafnesses' in Adult Speech Processing

Emmanuel Dupoux and Sharon Peperkamp

7.1. INTRODUCTION

Recent research has demonstrated that language acquisition begins at a very early age and proceeds at an amazingly fast pace. During the first year of life, infants find out important parts of the phonological structure of their maternal language and begin to recognize and store frequent words. One crucial question for models of language acquisition concerns the mechanisms underlying these developments. In particular, the question arises as to what type of learning algorithm infants use to extract phonological and lexical

The names of the authors are in alphabetic order. Research for this chapter was supported by a Fyssen grant to the second author. We would like to thank Leticia Maria Sicuro Correa, Anne Christophe, François Dell, Jacques Mehler, Marina Nespor, and Franck Ramus for comments and discussion.

information. The more specific question we are interested in is whether learning the words of one's language is independent from learning the phonology, or whether the two processes are interleaved and interdependent.

In this chapter, we claim that cross-linguistic studies of the end-state in adults can shed light on these developmental questions. We rest our claim on the finding that early exposure to a language has a lasting impact on speech processing routines in adults. That is, listeners use a processing apparatus specifically tuned to their maternal language. Consequently, they have a lot of difficulty in dealing with sound structures that are alien to the language they heard as infants. They display what we call phonological 'deafnesses'; that is, they have trouble discriminating phonological contrasts that are not used in their native language. Moreover, the phonological 'deafnesses' are robust, in that—analogously to patterns of foreign accent in production—they are resistant to learning a second language, and even to specific training. We hypothesize that phonological 'deafnesses' originate in the acquisition during the first few years of life. We therefore propose to look at perception in adults cross-linguistically, in order to gain insight into the acquisition processes that they went through during these first years. Crucially, we propose to test the predicted 'deafnesses' in various languages according to different theoretical options regarding early language acquisition.

The outline of this chapter is as follows. In section 7.2, we provide some background data regarding, on the one hand, phonological processing and acquisition, and, on the other hand, lexical processing and acquisition. In section 7.3, we present two hypotheses concerning the relationship between phonological and lexical acquisition, i.e. Bottom-up Bootstrapping and Interactive Bootstrapping. In section 7.4, we propose to test these hypotheses by means of a cross-linguistic study on the perception of stress by speakers of languages that differ crucially in their stress rules. That is, we consider four types of regular stress systems the acquisition of which requires different sources of information, and we discuss the predictions following from the two hypotheses regarding the pattern of stress perception of adults. Finally, a summary and some concluding remarks are presented in section 7.5.

7.2. EXPERIMENTAL DATA

7.2.1. Phonological processing and acquisition

During the first year of life, infants acquire many phonological properties of their native language and lose their sensitivity to phonological contrasts that are not pertinent. In this section, we review data concerning language-specific phonological processing in adults and its relation to phonological acquisition. In particular, we deal with the segmental inventory, phonotactics, and suprasegmentals, respectively.

7.2.1.1. *Segments*

It has long been known that speech perception is influenced by phonological properties of the maternal language (Sapir 1921, Polivanov 1974). Much experimental evidence has been gathered concerning this influence. For instance, Goto (1971) has documented that Japanese listeners map American [l] and [r] onto their own, single, [r] category, and, as a result, have a lot of difficulties in discriminating between them. Similarly, the contrast between the retroflex and dental stops [ʈ]—[t̪] is very difficult for the English, but not for the Hindi speaker (Werker and Tees 1984*b*). This contrast is, in fact, phonemic in Hindi, whereas neither of the stop consonants involved occurs in English; rather, English uses the alveolar stop [t]. Note, however, that not all foreign contrasts are difficult (Polka 1991, Best, McRoberts, and Sithole 1988). For instance, Best et al. found that English subjects do not have difficulties in discriminating different Zulu clicks from one another.

The Perceptual Assimilation Model (Best 1994) aims at explaining these differences. In particular, it states that a foreign sound is assimilated to an existing segment in the native language if the acoustic characteristics of both sounds are close enough. In this case, listeners are only able to judge whether the foreign sound is a good or a bad exemplar of the segment to which it has assimilated, but they do not have access to its detailed phonetic character-istics. Consequently, two distinct foreign sounds that are assimilated to the same segment in the native language and that are equally bad exemplars of this segment will be very difficult to discriminate. Such is the case for Japanese speakers with the American [l]—[r] contrast, both [l] and [r] being assimilated to Japanese [r], as well as for the English speakers with the Hindi [ʈ]—[t̪] contrast, both [ʈ] and [t̪] being assimilated to English [t]. By contrast, foreign sounds that are too distant from all of the native segments will not be assimilated at all and listeners will be able to make fine phonetic discriminations between them. This is illustrated by the successful discrimination of different Zulu clicks by native speakers of English.

The effects of the maternal inventory on adult perception are very robust, and resist the acquisition of a second language. Thus, even early and highly fluent bilinguals have difficulties with non-native vowel contrasts, as shown in Pallier, Bosch, and Sebastián-Gallés (1997). In this study, subjects are Spanish-Catalan bilinguals who have begun to acquire their second language between 4 and 6 years of age, and have used it extensively thereafter. The two languages differ as to the number of vowel phonemes; Spanish has a five-vowel system, while Catalan uses two more vowels. Crucially, subjects whose native language is Spanish are shown to use exclusively the more restricted Spanish vowel system for the purposes of speech perception and spoken word recognition.

Finally, electrophysiological studies suggest that effects of the phoneme inventory occur very early during on-line speech processing. Thus, Näätänen et al. (1997) presented repeated sequences of the same vowel, followed occasionally by a change in vowel. They found that the Mismatch Negativity (an electrophysiological component that correlates with detection of a change in stimulation) is modulated as a function of whether the vowel is part or not of the phoneme inventory of the language. That is, 100 to 240 ms after the vowel onset, the perceptual system is already influenced by the vowel inventory of the native language.

All in all, these data suggest that listeners use a set of language-specific phoneme categories during speech perception. This raises the question as to how and when infants acquire their native segmental inventory. Concerning the age at which infants tune to the inventory of their language, Kuhl et al. (1992) have shown that American and Swedish 6-month-old infants react specifically to vowels that are prototypic in their maternal language. Furthermore, Polka and Werker (1994) found that at the same age, infants begin to lose their sensitivity for non-native vowel contrasts. That is, 6-month-old English-acquiring infants fail to discriminate between the German lax vowels /ʏ/ and /ʊ/ as well as between their tense counterparts /y/ and /u/; the first, front, vowel in each pair is not part of the English inventory. Between 10 and 12 months, infants similarly lose the ability to discriminate non-native consonantal contrasts (Werker and Tees 1984*a*). Regarding the way in which infants acquire their segmental inventory, Kuhl et al. (1997) found that mothers addressing their infants produce acoustically more extreme vowels than they do when addressing adults, resulting in a 'stretching' of the vowel space. This shows that language input to infants provides well-specified information about the phonemes, and suggests that a purely statistical extraction algorithm could establish prototypes for the sounds of the native language.

7.2.1.2. *Phonotactics*

Language phonologies differ in properties other than the inventory of phonemes. Notably, they differ in the way in which phonemes can co-occur in words. These *phonotactic* properties appear to influence speech processing routines, in that non-words with a high phonotactic probability are processed faster and more accurately than non-words with a low phonotactic probability (Brown and Hildum 1956, Vitevitch et al. 1997, Gathercole et al. 1999). Furthermore, phonotactics have been shown to bias the perception of individual segments. For instance, Massaro and Cohen (1983) found that synthetic stimuli that are ambiguous between [r] and [l] tend to be perceived as [r] when preceded by [t] and as [l] when preceded by [s]. The interpretation given by Massaro and Cohen is that perception is biased towards segments that yield the legal clusters [tr] and [sl], rather than the illegal clusters [tl] and [sr] (see also Pitt 1998). Similarily, Hallé et al. (1998) found that illegal onset clusters in French are perceived as legal ones. In particular, illegal [dl] and [tl] are perceived as legal [gl] and [kl], respectively.

It has even been reported that in some contexts, illegal sequences of phonemes yield perception of illusory segments. For instance, Japanese syllables cannot have complex onsets (except for consonant-glide onsets) and cannot have codas (except for nasal consonants and the first half of geminates). Dupoux et al. (1999) found that Japanese subjects report the presence of an epenthetic vowel [u] between consonants in non-words like [ebzo]. They also found that Japanese subjects have problems discriminating between, for instance, [ebzo] and [ebuzo]. This was found even in subjects who were quite proficient in French, a language which authorizes both coda consonants and complex onsets. Moreover, in an electrophysiological study, Dehaene-Lambertz, Dupoux, and Gout (2000) found that the effect for phonotactics arises as early as that of the phoneme inventory investigated by Näätänen et al. (1997) and reported above. These results, then, suggest that phonotactics plays a role so important as to create the illusory perception of segments.

As to infants' sensitivity to phonotactic properties, there is evidence that it equally arises during the first year of life. For instance, Friederici and Wessels (1993) showed that 9-month-old Dutch infants prefer to listen to phonotactically legal words rather than to illegal ones. Similarly, Jusczyk, Luce, and Charles-Luce (1994) found that 9-month-old American infants, when listening to monosyllabic non-words, prefer those with a high-probability phonotactic pattern rather than those with a low-probability phonotactic pattern. Jusczyk et al. (1993) reported, furthermore, that 9-month-old American infants listen longer to unfamiliar English words than to Dutch words. The latter contain segments and sequences that are illegal in English, suggesting again that infants of this age are sensitive to the phonotactics of their language. This is corroborated by the finding that no differences are found when the stimuli are low-pass filtered, hence do not contain any segmental information. Note, however, that we do not yet know whether at the same age, the presentation of illegal clusters yields the perception of illusory segments as documented for adults.

7.2.1.3. *Suprasegmentals*

Finally, languages differ in suprasegmentals and, in particular, in the use of word-internal prosody. Two examples might illustrate this. First, consider stress in Spanish and French. In Spanish, stress falls on one of the word's last three syllables (Navarro Tomas 1965), and there are minimal pairs of words that differ only as far as the location of stress is concerned, for instance *bébe* '(she or he) drinks'—*bebé* 'baby'. In French, by contrast, stress does not carry lexical information. Rather, it predictably falls on the word's final vowel (Schane 1968, Dell 1973). Thus, speakers of Spanish have to process and represent stress to identify the lexical item(s) intended by the speaker. Speakers of French, by contrast, do not need to process stress, at least not in the same way.[1] Dupoux et al. (1997) found that French listeners are 'deaf' to stress. That is, French listeners—as opposed to Spanish listeners—exhibit great difficulties in discriminating non-words that differ only in the location of stress. Another example of word-internal prosody concerns the use of vowel length. In Japanese, but not in French, vowel length is contrastive. Thus, we find minimal pairs in Japanese such as [to] 'door' and [too] 'tower'. In French, by contrast, vowel length is not used to make lexical distinctions. Accordingly, Dupoux et al. (1999) found that French, but not Japanese listeners, have great difficulties in distinguishing between non-words that differ only in vowel length.

Little is known about the acquisition of suprasegmentals in young infants. However, there is evidence that newborns are already sensitive to some global suprasegmental properties. In particular, it appears that on the basis of these properties, they distinguish between their native language and a foreign language, as well as between different foreign languages. Thus, Mehler et al. (1988, 1996) found that French infants discriminate both between French and Russian utterances and between English and Italian utterances. The stimuli were low-pass filtered, indicating that discrimination can be achieved on the basis of suprasegmental information only. Similarly, Moon, Cooper, and Fifer (1993) found that English-acquiring newborns prefer to listen to English rather than to Spanish sentences, while Spanish-acquiring newborns show the reverse preference pattern (see also Nazzi, Bertoncini, and Mehler 1998).

---

[1] Rather, stress may be used as a cue to word segmentation (Trubetzkoy 1939, Rietveld 1980).

Furthermore, Jusczyk et al. (1993) showed that 6-month-old American infants prefer to listen to English rather than to Norwegian words, while they fail to show a preference for English words as opposed to Dutch words. These results also hold when the stimuli are low-pass filtered, suggesting that infants are sensitive to suprasegmental properties that are typical of their native language; English and Dutch indeed share many of these properties, whereas Norwegian suprasegmentals differ substantially from those of English. Along the same lines, Jusczyk, Cutler, and Redantz (1993) found that 9-month-old American infants prefer to listen to disyllables with the metrical pattern which is predominant in English, i.e. with stress on the first rather than on the second syllable. However, this experiment has not been carried out with a language that shows the reverse metrical pattern. It could, therefore, be the case that the obtained preference of American infants stems from a universal bias, rather than being related to the predominant metrical pattern of disyllables in the native language.

Finally, it is currently unknown at what age infants begin to exhibit the type of 'deafness' to foreign prosodic contrasts that has been found in adults.

7.2.2. Lexical processing and acquisition

During the first year of life, infants not only acquire many phonological properties of their language, they also begin to build a lexicon. In this section, we review data regarding lexical processing and acquisition.

It has been argued that in adult speech processing, function words and content words are processed differently. For instance, Friederici (1985) reported that in a word-monitoring experiment, responses to function words were faster than responses to content words. This suggests that function words and content words are not stored together. In fact, given that the set of function words is extremely limited, search procedures within this set are faster than within the set of content words. Similarly, Neville, Mills, and Lawson (1992) found that the brain elicits qualitatively different electrophysiological responses to function words and content words, respectively.

There is recent experimental evidence that the distinction between function words and content words is acquired early in life. In particular, Shady, Jusczyk, and Gerken (1988) (cf. Jusczyk 1999) found that 10½-month-old American infants listen for a shorter time to passages in which function words are replaced by non-words having the same phonological properties. By contrast, they do not listen for a shorter time if content words are replaced by non-words having the same phonological properties. This suggests that, at this age, infants not only make a distinction between function words and content words, but also recognize the actual function words of English. By contrast, they do not know the semantics of these words, as evidenced by a follow-up experiment. That is, infants listened equally long to normal passages and to passages in which the function words were exchanged among each other, leading to ungrammatical sentences.

Gerken (1996) and Morgan, Shi, and Allopenna (1996) proposed that infants acquire function words before content words and that they do so on the basis of phonological cues. Specifically, function words typically share phonological properties that set them apart from content words. In English, for instance, function words are characterized by having a short duration and low relative amplitude, a simple syllable structure, and centralized vowels. Moreover, they tend to occur utterance-initially. Shi (1995) showed that taken together, these cues are sufficient for a self-organizing neural network to classify words as function words or content words with an accuracy of 85–90 per cent. Shi, Morgan, and Allopenna (1998) obtained similar results with two unrelated languages, i.e. Mandarin Chinese and Turkish, suggesting that function words can universally be set apart from content words on the basis of acoustic, phonological and distributional cues only.

As to the beginning of the compilation of a lexicon of content words, Jusczyk and Aslin (1995) showed that it could lie as early as 7½ months of age. That is, infants of this age listen for longer to passages containing a word to which they are habituated than to passages that do not contain such a word. The same results are obtained if infants are habituated to passages containing several instances of certain words and tested on these words in isolation. Thus, infants listen for longer to words that are contained in the passages they have heard previously than to words that are not contained in the passages. Moreover, words appeared to be stored in a detailed phonetic representation. For instance, when trained on *cup*, infants show no recognition of *tup*, which differs only as far as the place of articulation of the first segment is concerned.

Benedict (1979) reported—on the basis of comprehension tests as well as observational data in mothers' diary notes—that English-learning infants of 10 months comprehend around ten words; this figure grows to around forty at 12 months, and to 100 or more at 16 months. Recent experimental work is consistent with this report. For instance, Hallé and Boysson-Bardies (1994) found that at 10 months of age, French infants prefer to listen to a list of twelve familiar rather than to a list of twelve unfamiliar words. More surprisingly, Mandel, Jusczyk, and Pisoni (1995) reported that 4½-month-old infants recognize their own name. Specifically, infants were shown to prefer to listen to their own name rather than to names with the same number of syllables and the same stress pattern. Moreover, such preference disappears if the initial phoneme of the infant's name is changed (Nazzi and Jusczyk, personal communication). Hence, recognition of the proper name of the infant seems to be based on precise segmental information rather than on global prosodic properties.

7.2.3. Open questions

As is apparent in the above review, both phonological acquisition and lexical acquisition begin very early in life and develop rapidly. However, many questions regarding the mechanisms that are responsible for such speedy acquisition remain open and the proposed learning mechanisms contain paradoxical circularities. On the one hand, the acquisition of certain phonological properties, such as phonotactics or the typical prosodic shape of words, seems to require the prior acquisition of a lexicon of a reasonable size in order to extract some stable statistics. On the other hand, lexical acquisition itself seems to require some prior phonological knowledge, such as phoneme categories and language-specific word boundary cues. This raises questions regarding the relative time-course of phonological and lexical acquisition, as well as the potential interactions between the two processes. In the next section, we examine the various theoretical alternatives.

7.3. SETTING UP THE RESEARCH FRAMEWORK

7.3.1. Assumptions and hypotheses

Before discussing different theoretical pathways in early language acquisition, let us first describe three underlying assumptions (cf. Mehler, Dupoux, and Segui 1990). First, infants have an innate *universal phonetic representation*. This representation encodes speech sounds and keeps all phonetic distinctions that can in principle be used contrastively, while reducing the importance of non-linguistic variables such as talker voice, length of vocal tract, and background noise. Second, infants similarly acquire a *lexicon* of word forms during the first years of life. This lexicon distinguishes between content words and function words. Third, during the first years of life, infants acquire a language-specific *prelexical representation*. This representation is intermediate between the universal phonetic representation and the lexicon. It is discrete and encodes only a small subset of those segmental and suprasegmental distinctions that are available at the universal phonetic level. It thus specifies the format under which the lexical items are stored. Once acquired, the prelexical representation is assimilatory; that is, foreign sound patterns are assimilated to the closest native sound pattern.[2] This holds not only for the segmental inventory, as in the Perceptual Assimilation Model of Best (1994), but also for all other aspects of phonological structure, such as phonotactics and suprasegmentals. For instance, foreign words that contain illegal syllabic structure will be regularized through the assimilation to existing syllables in the native language (Dupoux et al. 1999). Finally, the prelexical representation is crystallized in the adult; that is, it remains stable even after extensive exposure to a second language. All these properties result in patterns of phonological 'deafness' for certain non-native contrasts, i.e. those contrasts involving sounds that are assimilated to a single sound pattern in the prelexical representation.

Within this framework, the acquisition problem can be stated as follows: at birth, the language-specific prelexical representation and lexicons of content words and function words are unavailable to the infant, while a few years later, the acquisition of these components has been completed; how, then, has this been accomplished? The paradox is that each one of these components of the processing system seems to require the prior acquisition of the other one before it can itself be acquired. On the one hand, lexical acquisition seems to require a language-specific prelexical representation. In fact, a given word can surface in a near infinity of phonetic forms that—if the lexicon were constructed on the basis of a universal phonetic representation—would all be mapped onto separate lexical entries. On the other hand, in order to acquire a prelexical representation, infants seem to need access to word meanings in order to decide which variation is pertinent; that is, they need to have a lexicon. This bootstrapping problem is one of the most puzzling questions in early language development. In the following, we discuss two theoretical possibilities to solve the puzzle. The first one we dub *Bottom-up Bootstrapping*, the second one *Interactive Bootstrapping*.

In Bottom-up Bootstrapping, acquisition begins on the basis of the acoustic signal only, and proceeds sequentially; once a component is acquired, the next component comes into play, using only information available at lower levels (cf. Mehler, Dupoux, and Segui 1990, Christophe and Dupoux 1996, Mehler et al. 1996). In our framework, this would mean

[2] If the foreign sound is too far away from any native sound (as in the case of Zulu clicks for English speakers), it is not assimilated but perceived on a purely phonetic basis (see Best, McRoberts, and Sithole 1988).

that the prelexical representation would be acquired first, exclusively on the basis of information that is available in the universal phonetic representation. This representation would then be used to extract words. Given that only partial linguistic information would be available for the compilation of the prelexical representation, it would not necessarily be fully optimized for the native language. In particular, in the absence of lexical information, evidence based on word meanings would not be taken into account. Allophones, for instance, would generally be encoded separately rather than as instances of their corresponding phonemes.[3] In other words, the prelexical representation would contain some redundancy.

In Interactive Bootstrapping, by contrast, lexical and phonological acquisition begin simultaneously and interact with one another. In our framework, this would mean that part of the phonological representation would be acquired bottom-up through inspection of the phonetic representation, and part would be acquired on the basis of lexical information. Similarly, the first words would be acquired from the universal phonetic representation, while they would be recoded more and more abstractly as more phonology becomes available. Thus, in Interactive Bootstrapping, each component could in principle be optimized for all language-specific properties, all relevant sources of information being available. As to the prelexical representation, its acquisition would continue until all redundancy had been removed. In other words, all and only those distinctions that are used contrastively would be encoded.

7.3.2. The acquisition of the prelexical representation: a typology

In the remaining part of this chapter, we compare Bottom-up Bootstrapping and Interactive Bootstrapping by focusing on the acquisition of the prelexical representation. The question we investigate concerns the types of information that allow infants to compile the prelexical representation and decide whether a given phonological distinction is to be kept or not in this representation. The prelexical representation is shown in Fig. 7.1; the square brackets represent the utterance boundaries. The four types of information that could be taken into account during the compilation of the prelexical representation are numbered in increasing order of complexity. First of all, Type I information can be extracted from the universal phonetic representation. Type II information can be extracted from the prelexical representation

---

[3] In Peperkamp and Dupoux (in press *a*), we argue that certain allophones can be detected on the basis of the phonetic representation only.

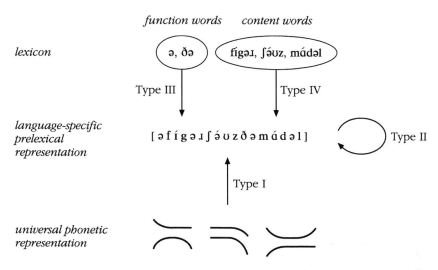

F IG. 7.1. Compilation of prelexical representation in early language acquisition.

itself by making reference to already acquired phonological properties. Type III information regards the distribution and shape of function words. Finally, Type IV information concerns the location of content word boundaries in the utterance.

Bottom-up Bootstrapping and Interactive Bootstrapping make different predictions as to the types of information that can affect the compilation of the prelexical representation. That is, according to Bottom-up Bootstrapping, only low-level information, i.e. Type I and Type II, can affect prelexical acquisition; according to Interactive Bootstrapping, by contrast, high-level information, i.e. Types III and IV, might also come into play. 'Deafnesses' originating from Type I and Type II information, then, would support both Bottom-up Bootstrapping and Interactive Bootstrapping, while 'deafnesses' originating from Type III and Type IV information would provide evidence in favour of Interactive Bootstrapping only.

We can now classify phonological generalizations according to the type of information that is required in order for them to be observed. Thus, a phonological generalization of Type I is a generalization that can be observed on the basis of Type I information, and so forth. We exemplify one by one the four types of generalizations and determine the corresponding deafnesses that are or might be attested. First, regarding Type I, certain generalizations relevant to the prelexical representation are directly observable on the basis of the universal phonetic representation. For instance, there is some evidence that the distribution of vowels around language-specific prototypes is observable at an acoustic level (Kuhl et al. 1997). Consequently, one observes an early prelexical acquisition of prototypic vowels in the language (Kuhl et al.

1992), yielding language-specific 'deafnesses' to contrasts of vowels that are phonetically different but map onto the same prototype (e.g. Pallier, Bosch and Sebastián-Gallés 1997).

Second, Type II generalizations require the prior acquisition of other aspects of the phonology of the language. For instance, German has both voiced and unvoiced obstruents, but syllable-finally only the latter can occur (Wiese 1996). In order for German infants to observe this regularity, they should have access to German syllable structure. Thus, once syllable structure is encoded in the prelexical representation, the regularity concerning the absence of syllable-final voiced obstruents can be made. Provided that the latter observation feeds back on the compilation of the prelexical representation, the voicing feature will not be encoded in the prelexical representation for syllable-final consonants. German adults, then, are predicted to exhibit a 'deafness' to syllable-final voicing contrasts.

Similarly, in Italian, vowel length is allophonic: vowels are lengthened if and only if they occur in an open stressed syllable (Vogel 1982). In order to find this regularity, infants need to have acquired both the distinction between open and closed syllables and the distinction between stressed and unstressed syllables in their language. Once such information is contained in the prelexical representation, the higher-order observation (that is the correlation of syllable structure, stress, and vowel length) becomes available. Again, provided that this higher-order observation can feed back on the compilation of the prelexical representation, vowel length is predicted to be removed from the prelexical representation. As a consequence, Italian-speaking adults should have difficulties distinguishing between short and long vowels; that is, they should exhibit a 'deafness' to vowel length contrasts.

Third, Type III generalizations can be observed only once the distinction between content words and function words is made. For instance, in Dutch, words can begin with any vowel except schwa. The prohibition on word-initial schwa, though, does not hold for function words, witness examples such as *een* [ən] 'a' and *het* [ət] 'it' (Booij 1995). Once infants can extract function words out of the speech stream, they can observe that the remaining strings do not begin with schwa. If this regularity is taken into account during the compilation of the prelexical representation, we might expect that in adult speech perception, foreign content words with an initial schwa are misperceived and assimilated to a legal word-initial vowel.

Fourth, in order for Type IV generalizations to be observed, the boundaries of content words have to be available. For instance, in northern varieties of Standard Italian, the contrast between [s] and [z] is allophonic; that is, within words, [z] surfaces before voiced consonants and in intervocalic position, while [s] occurs everywhere else (Camilli 1965, Nespor and Vogel

1986). In intervocalic position within phrases, then, both [z] and [s] occur, depending on the presence or absence of a word boundary within the sequence. This is illustrated in (1).

(1) *a.* bu[z]ecca   'bovine tripes'
     b. bu[s] ecologico   'ecological bus'

Therefore, infants need to segment utterances into separate words in order to find the generalization concerning the distribution of [s] and [z].[4] If word boundaries or lexical knowledge can influence the compilation of the prelexical representation, one might expect that intervocalic [z] will be recoded as underlying /s/. Italian-speaking adults, then, should exhibit 'deafness' to the contrast between word-internal intervocalic [s] and [z].

The inventory presented above does not exhaust the type of 'deafnesses' that could theoretically arise. We might envision cases where only knowledge of syntactic categories or morphological decomposition can inform the prelexical level that some distinction is irrelevant and hence can be removed from the representation. The predictions are the same: if such high-level information is available to infants while they are compiling the prelexical phonological representation, then a 'deafness' to this type of distinction should be observed in adults.

In the examples given above, different phenomena (neutralization, allophonic variation, phonotactics) were involved. Hence, testing these four types of predicted 'deafness' would involve using different materials and experimental paradigms. In the remaining part of this chapter, we exemplify the four-way distinction with the stress system, which allows us to construct a single experimental test that can be applied cross-linguistically.

7.4. A CROSS-LINGUISTIC TEST CASE: STRESS 'DEAFNESS'

One domain in which we find limited capacities to perceive phonological contrasts that are not pertinent in the native language is that of stress. For instance, recall from section 7.2.1.3 that French listeners have great difficulties perceiving the difference between non-words that are distinguished only with regard to the position of stress, such as

---

[4] We abstract away from problems posed by prefixes for the distribution of [s] and [z] (see e.g. Nespor and Vogel 1986, Peperkamp 1997).

vásuma—vasúma—vasumá (Dupoux et al. 1997). In contrast, Spanish subjects have no problem in making this distinction.

In our framework, the stress 'deafness' in French adults could arise as a consequence of the way infants acquire stress. In French, stress is predictable in that main stress always falls on the word's final syllable (Schane 1968, Dell 1973), a generalization that can be inferred by infants on the basis of the universal phonetic representation. Indeed, since—as we will show in detail in section 7.4.1—all utterances end with a stressed syllable, infants can deduce that stress is not contrastive by paying attention to the ends of utterances only. Therefore, they will not encode stress in the prelexical representation, and as adults they will exhibit a 'deafness' to stress contrasts. In Spanish, by contrast, stress falls on one of the word's last three syllables. Although there are certain restrictions on stress placement, the existence of minimal pairs such as *bebé* 'baby' – *bébe* 'drinks' shows that there is no way to reliably predict the stress location in all cases. Consequently, stress will be encoded in the prelexical representation.

French and Spanish hence represent two extreme cases: one in which stress is Type I predictable, and one in which it is unpredictable. In this section, we will explore languages that display stress regularities of the four types defined in section 7.3. The patterns of stress perception by adult speakers of these languages will help to determine the types of information that are taken into account in the compilation of the prelexical representation during infancy, and hence to draw conclusions regarding the validity of the two bootstrapping hypotheses.

Before going into this, however, we should define what is meant exactly by studying the perception of stress cross-linguistically. We will examine stress as it is realized in the subjects' native language, and hence test the perception of the acoustic cues that are typical of stress in the language under consideration. Crucially, we make sure that we do not manipulate variables that could be perceived as something else than stress in that language. The acoustic correlates of stress are loudness, pitch, and duration (Lehiste 1970), but not every language uses all three cues to realize stress. For instance, in languages with contrastive vowel length, duration is avoided as a correlate of stress (Hayes 1995). Therefore, when processing a foreign language with duration as phonetic correlate of stress, speakers of languages with contrastive length might map stressed vowels onto long vowels and unstressed vowels onto short vowels. Thus, they can assimilate stress to length, and consequently, stress 'deafness' will not be observed. Similarly, tone languages typically avoid pitch as a correlate of stress. Thus, when processing a foreign language with pitch as phonetic correlate of stress, speakers of tone languages might map stressed vowels onto high-tone vowels and unstressed vowels onto low-tone vowels. In other words, they can assimilate stress to tone, and again, stress 'deafness' will not be observed. For convenience's sake, we will continue to use the term stress 'deafness' in referring to 'deafness' to the phonetic correlate(s) of stress as present in the subject's native language. For an experimental paradigm that enables testing the perception of stress in adult speakers, see Dupoux, Peperkamp, and Sebastián-Gallés (2001).

We will now turn to languages with different stress rules and spell out our predictions concerning the perception of stress by native speakers of these languages. The languages are classified according to the type of regularity presented by their stress rules.

7.4.1. Type I

First, let us look at languages in which the stress rule corresponds to a Type I generalization. French is a case at hand, the stress rule ('stress the final vowel') making reference only to phonetic notions. Notice that even clitics, which are typically unstressed elements, attract stress if they are phrase-final.[5] This is illustrated in (2).

(2) *a.* coupez   [kupé]   'cut$_{IMP-PL}$'
    b. coupez-les   [kupelé]   'cut$_{IMP-PL}$-them'
    c. coupez-vous-en [kupevuzá]   'cut$_{IMP-PL}$-yourself$_{PL-DAT}$-of them'

Moreover, although eurhythmic principles induce destressing rules in French, the final and strongest stress of an utterance is never reduced (Dell 1984). Hence, neither the occurrence of enclitics nor destressing interferes with the phonetic observability of the stress rule. Therefore, all utterances in French have stress on their final syllable.[6] Infants, then, can infer that stress is not contrastive, hence, need not be encoded in the prelexical representation.

[5] Exceptions are *je* 'I' and *ce* 'it'. These clitics have schwa as their vowel, which is deleted in phrase-final position, as in *suis-je* [sɥíʒ] 'am I' and *est-ce* [és] 'is it'. In other words, these two clitics do not undermine the surface observability of stress falling on the final vowel either.

[6] In southern varieties of French, utterance-final words can end in an unstressed schwa. In these varieties, the acquisition of the stress regularity is more complex, in that infants first have to acquire the difference between full vowels and schwa. Consequently, the stress 'deafness' is of the second rather than of the first type.

Note also that, alternatively, French has been characterized as having phrasal stress, with stress falling on phrase-final syllables (Grammont 1965). The question as to whether French has word stress or phrasal stress is irrelevant to our point, given that under both assumptions, all utterances end in a stressed syllable.

Pitta-Pitta (Blake 1979, Hayes 1995) is another example of a language with a stress rule that should give rise to Type I 'deafness'. This Australian language has fixed word-initial stress (3), and there are no proclitics.

(3) *a.* kárru   'boy'
     b. mílilpu   'eyebrow'
     c. yápariri   'young man'

Pitta-Pitta has no monosyllabic words; stress clash, therefore, never occurs. Thus, all utterances have stress on the first syllable. Given that stress is predictable and observable on the basis of the universal phonetic representation, both the Bottom-up Bootstrapping hypothesis and the Interactive Bootstrapping hypothesis predict that stress is not encoded in the prelexical representation and that speakers of Pitta-Pitta exhibit stress 'deafness'.

7.4.2. Type II

An example of a stress system involving a Type II regularity is presented by Fijian (Schütz 1985, Dixon 1988, Hayes 1995). In this Austronesian language, word stress falls on the final syllable if it is heavy; otherwise stress is penultimate. The language has only two syllable types, (C)VV and (C)V, where the former is heavy and the latter is light. Suffixes are within the stress domain,[7] and there are no enclitics. Examples from Dixon's (1988) description of the Boumaa dialect are given in (4); syllable boundaries are indicated by dots.

(4) *a.* lú.a   lu.á.ca   'vomit—vomit on$_{TR}$'
     b. te.ʔe.vúː   te.ʔe.vúː.na   'start—start$_{TR}$'
     c. pu.lóu   pu.lóu.na   'be covered—cover$_{TR}$'

The language permits monosyllabic words provided they are heavy. If a monosyllable is preceded by a word ending in a long vowel or a diphthong, a stress clash arises. We do not know if and how stress clash is resolved in Fijian. Clearly, if the second stress undergoes destressing, utterance-final stress clash configurations disrupt the surface stress pattern. Abstracting away from this potential disturbance, however, we can formulate the following surface generalization: in utterances that end in a word with a final long vowel

---

[7] Some suffixes and sequences of suffixes, however, form separate stress domains. That is, they behave as independent words phonologically (cf. Dixon 1988).

or a diphthong, the final syllable is stressed, while in utterances that end in a word with a final short vowel, the penultimate syllable is stressed. Once infants have acquired the distinction between heavy and light syllables, they can observe the stress regularity. Speakers of Fijian, then, are predicted to exhibit stress 'deafness' if this regularity is taken into account during the compilation of the prelexical representation. As with the Type I regularities, this follows from both the Bottom-up Bootstrapping hypothesis and the Interactive Bootstrapping hypothesis.

7.4.3. Type III

In many languages, stress is predictable and observable *modulo* the occurrence of clitics. In fact, contrary to the situation in French described in section 7.4.1, clitics are typically unstressed, regardless of their position in the utterance. Consider, for instance, the case of Hungarian. In this language, stress falls on the word-initial syllable, and clitics are systematically unstressed (Vago 1980). This is illustrated in (5).

(5) *a.* emberek   [émberek] 'men'
    b. az emberek [azémberek] 'the men'

In Hungarian, then, utterances that begin with a clitic have stress on the second syllable, while all other utterances have stress on the first syllable. Hungarian has monosyllabic content words, but stress clash resolution does not interfere with this surface stress pattern (Vogel 1988).

In order for prelexical infants to discover the stress rule of Hungarian, they should strip off utterance-initial function words and look for generalizations in the remaining string. That is, after removing the initial function word(s), infants can discover that the remaining string of content words always begins with a stressed syllable. Bottom-up Bootstrapping states that such a discovery cannot affect the compilation of the prelexical representation. In fact, according to this hypothesis, only low-level phonetic and phonological information is taken into account during the compilation of the prelexical representation. As a consequence, adult speakers of Hungarian should not exhibit stress 'deafness', even though stress is not contrastive in their language. By contrast, Interactive Bootstrapping states that all possible sources of information—including those pertaining to the distinction between function words and content words—are used in order to determine which contrasts are pertinent in the language. According to this latter hypothesis, stress would not be encoded in the prelexical representation; hence, adult Hungarians should exhibit stress 'deafness'.

7.4.4. Type IV

Certain stress rules are observable only if the boundaries of content words are available. Consider, for instance, Piro, an Arawakan language in which word stress is on the penultimate syllable (Matteson 1965, Hayes 1995). Examples from Matteson (1965) are given in (6).

(6) *a.* nsó   'genipa'
     b. wálo   'rabbit'
     c. ruʈɕíʈɕa   'he observes taboo'
     d. ʧiyaháta   'he cries'

Given that there are no enclitics, the following generalization emerges. In utterances ending in a monosyllabic word, the final syllable is stressed, whereas in all other utterances, the penultimate syllable is stressed. In order to extract the rule regarding penultimate stress, prelexical infants should have access to content word boundaries. Therefore, the Interactive Bootstrapping hypothesis but not the Bottom-up Bootstrapping hypothesis predicts that speakers of Piro exhibit stress 'deafness', since only in the former can word boundaries influence the compilation of the prelexical representation.[8]

Another example of a purely phonological stress rule that is observable only if the boundaries of content words are available is presented by Nyawaygi (Dixon 1983, Hayes 1995). In this Australian language, stress is assigned at the left edge of words, as follows. In words beginning with a heavy syllable, stress falls on the first syllable (7a). In words beginning with a light syllable, stress falls on the second syllable if the word contains three or five syllables (7b) and on the first syllable if the word contains two or four syllables (7c). Notice that coda consonants are weightless in Nyawaygi; heavy syllables are syllables containing a long vowel.

(7) *a.* *heavy initial syllable*:
          ŋú:ɟu   'fish'
          ɟíːbaʈi   'south'
     b. *light initial syllable, uneven number of syllables*:
          bulbíri   'quail'
     c. *light initial syllable, even number of syllables*:
          ɟíɲa   'man'
          bíyaɟala   'water snake'

---

[8] For the sake of simplicity, we deliberately chose a language without enclitics. Of course, a language with penultimate stress that has enclitics would fall into the same class of our 'deafness' typology, since lexical segmentation includes clitic stripping.

Stress clash does not occur, since all words are minimally disyllabic and no word has final stress. Furthermore, there are no proclitics. Thus, all utterances whose first word begins with a heavy syllable have initial stress, whereas all other utterances have stress on either the first or the second syllable, depending on the number of syllables in the first word. In order to extract this generalization, infants not only need to be sensitive to syllable weight, but they also need to have access to the number of syllables in the utterance's first word; hence, they must be able to segment the first word out of the utterances. Therefore, as with speakers of Piro, native speakers of Nyawaygi are predicted to exhibit stress 'deafness' according to Interactive Bootstrapping but not according to Bottom-up Bootstrapping.

7.4.5. A caveat

Before closing our typology of stress 'deafness', we would like to raise the following caveat. Our reasoning is based on the assumption that the stress pattern at utterance edges allows infants to make inferences about the general stress rule of their language. For instance, we postulate that from the observation that all *utterances* end with a stressed syllable, infants will infer that all *words* end with a stressed syllable. This, of course, may be unwarranted. Phonological rules can indeed apply at some phrasal edge only. In that case, a regularity appears at some utterance edge which does not hold, however, for individual words. An example is provided by the tonal system of Slave. In this language, there are two tones, high and low. At the end of intonational phrases, the distinction is neutralized; the final word necessarily surfaces with a low tone (Rice 1987). If infants were to examine the end of utterances only, they would incorrectly conclude that there is no tone in their language.

Yet, stress seems to be special, in that—to the best of our knowledge—this kind of situation does not arise with stress rules. On the contrary, in the cases in which stress is modified at a phrasal edge, the modification seems to enhance the regularity of the stress pattern instead of obscuring it. For instance, recall from section 7.4.1 that in French, phrase-final enclitics are stressed. This pattern reinforces the utterance-final regularity caused by the word-final stress pattern of French. By contrast, we have found no language in which, analogously to tone in Slave, contrastive stress is neutralized at a phrasal edge. It should be noted that if our model is correct, there cannot be such a language. In fact, if it existed, infants would use the edge regularity to infer that stress is predictable, and hence they would become stress 'deaf';

this, then, would have the effect that stress contrasts would be lost within one generation.

To conclude, the absence of languages with contrastive stress that is neutralized at some phrasal edge is quite critical for our model. If such languages exist, we have to revise our proposal, by offering another, more complex, learning principle that allows infants to acquire the stress rule of their language. Note that even in that case, our hierarchy of languages would still be pertinent to describe the relative observability of these stress rules from the infant's viewpoint. For instance, stress in French (Type 1) would still be easier to acquire than stress in Nyawaygi (Type 4).

7.5. SUMMARY AND CONCLUSION

We have shown that cross-linguistic research of adult speech perception can be brought to bear on issues of language acquisition. In particular, it might allow us to solve some of the most puzzling issues in early language development, namely, the paradoxical fact that the acquisition of each processing component seems to require the prior acquisition of the other components.

As a first step to solve the acquisition paradox, we proposed to distinguish two hypotheses, i.e. Bottom-up Bootstrapping and Interactive Bootstrapping. The former states that acquisition proceeds step by step; specifically, the acquisition of each level exclusively relies upon information that is available in the shallower levels of representation. According to the latter hypothesis, in contrast, all levels begin to be acquired independently and there is interaction between levels until a stable state is attained.

We set up our methodology to explore the acquisition of the prelexical representation and focused on the stress system, since it allows a uniform way of distinguishing the various sources of information that could in principle be taken into account in the compilation of the prelexical representation. We thus proposed to test whether stress is encoded in this representation by speakers of a variety of languages. In particular, we argued that the *presence* of stress 'deafness' is an indication of the *absence* of stress in the prelexical representation. The underlying assumption is that stress should only be encoded in the prelexical representation if it is useful to distinguish lexical items. The infant's problem is to decide, on the basis of a limited amount of information, whether stress should be encoded or not.

We distinguished four classes of languages, corresponding to four types of information that infants could use in order to make this decision. That is, in

TABLE 7.1. Summary of predictions for the four classes of stress systems

Regularity	Language	Stress rule	Interfering destressing	Clitics	Stress 'deafness'
Type I	French	stress final syllable	no	stressed enclitics	attested (Dupoux et al. 1997)
	Pitta-Pitta	stress initial syllable	not applicable	no proclitics	predicted by both Bottom-up and Interactive Bootstrapping
Type II	Fijian	stress heavy final, otherwise penultimate syllable	?	no enclitics	predicted by both Bottom-up and Interactive Bootstrapping
Type III	Hungarian	stress first syllable	no	unstressed proclitics	predicted only by Interactive Bootstrapping
Type IV	Piro	stress penultimate syllable	?	no enclitics	predicted only by Interactive Bootstrapping
	Nyawaygi	stress initial syllable if heavy or if word contains even number of syllables; otherwise, stress second syllable	not applicable	no enclitics	predicted only by Interactive Bootstrapping

the first class of languages (Type I), the stress rule can be acquired on the basis of a universal phonetic representation only; in the second class (Type II), it can be acquired once certain language-specific phonological information has been extracted; in the third and the fourth class (Types III and IV, respectively), it can be acquired only after function words and content words, respectively, can be segmented out of the speech stream. We then made contrasting predictions regarding the presence of stress 'deafness' in adults of these four language classes. The reasoning is as follows. Whenever stress 'deafness' is exhibited by speakers of a certain language, we take this as evidence that the stress regularity is taken into account during the compilation of the prelexical representation. According to the Bottom-up Bootstrapping hypothesis, only the universal phonetic and the prelexical representation itself can enter the scene during the compilation of the prelexical representation, hence only 'deafnesses' of Types I and II are predicted. In contrast, the Interactive Bootstrapping hypothesis states that all processing components are allowed to interact till a stable state is attained. Hence, one would expect all four types of 'deafnesses' to be observed. A summary of the languages with their characteristics and the various predictions is given in Table 7.1. The empirical investigation that we propose thus allows us to test models of early language acquisition. Such empirical investigation is now under way.

   As a final note, we would like to mention that although we have focused on the acquisition of the prelexical representation, our approach can be transposed to other processing components that are involved in early language acquisition, such as word segmentation or lexical access. Provided that these components show clear language-specific properties in adults, a cross-linguistic comparative study can probe what types of information are used by infants to compile such language-specific routines. In other words, the comparative psycholinguistics approach using only adult data is a potentially useful tool that can be added to the panoply of techniques currently used to investigate first language acquisition.

8

Syllabic Constraints and
Constraint Conflicts in Loanword
Adaptations, Aphasic Speech,
and Children's Errors

Carole Paradis and Renée Béland

8.1. INTRODUCTION

In a longitudinal case study, Béland and Paradis (1997) compared the
syllabic errors—defined as segment insertion and deletion (as opposed to

We would like to thank the audience at the 'Current Trends in Phonology II' Conference,
held at the Abbey of Royaumont near Paris in 1998, where a preliminary version of this
chapter was presented. We are particularly grateful to Steve Anderson, John Goldsmith, Janet
Pierrehumbert, Jean-François Prunet, and Annie Rialland for their illuminating comments
and challenging questions. We are also deeply indebted to Isabelle McClish and Joël Macoir
for their work with the second aphasic patient of our study, to Claudine Blouin, André
Courcy, Yannique Laplame, and Myriam Babaï for their work with the children of our study,
and to Darlene LaCharité for her feedback on this version of the article vis-à-vis both substance
and exposition. We acknowledge SSHRC grants 410–97–1446 (C.P.) and 410–96–1467
(R.B.) and FCAR grant 98-ER-2305 (C.P. and R.B.).

segment substitution)—produced by a French-speaking patient suffering from Primary Progressive Aphasia (henceforth PPA) to the syllabic adaptations (segment insertion and deletion) of French borrowings in different languages (Fula, Kinyarwanda, and Moroccan Arabic). The results of this comparison revealed both similarities and dissimilarities in the patient's data and the borrowing data.

With respect to the similarities, first, the syllabic errors of the aphasic patient as well as the syllabic adaptations of loanwords were found in marked syllabic contexts, i.e. the six syllabic contexts that do not correspond to the universally unmarked CV-syllable (codas, branching onsets, branching codas, hiatus, diphthongs, and word-initial empty onsets). Second, the repair strategies applied by the patient in the marked syllabic contexts were very similar to those applied by the borrowers, i.e. normal speakers, when they adapt French words containing marked syllabic contexts disallowed in their mother tongue. Syllabic paraphasias (errors) and loanword adaptations are both governed by two principles of the Theory of Constraints and Repair Strategies (henceforth TCRS; see e.g. Paradis 1988*a*, 1988*b*, LaCharité and Paradis 1993), i.e. the Preservation and the Tolerance Threshold Principles, presented in section 8.2.

As for the dissimilarities, they appeared to be the following. First, the rate of segment insertion was by far lower in the syllabic paraphasias of the patient than in the syllabic adaptations of loanwords. Second, with the progression of the deficit, the type of repair strategy applied by the patient changed: segment deletion, which was already more frequent in paraphasias than in loanword adaptations, still increased significantly in the latest stages of the illness. This change in the error pattern contrasted with loanword adaptations, where segment insertion is overwhelmingly preferred over segment deletion (see Paradis and LaCharité 1997), as will soon be shown in detail. The change in the patient's error pattern was accounted for by a tendency, with the progression of the illness, to reject complex (multi-step) repairs. Indeed, in many syllabic contexts, as we will see in section 8.2, segment insertion involves a larger number of phonological operations than segment deletion. This account makes sense, given that PPA, a precursor of a more generalized dementia of the Pick-Alzheimer spectrum, is characterized by a progressive language deterioration leading to phonological dissolution.

A first objective in this study is to verify the results reported in Béland and Paradis (1997) with a second PPA case, whose errors were studied in Paradis et al. (2001), and to measure a factor which is frequently influential but which was not investigated in the first study, the word length effect. A second objective is to extend the analysis to children's errors in order to show more conclusively that syllabic errors are not random but triggered by universally conditioned syllabic constraints that commonly apply in native and nativized words of natural languages. In a sense, we follow the steps of Jakobson (1971) in relating children's errors to paraphasias. Finally, a third objective is to show that the repairs applied by our two aphasic patients and the children of this study are governed by the same principles of TCRS as those which apply in loanword adaptation, here the Preservation and Threshold Principles.

The chapter is divided into three parts. In section 8.2, the theoretical framework is presented along with statistics in loanword adaptations showing that insertion is much more frequent (96.7 per cent) than segment deletion (3.3 per cent). In section 8.3, the syllabic adaptations of our corpora of loanwords are compared to the syllabic errors produced by our two aphasic patients. The investigation of our second PPA case suggests that the higher rate of segment deletion in syllabic paraphasias might be partly accounted for by a metrical constraint on word length. Finally, the analysis of children's errors is reported in section 8.4. We examine two populations of pre-school children, normal children and children suffering from Phonological Awareness Disabilities (PAD). The results indicate that the syllabic errors of children are triggered by the same syllabic constraints as those which apply in loanword adaptations and paraphasias (the error rate is lower in CV than in marked syllabic structure), and that the error rate in the form of segment deletion (as opposed to segment insertion) is higher in children than in PPA patients, and higher in PAD children than in normal children. The difference in the rate of segment deletion, which is clearly higher in both children's and aphasics' syllabic errors than in syllabic adaptations of loanwords, is attributed to two factors: (*a*) the tolerance threshold of children and aphasics is lower than that of normal adults, and (*b*) aphasics and children, and especially PAD children, have metrical limitations that normal adult subjects (including borrowers) do not have.

8.2. LOANWORD ADAPTATION

The seven studies conducted by Paradis (1995*a*, 1995*b*), Paradis and LaCharité (1997), and Paradis and Prunet (1998, 2000), among others, on the phonology of loanwords have shown the predictability of loanword adaptation, i.e. segment preservation and segment deletion in borrowings. As can be seen in Table 8.1, malformations from a syllabic or segmental point of view are adapted, i.e. preserved, in the vast majority of cases. Together adaptations and non-adaptations represent 96.7 per cent of cases, i.e. 19,847 cases out of 20,558 malformations contained in 13,945 forms[1] from 6,039 borrowings from English in Quebec City French, Montreal French, and Mexican Spanish, and from French in Moroccan Arabic, Kinyarwanda, Lingala (two Bantu languages), and Fula (a West Atlantic language). These findings are supported by those obtained by Ulrich (1998), who reports very similar results from his study based on 614 French and English loans in Lama, a Gur language, with a rate of adaptation, i.e. segment preservation over segment deletion, of 94.4 per cent. As can be seen in the penultimate column, the rate of segment deletion is extremely low, representing only 3.3 per cent of cases. This is attributed to the Preservation Principle, in (1), which states that:

(1) PRESERVATION PRINCIPLE: Segmental information is maximally preserved within the limits of constraint conflicts.

The Preservation Principle, which resists the loss of phonological information, favours viewing a problematic structure as a lack of content or structure, giving precedence to insertion over deletion (of content or structure). TCRS, the framework in which the analyses presented in this chapter are couched, nevertheless posits limits to preservation, that is, to the price languages are ready to pay to conserve segmental information. One of these limits is expressed in the form of the Threshold Principle, shown in (2).

(2) THRESHOLD PRINCIPLE:
    a. All languages have a tolerance threshold to segment preservation.
    b. The tolerance threshold of a language sets the limit on the procedural weight (i.e. the number of steps)[2] a repair is allowed within a constraint domain.

As shown extensively in Paradis and LaCharité (1997), a conflict between the Preservation Principle and the Threshold Principle results systematically in a segment loss. The Threshold Principle restrains the procedural weight of

---

[1] A 'form' is a borrowing found in a given source or pronounced by an informant, i.e. the concrete realization of an abstract entity, the borrowing. This distinction between 'form' and 'borrowing' is essential since not all informants know all borrowings nor realize a single borrowing in the same way.

[2] The notion of procedural weight in psycholinguistics refers essentially to the number of operations required to handle linguistic information. For instance, Macoir and Béland (1998) have shown that both the number and the patterns of errors produced by two aphasic patients in the contexts of verbal and adjectival inflexion are directly related to the number of morphophonological operations necessary for their production.

TABLE 8.1. Statistics on loanwords from seven corpora

Corpora	Loans	Forms	Malformations	Adaptations	Deletions	Non-adaptations
English loans in:						
Quebec City French	948	2412	3076	2326 (75.6%)	90 (2.9%)	660 (21.5%)
Montreal French	948	2245	2864	1687 (58.9%)	78 (2.7%)	1099 (38.4%)
Mexican Spanish	1045	1514	2108	1405 (66.6%)	1 (0.1%)	661 (31.4%)[a]
French loans in:						
Moroccan Arabic	1127	2691	3917	3047 (77.8%)	351 (9%)	519 (13.2%)
Kinyarwanda	756	2130	4208	4120 (97.9%)	62 (1.5%)	26 (0.6%)
Lingala	670	1917	3571	3378 (94.6%)	31 (0.9%)	162 (4.5%)
Fula	545	1036	814	741 (91%)	57 (7%)	16 (2%)
Total (7 corpora)	6039	13945	20558	16704 (81.3%)	670 (3.3%)	3143 (15.3%)[a]

[a] Forty-one marginal cases, i.e. 1.9%, must be added in Mexican Spanish, which represents 0.2% in the total line.

a repair within a constraint domain, a notion which is addressed in detail in Paradis (1996). Roughly stated, a 'constraint domain' consists of the scope of a constraint, i.e. the segmental material that must be scanned horizontally (i.e. phonotactically) and vertically (within a segment) by a constraint before a violation is declared. For this study, it suffices to know, as we will see later, that an ill-formed segment which is also 'unsyllabifiable' usually represents an offence great enough to yield its deletion. Thus it is not the number of malformations within a word which is responsible for segment deletion—indeed, a borrowing may contain over ten malformations without undergoing any segment deletion—but, as we will soon see, the presence of a malformation (normally a segmental one) embedded within another one (usually a syllabic one).

The (French) syllabic contexts which are often problematic, i.e. unsyllabifiable, in loanwords in the borrowing language are the six marked structures in (3), i.e. branching onsets, branching codas, simple codas, diphthongs, hiatus, and word-initial empty onsets. In fact, any syllable other than CV, the most neutral syllable, is potentially problematic.

(3) The six marked syllabic structures with examples from French:
- *a.* branching onsets (e.g. *place* /p̲l̲as/ 'place')
- *b.* branching codas (e.g. *contre* /kɔ̃t̲r̲/ 'against')
- *c.* simple codas (e.g. *patte* /pat̲/ 'paw')
- *d.* diphthongs (e.g. *boisson* /bw̲as̲ɔ̃/ 'drink')
- *e.* hiatus (e.g. *mosaïque* /moz̲a̲i̲k/ 'mosaic')
- *f.* word-initial empty onsets (e.g. *ambassade* /ãbasad/ 'embassy')

Those syllabic structures are often prohibited in languages of the world, and in the languages of our database of borrowings. For instance, branching onsets and codas are prohibited in Fula, Lingala, and Kinyarwanda. Simple codas and diphthongs, too, are prohibited in Lingala and Kinyarwanda while hiatus is prohibited in Fula and Moroccan Arabic (henceforth MA), as well as in Kinyarwanda and Lingala. The distribution of syllabic adaptations (i.e. segment insertions), non-adaptations, and segment deletions for the six marked syllabic contexts in French borrowings can be observed in Table 8.2.

As can be seen in Table 8.2, the rate of segment deletion is very low for all languages except MA, which has an unusually high rate of segment deletion in word-initial empty onsets, i.e. 43.2 per cent. As will be discussed below, there is a word length effect at work in this language which is in large measure responsible for its higher rate of segment deletion.

The prohibition of the marked syllabic contexts in Table 8.2 is due to negative parameter settings, such as that in (4), which act as constraints.

TABLE 8.2. Marked contexts and repairs in the French borrowings of our database

	Kinyarwanda		Fula		MA		Lingala		Total	
Branching onset	443		94		N.A.		229		766	
Adaptations	428	96.6%	88	93.6%			229	100%	745	97.3%
Non-adaptations	12	2.7%	6	6.4%			0	0%	18	2.3%
Deletions	3	0.7%	0	0%			0	0%	3	0.4%
Branching coda	156		98		N.A.		93		347	
Adaptations	139	89.1%	70	71.4%			93	100%	302	87%
Non-adaptations	4	2.6%	16	16.3%			0	0%	20	5.8%
Deletions	13	8.3%	12	12.3%			0	0%	25	7.2%
Simple coda	1524		N/A/		N.A.		851		2375	
Adaptations	1490	97.8%					848	99.6%	2338	98.4%
Non-adaptations	6	0.4%					0	0%	6	0.3%
Deletions	28	1.8%					3	0.4%	31	1.3%
Diphthongs	252		121		N.A.		213		586	
Adaptations	234	92.9%	61	50.4%			212	99.5%	507	86.5%
Non-adaptations	4	1.6%	24	19.8%			1	0.5%	29	5.0%
Deletions	14	5.5%	36	29.8%			0	0%	50	8.5%
Hiatus	43		12		44		26		125	
Adaptations	41	95.3%	8	66.6%	31	70.5%	26	100%	106	84.8%
Non-adaptations	0	0%	2	16.7%	0	0%	0	0%	2	1.6%
Deletions	2	4.7%	2	16.7%	13	29.5%	0	0%	17	13.6%
Word-initial empty onset	N.A.		N.A.		333		N.A.		333	
Adaptations					180	54.1%			180	54.1%
Non-adaptations					9	2.7%			9	2.7%
Deletions					144	43.2%			144	43.2%

N.A. = non-applicable

(4) Branching onsets?   *Yes*   *No* (constraint)
                         French   Fula
                                      Kinyarwanda
                                      Lingala

In TCRS, constraints stem from negative answers to universal options, the parameters, and from principles, i.e. universal constraints. A constraint violation is taken care of by a repair strategy, which is defined in (5).

(5) Repair strategy: A universal, non-contextual phonological operation that is triggered by the violation of a phonological constraint, and which inserts or deletes content or structure to ensure conformity to the violated constraint.

The French loans in Fula, shown in (6), exemplify the application of a repair, here vowel insertion, as well as obedience to the Preservation Principle, which gives precedence to insertion over deletion.

(6) Repair by vowel insertion in Fula (Preservation Principle)
    French *place* [plas]   'place'   → Fula [palas] (*[pas])
    French *tracteur* [traktœr] 'tractor'   → Fula [taraktɔr] (*[taktɔr])

Nonetheless, segment insertion is not always the strategy selected. As already mentioned, the Preservation Principle may conflict in some cases with the Threshold Principle, in (2). This principle states that each language establishes a limit on the cost of rescuing a segment. Infringement yields segment deletion. As addressed in Paradis and LaCharité (1997), the tolerance threshold of Fula and Kinyarwanda for a repair is two steps, the limit beyond which segment deletion occurs. By contrast, Lingala is a little more tolerant with a threshold set at three steps (see Bambi 1998). This is summarized in (7).

(7) Tolerance threshold for a repair: Fula, Kinyarwanda: 2 steps
                                         Lingala: 3 steps

It is important to understand that the Threshold Principle does not entail the serial counting of repair steps (one, two, three, etc.). We suggest that the procedural weight of a repair is established canonically, i.e. globally. The recognition of a canonical pattern of numbers is well known in psychology and called 'subitization'. According to Wynn (1990: 158) 'Adults and children can "subitize" small numerosities, up to four or five for adults and two or three for 3-, 4-, and 5-year-olds.'[3]

Typically, segment deletion occurs in Fula when a segment contained within an unsyllabifiable sequence is itself identified as ill formed. For instance, the adaptation of the sequence *kɥ* in a French word such as *biscuit* [biskɥi] 'cookie', in (8), is problematic in Fula because the sequence contains two malformations: (a) an unsyllabifiable CC onset, *kɥ*, and (b) the disallowed labio-coronal glide *ɥ*.

(8) Loss of a consonant: violation of the tolerance threshold of Fula

French			Fula		gloss
biscuit	[biskɥi]	→	biski	*biskuwi	cookie
cuisinier	[kɥizinje]	→	kisiⁿge	*kuwisiⁿge	cook

In (9), *ɥ* is not contained in an unsyllabifiable cluster. Indeed, the lateral *l* is syllabified within a coda, a permitted syllabic constituent in Fula, and the glide *ɥ* forms the onset of the following syllable. Therefore it is not deleted but merely adapted (to *w*) because its adaptation requires only one step, i.e. deletion of the articulator Coronal from the glide, which yields the labio-velar glide *w*.

(9) Segment adaptation: no violation of the tolerance threshold of Fula

French			Fula		gloss
(de l') huile	[dəlɥil]	→	dilwil	*dilil	oil
minuit	[minɥi]	→	minwi	*mini	midnight

Segment deletion in (8) is due to the procedural weight that segment preservation would entail. By contrast with the first *l* in French *de l'huile*, in (9), *k* in [biskɥi] cannot be syllabified into the coda of the first syllable, since this syllable already has a coda consonant, *s*. The sequence *skɥ* in [biskɥi] is thus unsyllabifiable. Recall that branching codas and branching onsets are disallowed in Fula. To adapt the ill-formed structure, a nucleus would have to be inserted in a first stage, as in (10*a*). In a second stage, the epenthetic nucleus would have to be filled with segmental material, as in (10*b*). Finally, in a third stage, the ill-formed consonant *ɥ* itself would have to be adapted to *w*, as in (10*c*).

---

[3] She adds (p. 191) that 'Infants may have an innate concept of numerosity, or at least of the numerosities one, two, and three, which they must map onto the correct number words.'

(10) Three-step rescue: Cч → Cuw
    a. nucleus insertion   *b. ч* spreading   *c. ч* adaptation

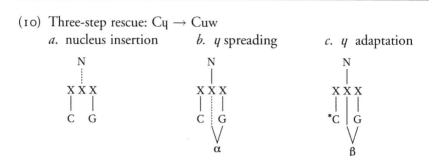

   This three-step rescue is rejected by Fula because it violates its tolerance threshold, which is limited to two steps, as seen in (7); this explains why consonant deletion applies instead of vowel insertion.
   A constraint conflict may also arise between the Preservation Principle and a metrical constraint which imposes a limit on word length. In such a case, the conflict is resolved by the Precedence Convention, in (11), which states that precedence is always given to the conflicting constraint dealing with the highest level of the phonological organization.

(11) PRECEDENCE CONVENTION: In a situation involving two or more violated constraints, priority is given to that constraint referring to the highest level of the Phonological Level Hierarchy.

   The Phonological Level Hierarchy, given in (12), is not an additional tool of TCRS but simply the reflection of a universally recognized phonological organization required independently of TCRS, which states that the metrical level is more organizational than the syllabic one, and so forth.

(12) PHONOLOGICAL LEVEL HIERARCHY (simplified version):
    metrical level > syllabic level > skeletal level > root node > feature

   The Precedence Convention gives priority to metrical constraints over syllabic ones in a constraint conflict. A constraint conflict occurs in borrowings—and in language errors, as we will see later—when the language imposes a maximal limit on the length of words, on one hand, and the repair of a syllabic malformation by segment preservation/insertion would entail infringing upon this limit by adding a syllable.
   An example of conflict between the Preservation Principle and a metrical constraint is found in MA. We have seen in Table 8.2 that MA does not allow empty onsets. In word-initial position, a consonant may be inserted in the onset—either the glottal stop or the French/MA definite article *l*—but very often the vowel is deleted. The rate of vowel deletion in word-initial position

is unexpectedly high at 43.2 per cent. While we cannot account entirely for why the rate of vowel deletion is so high—the metrical constraint on word length in MA is obviously not absolute—it is clear that vowel deletion increases significantly with the number of syllables within the word. As shown in (13), the longer the word, the more vowel deletions we observe.

(13) Word-initial vowel deletions per number of syllables within loan forms in MA

Number of syllables	1	2	3	4	5
Number of V deletions	0/3	25/106	86/162	26/40	7/9
Percentages	0%	24%	53%	65%	78%

Word-initial vowel deletions range from 24 per cent in bisyllabics to 78 per cent in words with five syllables. The word length effect is even stronger in verbs alone, as can be seen in (14).

(14) Word-initial vowel deletions per number of syllables within loan forms in MA

Category	2 syllables	3 syllables	4 syllables
Verbs	0/2	24/26	0/0
	0%	92%	
Nouns	25/104	62/136	26/40
	24%	46%	65%

It is well known that the prototypical roots of MA, like those of Arabic in general, are triliteral, i.e. with three consonants ($C_1C_2C_3$), or quadriliteral, i.e. with four consonants ($C_1C_2C_3C_4$) (see Heath 1989: 19). Does the word length effect in MA ensue in reality from a constraint on the number of consonants within roots instead of a constraint on the number of syllables? It does not seem so as seen in (15). For instance, if we consider vowel-initial trisyllabic borrowings alone—the word length category which obtains the greatest number of examples for both nouns and verbs—the number of word-initial vowel deletions does not increase linearly with the number of consonants within the root. Triliteral roots undergo 55.9 per cent of deletions whereas roots with five consonants undergo a little more, 62.5 per cent, but word-initial vowel deletion drops to 42.1 per cent in quadriliteral roots.

(15) Word-initial vowel deletions per number of consonants within MA
trisyllabic loans

1 C	2 Cs	3 Cs	4 Cs	5 Cs	6 Cs
0/0	13/23	52/93	16/38	5/8	0/0
	56.5%	55.9%	42.1%	62.5%	

We do not totally dismiss the possibility that word-initial vowel deletion is also conditioned by a soft constraint on the number of consonants within roots—the data in (15) reveal a slight increase in the number of word-initial vowel deletion if we compare triliteral roots to roots with five consonants—but the influence of such a constraint would obviously be too mild to account for as much as 43.2 per cent of vowel deletion in word-initial position (see Table 8.2). As seen in (13), the number of syllables within words seems to be a much more deterministic factor than the number of consonants, and thus more suited to expressing the word length effect in that language.

Languages limiting the syllables in words are not uncommon. In Gere—a Kru language spoken in the Ivory Coast—non-compound words are maximally bisyllabic, as in Kru languages in general (see Paradis 1983). The metrical constraint of Gere can be formulated as in (16).

(16) Metrical constraint in Gere
    a. Maximal non-compound word: one foot
    b. Maximal length of a foot: binary, i.e. with two syllables

In Jamaican Creole, reduplicated derivational adjectives are maximally and minimally bisyllabic (see Kouwenberg and LaCharité 1999). There is also a strong preference for bisyllabic words in Cantonese Chinese, although it is not an absolute constraint (see Yip 1993). The metrical constraint in MA is certainly not as strict as in Gere. We suggest that it is nonetheless responsible in large measure for word-initial vowel deletion in that language, and propose to express it in a form similar to that in (16).

8.3. A COMPARISON BETWEEN LOANWORD ADAPTATIONS AND PARAPHASIAS

As mentioned in section 8.1, Béland and Paradis (1997) compared the syllabic errors produced by a French-speaking PPA patient to the syllabic adaptations of French borrowings in different languages. In 8.3.1, we briefly present the case history of the first PPA patient, here referred to as Patient 1, along with the working hypotheses of Béland and Paradis (1997), our specific objectives in the present study regarding those hypotheses, the methodology followed by Béland and Paradis (1997), as well as the results they obtained. We also present a large sample of the examples provided in Béland and Paradis (1997). In section 8.3.2, we present the preliminary information regarding our second patient, referred to as Patient 2, and the results we obtained.

8.3.1. Patient 1

A summary of the case history of Patient 1 is presented in what follows.

(17) Case history of Patient 1: A university educated right-handed female and a native speaker of French with a familial history of probable dementia of Alzheimer type. She developed a progressive language impairment at the age of 58 years. H.C. presented in April 1987 with a 12-month history of language disorder. She consulted because she was worried by her frequent word mispronunciations. A CT scan showed a mild atrophy affecting the left hemisphere without signs of a focal lesion in 1987 and a severe left atrophy in 1992.

The hypotheses formulated by Béland and Paradis (1997) with which we will be concerned in this study are those presented in (18). They are partly reworded for ease of exposition.

(18) Hypotheses of Béland and Paradis (1997)
   a. Syllabic paraphasias should be much more frequent in the six marked syllabic contexts in (3) than in the unmarked CV syllabic context.
   b. If this were indeed the case, it would show that paraphasias originate from the same universally conditioned constraints as those that govern natural languages. In other words, if phonemic paraphasias result from the patient negatively setting parameters of UG (Universal Grammar), the authors would expect the negative constraints from which paraphasias originate to exist in natural languages.
   c. The authors also hypothesized that if phonemic paraphasias result from the patient negatively setting parameters of UG, loanword adaptations and paraphasias should be very similar in nature.

  d. They also hypothesized that loanword adaptations and paraphasias should be similar in proportion. In other words, if paraphasias are governed by the principles of UG, insertion of a segment (adaptation) should be preferred to segment deletion in syllabic paraphasias as well as in the syllabic adaptation of borrowings, as a consequence of the Preservation Principle.

  e. With the progression of the deficit, the patient's tolerance threshold should be lowered below that of normal native speakers. Therefore, Béland and Paradis expected a malformation perceived by the patient to trigger segment deletion much more frequently in the later stages of the illness than in the earlier ones.

In this chapter, we broadly endorse the hypotheses of Béland and Paradis (1997) presented in (18). They will be discussed in some detail in the remainder of the chapter. Our specific objectives regarding those hypotheses, however, are displayed in (19).

(19) Our specific objectives: to show that
  a. syllabic errors in aphasic speech as well as in acquisition are triggered by universally conditioned syllabic constraints (i.e. constraints that exist in natural languages);
  b. preservation of segments is not as great in aphasic speech and acquisition because the Preservation Principle is in conflict with other constraints in those cases, namely the Threshold Principle and a metrical constraint on word length.

The methodology followed by Béland and Paradis (1997) is the following. They collected the syllabic errors (insertions or deletions of a segment) produced by the patient in the six marked syllabic contexts displayed in (3). A total of 638 syllabic errors were collected in syllabically marked stimuli from different language tests, including oral reading, repetition, spontaneous speech, oral and written picture naming, and dictation. The corpus also includes 63 syllabic errors collected in control stimuli, that is, stimuli comprising only CV-syllables (CV(CV)), which overall yields a total of 701 syllabic errors for both marked and unmarked syllabic contexts. The corpus of errors was gathered over three and a half years and divided into two phases, Phase 1 and Phase 2, in order to test Hypothesis (18*e*) on the increase of segment deletion correlated with the progression of the illness. Those phases correspond, as shown in (20), to a little more than a year and a half each. There was no other justification for this dichotomy apart from a concern for time-length symmetry between the phases.

(20) Patient 1: Phase 1: from March 1989 to November 1990
                 (337 syllabic errors in marked contexts and 40 in control
                 stimuli)
                 Phase 2: from January 1991 to August 1992
                 (301 syllabic errors in marked contexts and 23 in control
                 stimuli)
                 Phases 1 and 2: 701 syllabic paraphasias

The results obtained by Béland and Paradis (1997) are very clear. The six marked syllabic contexts yield a significantly greater number of errors than the CV(CV) control stimuli. As shown in (21), syllabic errors in marked contexts represent 97.8 per cent of all errors, i.e. 638 syllabic errors out of 652 including substitution errors, vs. 17.6 per cent of errors for control stimuli, i.e. 63 syllabic errors out of 357 general phonemic errors. The difference in the number of syllabic errors between marked and control stimuli is significant ($\chi^2 = 696$, p < .001).

(21) Patient 1:
       six marked syllabic contexts: 638/652 errors, i.e. 97.8 per cent are
       syllabic
       control CV(CV) stimuli: 63/357 errors, i.e. 17.6 per cent are syllabic

These results confirmed the first hypothesis of Béland and Paradis (1997) in (18), according to which syllabic paraphasias should be much more frequent in the six marked syllabic contexts than in the unmarked CV-syllabic context. Furthermore, the examples in (22) show that violations of the constraints prohibiting the six marked syllabic structures are repaired in the same way in syllabic paraphasias as in syllabic loanword adaptations. This confirms Hypotheses (18b) and (18c), according to which paraphasias originate from constraints that exist in natural languages (see (18b)) and loanword adaptations and paraphasias should be very similar in nature (see (18c)). Indeed violations of syllabic constraints trigger either segment insertion or deletion in both cases. For example, in (22), French *place* [plas] yields [p̲alas] in Fula, and *citron* [sitr5] is pronounced [sit̲er5] by the patient. In both cases, the problematic French branching onset undergoes vowel insertion. We do not provide examples of segment deletions in borrowings since there are very few examples, as seen in (Table 1). Apart from the special case of word-initial vowel deletions in MA, phonologically conditioned deletion in the borrowings of our database is almost exclusively restricted to consonants in the context of branching onsets and codas. Those cases are identical to the deletion cases of the patient, i.e. they result in a consonant loss, as seen in (8) with Fula (see Paradis and LaCharité 1997 for more examples and a thorough discussion).

(22) Syllabic adaptations in borrowings compared to syllabic paraphasias

    a BRANCHING ONSET

	BORROWINGS		
Fr. *place* [pl̲as]	'place'	→	F. [pa̲las]
Fr. *projet* [pr̲ɔʒɛ]	'project'	→	K. [po̲roʒe]

(Fr. = French, F. = Fula, K. = Kinyarwanda)

Patient 1

V insertion: CC → CV̲C
Fr. *citron* [sit̲rɔ̃]	'lemon'	→	patient [sit̲ɛrɔ̃]
Fr. *crocodile* [kr̲ɔkɔdil]	'crocodile'	→	patient [k̲ɔrɔsil]

C deletion: CC → CØ
Fr. *bleu* [bl̲ø]	'blue'	→	patient [b̲ø]
Fr. *fromage* [fr̲ɔmaʒ]	'cheese'	→	patient [f̲ɔmaʒ]

    b. BRANCHING CODA

	Borrowings		
Fr. *carde* [kar̲d]	'card (comb)'	→	F. [kar̲da]
Fr. *carte* [kar̲t]	'card'	→	F. [kar̲tal]

Patient 1

V insertion: CC# → CCV#
Fr. *parc* [par̲k]	'park'	→	patient [park̲ə]
Fr. *meuble* [mœbl̲]	'furniture'	→	patient [mœbl̲y]

C deletion: CC# → C#
Fr. *porte* [pɔr̲t]	'door'	→	patient [pɔt̲]
Fr. *parle* [par̲l]	'speak'	→	patient [pal̲]

    c. CODA

	Borrowings		
Fr. *mine* [mi̲n]	'mine'	→	K. [mi̲ni]
Fr. *docteur* [dɔ̲ktœr]	'doctor'	→	K. [doɩiteer̲i]

Patient 1

V insertion: C# → CV#
Fr. *fougère* [fuʒɛr̲]	'fern'	→	patient [fuʒɛr̲ə]
Fr. *bol* [bɔl̲]	'bowl'	→	patient [bɔl̲ə]

C deletion: C# → Ø#
Fr. *facteur* [fak̲tœr]	'mailman'	→	patient [fat̲œr]
Fr. *bail* [baj]	'lease'	→	patient [ba̲]

d. DIPHTHONG

	Borrowings		
Fr. *boîte* [b<u>wa</u>t]	'box'	→	K. [ßu<u>waa</u>ti]
Fr. *lieutenant* [lj<u>øt</u>nã]	'lieutenant'	→	K. [ri<u>je</u>tona]

Patient 1

C insertion: CVV → CVCV

Fr. *fouet* [f<u>wɛ</u>]	'whip'	→	patient [fu<u>l</u>ɛ]
Fr. *piéton* [pj<u>e</u>tɔ̃]	'pedestrian'	→	patient [pi<u>te</u>tɔ̃]

V deletion: CVV → CV

Fr. *celui* [səl<u>ɥi</u>]	'the one'	→	patient [sə<u>li</u>]
Fr. *télévision* [televiz<u>jɔ̃</u>]	'television'	→	patient [tiliviz<u>ɔ̃</u>]

e. HIATUS

	Borrowings		
Fr. *mosaïque* [moz<u>ai</u>k]	'mosaic'	→	MA [møz<u>a</u>jik]
Fr. *Noël* [n<u>ɔɛ</u>l]	'Christmas'	→	MA [n<u>ɔw</u>ɪl]

Patient 1

C insertion: VV → VCV

Fr. *véhicule* [v<u>ei</u>kyl]	'vehicle'	→	patient [f<u>e</u>tɪl]
Fr. *jouer* [ʒ<u>ue</u>]	'to play'	→	patient [ʒ<u>uwe</u>]

V deletion: VV → V

Fr. *pays* [p<u>ei</u>]	'country'	→	patient [p<u>e</u>]
Fr. *Joël* [ʒ<u>ɔɛ</u>l]	'Joel'	→	patient [ʒ<u>œ</u>l]

f. WORD-INITIAL EMPTY ONSET

	Borrowings		
Fr. *ambassade* [<u>ã</u>basad]	'embassy'	→	MA [<u>lã</u>mbaṣaḍ] or [ʔambaṣaḍ]
Fr. *ouvreuse* [<u>u</u>vrøz]	'usherette'	→	MA [<u>lø</u>vrøz] or [ʔøvrøz]

Patient 1

C insertion: #V → #CV

Fr. *hache* [<u>a</u>ʃ]	'axe'	→	patient [<u>wa</u>ʃ]
Fr. *université* [<u>y</u>niversite]	'university'	→	patient [<u>ny</u>nivɛrsite]

V deletion: #V → #∅

Fr. *orange* [<u>ɔ</u>rãʒ]	'orange'	→	patient [<u>r</u>ãʒ]
Fr. *échelle* [<u>e</u>ʃɛl]	'ladder'	→	patient [<u>ʃ</u>ɛl]

The examples in (22) (and (8)) show that the same processes, i.e. insertion and deletion, are applied in paraphasias and borrowings, but do they apply in

TABLE 8.3. Patient 1: Distribution of error types in the six marked syllabic contexts and level of significance of the Chi-Square (χ^2) test for the difference in the proportion of error types collected in Phase 1 vs. Phase 2

a.

Context	Phase	V insertions	C deletions	χ^2
Branching onset	1	19 (**54.3%**)	16 (45.7%)	
	2	4 (7.8 %)	47 (92.2%)	*
Branching coda	1	40 (**62.5%**)	24 (37.5%)	
	2	1 (16.7%)	5 (83.3%)	n.s.
Simple coda	1	103 (**68.7%**)	47 (31.3%)	
	2	29 (39.7%)	44 (60.3%)	**

b.

Context	Phase	C insertions	V deletions	χ^2
Diphthong	1	21 (**51.2%**)	20 (48.8%)	
	2	10 (20%)	40 (80%)	*
Hiatus	1	8 (**47%**)	9 (53%)	
	2	45 (83.3%)	9 (16.7%)	*
Word-initial empty onset	1	21 (**70%**)	9 (30%)	
	2	40 (59.7%)	27 (40.3%)	n.s.

Note: ** indicates p < .001, * indicates p < .01, n.s. indicates not significant (p > .05).

the same proportions in both cases, as predicted by Hypothesis (18*d*)? In other words, does the Preservation Principle govern paraphasias as much as it rules borrowings? The distribution of segment insertions and deletions produced by Patient 1 in the six marked contexts in Phases 1 and 2 is given in Table 8.3, which is a simplified version of that provided by Béland and Paradis (1997: 1186).

The results in Table 8.3 show that, in the six contexts in both phases, the proportion of segment deletion is more important in syllabic paraphasias than in loanword adaptations, where a low percentage of 3.3 per cent of segment deletion was reported in Table 8.1. At first sight, those results falsify Hypothesis 18*d*, according to which insertion of a segment should be preferred to its deletion in syllabic paraphasias as well as in syllabic adaptations of borrowings, a consequence of the Preservation Principle.

Nonetheless, the results in Table 8.3 do not necessarily entail that the Preservation Principle is not active in aphasic speech. Let us examine the facts more closely. We have seen in section 8.1 that the Preservation Principle can conflict with another constraint. For instance, we have seen that a conflict between the Preservation Principle and the Threshold Principle is responsible for consonant deletion in Fula (see (8)). We have also seen that a conflict between the Preservation Principle and a metrical constraint on word length triggers vowel deletion at the beginning of words in MA.

Let us put aside Hypothesis (18*d*) for now (we will return to it in section 8.3.2), and consider Hypothesis (18*e*). It predicts that the patient's tolerance threshold should drop below that of normal native speakers with the progression of the deficit, and consequently cause more segment deletions in the later stages of the illness than in the earlier ones. What is of particular interest in Table 8.3 is that segment preservation, i.e. segment insertion, drops in five of the six tested contexts in Phase 2, and that this decrease is significant in three contexts. Decrease in segment insertion in Phase 2 is accounted for by the lowering of the tolerance threshold of the patient (see (18*e*)) to one step. Indeed, segment deletion is observed whenever an adaptation requires more than one repair.

In four of the six contexts examined (branching onset, branching coda, simple coda and diphthong), adaptation of the ill-formed syllabic structure into a CV-syllable requires a minimum of two repairs, as shown in (23).

(23) Two-step repair
    a. the insertion of a nucleus, that is, the creation of a new syllable, and
    b. segmental filling of the inserted nucleus.

In the hiatus context, the patient produced more consonant insertions than vowel deletions in Phase 2. Béland and Paradis (1997) argued that this difference in the patient's behaviour stems from the fact that consonant insertion in the hiatus context is less costly than vowel insertion in, for instance, the branching onset context. Vowel insertion necessarily results in the addition of a whole syllable in branching onsets whereas that is not the case for consonant insertion in hiatus. The only context in which consonant insertion consists of the addition of a new syllable is the diphthong context. For example, *fouet* [fwɛ] 'whip' in (22), a monosyllabic word, becomes bisyllabic (i.e. [fulɛ]) after the liquid *l* is inserted in the nucleus, and thus splits up the two parts of the diphthong. They thus correctly predicted that, in this context, contrary to the hiatus context, consonant insertion should be less frequent in Phase 2 than in Phase 1.

However, one might wonder about word-initial empty onsets, where consonant insertion should be no more of a problem than in the hiatus context—since it does not create a new syllable—and where consonant insertion still decreases in Phase 2. Nonetheless, what matters here is that, in spite of the decrease between Phases 1 and 2—which is, incidentally, not significant—consonant insertion is still greater than vowel deletion in Phase 2, with almost 60 per cent, vs. 40 per cent for vowel deletion. This indicates that hiatus and word-initial empty onsets pattern together: segment insertion in those contexts is not as costly as in the other four contexts. These results suggest a word length effect, that is, a tendency for the patient to resort to repairs that do not increase the number of syllables of the target, despite the Preservation Principle. The confirmation of this hypothesis constitutes the main objective of the next section, where we present our second PPA case study.

8.3.2. Patient 2

A summary of the case history of Patient 2 is presented in what follows.

(24) Case history of Patient 2: The patient, a right-handed native speaker of French, was 74 years old at the time of testing. He was high-school educated and had no familial history of Alzheimer's disease. He began to display language impairment at the age of 68 (word-finding difficulties followed by a progressive disorder affecting writing and speech production (hesitant speech)). A CT scan in 1996 revealed a subcortical atrophy and a cortical left fronto-parietal atrophy.

As formally expressed in (19*b*), one of our two objectives in this chapter is to show that preservation of segments is not as great in aphasic speech and acquisition as in loanword adaptation because the Preservation Principle is in conflict with the Threshold Principle and a metrical constraint on word length in the two former cases.

As mentioned in section 8.1, the stimuli and tests that were administered to Patient 2 were more suited to measure the word length effect than those administered to Patient 1, since Béland and Paradis (1997) did not expect such an effect when they started to work on the first case in 1989. A set of word and non-word stimuli corresponding to different syllabic lengths (one to four syllables) and structures (the six marked syllabic contexts in (3) and the CV unmarked context) was constructed and administered to the patient in oral reading and repetition tasks. As in the first case study, the data collected during the two kinds of task were collapsed in all the tables presented in this chapter, since there was no significant difference between the results for each task. The corpus of errors was collected over a period of eight months, with five months between the end of the first period of tests and the beginning of the second one. The tests could not be extended over a longer period of time since the language faculty and the general condition of Patient 2 were already quite deteriorated when the tests started, and worsened rapidly. As in the first case study, the corpus was divided into two phases, identified in (25), in order to assess Hypothesis (18*e*), regarding the decrease of the patient's tolerance threshold with the progression of the illness. This ultimately meets Objective (19*b*) by showing conflicts between the Preservation Principle and other constraints, among which are the Threshold Principle and metrical limitations.

(25) Patient 2: Phase 1: January 1997 (108 syllabic paraphasias)
              Phase 2: September 1997 (107 syllabic paraphasias)
              Phases 1 and 2: 215 syllabic paraphasias

Since the errors of Patient 2 are very similar to those of Patient 1, we will not provide further examples of patient's errors in the next sections. However, the reader willing to examine more examples is referred to McClish (1999), to which the corpus of Patient 2 is appended, along with details of the tests and analyses.

The results obtained by Paradis et al. (2001) and McClish (1999) meet Objective (19*a*), whose purpose is to show, along with Béland and Paradis's (1997) Hypotheses (18*a*) and (18*b*), that syllabic paraphasias are triggered by universally conditioned syllabic constraints, i.e. constraints that exist in natural languages. Indeed, the six marked syllabic contexts, in Patient 2 as well as in Patient 1, yield a significantly greater number of errors than the CVCV control stimuli. As shown in (26), syllabic errors in marked contexts represent 23 per cent of all errors, i.e. 200 errors out of 868, vs. 7.7 per cent for control stimuli, i.e. 15 errors out of 195. The difference in the error rate between marked and control stimuli is highly significant ($\chi^2 = 22.3$, $p < .001$).

(26) Patient 2
         six marked syllabic contexts: 200/868 errors, i.e. 23 per cent are
                                            syllabic
         control CV(CV) stimuli: 15/195 errors, i.e. 7.7 per cent are
                                            syllabic

Furthermore, as predicted by Béland and Paradis (1997) in Hypothesis (18*e*), segment insertion in the second study, as in the first one, is greater in Phase 1 than in Phase 2. The difference between the two phases is clear in the marked syllabic contexts where a preserving repair (i.e. vowel insertion) would increase the number of syllables within the word, as is the case with branching codas, branching onsets, simple codas, and diphthongs. We call those contexts the 'lengthening marked syllabic contexts'. As shown in (27), insertion in bisyllabic stimuli with lengthening marked syllabic contexts represents 51.1 per cent of cases in Phase 1 vs. 43.2 per cent in Phase 2.

(27) Patient 2: number of insertions vs. deletions in lengthening marked
     syllabic contexts (branching onset/coda, simple coda, diphthong) in
     bisyllabics

Phase 1	insertions	deletions
number of syllabic errors: 45	23 (51.1%)	22 (48.9%)
Phase 2		
number of syllabic errors: 44	19 (43.2%)	25 (56.8%)

The difference in the type of errors (insertions vs. deletions) between Phase 1 and 2 in (27) is not statistically significant—most likely because there was only five months between the first battery of tests and the second—but it goes in the right direction, i.e. there are fewer insertions and more deletions in Phase 2. The hypothesis that the Preservation Principle is more liable to conflict with other constraints (i.e. the Threshold Principle and metrical constraints) in the late stages of the illness, and thus to be violated more often in Phase 2 (see Objective (19b)), is further supported by the results in (28). As expected, segment insertion applies in 100 per cent of cases in non-lengthening marked syllabic contexts, i.e. word-initial empty onsets and hiatus, contained in bisyllabic stimuli in both phases.

(28) Patient 2: number of insertions vs. deletions in a non-lengthening
     marked syllabic context (word-initial empty onset and hiatus) in
     bisyllabics

Phase 1	insertions	deletions
number of syllabic errors: 6	6 (100%)	0 (0%)
Phase 2		
number of syllabic errors: 5	5 (100%)	0 (0%)

While there is a striking difference in the error type between lengthening vs. non-lengthening marked syllabic contexts, these results do not clearly indicate to us which constraint is conflicting with the Preservation Principle, the patient's low tolerance threshold or a metrical constraint of his own on word length. It might be one or the other, or both. If we take for granted that the patient's tolerance threshold for repair is increasingly limited to one step with the progression of the illness, segment deletions in Phase 2 in (27) might be attributed to the fact that a segment-preserving repair would necessarily be a complex (multi-step) repair (see (23)) in lengthening contexts, which would violate his tolerance threshold. In non-lengthening contexts, as in (28), segment insertion consists only in filling an empty onset, whereas in lengthening contexts, a new syllable must be created, and its nucleus segmentally filled, which constitutes two operations instead of one, as in the former case. Alternatively, if we take for granted that the patient has an increasingly strong metrical constraint such as that of Gere, in (16), which restrains his maximal word to two syllables, segment deletions in Phase 2 in (27) might be due to the fact that a preserving repair (i.e. vowel insertion here) would violate such a constraint by adding a third syllable to the stimuli. More generally, the question is: does the difficulty for both Patient 1 and Patient 2 in Phase 2 reside in the result (i.e. a constraint conflict between the Preservation Principle and a metrical constraint) or the process (i.e. his/her tolerance threshold to complex repair)?

Before addressing this question more thoroughly, let us point out that it is at least obvious that segment deletions in Phase 2 in (27) do not stem from a mere deactivation of the Preservation Principle in the late stages of the illness. If that were the case, segment deletion would be as frequent in non-lengthening contexts (see (28)) as in lengthening ones (see (27)). The fact that consonant insertion is greater than vowel deletion in Phase 2 in the two non-lengthening contexts in both studies shows that the two patients complied with the Preservation Principle until late in the evolution of the disease, as long as preservation (i.e. segment insertion) did not entail the addition of a syllable, that is, word lengthening and/or a complex repair procedure. Thus although Hypothesis (18*d*) is not accurate in predicting that segment insertion should be similar in proportion in paraphasias and loanword adaptations— segment insertion is obviously more frequent in loanword adaptation— it correctly states that segment insertion is the preferred strategy in both cases, although it is not always within the reach of the aphasic patient, due to constraint conflicts.

It is also evident that there is a word length effect at work in the paraphasias of Patient 2. This word length effect can be observed in Table 8.4, where the error rate increases with the number of syllables in each phase for each marked syllabic context. This increase is statistically significant ($p < .05$) in the first four contexts in Table 8.4. As can be seen in (29), the error rate increases with the number of syllables even in control stimuli, although the difference in the error distribution is significant only in Phase 2.

TABLE 8.4. Patient 2: distribution of error rates (number of errors/number of stimuli) in the six marked contexts as a function of the stimulus length (1 to 4 syllables)

Phase 1 and 2 collapsed	1 syllable	2 syllables	3 syllables	4 syllables
Branching onsets $\chi^2 = 13.41$, p < .01	14/43 (32.6%)	75/187 (40.1%)	39/59 (66.1%)	
Simple codas $\chi^2 = 7.83$, p < .05	10/33 (30.3%)	89/200 (44.5%)	19/29 (65.5%)	
Diphthongs $\chi^2 = 20.95$, p < .01	5/32 (15.6%)	72/129 (55.8%)	37/58 (63.8%)	
Hiatus $\chi^2 = 6.63$, p < .05		20/51 (39.2%)	87/151 (57.6%)	14/21 (66.6%)
W-initial empty onsets $\chi^2 = 0.44$ p > .05		35/85 (41.2%)	64/137 (46.7%)	
Branching codas $\chi^2 = 0.114$ p > .05	69/161 (42.9%)	35/62 (56.5%)		

(29) Patient 2: distribution of error rates (number of errors /number of stimuli) in CVCV control stimuli as a function of the stimulus length

Control stimuli	1 syllable	2 syllables	3 syllables
Phase 1 $\chi^2 = 4.24$,			
p > .05	11/58 (19%)	77/307 (25.1%)	22/63 (34.9%)
Phase 2 $\chi^2 = 6.5$,			
p < .05	8/42 (19.1%)	73/227 (32.2%)	22/50 (44%)

This undoubtedly indicates that Patient 2 faces metrical limitations on word length. Yet the lower tolerance threshold cannot be totally discarded as an explanation for the increase of segment deletions in the lengthening marked syllabic contexts in Phase 2 in (27). Our argument is based on the nature of insertions in diphthongs. As can be seen in (30a), insertions in diphthongs consist in all cases but one, i.e. 92.3 per cent of cases, in the insertion of a nucleus, to which the second part of the diphthong attaches, not in the insertion of a consonant between the two vowels. For instance, *buisson*, in (30b), is pronounced [py.isɔ] by the patient, that is with a hiatus (a hetero syllabic VV sequence) instead of a diphthong.

(30) Patient 2: insertions of a nucleus in diphthongs
    a. statistics

Phases 1 and 2	nucleus insertions (hiatus creation)	consonant insertions
total: 13	12 (92.3%)	1 (7.7%)

    b. examples

French stimuli		gloss	patient	error type
(i) *buisson*	[bɥisɔ]	'bush'	[py.isɔ]	hiatus
(ii) *muissant*	[mɥisā]	non-word	[my.isāstā]	hiatus
(iii) *pion*	[pjɔ]	'pawn'	[piju]	C insertion

This suggests that the patient is sensitive not only to the length result of the stimuli but also to the complexity of the repair. Repairing a diphthong by creating a hiatus (i.e. a heterosyllabic VV-sequence), as in (30bi) and (30bii), is less demanding in terms of operations than inserting a consonant between the two nuclear segments in order to generate a VCV sequence, as in (30biii). As shown in (31a), hiatus creation requires only the insertion of a nucleus. It does not necessitate the insertion of any new segmental material since its very purpose is to resyllabify one of the two segments of the diphthong. Whereas inserting a consonant between the two parts of the diphthong requires, as shown in (31*b*): (i) insertion of a nucleus, as in the first case, but also (ii) insertion of an epenthetic consonant in the empty onset of the newly created syllable.

(31) Hiatus creation vs. consonant insertion: the procedural weight
      a. creation of a hiatus   *b.* insertion of a consonant in the
                                             diphthong
          (i) insertion of a nucleus   (i) insertion of a nucleus
          ————   (ii) filling of the empty onset
                                                   (with a consonant)

Interestingly, the patient is willing to create a marked syllabic context, i.e. a hiatus, in order to ease the repair of another marked syllabic context, the diphthong. In other words, the patient prefers a marked result to a heavy procedure. This suggests that not only do paraphasias obey metrical considerations, but that they are also governed by the lowering of the patient's tolerance threshold to costly repairs—although our current results do not permit us to assert with certainty that this factor is exclusively or jointly (with metrical limitations) responsible for the increase in segment deletions in Phase 2 in (27).

Before concluding, note that hiatus creation is not restricted to Patient 2 in any respect. Diphthongs were also adapted in hiatus in a considerable number of cases in Study 1 (e.g. *avion* [avjɔ̃] 'plane' → patient [avi.ɔ̃], *piéton* [pjetɔ̃] 'pedestrian' → patient [pi.etɔ̃]), even though Béland and Paradis (1997) did not interpret hiatus creation as insertion (namely of a nucleus) at the time of Study 1. Repair of diphthongs by hiatus creation is also frequent in acquisition. We will see striking results with the presentation of our children's errors in the next section.

We conclude that the results presented in this section allowed us to reach our two objectives in (19). In showing that syllabic errors are very seldom in CV(CV) control stimuli in both the first and second study, while clearly prominent in marked syllabic contexts, we have demonstrated that syllabic errors in aphasic speech along with syllabic adaptations in loanwords are triggered by universally conditioned syllabic constraints, i.e. constraints that exist in natural languages, and whose purpose is to rule out marked syllabic contexts (see (19*a*)). We have also partly attained our second objective in showing that the reason segment preservation is not as great in aphasic speech as in loanword adaptation might be because the Preservation Principle conflicts with the Threshold Principle and metrical limitations in aphasic speech. Indeed, there are very good reasons to believe that the effect of the

Preservation Principle is reduced either by the patient's low tolerance threshold to complex repair or by a metrical constraint activated by the patient on word length, or both of these factors.

8.4. A COMPARISON BETWEEN CHILDREN'S ERRORS AND PARAPHASIAS

In the course of our studies on paraphasias, we became increasingly intrigued about whether the errors produced by aphasics were comparable to those produced by children. In order to test this hypothesis, we studied the errors produced by two groups of French-speaking children, aged between 6 and 6.75 years.

The first group contained 30 normal children and the second group 26 children with PAD (Phonological Awareness Disabilities), who were selected on the basis of the criteria list proposed by Catts (1997) for identifying children at risk for reading disabilities. The 56 children were administered 12 tests measuring their metaphonological abilities including rhyme production, rhyme recognition, syllabic and phonemic segmentation, phonemic and syllabic synthesis, phonemic and syllabic inversion (e.g. [bato] → [toba]). The 56 children were tested for verbal and non-verbal IQ, expressive and receptive vocabulary tests (EWOP (Gardner 1990) and EVIP (Dunn, Thériault-Whalen, and Dunn 1993), which are French adaptations of tests similar to the Peabody Vocabulary Test). Children were also tested for alphabet knowledge and sound-to-spelling correspondences. Those that were able to read were discarded. In all language tests, mean scores of children identified at risk (PAD) were significantly lower than mean scores of control children. All the PAD children were on a special programme, called 'classe de maturation' in French, a programme for children who are identified at risk for reading disabilities.

The tests comprised only non-words in order to maximally reduce interference with long-term memory. Two stimuli sets were elaborated: a first set was made up of 120 bisyllabic and trisyllabic non-word stimuli comprising one (two in the case of trisyllabic stimuli) CV-syllable and a syllable corresponding to one of the six marked syllabic contexts (described in (3)). There were 20 stimuli for each marked syllabic context. For instance, the stimulus set comprised 20 non-word stimuli such as [klora], a non-word with a word-initial branching onset, i.e. a marked syllabic context. The second stimuli set was made up of 80 control stimuli (i.e. stimuli with no marked syllabic context), including 20 bisyllabics (e.g. [mido]), 20 trisyllabics (e.g. [rogida]), 20 quadrisyllabics (e.g. [forekalu]), and 20 stimuli of five syllables (e.g. [gitunavose]).

The 200 stimuli were tape-recorded in three different randomized orders and administered to the children in a repetition test. In order to eliminate possible contamination of phonological processing by access to the orthographic representation, the study was conducted before the children received reading education, that is, either at the end of kindergarten, or at the very beginning of the first grade.

Our general objectives remain those presented in (19), that is, to show that syllabic errors in acquisition and aphasic speech, like loanword adaptations, are governed by universally conditioned syllabic constraints, i.e. constraints that exist in natural languages, (see (19*a*)), and that the reason preservation of segments is not as great in acquisition and aphasic speech as in loanword adaptation is because the Preservation Principle, in the two former cases, conflicts with other constraints, here the Threshold Principle and a metrical constraint on word length (see (19*b*)). Our specific hypotheses in relation to children's errors and our objectives in (19) are displayed in (32).

(32) Hypotheses on children's errors

    a. Both children's groups should produce more syllabic errors in marked syllabic contexts than in unmarked syllabic ones (see Objective (19*a*)).

    b. A strong stimulus length effect is expected. In control stimuli, the error rate should increase with the number of syllables in the stimuli, and the number of segment insertions should be much greater in non-lengthening marked syllabic contexts than in lengthening ones.

    c. If there is a word length effect, there should be more segment deletions in children's errors than in loanword adaptations, as the result of a conflict between the Preservation Principle and metrical limitations (see Objective (19*b*)).

    d. Having a less mature phonological system, PAD children's tolerance threshold should be lower than that of normal children, and their metrical constraint on word length stronger. Consequently, they should produce more errors in general, and more errors of the segment deletion type, since conflicts between the Preservation Principle and both the Threshold Principle and the metrical constraint are greater in PAD children than in normal ones (see Objective (19*b*)).

As predicted by Hypothesis (32*a*), both control and PAD children produced a significantly greater number of errors in marked syllabic contexts than in control CVCV stimuli, as can be seen in (33). The error rate for normal children in marked contexts is 40.9 per cent vs. 8.2 per cent in control stimuli, and, for PAD children, 58.4 per cent vs. 17.2 per cent in control stimuli. Here again we considered only bisyllabic stimuli to eliminate a word length effect in terms of number of syllables.

(33) Rate of errors in syllabically marked vs. control CVCV bisyllabic stimuli

normal children:	marked:	282/689	40.9%
$\chi^2 = 33.18$, p < .001	control:	7/85	8.2%
PAD children:	marked:	729/1249	58.4%
$\chi^2 = 102.13$, p < .001	control:	30/174	17.2%

Children with PAD, having a less mature phonological system (see Hypothesis (32*d*)), produced a greater number of errors than normal children, which is not surprising since normal children have acquired more of French syllabic structure. The difference in the results between marked and control stimuli in (33) demonstrates that children's errors are no more random than the errors produced by our two aphasic patients, i.e. children's errors as well as paraphasias are caused by syllabic constraints found in natural languages, which shows that they are as phonologically principled as are loanword adaptations.

Children fix up marked syllabic structures in the same ways as do borrowers with loanwords, and aphasics with stimuli: they insert or delete content. However, as can be observed in Table 8.5, segment deletion applies much more often in children's errors than in loanword adaptations. Segment deletions represent 87.6 per cent of cases for normal children and 94.5 per cent for PAD children. Thus, as expected (see Hypothesis 32*d*), PAD children produced more segment deletions than normal children. Deletions are even more frequent in children's errors than in the paraphasias produced by our two patients in the late stages of their deficit. This difference between aphasics and children in the number of segment deletions may be partly attributed to the fact that children were tested with non-words only. Non-words, having no lexical representation, are more difficult to handle, and usually yield more errors than words.

More generally, the very high rate of segment deletions in children's errors may be attributed, at least partly, to a metrical constraint on word/stimulus length, as predicted by Hypothesis (32*c*). The analysis of the errors produced in the eighty control stimuli revealed a strong stimulus length effect in both groups, that is, the mean number of errors increases dramatically with the

TABLE 8.5. Distribution of insertion and deletion errors in lengthening marked syllabic contexts for normal and PAD children

Lengthening contexts	Children's group	Insertions		Deletions	
Branching onsets	normal	1/28	(3.6%)	27/28	(96.4%)
	PAD	0	(0%)	97	(100%)
Simple codas	normal	0	(0%)	5	(100%)
	PAD	0	(0%)	37	(100%)
Branching codas	normal	10/139	(7.2%)	129/139	(92.8%)
	PAD	4/281	(1.4%)	277/281	(98.6%)
Diphthongs	normal	18/54	(33.3%)	36/54	(66.7%)
	PAD	27/149	(18.1%)	122/149	(81.9%)
Total	normal	28/225	(12.4%)	197/225	(87.6%)
	PAD	31/564	(5.5%)	533/564	(94.5%)

number of syllables in the stimuli, as predicted by Hypothesis (32*b*). This is indicated by Fig. 8.1.

Note, however, that although the mean number of errors is higher in the PAD than in the normal group, the gap between the two groups does not increase with stimulus length. This indicates that the higher number of errors in the PAD group cannot be attributed solely to an eventual deficit of working memory in PAD children. If a span reduction in working memory was responsible for the difference between the two groups, the difference between the two groups would increase with the stimulus length. Clearly, a metrical constraint is at work for both groups of children. We suggest that this metrical constraint is responsible, at least in large measure, for the very

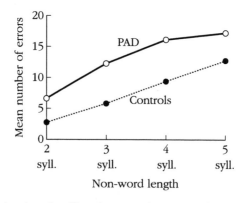

FIG. 8.1. Stimulus length effect (non-word repetition) in control stimuli for both groups.

high rate of segment deletions in the errors produced by both groups of children (see Hypothesis (32c)), although we cannot prove it specifically at this stage of our research.

As can be seen in Table 8.6, when the repair of a marked syllabic structure does not conflict with metrical limitations, i.e. it does not entail an increase in the number of syllables within the stimuli, as is the case with non-lengthening marked syllabic contexts, there are considerably more segment insertions than segment deletions. This further supports Hypothesis (32b), according to which there should be a strong stimulus length effect in children's errors. In Table 8.6, the total number of insertions for the word-initial empty onset and the hiatus contexts represents 65.3 per cent for normal children and 76.8 per cent for PAD children, a drastic difference from the results in Table 8.5. Note that, surprisingly, PAD children produced a few more segment insertions than normal children, a fact for which we have no explanation at this point.

The high rate of segment insertions indicates that the Preservation Principle is as active in children as in borrowers, but that it might conflict with a strong metrical constraint on word/stimulus length in children (see Hypothesis (32c)). Now does the tolerance threshold of children play any role at all in those results or is the metrical constraint the only factor responsible for segment deletions? Again, the way diphthongs are repaired provides an answer. As can be seen in (34), diphthongs undergo many more insertions than the three other contexts (branching onsets, branching codas, and simple codas). If we add those three contexts, as in (34), we notice that segment insertion represents, for those three contexts, 6.4 per cent and 1 per cent for normal and PAD children, respectively, whereas, for diphthongs, it represents up to 33 per cent and 18 per cent for normal and PAD children, respectively.

Table 8.6. Distribution of insertion and deletion errors in the non-lengthening marked syllabic contexts for normal and PAD children

Non-length. contexts	Children's group	Insertions	Deletions
Word-initial empty onsets	normal	4/9 (44.4%)	5/9 (55.6%)
	PAD	16/18 (89%)	2/18 (11%)
Hiatus	normal	30/43 (70%)	13/43 (30%)
	PAD	80/107 (75%)	27/107 (25%)
Total	normal	34/52 (65.3%)	18/52 (34.7%)
	PAD	96/125 (76.8%)	29/125 (23.2%)

(34) Insertions vs. deletions in diphthongs vs. the three other lengthening
     contexts

Lengthening contexts	Children's group	Insertions	Deletions
Diphthongs	normal	18/54 (33%)	36/54 (67%)
	PAD	27/149 (18%)	122/149 (82%)
Three other lengthening contexts	normal	11/172 (6.4%)	161/172 (93.6%)
	PAD	4/415 (1%)	411/415 (99%)

Why such a big difference between diphthongs and the three other
lengthening contexts? Why is it that adding a syllable in diphthongs is not
as big a problem as adding a syllable in the other three contexts? As seen in
section 8.3.2 with the paraphasias of Patient 2, the answer resides in the way
the repair is done. As shown in (35), diphthongs are repaired in the majority
of cases—80 per cent and 72 per cent of cases for normal and PAD children,
respectively—by the creation of a hiatus, i.e. by the insertion of a nucleus for
which no segmental filling is required. Diphthongs are repaired by children
in the same way as in aphasic speech, i.e. with a minimum number of steps.
As was shown in (31), hiatus creation requires only the insertion of a nucleus,
whereas consonant insertion necessitates the insertion of a nucleus in addition
to onset filling.

(35) Children's errors: insertions in diphthongs

	Nucleus insertions (hiatus creation)	Consonant insertions
Normal	16/20 (80%)	4/20 (20%)
PAD	26/36 (72%)	10/36 (28%)

Note that PAD children produced a slightly higher rate of consonant
insertions than normal children. We suggest that this may be due to PAD
children having greater difficulty handling a marked result than coping with a
heavy procedure. In other words, we suggest that PAD children may have a
lower tolerance for hiatus, the marked syllabic context which results from the
mere insertion of a nucleus in diphthongs, than normal children. As can be

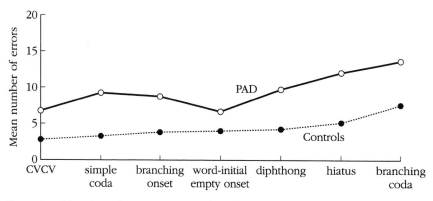

F I G. 8.2. Number of errors per control and marked syllabic context in PAD and normal children (structure effect).

seen in Fig. 8.2, indeed, PAD children produced a very high rate of errors in the hiatus context, a much higher rate than normal children.

In line with Hypothesis (32*d*), we conclude that the Preservation Principle is as active in children's errors as in loanword adaptations. However, in acquisition as in aphasic speech, preservation is more prone to conflicts, namely with the Threshold Principle and metrical limitations.

8.5. CONCLUSION

In this chapter, we have endeavoured to show that syllabic paraphasias, as well as children's errors, are not random, i.e. they are triggered by syllabic constraints that are commonplace among languages, and that the ill-formed syllabic structures responsible for the syllabic errors observed in our corpora of paraphasias and children's errors are repaired in ways comparable to those found in syllabic adaptations of loanwords (insertion and deletion of material/structure). This chapter was also devoted to showing that paraphasias and children's errors obey the same principles as loanword adaptation, that is, the Preservation Principle and a limit to its cost, in the form of a metrical constraint and/or the tolerance threshold of the borrower, the aphasic, or the child. Those two objectives were formally expressed in (19). However, the analysis of the errors produced by our two aphasic patients and our two groups of children, presented in sections 8.3 and 8.4, respectively, indicate that children and PPA aphasics seem to face a metrical constraint that is not generally found in the adaptations of the borrowings of our database (see however the case of word-initial vowels in MA in section 8.2). Thus, one might wonder why it is the case in aphasic speech and acquisition, but not in loanword adaptation.

We suggest that the child and aphasic language is ruled by the default settings of UG (Universal Grammar), which say 'no' to any sort of marked material, such as words longer than two or even one syllable—depending on the acquisition stage of the child or the involution stage of the aphasic. This is not the case of borrowers whose mother tongue does not have a strict limit on word length: they have reset the default (unmarked) metrical parameters of UG with marked settings a long time ago. Thus, in the case of borrowers, the Preservation Principle, most of the time, does not conflict with a metrical constraint. This proposal accounts for the very high rate of segment preservation that we observed in the statistics of Tables 8.1 and 8.2, which contrasts with the generally low rate of segment preservation in aphasic speech and acquisition. Our position may be schematized as in (36). As shown in (36*a*), borrowers who do not have a metrical constraint (MC) on word length in their language are obviously not expected to enforce one in the adaptation of borrowings. As can be observed in (36*b*) and (36*c*), this contrasts with children and PPA aphasics, who are both influenced by the default settings of UG. In the case of children, this is so because they have not yet acquired or have not totally mastered the marked metrical settings of their mother tongue (i.e. they are still left with the unmarked metrical settings of UG, which limits the length of words to one or two syllables), whereas in the case of PPA aphasics, this is so because they are no longer able to handle the marked metrical settings of their mother tongue (i.e. they are returning to the unmarked metrical settings of UG).

(36) Explanations for the difference in the rates of segment deletion in adaptations and errors produced by children and PPA cases

a. borrowers	*b.* children	*c.* PPA aphasics
Source language (no MC) → target language (no MC)	UG (MC)→ 1st language (no MC)	1st language (no MC) → UG (MC)

This general approach allows us to make the predictions in (37) that we leave for further investigation.

(37) Predictions following from (36):

    a. A borrowing language which is ruled by a metrical constraint on word length similar to that of Gere, in (16), should present rates of deletion similar to those found in child and aphasic language. This seems to be the case of word-initial vowels in MA in section 8.2, although the metrical constraint that we posit in MA is not absolute.

    b. Since learning a language involves resetting parameters, it is expected that normal children will reset parameters (i.e. they will lift the metrical constraint of UG) earlier than PAD children, which is confirmed by our results in section 8.4, provided the high rate of segment deletions in the errors of our children is at least partly due to metrical limitations. In the same line of reasoning, this leads us to predict that the error pattern in younger normal children should be similar to that of PAD children.

    c. Since PPA aphasia involves the regressive resetting of parameters, we expect the metrical constraint of UG to show stronger effect in the later stages of the disease, and yield increasing segment deletion. This prediction is confirmed by our results in section 8.3, provided, as in the case of children, that the high rate of segment deletions in the errors produced by our aphasic patients in Phase 2 is at least partly due to metrical limitations. Conversely, we predict that the reverse effect should be observed in the case of aphasia recovery (progressive resetting).

9

What Can the Utterance 'Tan, Tan' of Broca's Patient Leborgne Tell Us about the Hypothesis of an Emergent 'Babble-Syllable' Downloaded by SMA?

Christian Abry, Muriel Stefanuto, Anne Vilain, and Rafael Laboissière

We wish to thank the following people for comments and references: Monica Baciu-Raybaudi, Pierre Badin, Pierre Bessière, Catherine Best, Gerhard Blanken, Driss Boussaoud, Bénédicte de Boysson-Bardies, Stéphanie Brosda, Marie-Agnès Cathiard, Patrick Chauvel, Barbara Davis, Jean Decety, Jean-François Démonet, Jacques Durand, Christopher Frith, Vincent Gracco, Julie Grèzes, Pierre Hallé, Marc Jeannerod, Jean-Pierre Joseph, Catherine Liégeois-Chauvel, Hélène Lœvenbruck, Peter MacNeilage, Jean-Luc Nespoulous, David Ostry, Yohan Payan, Claude Prablanc, Giacomo Rizzolatti, Jean-Luc Schwartz, Christoph Segebarth, Saul Sternberg, Carol Stoel-Gammon, Jacques Vauclair, Marilyn Vihman; we also received the help of the teams involved in the 'Speech Emergence and Robotics' project (ARASSH, Lyon) and in the French Cogniscience Programme (Paris).

9.1. WHAT IS AT ISSUE FOR NEUROPHONETICS AND THEORIES IN PHONOLOGY?

Brain studies are often considered as irrelevant for linguistic theory *per se*, even by some proponents of the most 'language organicist' Chomskyan school, who have been known to disqualify researchers using brain imaging facilities, by simply claiming that they borrow naive theories in designing their experimental exploration of the brain (see the debate raised by Poeppel 1996*a*, 1996*b*, vs. Démonet et al. 1996). From our point of view these neuropsychological models certainly have biases. First and foremost such a secondary skill as *reading* is considered at least as central for them as speech phonology and language semantics (as exemplified by Posner and Raichle 1994, and even more recently in Price 1998). Consequently when they explore the link—direct or through intermediate units, forward or backward—between semantic classes and symbolic representations of the speech input, they conceive this input as a somewhat elaborated variant of the orthographic model (with the notable exception of a small set of studies on lexical access through experimentally controlled coarticulation). But this is not to say that 'naive' theories cannot make an important contribution to our understanding of language. In particular, we do not think that empirical data (be they descriptively or experimentally elicited) which were designed for the purpose of testing one theory, would *ipso facto* be irrelevant for another type of investigation.

It is true that phoneme categorization and monitoring tasks have evidenced, quite surprisingly for such typical *perception* tasks, activations in the left inferior frontal gyrus, which includes the *classical production* Broca's area.[1] The best explanation for the moment is that it is only when such phonological tasks are *difficult* (Démonet et al. 1996, this volume) that they call for working memory, specifically the components of Baddeley's articulatory loop, a network including Broca's area. We will leave out of the debate here a growing set of studies which evidence the non-language-specific involvement of Broca's area and surrounding regions (from the frontal left inferior gyrus to the ventral part) in working memory for the semantics of recognition or action identification (Rizzolatti et al. 1996*a*, Grafton et al. 1996). Nor will we consider one hyperspecific claim that Broca's area itself is dedicated only to the Chomskyan operation of syntactic movement transformation, for comprehension, and to tense inflection, for production (Grodzinsky 2000). As far as working memory is concerned, one could conclude that these frontal activations are more revealing of 'general'

---

[1] Editors' note: for further discussion of the brain, see Ch. 10.

processes than of linguistic ones (Poeppel 1996*a*). But it remains true that, not for general but for precise phonological tasks, when these frontal/non-frontal relationships are put into the classical issue of interhemispheric transfers, imaging results reinforce classical EEG data on speech category acquisition. Frontal vs. non-frontal (temporo-parietal) and left vs. right hemispheric specializations are thus at issue, for speech vs. non-speech sounds, common vs. uncommon speech mechanisms (e.g. Zulu clicks), native vs. non-native contrasts, between-category vs. within-category perception and production (for perception, see Best et al. in preparation; and for production, Abry et al. in preparation).

In short, we see the exploration of the brain universe as cumulative and growing exponentially in the same way as the discovery of the stars and planets, just comparable to the exploration of the surface of the earth, speeding during the last centuries . . . but advancing very slowly in neurophonetics (see the very small number of brain imaging communications within and outside the neurophonetics session at the 1999 International Congress of Phonetic Sciences). Consequently, if one wants to make some cumulative progress in phonetic cognition—in other words (borrowed from Marr 1982), if one wants to advance knowledge about *representations* (from on-line to long-term ones), *processes*, and *constraints*, constitutive of speech, in its full auditory-visual bimodality (partially handicapped for the deaf, *and* the blind, Mills 1987), or exceptionally haptic (tactile, proprioceptive, and kinaesthetic) for deaf-blind users of Tadoma (Reed et al. 1992)—one has to ask new questions both from old and brand new data (for this integrative view of phonetic cognition, see Schwartz et al. this volume).

9.2. BABBLE, THEN SYLLABLE

For us a rather new fundamental question about the organization of speech—as promoted for a long time by Peter MacNeilage's theory (we will come back below to the main debate about it)—is to consider that basic phonological units, be they syllables, phonemes, or features/gestures, are by-products and not primes. This runs contrary to any of the current phonological approaches, which all build syllables from smaller units, a legacy from the *free monoid* of Schützenberger and Chomsky (and its successors, including GEN in Optimality Theory). In the view to which we adhere here, all these units are the result of the development in the child of two main control components. As in many other types of behaviour, like walking, grasping, etc., the speech signal is biocybernetically a compound of (i) a carrier control, on proximal effectors, and (ii) a carried control, on distal end-effectors. The carrier component of speech generates an open–close cyclicity, depending on the control of the mandible (in fact an oro-laryngeal coordination, recruiting the *hyoid-mandibular carrier system*, Laboissière, Ostry, and Feldman 1996). Starting from the sparse degrees of freedom of jaw waggles in babbling (not the maximum 6 degrees, for sure), the carried articulators, the tongue and the lower lip, produce contacts, labial or (and) coronal [baba, dada, bdadba], depending on the baby's anatomy and current on-line, state-to-state, presetting behaviours. Then, for these carried articulators, independence from the jaw will emerge, as observed in the hand development, from the grasp reflex to common fingering skills. This is what we call 'babble-syllable', to avoid identifying this true precursor of the syllable with what current phonology calls a syllable.

A valuable example of a [bababa] movement pattern has recently been made available by Munhall and Jones (1998: 524; even if they call it 'anecdotal', since their OPTOTRAK system is obviously not easy to use with an 8-month-old baby babbling):

The most important point to note . . . is that the movement does not appear to involve the upper lip actively. The only upper lip movement occurs in phase [in the same upward direction] with the lower lip motion and is presumably caused by the lower lip forces pushing the upper lip upward after contact. This pattern is consistent with [MacNeilage's] proposal that initial babbling primarily involves mandibular motion; the lower lip rides on the jaw and deforms [the] upper lip on contact [by simple compliance]. In contrast [for] an adult producing the same sequence . . . , the upper and lower lip both produce opening gestures [i.e. in opposite directions along the vocalic phase]. In addition, some deformation of the upper lip can be observed at the lower lip's upward displacement peak [but the upper lip is obviously less compliant, or more counteracting].

The achievement of this independence can be biocybernetically demonstrated to be viable through the computation of what we called a *no-motion manifold* (Laboissière, Ostry, and Feldman 1996). The general functional question was: 'How is it possible to recover our *given* anatomical degrees of freedom of our articulators, the jaw, the tongue, and the lips, in the same way as the *given* degrees of freedom of our hand are finally recovered with enough practical skill?' When applied to the hyoid-mandibular carrier system, it appeared that in spite of the high non-linearity of the muscle system which drives the jaw and hyoid degrees of freedom recruited in speech movements, there was a simple solution to control *independently* each of these *given* distal degrees of freedom (Laboissière, Ostry, and Feldman 1996, for the tongue see Sanguineti, Laboissière, and Ostry 1998). This control is probably neurally achieved by transfer, along the learning process, of the cortical maps corresponding to the coordinated articulators to the cerebellum (Wolpert, Miall, and Kawato 1998). This issue will not be addressed here (for a possible developmental scenario, see Vilain et al. 1999). As a result, this emergence of articulator independence will be the basis, in the phonological literature accounts, of featural or gestural descriptions, from which the jaw is steadily absent, in spite of its original role for syllable pacing and its synergetical role in coarticulation (and this even when its behaviour is crucial for an output-oriented aeroacoustic control, as for [s], e.g. Lee, Beckman, and Jackson 1994).

Since it is probable that, after normal integration in the child's development of the two fundamental components of speech, some brain diseases will give rise to dissociation or disintegration of these two components, we dedicated our meta-analysis of the literature in aphasiology to the search for such cases.

9.3. AN INSUPERABLE PROBLEM . . .

In the debate which took place in *Behavioral and Brain Sciences* (*BBS*), in which we participated around Peter MacNeilage's *Frame/Content Theory of the Evolution of Speech Production* (MacNeilage 1998), we supported the author's point of view, that the so-called typical 'canonical babbling' of the [bababa] or [dadada] type—a *frame* without segmental *content* in MacNeilage's terms, emerging suddenly at about 7 months of age—could be controlled by the Supplementary Motor Area (SMA), and not classical Broca's. In actual fact, we contributed 'negatively', as it were, by adding only one study, among a very small strand of studies in aphasiology, to the arguments against a control of babbling by Broca's area, which is different from a positive claim in favour of SMA (Abry et al. 1998: 513).

MacNeilage's reaction to our commentary on this point was formulated in a rather decisive way:

Abry et al. seem to have unearthed an insuperable problem for the three commentators who conclude that both frame and content are controlled in lateral premotor cortex [where Broca's area is]—Abbs and DePaul [1998], Jürgens [1998], and Lund [1998]. They [Abry et al. 1998] refer to the work of Poeck et al. (1984), who distinguish two classes of global aphasics, the classical type with negligible comprehension or production of language and a single repeated syllable form, much as Broca's famous patient repeated 'tantantan'. As global aphasia is associated with relatively complete destruction of the perisylvian cortex of the left hemisphere, the subgroup who produced syllabic sequences could not be producing their simple frames under control of left lateral premotor cortex. (MacNeilage 1998: 536).

We will not repeat here the main arguments against SMA by such prominent researchers in the field as Uwe Jürgens for animal vocalization, James Lund for mastication, and James Abbs for speech (and also hand) motor control. It will be sufficient to refer to the debate for both their separate and converging criticisms, since what is at stake here is their proposal to control *both frame and content* in the lateral system, with no contribution from another system like SMA (Abbs and DePaul 1998: 512 admit that this SMA control could be, in humans, a 'primitive residual' coming from monkey vocalization, restricted to children's vocalization/babbling, but not active in human adults). Their argument rests mainly on the fact that both the carrier mandibula and the carried tongue and lip are actually controlled in the lateral system for mastication. This is of course uncontroversial and for our part we do not take as our own the problem faced by MacNeilage's hypothesis in considering that during phylogeny this lateral system would have to be integrated together with the primitive medial vocalization system (Jürgens, 1998: 519 has good arguments for dissociating in the monkey's brainstem the mastication and vocalization systems). For, whether mastication is integrated or not in speech, by a descent with modification evolution, it remains possible for adult humans to produce such babble-like utterances, in spite of the fact that their *speech lateral system* is impaired. And that is the insuperable problem for the proposal of these three eminent opponents (the other twenty-four commentaries not considering this SMA topic, except ours).

Just anticipating MacNeilage's defence, which makes use of the work of Ziegler, Kilian, and Deger (1997), we will emphasize that SMA can take care of the *frame* without coping with the *content* of the syllable. Is this frame mandibular-based and motorically driven by SMA? This is another double set of questions. The jaw can obviously move without lateral control in primate vocalization, including human emotional sounds, and in the speech of humans with a large lesion in the domain of the middle cerebral artery; and the same for the carried articulators. Finally SMA proper or other regions nearby could have very little to do with motor execution, as we will see later.

One must emphasize with MacNeilage (1998: 532) that the debate is still about the neural structures underlying the two components. 'The lack of an explicit objection [among the twenty-seven commentaries] to the frame/ content characterization of modern speech production would seem to be a very important outcome of the target article. The credit for the survival of this dichotomy goes primarily to the branch of psycholinguistics concerned with speech errors at the phonological level [as re-emphasized by Levelt 1999]. This outcome gives support to my contention . . . that "no theory of . . . the organization of speech . . . that does not include the dual components metaphorically labelled frame and content . . . is a viable one".' We will take here the opportunity to be more precise in what can be meta-analysed in the literature in order to be linked as evidence for the re-emergence of the carrier component of speech and the syllable in speech disorders.

9.4. REMEMBERING THAT TAN SAID: 'TAN, TAN'

The reputation of Broca's patient Leborgne is worldwide. But what he said has not always been reported *verbatim*. Just take two recent 'handbooks'. In the English tradition, Ray Kent (1997) wrote on p. 287 of his well-documented volume *The Speech Sciences*: 'So severe was the disorder that Broca's patient could say only a single word—"tan".' (Who said it was a word . . . or a proposition?) In the French tradition, Marc Jeannerod (1996: 49) commented in his reference book *De la physiologie mentale* (a history of the relationships between biology and psychology): 'il [Leborgne] ne disposait plus que de rares phonèmes qu'il répétait en toutes circonstances, ce qui lui avait valu le surnom de "Tan".'[2] (Who said he pronounced phonemes . . . or rather a syllable, as labelled by Broca?)

In fact, Broca met Leborgne for the first time on 12 April 1861. The patient died on the 17th. The following day, Broca carried out a post-mortem examination of his brain and displayed the latter at his Society of Anthropology. Section II of Broca (1861) is entitled *Aphémie datant de vingt et un ans* [Aphasia having started twenty-one years earlier], *produite par* [caused by] *le ramollissement chronique et progressif* [the chronic and progressive degeneration] *de la seconde et de la troisième circonvolution de l'étage supérieur du lobe frontal gauche* [of the second and third gyri of the upper part of the left frontal lobe]. The first paragraph reads: 'Aux questions que je lui adressai . . . , il ne répondit que par le monosyllabe *tan*, répété deux fois de suite [In answer to all the questions I put to him he just uttered the monosyllable *tan* repeated twice].' And in the third paragraph: 'quelle que fût la question qu'on lui adressât, il répondait toujours: *tan, tan* [Whatever the question put to him, his answer was always: *tan, tan*].' Hence even if Broca never wrote that Leborgne said 'tantantan', as MacNeilage emphasizes about our reminder in *BBS*, this is probably the closest account of his actual speech performance. In fact, what was remembered by posterity was his derived

---

[2] Editor's translation: 'He [Leborgne] could only use rare phonemes which he repeated in all circumstances, which is why he had been nicknamed "Tan".'

nickname: 'Il allait et venait dans l'hospice où il était connu sous le nom de *Tan*. [He would come and go in the hospital where he was known under the name of *Tan*.]'

More has been written about Leborgne by Broca. From his youth, he had been an epileptic; in spite of a paralysis of the right arm and leg, and to some extent of the left side of the face, his tongue was not twisted, neither to the left nor to the right, and it remained free to perform common movements; he understood everything and was 'obviously more intelligent than was needed for speaking'; while uttering *tan, tan*, with a perfectly clear pronunciation, he gestured with his left hand in order to be understood; in addition to his 'monosyllable', Broca heard once the stereotypical curse *Sacré nom de Dieu*; etc. And finally his brain was scanned by Castaigne et al. (1980): Leborgne's lesion extended farther and deeper than Brodman 44–5 . . . But SMA was intact.

9.5. TAN'S BROTHERS?

In our *BBS* commentary we claimed that we considered patients with SMA lesions reviewed by Jonas (1981) as 'brothers' of Broca's 'Tan-tan'. This was of course in order to connect another trend of studies with the seminal work of Penfield (Penfield and Welch 1951) and his inheritors such as Jonas in the literature that MacNeilage referred to over a couple of years.

This trend has been concerned for a long time with *speech automatisms* in aphasia (for this term see Huber, Poeck, and Weniger 1989, and for reviews, Blanken 1991, Code 1994, Lebrun 1986, Wallesh 1990), more specifically *recurrent utterances*, comprising both real word recurrent utterances (RWRUs, e.g. 'funny thing, funny thing'), as well as non-meaningful ones (NMRUs, e.g. 'da da da'). In the 19th Hughlings Jackson Lecture, delivered in 1954 at the Neurological Institute of McGill University, at Montreal, the great French aphasiologist Théophile Alajouanine (1956: 4) acknowledged: 'Broca has given the first observation with his patient retaining only the stereotyped expression "TAN-TAN". But Jackson (1915; 1st pub. 1874) was the first who described its chief aspects; he called them first "stock utterances" and later preferred the term "recurring utterances" [or "recurrent utterances"].' Among them can be included what Alajouanine called 'permanent verbal stereotypies': 'The "TAN-TAN" of the first of Broca's patients, or the "TITI-TITI" of one of our cases are examples of iterative stereotypies' (Alajouanine 1956: 5). In fact Alajouanine published few such examples (notice the use of capitals in these repetitions).

One must wait until the British aphasiologist Chris Code to have the first sizeable corpus published (Code 1982*a*, 1982*b*, 1983), both of RWRUs and NMRUs (these are his own terms). Non-meaningful utterances were listed for 22 subjects (Code 1982*a*: 143), in orthographic and 'phonemic' transcription, given by a questionnaire answered by British clinicians, with the number of repetitions produced in an average utterance. [də də də] for 3 patients; [æbɪ dæbɪ]; [hɒlətəuz]; [tɑ tɑ]; [si si]; [pi pi]; [es es es]; [bi bi bi]; [bəu bəu bəu]; [sətɑ sətɑ]; [wi wi wi]; [ɪs]; [nəusi nəusi nəu nəu nəu]; [kɪ kɪ kɪ kɑ]; [əzəz əzəz]; [bi bi]; [eɪ weɪ eɪ weɪ wi wi wi weɪ mmm eɪ weɪ weɪ weɪ]; [dɪ dɪ dɪ]; [kɑ]. An additional subject had various NMRUs: [də də də], [tu tu tu uuuu], [du du du də du], [nə nə nə], [ini ini], [əubɑbrɜ əubɑprɜ], [ibi ibi]. Code (1982*a*: 146) noted that the predominance of dentals and alveolars, i.e. coronals, in RU (62.5 per cent for NMRUs) reflected the English distribution (60.93 per cent).

This work was immediately criticized by the German group in Aachen, led by the great aphasiologist Klaus Poeck (De Bleser and Poeck 1983). They questioned the indirect method used (the questionnaire) for the reliability of the 'phonemic' transcription, incidentally insisting on the fact that 'the sounds produced as NMRU do not fulfill the linguistic criteria of phonemes' (p. 260), a point on which Code (1983) easily agreed. As a whole, it was easy for him to reply that, with this method, he had published the largest corpus, whereas Poeck, De Bleser, and Graf von Keyserlingk (1984), with their direct observations, were on the point of publishing only eight NMRUs.

That is the work we referred to in *BBS* debate as defining *exclusive consonant-vowel recurring utterance aphasia*.[3] Poeck, De Bleser, and von Keyserlingk (1984: 199–200) were aware of the synthesis by Alajouanine (1956), recalling however that factually, within the recurring utterances classified by Jackson: 'it is curious that [he] did not mention an even more restricted class . . . where the patients produce exclusively CV syllables, such as *dada, didi, dodo, mama* . . . This is the language production found in Paul Broca's . . . first patient Leborgne, who was limited to saying "tan-tan" . . .' This reference to Leborgne will be regular in the publications of the German group (Code 1983: 262 just refers to 'Tan', in response to their reference to 'Tan-Tan').

In addition they insisted on the fact that, at that time, Hécaen and Albert (1978) was one of the rare textbooks mentioning the phenomenon of patients producing only 'meaningless phonemes or syllables' like 'Tan-Tan'. Importantly they emphasized again the point that 'there is only one

---

[3] An error was introduced within our abstract by the editor who printed a proof correction, which resulted in an indication 'wrong' before this definition.

recurring syllable, consisting of one and the same consonant and vowel which do not even have the status of phonemes' (p. 211), since they do not contrast. Certainly this argument takes us far from the *frame* concept, where there is not even a segment, not to mention a syllable. Anyway their eight patients uttered repetitively the following CVs: [mæ] (mä); [ta]; [an]/[al]; [od]/[or]; [do]; [di]; [sa]/[da]; [ma]. Poeck, De Bleser, and von Keyserlingk (1984: 200) noticed that 'the consonant was always a dental plosive or a nasal, except in the presence of dysarthria where it could also be a fricative [s] or a liquid [l], [r]'. Finally the dominance of coronals was as obvious as in Code's corpus.

Six years later, a related German group in Freiburg im Breisgau, in collaboration with a Milanese clinician, finally published the largest corpus currently available of twenty-seven aphasics with frequent production of what they called non-lexical speech automatisms, i.e. NMRUs (Blanken, Wallesh, and Papagno 1990: 45, reprinted in Blanken and Marini 1997: 20). For several patients they gave the corresponding sets of variants: [do-do], [da-da], [na-na], [no-no]; [vɛdi], [vidi], [vɛti], [viri]; [diːbn (di)], [tiːbn (di)], [diː]; *bitte sehr* (please); [bɔm], [bam], [mam]; [diː-diː], [siː-siː], [oː-iː], [oː-siː]; [doː-doː], [də-də], [de-de], [dɛ-dɛ], [deːs-deːs], [do-do]; [be-be]; [asa], [aso], [ase]; [na], [ta], [do]; [titetote], [tateto], [tetepi]; [dada]; [tsetsétsetsétsetsétsin]; [do-do]; [ɛː], [hie], [hia]; [da-da]; [ede], [dede]; [tau], [ʃau], [to], [ho]; [da-da], [do-do]; [də-də]; [nau], [deːs]; [da-da], [də-də], [ta], [tat]; [na-ta-ta-ta-ta], [nau]; [hia], [hie], [mama-oːoːma] (ma-grandma); [ti-ti]; [gel, gelel] (and variations). Once again this corpus corroborates the dominance of coronals as in Code's work.

In addition to these two major corpora other evidence remained comparatively anecdotal. In cortical stimulation studies of SMA, when speech was not arrested (i.e, *aphemia* or *aphonia*), *palilalia* was recorded: e.g. 'da da da da', in Penfield and Welch (1951: 300).[4] In the study of SMA irritative lesions by Jonas (1981), among the four cases he described directly: case 1 stuttered; case 2 kept some 'da, da' intrusions (p. 352); case 3 had two paroxysmal disorders uttering 'la, la, la, la' and 'da, da, da, da' (p. 355). Among the other cases he reviewed from the literature, eleven had, comparably with this case 3, paroxysmal utterances comprising, as in cortical stimulation, either a 'rhythmical repetitive emission of vowel sounds requiring only expiratory and vocal cord activity ("ah ah ah . . .") or a vowel or consonant-vowel sounds also requiring control of labial or lingual activity ("oh oh oh . . .", "la la la . . .", "da da da . . .", "ba baba ba", "tati, tati . . .")' (p. 359). Three other patients had a prolonged sound in paroxysmal vocalization, and two

---

[4] Cf. too the earlier study by Brickner (1940); the simultaneous contribution by Erickson and Woolsey (1951); and later, Chauvel (1976), or Dinner and Luders (1995).

repeated a word (like 'oui oui oui . . .', reminiscent of what was said above for verbal stereotypies). In brief Jonas (1981) collected a total of 17 patients with RWRUs (only 2) and NMRUs (15, with 12 producing rhythmic or repetitive utterances).

These rather anecdotal SMA data, comparatively speaking, do not undermine the coronal dominance of the two documented corpora. This is just to say that comparison with child production was not completely forgotten in the literature recognizing Tan's legacy (which excludes the SMA trend, since neither Penfield nor Jonas connected their 'da da da' utterances with 'tan, tan', or to babbling). One of the first objections to Code (1982*a*) was formulated by De Bleser and Poeck (1983: 260) as follows: 'Rather than comparing nonpropositional sounds to frequency counts in normal propositional English, it would have been better to investigate the inventory of sounds occurring in recurring utterances in comparison to the early acquisition of language specific sounds in child language'.[5] This 'early acquisition of language specific sounds' was in fact very far from the *frame* of babbling and their additional remark made this clear: 'There is one problem, however, in that children in the babbling stage always have a variety of CV- and other clusters in their inventory, in contrast to the stereotyped production of NMRU patients.' Without mentioning the controversy surrounding canonical and variegated babbling (Smith, Brown-Sweeney, and Stoel-Gammon 1989), *frames* at this stage are obviously not made of clusters. But the interesting point evidenced by both opponents and their successors is that they converged with consonant place preference data in babbling: coronals have been shown to be most common in English, Swedish, and Japanese (French having as many labials, and sometimes English, depending on the data set, Vihman 1992: 399).

9.6. WHEN *CONSONANT-VOWEL RECURRING UTTERANCE* APHASIOLOGY IS SILENT ABOUT SMA

Since the beginning of the collection of the English and German corpora, there has been a controversy about the definition of the related type of aphasia. Code was criticized by De Bleser and Poeck (1983) and Poeck,

---

[5] Code (1983: 262) saw this remark as asking him to re-examine his data in the light of the so-called regression hypothesis (degeneration recapitulating backward ontogeny) and considered it was out of his scope.

De Bleser, and von Keyserlingk (1984) for, in the reports he collected, patients with RUs were simply classified as Broca's aphasics. For Poeck, following proper testing of patient's performances, one must identify them first as global aphasics; and since, for him, there are two types of global aphasia—standard non-fluent and non-standard fluent—'CV patients' (i.e. with this precise type of NMRU) have to be named *non-standard fluent global aphasics*. Blanken, Wallesh, and Papagno (1990: 42) noticed that if, 'from 75 patients of [Code's] study, the majority was classified as Broca's aphasics by clinicians [they were] nearly evenly followed, however, by global aphasics'. As a matter of fact it was impossible for Poeck, De Bleser, and von Keyserlingk (1984) to distinguish by CT (Computerized Tomography) scans the two types of global aphasics, i.e. to identify a pattern of lesions corresponding to CV recurring utterance aphasia. And the same was true of speech automatisms in general, except that the lesioned structures were also in the depth of the area of supply of the left middle cerebral artery (Haas et al. 1988). It should be added that Poeck, De Bleser, and von Keyserlingk (1984) discarded Kornhuber's (Kornhuber, Brunner, and Wallesh 1979) hypothesis that such a repetitive behaviour was necessarily due to an additional lesion of the left basal ganglia (caudate and/or lenticular nuclei). Finally comparison with CT scans of Tan (Castaigne et al. 1980) led them to recognize that: 'Leborgne's lesion is compatible with the lesion of some patients in either group [CV patients and standard global aphasics]. On the other hand, the lesion in many of our patients is quite different from Leborgne's. Therefore, *Leborgne's lesion represents just one of the many variations we have found in both subgroups of global aphasia*' (our italics, Poeck, De Bleser, and von Keyserlingk 1984: 215–16).

So much for Tan's brotherhood . . . Some time after Code's reply (1983), Haas et al. (1988: 557), from the same German group, in spite of stating again that 'today, speech automatisms are considered a symptom of the most severe aphasic syndrome, global aphasia', acknowledged that 'this statement does not contradict the position of Alajouanine (1956) who described speech automatisms as occurring mainly with severe Broca's aphasia', since 'the traditional French classification of aphasia syndromes refers to global aphasia as "la grande aphasie de Broca"'.

But what about the insuperable impossibility of controlling CV recurring utterances with the lateral system (remember the proposal of MacNeilage's three opponents, Abbs and DePaul, Jürgens, and Lund)? 'The traditional view that the lesion underlying global aphasia is a large one, extending from Broca's to Wernicke's area, is only true for the cumulative representation [of all subjects]. However, when the individual lesions are compared with the cumulative ones, there is great variability in size and localization. Both in standard global aphasia and global aphasia with CV, the individual lesions are large and small, anterior and posterior, single and multiple' (Poeck, De Bleser, and von Keyserlingk 1984: 210). What is sure is that those among their subjects with deep anterior Broca's lesions were not prevented from producing CV utterances. Which is contrary to the prediction one can infer from Abbs and DePaul, Jürgens, and Lund's proposal.

But before throwing out the localizationist baby with the bath water, it must be emphasized that these CT scans in the perisylvian zone, considered as the language region, gave us no news about SMA: it was simply not a priority to scan this other region. More significantly neither Jonas's review, nor any relevant SMA study, was referred to.

9.7. SPEECH AUTOMATISMS: LEFT OR RIGHT?

Starting from Tan's performance, Broca and Jackson gave two different interpretations of speech automatisms. For Broca (1861), the language faculty, in the left hemisphere, was preserved and it was just the specific coordination of articulatory movements for speech that was handicapped. For Jackson, the dominant left hemisphere was controlling propositional speech, and since it was impaired by a lesion, automatisms were the product of the right, non-propositional, hemisphere (1874).

Code adopts the *two-source hypothesis* (Code 1987; see also Van Lancker 1987). For lexical automatisms (RWRUs) he elaborates that: 'an intention to communicate an emotional state is given an holistic phono-articulatory shape by right hemisphere motor Gestalt mechanisms which input the right motor strip' (Code 1983: 263). For non-lexical automatisms his elaboration is different. First: 'The data appears to reflect a simplification process under-lying the distribution of phonemes in RUs, which is most marked in NMRUs, where there is an increase in motorically "easier" articulations' (Code 1982*a*: 151). Hence, 'The origin of NMRUs is probably best explained in phonetic terms. NMRUs are linguistically very different to RWRUs; the majority being CV syllables or concatenations of CV syllables, mainly plosive + vowel. These NMRUs might be interpreted as phonetically "easy" utterances produced when expression was first attempted. This same articulatory pattern being repeated, due to inertia in the system, every time the speech production mechanism receives input' (Code 1982*b*: 162). For Code (1983: 263): 'NMRUs appear to be caused by a severe left-hemisphere lesion . . . Such a lesion may cause interhemispheric diaschisis which interferes with right hemisphere-limbic system interconnections so that a syllabic concatenation is produced of the motorically easiest and phonetically most accessible articulatory segments that the right hemisphere has access to.' Blanken and Marini (1997: 22) recently summarized Code's account as follows: 'The production of non-lexical forms is attributed to a severely damaged phonological system located in the left hemisphere . . . In agreement with the left hemisphere hypothesis, Code [1982a] found evidence that segmental processes are involved in the generation of non-lexical speech automatisms.' This segmental and syllabic concatenation process is, of course, very far from the *frame* concept.

The *common source hypothesis* is adopted by German groups and summarized by Blanken and Marini (1997: 23): 'the Aachen research group (see Haag et al. 1985) considered automatisms to be a product of disinhibited speech mechanisms. Articulatory patterns, be they lexical or not, are thought to directly feed the speech motor system without any control of the central language system.' For the Freiburg group, 'in the framework of Levelt's (1989) speech production model, Blanken (1991) suggested that an impairment of the "articulatory buffer" could be responsible for the generation of automatisms. Although established phonetic programs within the buffer can be (re)activated, the construction of new programs is severely disturbed. Following this hypothesis, the cause for automatisms lies at the interface between the phonological encoding (as part of central speech processing) and the articulatory processes.' After a thorough re-examination of corpora of lexical and non-lexical automatisms in the same patients, Blanken and Marini (1997: 29–30) concluded: 'According to the hypothesis of a common source for speech automatisms, lexical automatisms would also be caused by severely disturbed phonological planning mechanisms. This hypothesis would not have a problem with the parallel production of non-word and real-word automatisms since both patterns are traced back to a severely damaged left-hemisphere speech processing component.' Therefore, if we focus on the CV recurring utterances under examination here, the two hypotheses—both Code's and Blanken's—converge on this left hemisphere speech processing component. Jonas (1981) had something to say about this lateralization and, as we will see just below, so do Ziegler, Kilian, and Deger (1997) (needless to say, SMA studies are not referred to by the Aachen and Freiburg groups, even for Ziegler's German group in Munich). After a thorough examination of the literature, Jonas's (1981: 372) conclusion was straightforward: 'In summary, the nondominant (usually right) [SMA] probably plays no significant role in the control of speech emission.' And new lesional data have confirmed this claim: a right infarction does not disrupt speech (Dick et al. 1986), contrary to a left haemorrhage (Ziegler, Kilian, and Deger 1997).

As a whole, whatever the conceptions—Code's, Blanken's, or Jonas's—the origin of NMRUs or CV recurring utterances is supposed to be left. This discards the possibility of controlling such speech productions within the lateral system in the right hemisphere, which would have saved Abbs and DePaul, Jürgens, and Lund's proposal against MacNeilage.

9.8. SMA DOWNLOADING

In their recent handbook of human neuropsychology, Habib and Galaburda (1994: 323–4) entitled a part of their chapter: SMA the 'other' language area. In this view, SMA speech is part of an *endogenous* action network (be it G. Goldberg's MPS: Medial Premotor System, Goldberg 1985, or a 'willed action' system, following C. Frith 1992); contrary to Broca's speech, which is considered as part of a *responsive* action system (LPS: Lateral Premotor System in Goldberg's terminology). The structure and functions of SMA were reviewed some time ago for language by Caplan (1987) and from a more general point of view by Tanji (1996, for a summary of the new fractionation of SMA areas) and Picard and Strick (1996, for a review of different studies). Among the five functions proposed by Jonas (1981: 369)—(i) initiation of speech, (ii) suppression of automatic speech, (iii) pacing (rhythm control), (iv) control of articulation (supraglottal), (v) control of phonation (glottal)—some of them have become more firmly established. Generation of self-paced 'willed' actions (iii) has currently become part of brain imaging designs for SMA activation (e.g. Reed et al. 1997); its role in the control of the speech rhythm in respiration, phonation, and articulation (iv and v) has been evidenced (Murphy et al. 1997); initiation (i) will be below the main topic of 'downloading SMA'; notice especially this interesting property of suppressing automatic speech (ii), a problem directly related to our aphasic patients with recurring utterance.

Since an important part of the positive argumentation used by MacNeilage in his defence of SMA against his three opponents is taken from Ziegler, Kilian, and Deger (1997, a study published after commentaries, just in time for MacNeilage's response), we will briefly summarize the main results of this study. Their patient became a transcortical motor aphasic after a left anterior cerebral artery haemorrhage, which resulted in a lesion undercutting SMA, disconnecting the posterior part of SMA and the anterior cingulate cortex from the primary motor cortex. In addition transcallosal path was interrupted. For more than two weeks she was completely mute, and it took a month and a week after onset to have her respond with a complete sentence. At the time of testing, one year after onset, 'she was not aphasic and her spontaneous verbal output was no longer reduced', except that she had 'frequent and prolonged pausing, false start and repetitions' (Ziegler, Kilian, and Deger 1997: 1198). Two tests (1 and 3) corroborated each other, the length of the items in number of syllables being found to be more reaction-time consuming than their segmental content. Reaction times were longer for [dadada] than for [dada], while not significantly different when comparing repetitive [dada] vs. [daba]. In addition the onset latency of the second syllable relative to the first syllable was no longer for repeating [dada] than for switching from [da] to [ba] in [daba]. This means that the main problem was *frame* not *content*. 'This would imply that the SMA, while handling chains consisting of syllable units, is "blind" to the segmental make up of each syllable. The existence of a neuroanatomical structure specialized for syllabic chaining processes is consistent with the view that the syllable constitutes a basic unit in speech motor control (Gracco and Abbs, 1985) and in speech acquisition (MacNeilage and Davis 1990). This lends support to the idea that speech production branches into "metrical" and "segmental spellout" processes (Levelt, 1993), and that syllabic frames are conceptually separable from their phonemic content (Sevald et al. 1995)' (p. 1205).

The reference to Levelt's modelling of speech production was made just above by Blanken (1991). It is interesting to point out that Levelt and Schiller's (1998: 520) reaction to MacNeilage's target paper was rather positive. They agreed about the core point of his theory 'that there is a basic syllable cycle in speech'. In addition they agreed on the fact that such a 'basic cycle can run without the retrieval of stored syllable frames [frames meaning for them different constituent structures, CV, CVC, CCV, etc.].' This coincides with Levelt (1999) and colleagues' findings in Dutch and English that instead of retrieving differentiated syllable structures in phonological encoding, nothing more could be specified than the number of syllables and the word's main stress.

It is important to insist on the convergence of the study of Ziegler, Kilian, and Deger (1997) and another unrelated SMA study. For their patient, 'her problem was definitely related to the *initiation* and not to the programming or the execution of a sequence, and that sequence length was a major influencing factor [increasing reaction time]' (p. 1204). Recently Pridgen, Collins, and Fox (1999) concluded, in a key-press task: 'SMA is more likely involved in response initiation than in motor-programming, as TMS [transcranial magnetic stimulation]-induced interruptions of SMA processing affect RT but not performance accuracy.' The case studied by

Ziegler, Kilian, and Deger (1997: 1206) 'resulted from an impairment of initiating sequential articulations, particularly in association with the process of downloading temporarily stored multisyllabic strings from an articulatory buffer'. Surely, Blanken and Ziegler can no longer remain unaware of each other's studies. They share the same buffer hypothesis, stemming from Levelt (1989) and from previous seminal work in chronometry by Sternberg and colleagues (e.g. Sternberg et al. 1978).

9.9. REINFORCING CONNECTIONS TO GROUND THE SYLLABLE IN SPEECH NEURAL CONTROL

In order to evidence the main components of speech, and more specifically the emergence of the syllable from a speech carrier component, we have attempted to link studies which often remained unaware of one another. MacNeilage's theory had already connected in an illuminating way *babbling data* and *SMA studies*, i.e. cortical stimulation by Penfield, irritative lesions reviewed by Jonas, and the neuropsychology of SMA tested by Ziegler's group. Three eminent opponents (Abbs and DePaul, Jürgens and Lund)—not to MacNeilage's concept of *frame/content* for speech organization, but to his proposal concerning the neural support of SMA for the control of the *frame*—proposed to lump both *frame* and *content* into the lateral system (comprising of Broca's area), hence discarding SMA. We made MacNeilage aware of Poeck's—and now of Blanken's—group (both unaware of MacNeilage's theory and connections with SMA studies): these groups gathered valuable data on speech automatisms, with a slight precedence for Code. Poeck's patients helped us prove that a babbling-like aphasia—let's call it 'frame aphasia'—could produce typical CV recurring utterances, like Tan's 'tan, tan', without the lateral system, when it is lesioned in a severe case of Broca's aphasia (global aphasia). Code did not advocate so much for a related specific type of aphasia as Poeck did for CV recurring utterances (not followed by Blanken). But Code, like Blanken and Jonas, helped us in discarding a right hemisphere control for the *frame* production. All these connections reinforce positive claims in favour of a control of CV recurring utterances in the non-lateral left hemisphere. As concerns specifically left SMA, according to Ziegler's group, it seems to remain the best candidate, not for controlling action programming or execution, but for response initiation, downloading a motor sequence temporarily stored in an articulatory buffer.

A remaining question is how their common articulatory buffer hypothesis can account for both speech automatisms and reaction-time data. One group admits that one needs 'more detailed knowledge of the underlying processes than is currently available' (Ziegler, Kilian, and Deger 1997: 1203). This is precisely the conclusion given earlier by the Freiburg representative: 'It has to be emphasized again that the buffer account suggested . . . goes far beyond what the data allow for' (Blanken 1991: 126).

10

Towards Imaging the Neural Correlates of Language Functions

Jean-François Démonet, Guillaume Thierry, and Jean-Luc Nespoulous

Over the last twenty years, the study of the brain correlates of language functions has been marked by a profound mutation. Although the study of aphasia (the 'lesion-based model') prevailed until the 1980s, the evolution of functional neuroimaging techniques has led to new insights into implementation of language functions in the brain, yielding a new way of tackling and testing cognitive models. This new approach (the 'function-based model') is independent of and yet complementary to the previous one. It is based on recording subtle changes in brain activities (assessed via sophisticated imaging methods) that occur upon engagement of one's mind in any experimental cognitive task, such as processing language stimuli.

10.1. THE 'LESION-BASED' MODEL OR THE APHASIA PARADIGM

Following classical works by Broca or Déjerine who described brain lesions in aphasic patients, the main principle of the clinical anatomical method is to relate lesion sites to hopefully specific linguistic deficits. Ideally, the role of a given region in language functions would thus be inferred from the only cognitive deficit associated with damage to this particular site. However, such a one-to-one relationship is never observed in reality, and many factors account for the complexity of studying brain/language relationships especially in patients. Only the main factors will be outlined here. First, aphasic patients exhibit various language disorders and each of them may correspond to several cognitive mechanisms. Second, these symptoms are not just a consequence of damage to brain tissue; they also result from adaptive mechanisms, or strategies, taking place in undamaged parts of the mind/ brain so that considerable recovery from an initial severe aphasia is usually observed over weeks and months after the abrupt lesion onset. Third, aphasia is frequently associated with large brain lesions whose boundaries do not follow the exquisite limits of particular functional territories in the cortex. In spite of these important drawbacks, the clinical anatomical method has been used cleverly enough over several decades to sketch out a general, although indeed complex, model of the neural counterparts of language functions. The main feature of such a model consists in spatial distribution of language function(s) over distant cortical and subcortical sites. Indeed, a given language (sub)function is frequently subserved by a distributed network involving discrete parts of the cortical mantle that may be located centimetres apart from one another and even in different lobes of the brain.

10.2. THE 'FUNCTION-BASED' MODEL: INDEPENDENT AND COMPLEMENTARY OF APHASIOLOGICAL STUDIES

The emerging 'function' approach of a tentative neurophysiology of language has to rely on the massive amount of knowledge coming from the lesion-based model. In fact, not only does this new model complement the previous one by providing neurofunctional data that are independent of lesion-based studies, but the earlier and the new approaches can now also be used in combination with the study of aphasic patients (Karbe et al. 1998, Warburton et al. 1999).

These techniques have the potential to describe the defective and compensatory neural phenomena that can be correlated with the wide spectrum of impaired and preserved language processes in a particular patient. However, the combination of complex issues related to aphasia with other quite specific and technical aspects of the various neuroimaging

TABLE 10.1. Influencing factors for neuroimaging of language

Subject specific	Experiment specific	
	General	Language related
Gender	input modality (audition vision but also olfaction, taste, or touch)	levels of representation (phonemes, syllables, words, sentences, etc.)
Age	output modality (vocal, motor, inner, none)	lexicality (words, pseudo-words and non-words)
Handedness	task 'difficulty' (familiarity with the task, practice effects)	categories (nouns versus verbs, man-made versus natural, content word versus function word, etc.)
Literacy	rate of stimulation	lexical frequency
Motivation and stress	exposure duration	spelling-to-sound consistency

methods certainly makes this topic a difficult one and renders indispensable the close collaboration of many different disciplines from linguistics to physics, including neurophysiology, neurology, and statistics.

The neuroimaging techniques can be easily classified according to their ability to provide fine-grained information in either the space (anatomical) or the time domain.

Positron Emission Tomography (PET) and functional Magnetic Resonance Imaging (fMRI) are called tomographic techniques as they provide images which are brain slices that can be reconstructed in 3D to show the actual brain volume. These techniques allow us to localize quite precisely (in terms of cubic millimetres) variations of local vascular signals that are indirect indices of energy consumption in large ensembles of neural synapses (about 10^6 of them) in which changes in firing rates are induced by a given cognitive experiment. PET and fMRI make it possible to concentrate on particular brain regions when studying a cognitive function, and to study specific effects in terms of increases, or decreases, of blood flow under a particular experimental circumstance in comparison with another 'baseline' measurement. Although these techniques provide a fascinating insight into the working brain through 'visualization' of the anatomical localization of its activity, their results may be influenced by many factors that were frequently overlooked in previous studies (see Table 10.1) (for a review see Démonet 1998).

The tomographic methods cannot provide information about the timing of neural events subserving cognitive phenomena; the latter evolve over a millisecond time-scale whereas the former can hardly reach the level of seconds. Fortunately, other techniques, called neurophysiological, such as Event Related Potentials (ERPs) derived from ElectroEncephaloGraphic (EEG) recording or Event-Related Magnetic Fields from MagnetoEncephaloGraphic (MEG) recording do provide on-line information on the time-course of mental computations during a task, up to the millisecond level. However, such a high resolution in the time domain has its price and the localization of the sources of these rapidly evolving potentials in the brain is still imprecise. Resolution in both space and time can only be provided by the combination of the tomographic and the neurophysiological techniques.

10.3. AN EXAMPLE OF COMBINED SPATIAL AND TEMPORAL APPROACH TO THE NEURAL NETWORKS SUBSERVING PHONOLOGICAL AND LEXICAL SEMANTIC PROCESSES

As an illustration of a combined study in both space and time domains of the neural counterparts of language, the results of two studies of phonological and lexical semantic processes involved in single-word language comprehension tasks will be presented. The results were obtained via two different techniques, Positron Emission Tomography (PET) providing anatomical localizations of across-task changes in neural activities (Démonet et al. 1992, 1994*a*, 1994*b*) and multi-channel mapping of EEG event-related potentials (ERPs) showing the temporal dynamics of language-related neural activities in each task and its distribution over different locations on the scalp (Thierry, Doyon, and Démonet 1998).

10.3.1. Rationale

Whereas the techniques differed very much in terms of signal characteristics, the language tasks were kept constant in these two experiments conducted in small groups of right-handed, highly educated normal volunteers. Monitoring auditory tasks were chosen so that subjects remained deeply engaged in the tasks that they were given. They consisted in an auditory, non-verbal task using pure tones and two verbal tasks in which emphasis was put on either phonological or lexical semantic processes, respectively.

In all three tasks, stimuli were digitized, delivered binaurally, and consisted of 30 per cent of targets amongst distractors, and they were monitored by right fingers clicking on computer buttons.

In the phonological task ('Phoneme' task), subjects were presented with multi-syllable pseudo-words and were asked to press a designated button whenever they detected the presence of the phoneme /b/ if and only if preceded by the phoneme /d/ in a previous syllable, such as in /redozabu/. The majority of the distractors involved either /d/ but not /b/ ('dx' type (e.g. /idofupa/)) or /b/ but not /d/ before ('xb' type (e.g. /pimuviba/)) and the rest were fillers with neither /d/ nor /b/ ('xx' type (e.g. /moigajapo/)).

The structure of the lexical semantic task ('Word' task) paralleled that of the phonological task but involved adjective-noun pairs. Subjects had to click on the 'target' button when hearing names of small animals if and only if preceded by semantically 'positive' adjectives (e.g. 'kind mouse'). Three types of distractors were presented, positive-big (e.g. 'happy whale'), negative-small (e.g. 'unkind wasp'), and negative-big (e.g. 'awful lion').

Whilst having in common several features (twofold and sequential criterion for target identification, working memory and attentional resource requirements), these two language tasks were designed in order to tease apart as much as possible two different modes of language stimuli processing. The phonological task might be viewed as a phonological awareness task. It was thought to lead subjects to use a parsing strategy in which the phonemic and syllabic structure of the stimuli would be worked out in detail. On the other hand, the lexical semantic task was meant to require only superficial and automatic access to phonological representations upon lexical identification of words. Attentional resources were supposed to be mainly devoted to analysing the meaning of the heard words.

The choice of these tasks was also guided by neuro-anatomical considerations. From lesion-based studies, it has been suggested (Cappa, Cavalotti, and Vignolo 1981) that aphasic patients showing evidence of predominantly phonemic disorders suffered from lesions located close to the left sylvian fissure (e.g. located about Brodmann's areas (BAs) 44, 40, 22, see Fig. 10.1) whereas patients showing mostly lexical semantic symptoms tend to present lesions located in the inferior part of the left temporal or left parietal lobes (e.g. BAs 39, 37). Using functional imaging, we checked whether such a differential topography might also be observed in normal subjects whilst performing language tasks in which either phonological or lexical semantic processes would predominate.

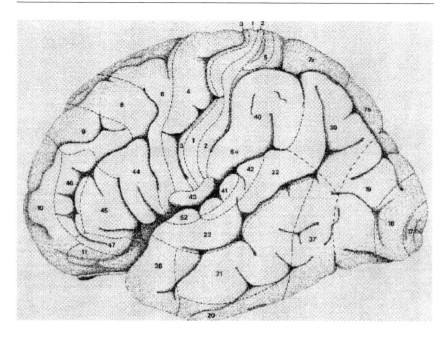

F IG. 10.1 Brodmann's areas.

10.3.2. The PET study

The PET study was conducted on nine volunteers using the Oxygen 15 method and the analysis of variations in regional cerebral blood flow (rCBF) was performed with the SPM software from Frackowiak and Friston (1994).

The analysis of error rates and reaction times in subjects showed that the phonological task, although correctly performed in all subjects, gave rise to more false positives and prolonged processing times than the other three tasks.

Because integration of radioactivity counts over a 60-second period is needed, the PET technique does not allow the analysis of the neural activities related to each type of stimuli that were identified in the task design. This technique only permits global comparisons across tasks to assess whether local increases of rCBF occurred while subjects underwent a given task, compared to another.

Whatever such a limitation in the time domain, these comparisons showed that different patterns of rCBF increase were generated by each of the two language tasks, respectively (Fig. 10.2). In accordance with lesion-based studies, the phonological task yielded activations localized in the vicinity of the left perisylvian areas (BAs 6, 4, 40). The lexical semantic task activated a more widespread pattern involving the middle and inferior temporal (BAs 21, 37) and the inferior parietal (BA 39, or angular gyrus) regions together with localizations that were not predicted by the lesion-based model, namely the left superior prefrontal (BA 9), the posterior cingulated (not shown on Fig. 10.1), and the right inferior parietal regions (BA 39).

This complex pattern of activation associated with our lexical semantic task was further confirmed by an analysis of the same results based on a correlational analysis (Démonet, Wise, and Frackowiak 1993) and by other studies using either PET (e.g. Vandenberghe et al. 1996) or fMRI (e.g. Binder et al. 1997)

Activations in the periphery of the left sylvian fissure in our phonological task were replicated in a further study (Démonet et al. 1994*b*) and proved to be congruent with several studies devoted to the functional anatomy of phonological processes (for critique, discussion, and review see Poeppel 1996*a* and Démonet et al. 1996). Of particular interest for the significance of our results is their high degree of convergence with those described by Paulesu, Frith, and Frackowiak (1993) in a study of phonological working memory. A small left-sided perisylvian network involving Wernicke's area (BA 22), the supramarginal gyrus (BA 40), and Broca's area (BA 44) was identified as the neural counterpart of the 'articulatory loop' in Baddeley's model (1986). More precisely, the inferior part of the left supramarginal gyrus (BA 40) was activated in Démonet et al. (1994*a*) in a location (stereotactic coordinates according to Talairach and Tournoux's atlas: x, y, z = −52, −26, 20) which is very close to that described by Paulesu, Frith, and Frackowiak (1993) (x, y, z = −44, −32, 24) as a focus corresponding to short-term phonological storage. This supports our view of a strong component of working memory in our phonological task. In this framework, short-term maintenance of phonemes or syllables is probably crucial to achieve this task and this might correspond to quite a precise localization in the left supramarginal gyrus (BA 40).

On the ground of a correlational analysis of rCBF changes in the lexical semantic task (Démonet, Wise, and Frackowiak 1993), we proposed, by analogy with our viewpoints on phonological tasks, that the activation of the left angular gyrus (BA 39) we found in this task might, at least in part, represent a similar short-term memory storage process related to lexical items. This would represent an equivalent of the phonological storage taking place in the left supramarginal gyrus.

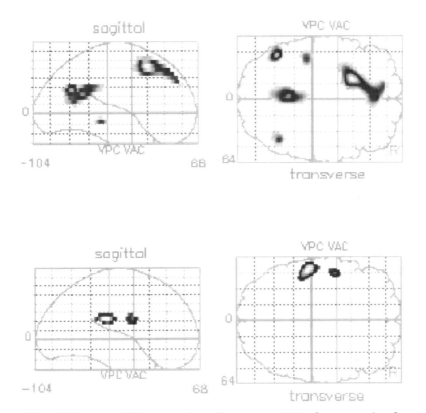

Fɪɢ. 10.2. PET study. SPM maps of significant (p < .001 after correction for multiple comparisons) increases of blood flow in the Word task compared to the Phoneme task (a), and conversely (b). Pixels are depicted in glass-views of a standardized brain space (Talairach and Tournoux 1988).

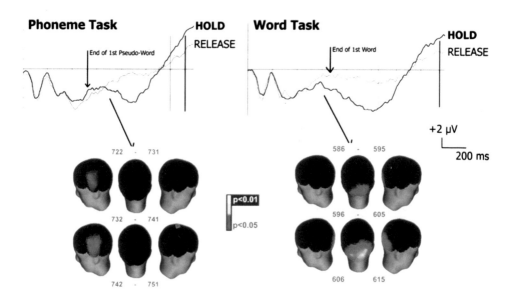

FIG. 10.3. Grand-average of ERPs recorded over the fronto-central electrodes of potentials respectively elicited by Hold and Release stimuli in the Phoneme and the Word tasks
(top) and interpolated mapping of the difference (paired t tests) between
Hold and Release following split points.

10.3.3. The ERP study

Using the same tasks, this part of our work allowed us to analyse the respective neural correlates of different types of stimuli within each task in terms of temporal dynamics and distribution over the scalp.

Because of their similarities in structure, the two language tasks may be achieved using the same, rather obvious, strategy. This strategy consists in attending only for the stimuli involving the conditioning item (i.e. the phoneme /d/ or a positive adjective) as potential target-bearing stimuli, that is, involving either the phoneme /b/ or the name of a small animal in its final part. We therefore labelled 'hold' these stimuli ('dx' and 'db' types, or 'positive-big' and 'positive-small' types) since, upon detection of the conditioning item, they require further maintenance of the heard sequence that will be loaded into the working memory system. On the contrary, the 'xb' and 'xx' pseudo-word or both the 'negative' word stimuli may be designated as 'release' stimuli since the absence of the conditioning item would preclude these stimuli from meeting the target criteria. Consequently, their identification as 'non-target' stimuli does not require further processing and their analysis may cease.

The ERP study was effected with twelve volunteers on a 32-electrode Neuroscan© system with continuous EEG sampled at 500 Hz and post-hoc 40 Hz low-pass filtering. After elimination of eye-blink artefacts, motion artefacts, and erroneous trials, at least 30 exemplars of each stimulus type and for each task corresponded to 1,800 ms epochs that were averaged.

Error rates and reaction times were similar to those observed in the PET study.

The analysis of the grand average of ERPs in the two language tasks led us to identify in both cases typical auditory components N1-P2 (i.e. a profound negative deflection occurring about 100 ms after stimulus onset followed by a positive deflection occurring about 200 ms), as well as further specific events that we characterized as split points since they consisted of divergence between ERPs respectively elicited by 'hold' and 'release' stimuli, in each task (Fig. 10.3). 'Hold' stimuli elicited a shift towards negative potentials whereas 'release' stimuli tended to elicit in turn positive shifts. This divergence seems to correspond to an ERP correlate of the decision taken by the subjects depending on whether or not a given stimulus should be further processed and maintained in the working memory system as a potential target, i.e. whether a conditioning item (phoneme /d/ or positive adjective) was detected or not.

Although this pattern of divergence was clearly observed in both tasks, this phenomenon differed from one language task to another in two ways. First, the split points differed in latency. Second, the distribution over the scalp of the release–hold differences was completely different (Fig. 10.3).

As a consequence of such a different timing of ERPs in the phonological and the semantic tasks, direct, between-task comparisons appeared of marginal relevance, unlike in the PET study. In turn, the within-task contrasts between 'release' and 'hold' ERPs turned out to be of crucial interest.

The mean duration of the first two syllables of the pseudo-words was shorter (512 ms) than that of the adjectives (684 ms). Despite this, the typical latency of the split recorded over fronto-central electrodes in the phonological task (782 ms) occurred *well after* the end of the trace of these first two syllables upon which subjects were to take their decision. On the contrary, the lexical semantic split was observed on fronto-central electrodes at 654 ms, that is 30 ms *before* the mean end of the acoustic traces of adjectives. This cross-over temporal pattern suggests that, in accordance with our theoretical views, the phonological task was performed in a sequential, step-by-step, parsing mode. This sequential processing is much slower than the probabilistic, non-exhaustive way of processing lexically valid items in the semantic task (Marslen-Wilson and Tyler 1980) so that semantic features of the heard words can be accessed quickly, ensuring faster processing in this task.

After the split points between 'hold' and 'release' stimuli, sustained divergences between ERPs were observed in both tasks for more than 200 ms. Differences between these potentials were computed and their distribution over the scalp was studied via t-maps interpolated between the electrodes. In the phonological task, the divergence first appeared and remained predominant over left-sided central electrodes, the maximum difference being centred on the T7 electrode. This is congruent with the left-sided perisylvian foci of activation in our PET study. In the lexical semantic task, the divergence first occurred on the posterior O1 electrode and quickly spread towards the homologous O2 electrode with further spreading to the entire set of posterior electrodes in both hemispheres. This bilateral and posterior distribution of ERP differences is compatible with the presence of activation foci in the left and right angular gyri in our PET study, although it does not account for the remaining aspects of the complex pattern observed in the left hemisphere.

In sum, the split phenomenon observed in both tasks is likely to relate, on the one hand, to common attentional and problem-solving mechanisms based on maintenance of potential targets in working memory and release of attention for irrelevant distractors, and, on the other hand, to language-specific modulations of this basic algorithm induced by the lexical status of the processed stimuli. Pseudo-words yield a slow, sequential process probably operated in the left hemisphere, via a perisylvian 'articulatory loop'. This mode of language processing is related to phonological awareness strategies that normal subjects may resort to when learning new words. Real words processing corresponds to a faster, automatized, and probabilistic mode of processing, relating to long-lasting exposure to lexical items that permits quick access to semantic representations.

These studies represent only a preliminary illustration of the multimodal neuroimaging approach to cognitive processes. By seeking anatomical and temporal indexes of the neural activities subserving two major modes of oral language comprehension, we gathered elements of functional information that complement one another but lack overlap in terms of time or space resolution. Very recent developments of new techniques such as event-related fMRI show that resolution in both time and space will come from the same data set or that EEG and MEG signal source analyses could be merged with MR data as future tools for the physiology of cognition.

11

Phonology in a Theory of Perception-for-Action-Control

Jean-Luc Schwartz, Christian Abry, Louis-Jean Boë,
and Marie Cathiard

INTRODUCTION

The whole story told in this book is likely to be a story of boundaries and links. The cognition programme was basically based on *links* between disciplines, while the phonology programme, on the contrary, started with the elaboration of *boundaries* . . . hence the interest of the present book. In fact, it is our deep belief that the whole story of *speech* itself is a story of links, and we shall attempt here to present an integrated framework in which it is the *relationships* between perception, action control, and phonology which are at the core of the study, rather than perception, action, or phonology independently of each other.

Let us start from a radical substance-based position (from MacNeilage 1998; see also comments by Abry et al. 1998), in which speech stems from a volitional vocalization system involving the cingular cortex and the supplementary motor area, and providing a basic *phonological principle*, a 'frame' consisting in syllabic oscillations; and from a vocal self-monitoring system, probably recruiting the Broca–Wernicke circuit, and allowing a 'content' to emerge and provide *phonological parameters*, specifying segments. In this view, the present contribution is rather focused on vocal self-monitoring. After the seminal work by Sperry on corollary discharge enabling one to predict the perceptual consequences of one's action, Frith's experiments (1992) extended this concept to the on-line following of one's own voice. The extrapolation towards the possible ability to follow on-line the vocal gestures of somebody else was suggested by the Motor Theory (Liberman and Mattingly 1985), and received some sort of echo in the so-called 'mirror neurons' recently discovered by Rizzolatti et al. (1996*a*) in the monkey's brain, and displaying similar kinds of responses to the monkey's action and action perception.

But whatever the claims about neurophysiological circuits, and considering that speech production involves stereotyped syllabic gestures (a 'rhythmer') and learnable segmental specifications through the acquirable control of timing and targets (a 'modeller'), a theory of speech perception must, in our view, be elaborated in this context. Such a theory should tell us how a listener might follow the vocalizations of his speaking partner, in order perhaps to understand them, but at least certainly to imitate and learn: in other words, how perception enables a listener to specify the control of his future actions as a speaker. On the other hand, this theory should also tell us how the perceptual representations of speech gestures transform, deform, shape the speaker's gestures in the listener's mind, and hence provide templates that in return also help to specify the control of the speaking partner's own actions. And lastly, this theory should be able to show how the choice of speech units inside the phonological system may be constrained and patterned by the inherent limitations and intrinsic properties of the speech perception system—and its indissociable companion, the speech production system.

To state this in more direct terms: speech perception is the set of perceptual (auditory, visual, if not tactile) processes allowing us, at the segmental level, to recover and specify the timing and targets of speech gestures, and supplying a set of representations for the control of one's own actions and the following of somebody else's actions, representations likely to intervene in the morphogenesis of phonological systems. Therefore, the research programme we shall try to illustrate here is concerned with the determination of processing and representations allowing action control and related, through perception–action interactions, to certain aspects of principles and parameter settings in phonology. It should be obvious, at this point, that our approach is centred on the *co-structuring of the perception and action systems in relation with phonology*, and hence is clearly different both from an 'auditory' theory in which the sensory-interpretative chain is considered independently of the patterning of sounds by speech gestures, in the search of some *'direct link' between sounds and phonemes*; and from a 'motor' theory (be it 'The' Motor Theory by Liberman and Mattingly 1985; or the direct realist theory by Fowler 1986) in which perception is nothing but a mirror of action, in the claim of a *direct link between sounds and gestures*.

11.1. ACTION-CONTROLLED PERCEPTUAL REPRESENTATIONS FOR ACTION CONTROL

11.1.1. Auditory-based event and formant detection for the recovery of timing and targets

The following of speech gestures must involve a way to capture and characterize the basic components of the speaker's vocal actions, that is, timing and targets. A series of influential works realized in the Pavlov Institute of Leningrad in the 1970s led Chistovich to propose a basic architecture for the auditory processing of speech sounds, quite consistent with this 'auditory programme'. This architecture consists of one system specialized in temporal processing and detection of acoustic events, and the other continuously delivering various analyses about the spectral content of the input (Chistovich 1976, 1980), and it seems clear that the neuro-physiological bases for this processing are already available in primary neurons in the auditory nerve, or secondary neurons in the cochlear nucleus (which is the first auditory processing centre in the central nervous system).

11.1.1.1. *Events*

The system specialized in event detection could be based on so-called 'phasic' units in the central nervous system, namely 'on' and 'off' units responding only to quick increases and decreases of the neural excitation in a given spectral region. Delgutte (1986) addressed the problem of detecting Chistovich's 'events' in a functional model of the auditory nerve with a neural adaptation component, and he obtained interesting results for the processing of French CVCV utterances, based on grouped responses in the low and high characteristic frequency regions (see also Chistovich et al. 1982). Later on, we developed a physiologically plausible module for the detection of articulatory-acoustic events such as voicing onset/offset, bursts, vocalic onset/offset (Piquemal et al. 1996, Wu, Schwartz, and Escudier 1996) in the cochlear nucleus. These events, which allow the labelling of every major discontinuity in the speech signal, are crucial for the control of timing in speech production (Abry et al. 1985, Abry, Orliaguet, and Sock 1990).

11.1.1.2. *Formants*

The system specialized in spectral processing would need so-called 'tonic' units responding continuously to a given stimulus, and then enabling precise statistics and computations about the variations of excitation depending on their characteristic frequency. The debate on the role of formants in the auditory processing of speech is not closed. Arguments in favour of distances computed on the whole spectrum cite the difficulties associated with formant detection (Bladon 1982), and the good fit with various types of perceptual data (e.g. Plomp 1970, Pols 1975, Bladon and Lindblom 1981), while several perceptual experiments point out the specific role of formants or spectral peaks in the determination of vowel quality (see e.g. Karnickaja et al. 1975, Carlson, Granström, and Klatt 1979, Klatt 1982). However, it seems clear that basic neurophysiological ingredients are available for formant detection in the auditory nerve, through spatio-temporal statistics (Delgutte 1984); and higher in the auditory chain, as early as the cochlear nucleus, through lateral inhibition mechanisms for contrast reinforcement. Then, from formant recovery, vowel articulatory targets can be specified quite efficiently, at least in terms of major constrictions in the vocal tract (except in the case of [u], which will be discussed later): this was demonstrated by Boë, Perrier, and Bailly (1992) on an articulatory model of the vocal tract. Formant trajectories should also provide a suitable tracking of the place of articulation of the closing gesture in plosives, as indicated by the recent and intensive work on locus by Sussman, Hoemecke, and Ahmed (1993) and Sussman, McCaffrey, and Matthews (1991), and confirmed by studies in our laboratory aiming at controlling an articulatory model from formant patterns through inversion algorithms (Bailly, Laboissière, and Schwartz 1991, Bailly 1995).

11.1.2. Audition shapes gestures

However, the view that audition provides a smart way to accurately follow the speaker's gestures is a bit misleading: audition does less and more than that.

11.1.2.1. *Gesture recovery is partial*

It does obviously less, since it allows the recovery of only *parts* of the
speech gestures: major parts probably, but still parts. This is first clear on
mathematical grounds: recovering articulatory gestures from sounds is an
'inverse' problem, and inverse problems are generally ill posed and unsolvable
because there is an excess of freedom degrees. Indeed, it is precisely this excess
which is exploited by the speech production system to prepare the next target
while achieving the present one, thanks to anticipatory gestures which often
benefit from their quasi-inaudibility. Non-linearities in the articulatory-to-
acoustic transform also play their part in this process. For example, Abry and
Lallouache (1995) have shown that in an [i]-towards-[y] gesture in French,
the lips may already begin their closing movement towards the rounded [y]
inside [i], while the sound stays perfectly stable all around the [i], since lip
closure begins to decrease F_3 only for rather small values of the lip area (Boë
and Perrier 1988). Notice that this kind of non-linear 'projection' of gestures
into the acoustic-auditory space has sometimes been taken as a case against
the motor or the direct realist theories of speech perception, with the
argument that 'speech perception is hearing sounds, not tongues' (Ohala
1996). In fact, we believe, as Fowler (1996) does, that it just demonstrates
that 'listeners do hear sounds, not tongues', which means that information
about gestures is sound, and processing of this information is audition.
Hence the basic task is to understand how audition processes and 'deforms'
gestures.

11.1.2.2. *From blurring to shaping*

This might appear as a limitation of the auditory recovery process, providing
only a 'blurred' view of speech gestures. In fact, audition processing should be
described as *shaping* rather than blurring. This is exactly Stevens's claim in his
famous Quantal Theory (1972, 1989). In this view, non-linearities in the
articulatory-to-acoustic or acoustic-to-auditory transforms define 'homogeneous' regions in which the output is more or less stable, contrasted by
transition areas defining natural boundaries, and Stevens claims that this
results in a so-called 'quantal' patterning of speech gestures, providing
substance-based principles for universal phonetic distinctions. Hence audition in this view achieves much more than a partial and blurred recovery of
speech gestures: it provides non-linear intrinsic mechanisms for categorization of a continuous articulatory substance, preparing the way for phonetic
distinctions to be exploited by phonology (see Petitot-Cocorda 1985).
    Such a kind of 'auditory patterning' of speech gestures can be illustrated,
still in the [i] vs. [y] contrast, in relation with the so-called 'perceptual second

formant' F'_2, which is known to represent a reasonable equivalent of F_2 and higher formants in the determination of vowel quality. This is demonstrated in various vowel perception experiments (e.g. Carlson, Granström, and Fant 1970, Bladon and Fant 1978) showing that it is possible to replace the set of high formants (F_2, F_3, F_4) by a single spectral peak located close to F_2 for back vowels, between F_2 and F_3 for central and front vowels, except [i] (and [e] to a lesser extent) for which F'_2 is between F_3 and F_4. We showed that this phenomenon could be explained by a 'large-scale integration' process (Schwartz and Escudier 1987) linked to the centre of gravity effect and the 3.5 bark critical distance described by Chistovich and colleagues at the end of the 1970s (Chistovich and Lublinskaya 1979, Chistovich, Sheikin, and Lublinskaya 1979). Indeed, this 'large-scale integration' mechanism provides an efficient basis for computing F'_2 from F_2, F_3, and F_4, and it is able to subsume formant variations around [i] and [y] into a quantal pattern with a stable F'_2 around 3,000 Hz for [i] and a stable F'_2 around 2,000 Hz for [y]. We also demonstrated that the quantal F'_2 pattern was really the result of a perceptual *pre-phonetic process* and not the *consequence* of a phonetic contrast (Schwartz and Escudier 1989), and that this pattern was able to group linguistic variations around the [i] vs. [y] contrast into a common framework (Schwartz et al. 1993).

Finally, this 'shaping' is crucial to be able to define gestures themselves. This is quite striking when reading the efforts by Mattingly (1990) to define phonetic gestures in the framework of articulatory phonology. Let us take his example of lip rounding (p. 447): 'in the phonetic gesture traditionally known as "lip rounding", not only are the lips protruded, but also the larynx is lowered. These two movements are surely part of a single gesture which serves to lengthen the vocal tract.' The conclusion comes later (p. 450): 'What is called for is a functional rather than an anatomical organisation, one in which the gestures are grouped according to the nature of their tasks.' This 'functional grouping' is part of what we call the auditory shaping of speech gestures.

11.1.3. Action constrains percepts

Pushing further the idea that speech gestures are shaped by auditory processing, we might be driven towards a 'pure auditory' theory of speech perception, in which action is functionally completely specified by auditory templates in relation with phonetic requirements. But is it the case that the auditory specification is complete? And what happens if it is not the case?

11.1.3.1. *Exploring the articulatory-auditory mapping around [u]*

A good test-case is provided by [u]. Indeed, the previously cited study by Boë, Perrier, and Bailly (1992) on the vocalic realizations of a geometrical model of the vocal tract show that, while the (F_1, F_2, F_3) set generally specifies without ambiguity the main constriction parameters of the vocal tract (constriction place Xc, constriction area Ac, lip area Al), the specification is ambiguous for [u]. In this case, there are two different articulatory strategies providing more or less the same acoustic output (that is, a low F_1 and F_2): the constriction in the first one is velo-palatal, while in the second one it is velo-pharyngeal (with rounded lips in both cases), and both are articulatorily feasible, as we will see later. Therefore, the acoustic-auditory specification is incomplete, and we could imagine that speakers are free to choose either of these two production strategies. In fact, it does not seem to be the case: [u] is decidedly a velo-palatal vowel, as shown in various studies, and confirmed by X-ray data available in a study by Savariaux, Perrier, and Orliaguet (1995) to which we shall come back soon.

What might be the reason for this articulatory choice? Articulatory costs can probably be discarded, since the velo-pharyngeal [u]* is quite close to [o], which shows that the corresponding tongue gesture is not unnatural. A possible response is suggested by Abry and Badin (1996; see also Boë et al. 1996). Indeed, in previous simulations with the articulatory model, Bailly et al. (1995) had shown that an optimization procedure searching for the correct articulatory route towards [u] provided a velo-palatal solution if the initial position was a neutral configuration close to centralized vowels around schwa, while a velo-pharyngeal solution would be reached starting from [o]. Therefore, we can assume that when a child 'learns' [u], starting from centralized vowels as seems to be typically the case in variegated babbling, he will reach the velo-palatal solution. Then, the memory of the adult [u] would keep the trace of the first [u] articulatory-to-acoustic mapping.

The fact that the acoustic characterization of [u] is incomplete, and must be 'regularized' by articulatory learning constraints, is reminiscent of a number of situations in visual perception, in which the visual representation of a scene is ambiguous, and is regularized by assumptions on the most likely physical input responsible for the sensory stimulation. The visual system interprets ambiguous retinian images thanks to deduction rules coming from regularities of the external world (Hoffman 1984). Could it be that the articulatory constraints on [u] intervene in the perceptual specification of action? This seems to be the case, according to the results of the perturbation study by Savariaux, Perrier, and Orliaguet (1995). In this study, our colleagues attempted to design a perturbation paradigm in which the sound-to-gesture link would be crucially modified in order to test whether speakers actually control sounds or gestures—while in the bite-block experiment by Lindblom, Lubker, and Gay (1979) the closing-opening gesture was not impeded by blocking the jaw, hence a complete articulatory reorganization was not necessary. Savariaux et al. used a labial perturbation of the French rounded [u], through a 20-mm diameter lip-tube inserted between the speaker's lips (eleven speakers took part in the study). Previous simulations on the articulatory model had shown that the velo-palatal [u] would have its acoustic output crucially disturbed, and particularly F_2 significantly increased, while a movement towards the back, reaching a velo-pharyngeal position with more constriction, would offer a solution with an acceptable acoustic pattern. Hence the question: would the perturbed speakers find this solution?

In fact, the results indicate that the speakers are guided by the auditory output. This is demonstrated by the trend to move in the correct direction (towards the back) from the first to the last utterance of a training set. A following perceptual study (Savariaux et al. 1999) showed that the main auditory specification can be summarized by an integrated parameter $F_1 + F_2 - F_0$, involving both a 'centre of gravity' of F_1 and F_2 computed by a large-scale integration process similar to the one previously described in section 11.1.2, and a normalizing term F_0 accounting for source modifications. This parameter should be low for [u], thus providing a plausible candidate for the major auditory cue of the 'grave' feature in this case. However, the study also showed that only one speaker was able at the end of the learning process to reach the velo-pharyngeal configuration and hence completely recover the low F_2 value, while the ten others were blocked in the neighbourhood of the velo-palatal initial articulation. The further perceptual study showed that some of them could achieve an acoustic correction through F_1 lowering or F_0 increase, but the trend remains clear: it seems that the articulatory specification of a velo-palatal constriction is part of the representation of [u] in the speaker's mind, just as the acoustic-auditory specification which can be summarized by the $F_1 + F_2 - F_0$ 'grave' feature.

11.1.3.2. *The role of regularities of speech movements*

Movement is generally considered as a crucial ingredient in perceptuo-motor interactions. This idea is well advocated outside speech by Viviani in the field of visual perception of tracing movements. Indeed, while Viviani and Schneider (1991) demonstrated the existence of a 'two-thirds power law' of tracing movements, relating in a systematic way the tangential velocity and the curvature radius in a lot of different kinds of human gestures, Viviani and Stucchi (1992) showed that this constancy in action was able to intervene in perception. Artificially modifying the velocity in a given movement changed the perception of the very shape traced by the movement, and the perceived shape had curvature radii more in line with velocity variations.

Is it possible to encounter such kinds of situations in speech perception? In fact, this is exactly the core of a long-standing debate in the field of vowel processing, about the possible 'dynamic specification' of vowel targets (beginning with Strange et al. 1976 vs. Macchi 1980; continuing with Strange 1989 vs. Nearey 1989; and more recently, Bohn and Strange 1995 vs. Nearey 1995). The debate is complex, and mixes various arguments dealing with consonantal coarticulation, speaker normalization, vowel dynamics, and vowel reduction. To quote a single point on which we have done quite a lot of work, vowel reduction involves articulatory and acoustic trajectories going towards vocalic targets but never reaching them, and it is appealing to wonder whether regularities in articulatory dynamics could enable a listener to infer the target from the trajectories, even reduced. The ability to extrapolate vowel trajectories is indeed in line with some perceptual data (see e.g. Darwin 1989, Schwartz et al. 1992), and experiments on our articulatory model showed that reduced trajectories were compatible with the assumption of a fixed target driving the behaviour of a second-order model based on the equilibrium point hypothesis (Lœvenbruck and Perrier 1996, 1997). Hence we suggest that motor knowledge could intervene in this case to compensate for lacking acoustic information (though see Van Son 1993, Pitermann and Schoentgen 1996, for different views). We shall come back to this idea in section 11.1.5.

11.1.4. Gesture recovery/shaping is multimodal

11.1.4.1. *Tracking speech gestures through ear, eye and touch*

The need for supplementary information when the auditory specification is incomplete opens another and very important field, the human ability to follow speech gestures through sensorial modalities other than audition, and eventually fuse multisensorial inputs for this aim. This can be demonstrated by successive arguments, which show step by step that this ability is not a marginal 'side effect' in speech perception, but on the contrary a core component of speech perception, in relationship with action control and phonology. Let us review these arguments.

First, it is possible to partly follow speech gestures when audition is lacking, particularly for the hearing impaired. The best-known system is speechreading. Of course, the visual information is incomplete. It is focused on the front of the vocal tract and mainly concerns place features related to the lips and jaw, while features related to voicing, nasality, and front–back tongue movements are hidden. Globally, with speechreading alone one can catch roughly 40 to 60 per cent of the phonemes, and 10 to 20 per cent of the words, but the variability at this level is enormous, the best speechreaders (generally, deaf people) achieving better than 60 per cent scores (see Bernstein, Demorest, and Tucker 1998, for a review). The speech gestures can also be directly perceived through the tactile sense, in the Tadoma method developed for deaf-blind subjects. In this method, the Tadoma user places a hand over the face of the speaker with the fingers making contact with the cheeks, lips, and throat. The features best perceived by touching the vocal tract are voicing, lip rounding, frication, and place for consonants; and lip rounding, tenseness, and lip separation for vowels, with overall the same amount of correct performances at the phonetic level as in visual speechreading, that is 40 to 60 per cent (Reed et al. 1982*a*, Reed, Durlach, and Braida 1982). Speech gestures can also be perceived indirectly, through recoding. Such recoding can be performed automatically through signal processing systems, as in the many tactile displays which provide various spectral or feature information extracted from the speech acoustic input, and then transformed into mechanical or electrocutaneous stimulation on some part of the body (finger, hand, forearm, or abdomen). The identification scores are much better for vowels than for consonants, with a global level of performances which seems similar to that of Tadoma (Reed et al. 1982*b*). Lastly, speech gesture recoding can be realized by the speaker himself, in the framework of the 'cued-speech method' developed by Cornett (1967). In this method, the speaker complements visible gestures with manual cues providing information about non-visible gestures, through hand shape for the consonants and hand position for the vowels. Cued-speech reception very significantly improves speechreading identification scores, up to levels comparable to those of normal hearing listeners (Leybaert et al. 1998).

Second, it is well known that speechreading improves speech intelligibility in noisy audio conditions, and all studies since the beginning of the 1950s (e.g. Miller, Heise, and Lichten 1951, Sumby and Pollack 1954, Neely 1956, Erber 1969, MacLeod and Summerfield 1987, Benoît, Mohamadi, and Kandel 1994) show that the audio-visual identification scores are higher than both audio-only and visual-only scores at all levels from words to syllables, phonemes, and even individual phonetic features (Robert-Ribes et al. 1998). The gain in intelligibility due to the visual input exploits the intrinsic complementarity of the audio and visual sensors: hard to hear (specially in noise), easy to see, both for consonants (Summerfield 1987) and vowels (Benoît et al. 1994, Robert-Ribes et al. 1998).

Third, the visual input is useful even with a perfect audio input (no hearing impairment, no acoustic noise), as demonstrated by Reisberg, McLean, and Goldfield (1987) in a 'close-shadowing' repetition task: repetition is more efficient when the visual input is present, if the audio input is complex (in the case of an arduous philosophical text) or if it is uttered in a foreign language (see a recent confirmation in Davis and Kim 1998).

Fourth, the visual input is used in gesture recovery even if it is conflictual with the audio input. This refers of course to the famous McGurk effect (McGurk and MacDonald 1976), in which a visual [ga] superimposed with an audio [ba] is perceived as [da] or [ða], while a visual [ba] superimposed with an audio [ga] is perceived as [bga]. This, and a number of further replications or refinements involving various vowel contexts, various consonantal targets, vowel targets instead of consonants, male faces mounted on female voices and vice-versa, etc. (see reviews in Green 1996, 1998) altogether show that 'whenever visual information is available we humans use it' (Burnham 1998: 2). In fact, it even seems to be the case with the tactile modality, according to similar kinds of auditory–tactile interactions with conflictual inputs demonstrated with the Tadoma method by Fowler and Dekle (1991).

Fifth, the visual input is obviously implicated in the speech perception module in everyday life as early as the beginning of speech, that is, acquisition. The importance of the visual speech input in language acquisition has been well displayed by Mills (1987) in her review on language acquisition in blind children, with data showing that blind children have difficulty in learning an easy-to-see and hard-to-hear contrast such as [m] vs. [n]. This effect has been demonstrated for German, Russian, and English children (with in this last case a similar difficulty for the [θ]–[f] contrast). She also cites data showing that blind children (between 12 and 18 years old) make less use of lip movements, while the acoustic output is normal, thus exploiting compensatory articulation. Other relevant data are those showing the predominance of bilabials at the first stage of language acquisition (Vihman et al. 1985), increased in hearing impaired children (Stoel-Gammon 1988), but decreased in blind ones (Mulford 1988). These data may be related to the ability that children have, as early as infancy (72 hours), to reproduce facial gestures, hence to convert movement vision into movement production, as demonstrated by the famous study by Meltzoff and Moore (1983).

Sixth, the vision of speech gestures, particularly with the supplementary timed information added through cued speech, enables deaf children to acquire a more or less complete phonological module (though no speech production ability) (see e.g. Alegria et al. 1992, Leybaert et al. 1998), as evidenced by their mastering of the 'three Rs': Remembering, involving serial recall experiments which display modality-independent recency effects typical of the phonological memory, together with an echoic modality-dependent component; Reading, including the ability to spell regular words even if they are unknown, and to acquire basic morphology; and Rhyming, e.g. making rhyme judgements about pairs of pictures.

11.1.4.2. *Multimodal fusion models for gesture characterization*

A number of models have been introduced in the literature for dealing with audio-visual speech perception and speech automatic recognition, and we have shown elsewhere that these models could be grouped into four basic architectures, differing in the nature of the internal representation involved (Schwartz, Robert-Ribes, and Escudier 1998).

The access to the phonological level can first be realized directly on bimodal inputs grouping auditory and visual parameters. In this 'Direct Identification' (DI) model, the categorization process operates on auditory, visual, or audio-visual configurations whether the input is acoustic, optic, or bimodal, but in this last case, there is no common representation of the sound and the lips where they could be compared before identification. In the second architecture, which we called 'Separate Identification' (SI), there are two separate phonetic decoding processes operating respectively on the auditory and visual inputs—even if the input is bimodal—defining two different phonetic representations, which can be compared if necessary. This first stage is followed by a 'late-integration' process fusing the two phonetic representations to access the phonological code.

In the last two architectures, it is still assumed that there is a common representation of the sounds and the lips somewhere in the brain and before the final identification stage—a 'common metric', as defined by Summerfield (1987)—but this representation is assumed to be pre-phonetic, instead of phonetic as in the SI model. Fusion occurs on this common pre-phonetic representation and precedes the final categorization process to access the phonological level, hence it is called 'early integration'. The question is to determine what could be the common format of this representation of hererogeneous sensory inputs, if it is not based on linguistic processes as in the SI model. The literature on various types of sensorial interactions in cognitive psychology provides two answers (Hatwell 1993). One may find, in a number of situations, a *dominant modality* imposing its format—this is likely to be the case for audio-visual interactions in spatial localization, vision providing the dominant format. In our case, considering that audition is more likely than vision to be the dominant modality—if any—the visual input would be 'recoded' through association processes into auditory parameters, typically characterizing the vocal tract transfer function, compatible with the lip and jaw configuration. Then, in this 'Dominant Recoding' (DR) model, 'auditory' parameters estimated both directly from the ear and indirectly from the eye would be fused before identification for phonological access. Finally, one may posit that the common format is *amodal*—as is likely to be the case in audio-visual interactions for the estimation of rhythm through an amodal representation of time. Amodal features can also be related to physical properties of the source, and in our case an action-based format could be a good candidate for fusing various sensory inputs due to the common gestural cause. This means that articulatory or motor characteristics of speech gestures would be estimated from both the auditory and the visual input. Then, after this 'Motor Recoding' (MR) process, a fused estimate would provide the basis for phonological access.

These four models can be implemented and their ability to recognize speech, particularly in noisy conditions, can be assessed and compared (see e.g. Robert-Ribes, Schwartz, and Escudier 1995, Teissier et al. 1999). From a theoretical point of view, it is important to study their compatibility with available perceptual data on audio-visual interactions for speech perception. The differences between them can be summarized by three questions.

First, is there a common representation in which the auditory and the visual input can be compared before fusion and identification? This question enables us to isolate the DI model—for which the answer is 'no'—from the three others. In fact, it seems that such a common representation does exist, as demonstrated by two sets of experiments performed on conflictual auditory and visual inputs for vowels. As soon as they are 4 months old, infants are able to choose the 'correct' video solution (a face producing [a] vs. [i] or [a] vs. [ɔ]) when hearing a voice uttering one or the other of the two possible vowels in the presented set (Kuhl and Meltzoff 1982, 1984). Later on, adult listeners keep the ability to detect and estimate on a continuous scale the incompatibility of auditory and visual vocalic inputs, while both are presented synchronously and fused for final identification, as demonstrated by the audio-visual percept, which is different from both the audio-only and the visual-only ones (Summerfield and McGrath 1984). Notice that the existence of a level where the sound and image may be compared before the final identification stage appears necessary to be able to discard the visual input in case of too large a conflict, e.g. dubbed films.

Second, since there is access to a common representation before the final decision, is it phonetic or pre-phonetic, that is, is fusion late as in SI, or early as in DR and MR? In fact, various perceptual data show that audio-visual interactions occur on pre-phonetic features such as estimates of speech gesture rate and timing. For example, Green and Miller (1985) showed that speech rate estimation integrates auditory and visual cues, and therefore seen speech rate affects the audio-visual identification of the voicing feature. In respect to gestural timing, experiments involving lip movements combined with sounds delivered by auditory pulse tones generated by vocal fold activity (Rosen, Fourcin, and Moore 1981, Grant et al. 1985, Breeuwer and Plomp 1986) demonstrate that subjects are able to identify the voicing feature audio-visually, despite identification failure with the ear or the eye alone. This indicates that they are able to extract temporal coordination of the auditory and visual signal (audio-visual Voice Onset Time: see Green and Kuhl 1989). Altogether, it is quite likely that there is a common pre-phonetic format where the auditory and visual pathways are projected for comparison and fusion before phonological access.

Lastly, if there is a common pre-phonetic representation, is it dominant or amodal? It seems difficult to defend the idea of a dominant auditory representation for speech gestures, since it would be very hard to reconcile this view with the intrinsic complementarity of the auditory and visual sensors for speech gesture tracking, suggesting that audition is not always dominant. Consider for example the study by Lisker and Rossi (1992) in which French-speaking speech researchers had to judge the rounding category of a vowel, through the ear alone, the eye alone, or the ear and eye together. Their data show that the ear is quite unhappy with this task. For example, the high back unrounded vowel [ɯ] presented auditorily was considered rounded 60 per cent of the time. On the contrary, the eye is at ease with this task which is exactly suited for it: the vowel when presented visually was considered an unrounded vowel in 99 per cent of the responses. When the two inputs were combined, the vowel was more frequently considered unrounded (75 per cent of the responses), thus following the eye decision. This, and other functional arguments, lead to a strong suspicion that the DR model is unlikely to be the right one for speech perception (Robert-Ribes, Schwartz, and Escudier 1995, Robert-Ribes et al. 1998).

In summary, an MR model in which the audio-visual interaction would be organized towards the recovery of speech gestures, and regularized and constrained by their characteristics, seems to provide the best framework for dealing with available audio-visual speech perception data (Robert-Ribes 1995). This model could also include a tactile input, as suggested by the Tadoma 'McGurk' data provided by Fowler and Dekle (1991) and interpreted by them in a way quite similar to ours.

11.1.5. The format of the visual representation of speech gestures

The nature of intermediate representations and low-level computational processes in the human brain has been extensively studied in vision, particularly in the last twenty years—see e.g. some major contributions by Marr (1982) introducing a general architecture for vision perception, Poggio (1984) defining low-level vision as inverse process needing regularization constraints, and Ullman (1979) and Pentland (1989) with the shape-from-motion and the shape-from-shading paradigms. Therefore, it is only logical to try to exploit some of this literature in relation with the visual perception of speech gestures in our group; this has been the approach followed by Cathiard for some ten years now. We shall review some major steps of this research, related to the primary visual contrast, that is, rounding, once more in the [i]–[y] region; the interest of the French language being that the lip rounding gesture can be controlled independently from the tongue front–back one.

11.1.5.1. *A basic ability to follow lip rounding visually*

To begin with, it is important to emphasize the accuracy of visual perception for this task: Cathiard (1988) showed that a protrusion modification of 1 mm suffices to determine a major shift from an [i] to an [y]. This accuracy enables the eye to track the anticipatory rounding gesture well before it has acoustic consequences (see section 11.1.2). This was demonstrated by Escudier, Benoît, and Lallouache (1990) in a perceptual study of [zV$_1$zV$_2$] French logatoms (V$_1$ and V$_2$ in the [i y] set). Their data show that when subjects are presented with [zizi] or [zizy] sequences and have to 'guess' the second vowel at some time before it is completed, the eye 'knows' the second vowel well inside the first one, thanks to anticipatory lip gesture; while the ear cannot guess the second vowel before the end of the first one. This confirms that the anticipatory rounding gesture is visible and not audible.

Cathiard et al. (1991) employed another paradigm, based on silent pauses, to study the perceptual ability to track anticipatory gestures. They used [i#y] transitions produced following two different pausing instructions, a short [#] and a long [#:] one. Subjects were able to follow the gesture correctly from [i] to [y] and identified the [y] rounded target during the pause, well before any [y] sound occurred. The capture of anticipated segmental information on rounding could occur by the eye up to 120 ms before the ear, and once more the regularity of the performance across the fifty tested subjects was remarkably stable, be they French or Greek—subjects for whom the rounding and front–back contrasts are not independent. The visual anticipation could reach as high as 200 ms for long pauses, and 40 ms were enough in the lip trajectory to switch from a lip configuration generally identified as [i] to another one generally identified as [y].

11.1.5.2. *Temporal and configurational coherence in relation to speech production*

The previous data display a 'natural desynchrony' between the sound and lips in an [i#y] gesture with the lips leading the sound because of coarticulation. In a later series of experiments, Cathiard et al. (1995) applied a desynchronization in the other sense, artificially setting the sound in advance of its natural occurrence, in an attempt to decrease the natural desynchrony. The perceptual influence of the temporal incoherence was marginal, until it led to configurational incoherence, that is, having a sound [y] happen while the lip area was still typical of that of an [i]. In this case, the authors showed that the response to the conflict through audio-visual fusion was much more subject-dependent than pure auditory or visual performance, with one group basing its decision on the visual input, and the other on a mixture of both inputs. This provides a confirmation that audition is not the dominant modality for rounding—notice that the role of audition for height tracking in another experiment focused on [i#a] was much greater than for rounding tracking in the present one. These data were related by Abry et al. (1996, Abry, Lallouache, and Cathiard 1996) to their speech production model of anticipatory gestures, that is, the Movement Expansion Model (MEM), thus offering a production rationale for the perceptual phenomenology of bimodal speech coherence.

11.1.5.3. *The role of dynamics*

Then, as for the auditory recovery of speech gestures, comes the question of the role of movement dynamics. In their first study on [i#y] and [y#i] sequences, Cathiard and Lallouache (1992) used face presentations, generally considered to be better than profile for lipreading (Neely 1956, Erber 1974). They found a small but significant gain due to movement: in the [i#y] case (but not in the other one) the [y] target could be identified slightly earlier when seeing the whole trajectory, from the beginning to a given image inside the transition, compared to the vision of the ending image alone. This result is in good agreement with another study by Kandel, Orliaguet, and Boë (1994) showing that subjects are able to exploit visually the dynamics of motor anticipation for guessing a target in the time-course of another motor task aimed at a linguistic objective, that is, handwriting.

However, a further study (Cathiard, Lallouache, and Abry 1996) showed that when replicating the experiment with profile instead of front speaker's views, the gain due to dynamics disappeared. Static and dynamic profile views provided exactly the same performances as the best front view condition, that is, the dynamic one. This confirms, by the way, other data showing that profile is not poorer than face for rounding visual perception (Wozniak and Jackson 1979). But, above all, it indicates that movement is not systematically useful. A contradictory position is defended by Rosenblum and Saldana (1996) from their McGurk data showing that static full mouth shapes were less efficient for biasing the auditory percept than scarce kinematic information on the face provided by temporal trajectories of a series of light dots. Hence their claim that movement rather than shape is the primitive of visual speech perception.

How can these complex phenomenological pieces be integrated into a common theoretical portrait? As an answer, Cathiard et al. defended the view that 3D shape is the basic component of the visual representation of speech gestures. Profile views of the lips would provide the least ambiguous information on the lip configuration, allowing a precise recovery of the 3D configuration thanks to shape-from-shading algorithms. Front views would be in this context non-optimal, providing an incomplete specification of the 3D lip shape, and dynamics would therefore be necessary to complete information through a shape-from-shading-and-motion paradigm. The gain due to dynamics would make it possible to achieve the same amount of performance of lip shape recovery as the best view, that is, profile, for which dynamics would be of no use. In the case of highly incomplete dot trajectories (Rosenblum and Saldana), movement would be crucial for shape tracking. Notice that the fact that static mouth shapes are less efficient for McGurk interference does not show that movement is a basic visual primitive: it just indicates that a coherence of movement reinforces the coherence of bimodal perception.

Finally, our most recent data (Cathiard 1998, Cathiard, Abry, and Schwartz 1998) show that even in the visual perception of rounding in glides vs. vowels, that is [ɥ] vs. [y], the basic correlate is a duration cue (duration of the static phase of rounding) rather than a dynamic one. A gating experiment indicates that the intrinsically dynamic nature of the glide is not visually exploited, unless expectancy is oriented towards motion processing by telling subjects that a glide might come after an [i], and asking them to guess if it is coming or not. Hence, even in this case, we cannot support an exclusive visual dynamic representation of the rounding gesture either for vowels or for glides.

11.1.6. An architecture for the perceptual representation of speech gestures

All this series of data and proposals, be they clear-cut arguments or complex reasoning, converges on the core of our 'theory of perception-for-action-control', centred on representations—or series of representations—which are intrinsically sensori-motor. These representations, aiming at recovering and specifying speech controls, are neither pure sensorial patterns, nor pure inferred motor objects, but multimodal percepts constrained by action regularities, or gestures shaped by multimodal perception.

We have proposed (Schwartz et al. 1992) a possible architecture for elaborating such representations, namely the timing-target model. This model is an elaboration of Chistovich's phasic-tonic model referred to in section 11.1.1, in which specific auditory and visual processes would be in charge to process the two major components that must be controlled to produce speech gestures, that is, *timing* and *targets*. Some auditory processes for timing recovery have been mentioned in section 11.1.1. The data, mentioned in section 11.1.4.2, demonstrate that the visual pathway also provides an input to the module for timing recovery. As for targets, the fact that both the auditory and the visual pathway contribute to their characterization is obvious from all the McGurk data. Our works, reported previously, on auditory and visual target specification, lead to the proposal that targets are characterized by their shape, recovered by shape-from-shading and shape-from-movement procedures, and patterned by non-linear properties of the auditory system providing some basis for 'intrinsic' substance-based categories.

This schema is compatible with a number of arguments provided by tenants of the two 'reference' theories of speech perception, from the 'motor' side with Liberman and Mattingly's Motor Theory and Fowler's Direct Realist Theory (see Fowler and Rosenblum 1991 or Liberman and Mattingly 1985 for the differences between these two theories) or from the 'sensory' side (see e.g. Greenberg 1995, or Hermansky 1998 for recent proposals on what should be the basic steps of the auditory processing of speech, independently of its production). To illustrate this, we shall review some of a classical series of arguments and controversies involving, among others, bird songs and human speech . . . or maybe the inverse, that is, bird speech and human songs!

Let us begin with the famous 'sine-wave speech' illusion, in which Remez et al. (1981) show that a set of three pure tones, modulated in frequency in order to follow the formant variations in a voiced utterance, may be perceived as speech and identified correctly. Subjects can be driven to perceive this kind of stimulus either as speech or as non-speech (typically, three bird songs such as a low-frequency owl, a medium-frequency chaffinch, and a high-frequency humming-bird) depending on the experimenter's explanations, and even to engage one of the sine-wave sounds (the highest) presented on a separate ear in a dichotic experiment into two different percepts, one speech-like and the other non-speech-like (the so-called 'duplex perception', see Liberman, Isenberg, and Rakerd 1981). This is taken by tenants of the motor theory as a proof that speech is special, and that the 'special' speech perception module is based on gestural representations.

However, birds are more often used as counter-arguments for a motor theory. Not mentioning all the arguments on Kluender's Japanese quail able to learn phonetic distinctions and solve some variability-to-invariance exercises (Kluender, Diehl, and Killeen 1987, Kluender 1991), a classical reasoning is that mynah birds are able to imitate speech, and we humans are able to understand this speech though no vocal tract was engaged in its production. This reasoning is not convincing. In fact, the mynah bird is able to track and reproduce the different frequency components of speech sounds (the formant trajectories) thanks to its bird larynx, that is a syrinx on which the animal can separately control the left and right parts, resembling two loudspeaker membranes. Therefore, in fact, the mynah bird perceives speech just as it is able to produce it: as a series of varying frequencies; while, in sine-wave speech, human listeners do the inverse: they perceive series of varying frequencies just as they are able to produce them, that is as various resonances produced by a moving vocal tract. In the first case, bird production knowledge leads the mynah bird to stream human speech in separate flows. In the second one, human production knowledge leads the listener to fuse two syrinx components into a common speech-like source.

The same kind of reasoning could be applied to explain another curious and less well-known illusion, that is, 'diphonic' song found in Mongolia. In this technique, the singer produces with his larynx a very stable low-frequency tone, and selectively reinforces various high-frequency harmonics thanks to appropriate vocal tract resonances achieved by appropriate tongue gestures. The illusion consists in the fact that this single source is perceived as two different streams, that is, a low-frequency fixed base and a high-frequency melody corresponding to the changing most intense harmonic. In this case, the listener, puzzled by this sophisticated technique, cannot accept the assumption of a single larynx+vocal tract source and prefers the more 'plausible' interpretation of two larynxes, hence two sources (two voices) superimposing their songs. Notice that this interpretation, once more relating perception to action, provides some convincing support to the illusion, while auditory theories would in such a situation be unable to provide any understanding. For example, Hermansky's 'perceptual linear prediction' spectral processing merging high-frequency components into gross characteristics (Hermansky 1998) would lose the harmonics melody, while popular 'Computational Auditory Scene Analysis' techniques (Bregman 1990, Rosenthal and Okuno 1998) would prefer merging all harmonics of a given fundamental frequency into a common stream, since harmonicity is one of the most efficient cues for grouping. The role of speech production constraints in auditory scene analysis is obvious when considering the heterogeneity of acoustic components of a speech utterance (including various formant trajectories not completely synchronized, the voicing bar with its own timing, bursts, and frication portions . . .), while the utterance is without doubt perceived as a single source (Remez 1996). It can also be observed in the inverse situation in which clicks in African languages are likely to be perceived by listeners of another language—without clicks—as a 'parallel' acoustic stream, because of these listeners' motor inability to produce the clicks.

In summary, all along this experimental journey, listeners (be they birds or humans) perceive sounds emitted by a living species (their own, or another one) in agreement with their ability to reproduce these sounds. This provides a good summary of our basic argument.

11.2. WHAT CAN THIS SPEECH PERCEPTION THEORY TELL US ABOUT PHONOLOGY?

In the second part of this chapter, we shall attempt to estimate what the consequences of this theory of perception-for-action-control might be for phonology. This is clearly part of a 'substance-based' approach to phonology which was born some thirty years ago, with the two seminal contributions by Liljencrants and Lindblom (1972), opening Lindblom's many variations about the 'dispersion' theme (Lindblom 1986, 1990, forthcoming), and by Stevens (1972) with his so-called Quantal Theory (Stevens 1989). This offered the starting point to a rich tradition of descriptive and theoretical phonetics, in which the aim is not to refute the existence of a formal phonological level with its intrinsic principles and rules, but to try to determine, and if possible quantitatively model, a set of constraints coming from the speech substance and able to have played a part in the emergence of this formal system—and therefore to throw some light on phonological facts which could sometimes appear arbitrary. We have already met some of the kinds of constraints we have in mind, such as learning processes setting [u] as a velo-palatal vowel, or perceptual quantal behaviour due to large-scale spectral integration mechanisms likely to play a part in the setting of the [i] vs. [y] contrast. In general terms, the question is: what part may the speaker-listener interactions, together with the involved representations, play in phonology?

11.2.1. What cannot be said on the origins of language

The two theoretical lines opened by Lindblom and Stevens both deal with the auditory distinctiveness of phonetic features. Lindblom's dispersion is related to the amount of information present in the acoustic signal. This can be viewed in line with our reasoning in section 11.1.2.1: acoustic information is what is necessary to recover the speaker's intention. A recent reformulation by Lindblom (1996) leads him to define auditory dispersion as the information provided by the speaker to enable the listener to disambiguate phonetic contrasts plausible at some epoch in a dialogue, considering external (contextual) information. Stevens's quantal processes introduce non-linear acoustic and auditory transformations shaping the continuous articulatory landscape and making auditory distinctions more salient.

   This view implicitly provides the basis to a long-standing and famous theory of the evolution of language proposed by Lieberman and his colleagues (Lieberman and Crelin 1971, Lieberman 1972, 1991; see also Laitman 1983, Laitman et al. 1990). In this theory, it is assumed that the low position of the larynx in adult human beings is a crucial component of Homo Sapiens's ability to communicate by speech. The reasoning is made in three steps. First, reconstructions of supralaryngeal vocal tracts of hominid Neanderthal fossils drove Lieberman and Crelin to suggest that they had a larynx position higher than that of the later Homo Sapiens. Second, acoustic simulations led Lieberman to claim that the vocal tract acoustic possibilities were reduced with a high larynx and small pharyngeal capacity: typically, the formant contrast (the 'dispersion') between the extreme [a], [i], and [u] vowels was poorer in this case. Lastly, this reduced acoustic contrast would have prevented the Neanderthaler from speaking, and their lack of speech would have played a crucial part in the selection pressure towards their disappearance. In this reasoning, auditory dispersion would provide a key for speech and language—and the final success of Homo Sapiens in the history of evolution— . . . through the larynx position.

In fact, we have recently shown that this theory was wrong (Boë et al. 1998). First, notice that the larynx position estimated by Lieberman and Crelin is debatable, as demonstrated by an increasing number of recent studies (Heim 1989, 1990, Honda and Tiede 1998), and there is no reason to believe that the larynx was higher for Neanderthaler than for Homo Sapiens. Second, the acoustic simulations themselves are wrong. In fact, a series of simulations involving articulatory models together with a model of vocal tract growth developed by Maeda (Variable Linear Articulatory Model, VLAM: see Boë and Maeda 1997) show that the 'maximal vowel space', characterizing the maximal available acoustic dispersion in the formant space for vowels (Boë et al. 1989), has similar auditory properties for adult or newborn humans, and for a vocal tract with a high larynx and small pharynx. Notice by the way that the relatively high larynx in women or children constitutes in no way an impediment for producing contrasted vowels. In conclusion, our search for substance-based constraints on language begins by a negative finding: the geometry and acoustics of the human vocal tract do not provide a crucial set of constraints on the birth of phonology. Of course, this is not to say that the 'speech production peripheral route' for language birth is of no interest, but it should involve other kinds of arguments— perhaps linked to achievable controls of the vocal tract—beyond our present understanding.

Also relevant in this discussion is the 'speech perception peripheral route', with the significant literature on the continuities and splits between human and animal audition. A long series of data demonstrated the ability of various animal species to classify speech sounds with 'similar' properties as we do: chinchillas being able to identify voiced vs. non-voiced stimuli on the basis of VOT (Kuhl and Miller 1975); with similar dependencies of the VOT boundary on the place of articulation as human listeners (Kuhl and Miller 1978); and even macaques displaying discrimination patterns typical of categorical perception, for both plosive place and voicing mode (Kuhl and Padden 1982*a*, 1982*b*); while a series of birds, including Japanese quails, budgerigars, and zebra finches, were able to discriminate and identify various phonetic contrasts (Dooling, Best, and Brown 1995, Dooling, Okanoya, and Brown 1989, Kluender, Diehl, and Killeen 1987, Kluender 1991, Lotto, Kluender, and Holt 1997). However, the recent finding by Kuhl of the so-called 'magnet effect' could provide a basis for a specifically human ability to generalize and prototypize (Grieser and Kuhl 1989, Kuhl 1991, Kuhl et al.

1992). Therefore, prototypes rather than boundaries of dispersion could be the first step towards language perception.

11.2.2. What can be said on vowel systems: the Dispersion-Focalization Theory

The failure of Lieberman's theory confirms that the question of the origin of language remains probably too far from our understanding. However, it is quite a different process to accept that language exists, implying the existence of a phonology, and then to attempt to determine whether this phonology is arbitrary, or whether it has something to do with possible sounds and gestures—just as the Morse code, far from being arbitrary, has something to do with the efficiency of communication with electrical signals. Considering that phonology should contain the set of formal structures characterizing conscious mechanisms for speech control, it is only logical to assume that it is not independent of the ability of the speech production system to produce gestures, and of the speech perception system to recover and shape these gestures. This is the basis of a theory we have developed for dealing with oral vowel systems, in the line of Lindblom's Dispersion Theory: the Dispersion-Focalization Theory.

Our theory is based on two principles, that is, dispersion and focalization. These principles specify two basic properties that vowel gestures should have in order to provide a viable sound system for communication. First, gestures should provide sufficiently different acoustic patterns to allow the perception system to be able to recover them without confusions or ambiguities: this is dispersion. Second, they should provide salient spectral patterns, easy to process and characterize in the ear: that is focalization. While auditory dispersion is a classical concept, focalization is a principle introduced by ourselves. Let us explain it in more detail.

In four-tube or coupled-resonator models providing a good first-order model for oral vowel production, affiliation exchanges, namely configurations in which there is a shift in the relation between a formant and the vocal tract cavity mainly responsible for this formant, lead to formant convergence in vowel spectra. These convergence regions, which we called *focal points* (Boë and Abry 1986), are not intrinsically stable for small variations of the place of articulation (Badin et al. 1991), but the formant displacements produced by these articulatory variations are frozen thanks to the already-mentioned large-scale spectral integration process integrating close formants (Schwartz and Escudier 1987, 1989). Furthermore, we demonstrated in a discrimination experiment that patterns with the greatest formant convergence (namely, in our case, with F_3 close to either F_2 or F_4) were more stable in short-term memory (lower index of false alarms), while patterns with less convergence (namely with F_3 at an equal distance from both F_2 and F_4) were more difficult to memorize (Schwartz and Escudier 1989). This led us to propose that formant convergence could result in an increased 'perceptual value' for a given spectral configuration because of acoustic salience. This 'focal' quality can be related to 'focal colours' (Brown and Lenneberg 1954), for which there seems to be general (cross-linguistic) perceptual agreement (Rosh-Heider 1972).

In the Dispersion-Focalization Theory (DFT), we characterize oral vowels by their formant values in the maximum available formant space, we define a vowel system by a set of vowels, and we associate to each system an energy function consisting of the sum of two terms, namely a structural dispersion term based on inter-vowel perceptual distances and a local focalization term based on intra-vowel perceptual salience, which aims at providing perceptual preference to vowels showing a *convergence between two formants*. Then, for a fixed number of vowels in a system, we implemented various algorithms to select optimal systems, that is, systems with the lowest energy (the best compromise of dispersion and focalization), either locally ('stable systems') or globally ('best systems') (Schwartz et al. 1997*b*). Our predictions of optimal vowel systems were then systematically compared to vowel inventories (Schwartz et al. 1997*a*), according to the UCLA UPSID Database (Maddieson 1984).

Beyond these two basic principles, our theory incorporates two parameters setting quantitative weights in the dispersion-focalization energy function. The first parameter, *lambda*, sets the relative weights of $F1$ and $F'2$ (grouping F2, F3, and F4 into a common perceptual parameter) for estimating a distance between two vowel spectra. *Lambda* varies between 0, for which $F'2$ plays no part, and 1, for which $F1$ and $F'2$ play the same part. Psychophysical data coming both from introspective estimates of high–low vs. front–back displacements of the tongue, and from low-to-high-frequency masking effects in psychoacoustics, indicate that the correct *lambda* value should be around 0.3, that is, $F1$ is three to four times more important than $F'2$ in spectral distances. The second parameter, *alpha*, sets the relative weight of the 'focalization' term in the energy function of a given system. *Alpha* can take any value higher than 0, since no psychophysical data exist enabling us to estimate it, except the mere fact that focalization may be demonstrated in the above-cited discrimination experiment.

We performed a number of experiments with this theory, using classical tools borrowed from physics, such as stability, optimality, and 'phase spaces', that is, domains in the (*lambda, alpha*) space in which a given vowel system is optimal for a fixed value of its number of vowels, *n*. Then, we attempted to estimate a (*lambda, alpha*) pair providing a series of optimal systems compatible with phonetic data for a large set of values of *n*: we showed that such a pair may be found, with *lambda* around 0.3 and *alpha* around 0.3, leading to predictions compatible with the most frequent systems in UPSID, for *n* varying between 3 and 9 (Schwartz et al. 1997*b*). Then, it can also be demonstrated that other values of our (*lambda, alpha*) parameters lead us to predict systems which, though non-optimal, are still plausible and observed in vowel system inventories (Vallée et al. 1999). To quote some major achievements of this theory, let us mention its ability to explain why peripheral systems are among the most popular in the languages of the world, because of the higher importance of F_1 relative to F_2 and higher formants, thanks to the low *lambda* value; why, among peripheral vowels, unrounded front vowels are slightly more frequent than rounded back ones, because of the larger available 'auditory space' in the corresponding region, due to the role of F_3 and F_4 in the computation of F'_2; why the [i y u] series of high vowels is viable—and often observed—because of the F_2–F_3 proximity in [y] diminishing the energy of corresponding systems through the focalization component, hence counterbalancing the high dispersion cost due to the strong [i]–[y] acoustic proximity. Finally, while trying to understand why schwa is observed so frequently, though its acoustic configuration at the centre of the vowel space makes it an unstable vowel, we provided typological analyses showing that schwa in fact does not interfere with the other vowels in the system, and hence should be considered as part of a parallel system with a special phonetic status (Schwartz et al. 1997*a*).

11.2.3. The potential role of the visual output in phonological settings

A basic component of our theory of perception-for-action-control is that gesture recovery and specification involves multisensorial inputs, and particularly that gestures can be not only heard but also seen (if not touched). The logical consequence is that visual dispersion could also intervene in the substance-based constraints on phonological systems. First, it is important to notice that not only does a listener use the visual input, but also a speaker is able to 'speak to be seen in order to be understood', to paraphrase the famous citation by Jakobson (in French, as early as 1942; see Jakobson 1976). This is obvious when thinking of the situation, experienced by all of us, in which you have to say something to somebody without being heard, e.g. as a pupil or student in a classroom! In this case, you will be able to hyperarticulate visually while using a quasi-silent voice—notice however that the ability to increase selectively the intelligibility of the visual output, as can be done with the auditory output, has still not been directly demonstrated (see Benoît, Fuster-Duran, and LeGoff 1996). Therefore, is there some reason to believe that some phonetic contrasts would be preferred in human languages because of their visibility?

In the case of vowel systems, it is difficult to propose a firm answer. One may define a 'visible triangle' based on the two main dimensions of the lip geometry, that is, lip rounding and lip opening, just as there is an auditory triangle based on formant values. The corners of this visible triangle are the retracted shape typical of an [i], the open shape typical of an [a], and the rounded shape typical of an [u] (Abry and Boë 1986, Benoît et al. 1992); hence the visible triangle for vowels is more or less redundant in conjunction with the auditory triangle. The ability of visible shapes for vowels to reinforce the role of the high–low contrast in respect to the front–back one, and perhaps to play a part in the already mentioned efficacy of the [i y u] series for communication, could be mentioned (Robert-Ribes et al. 1998), but it does not provide a clear-cut argument.

The situation is perhaps different for consonants. It is still difficult to find a decisive argument for plosives (for which bilabials are not privileged over dentals or velars) or fricatives (no predominance of labio-dentals), but the portrait is much clearer for nasal plosives. Indeed, the UPSID-451 Database (Maddieson and Precoda 1989) shows that 94 per cent of the 451 languages studied contain a contrast between a bilabial [m] and a coronal [n]. This contrast is acoustically very poor: remember that blind children are often unable to learn it (Mills 1987). Hence it is not unreasonable to assume that the high visibility of this contrast plays a part in the fact that it is almost universal.

11.3. CONCLUDING REMARKS

There have been a number of approaches aiming at defining an input for linguistic models into the framework of Information Theory, or at basing language theories on information processing tools. In the field of speech perception, the best-known proposal is Massaro's Fuzzy Logical Model of Perception (Massaro 1989). More recently another 'fitting modelling' is Nearey's well-named 'double-weak' theory (Nearey 1997), using logistic functions (see Kluender and Lotto 1999, for a debate). More explicitly related to phonology, recent proposals by Pierrehumbert, Hay, and Beckman (MS) claim that statistical knowledge is part of linguistic knowledge, rejoining the exemplar issue in psychological models of memory and statistical learning in speech technology (HMM and ANN). In the last conference 'Current Trends in Phonology II', held at Royaumont (22–4 June 1998), John Goldsmith took the very same stance in his talk 'Phonology with and without information theory', arguing that phonology must come back to the notion of entropy. But all these approaches might suffer precisely from their weakly constrained framework, in which the core of the models is intrinsically provided by relational structures between informational patterns.

At this point it is not unimportant to recall that Wiener's cybernetics were part of Shannon's Information Theory programme, but added constraints on *regulation* and *control*. This is precisely the goal of this chapter: to attempt to propose constraints coming from Control Theory into weakly constrained General Information Theory approaches. Our Theory of Perception-for-Action-Control aims at installing the perception–action link at the core of the relationships between phonetics and phonology, providing naturally the 'interface' anxiously searched for in a number of old and new papers (see e.g. the special issue of *Journal of Phonetics*, 18, 1990). We hope that this chapter will possibly contribute to add some substance to this sometimes formal but always crucial research theme.

References

Abbs, J. H., and DePaul, R. (1998). 'Motor cortex fields and speech movements: simple dual control is implausible'. Commentary to P. MacNeilage, 'The frame/content theory of evolution of speech production'. *Behavioral and Brain Sciences*, 21: 511–12.

Abercrombie, D. (1991). *Fifty Years in Phonetics*. Edinburgh: Edinburgh University Press.

Abry, C., and Badin, P. (1996). 'Speech Mapping as a framework for an integrated approach to the sensori-motor foundations of language'. *4th Speech Production Seminar, 1st ESCA Tutorial and Research Workshop on Speech Production Modeling: From Control Strategies to Acoustics*, 21–4 May 1996, Autrans: 175–84.

——and Lallouache, T. (1995). 'Le MEM: un modèle d'anticipation paramétrable par locuteur. Données sur l'arrondissement en français'. *Bulletin de la communication parlée*, 3: 85–99.

————and Cathiard, M.-A. (1996). 'How can coarticulation models account for speech sensitivity to audio-visual desynchronization?' In D. Stork and M. Hennecke (eds.), *Speechreading by Humans and Machines*. NATO ASI Series F: Computer and Systems Sciences 150. Berlin: Springer-Verlag: 247–55.

——Orliaguet, J. P., and Sock, R. (1990). 'Patterns of speech phasing: their robustness in the production of a timed linguistic task: single vs double (abutted) consonants in French'. *European Bulletin of Cognitive Psychology*, 10: 269–88.

——Benoît, C., Boë, L.-J., and Sock, R. (1985). 'Un choix d'événements pour l'organisation temporelle du signal de parole'. *14èmes journées d'études sur la parole, Société Française d'Acoustique*: 133–7.

——and Boë, L.-J. (1986). 'Laws for lips.' *Speech Communication*, 5: 97–104.

——Cathiard, M.-A., El Abed, R., Lallouache, M.-T., Leroy, M.-C., Perrier, P., and Poveda, P. (1996). 'Silent speech production: anticipatory behaviour for 2 out of the 3 main vowel gestures/features, while pausing'. *4th Speech Production Seminar, 1st ESCA Tutorial and Research Workshop on Speech Production Modeling: From Control Strategies to Acoustics*, 21–4 May 1996, Autrans: 101–4.

————Laboissière, R., and Schwartz, J.-L. (1998). 'A new puzzle for the evolution of speech?' *Behavioral and Brain Sciences*, 21: 512–13.

——et al. (in preparation). 'Motor equivalence and hemispheric dominance in compensatory vowel production: a fMRI study'.

ALAJOUANINE, T. (1956). 'Verbal realization in aphasia'. *Brain*, 79: 1–28.

ALEGRIA, J., LEYBAERT, J., CHARLIER, B., and HAGE, C. (1992). 'On the origin of phonological representations in the deaf: hearing lips and hands'. In J. Alegria, D. Holender, J. Junca de Morais, and M. Radeau (eds.), *Analytic Approaches to Human Cognition*. Amsterdam: Elsevier Science Publishers: 107–32.

ALLEN, W. S. (1953). *Phonetics in Ancient India*. London.

ALTMANN, G. T. M. (1997). *The Ascent of Babel: An Exploration of Language, Mind, and Understanding*. Oxford: Oxford University Press.

ANDERSON, J. M. and DURAND, J. (1988). 'Underspecification and dependency phonology'. In P. M. Bertinetto and M. Loporcaro (eds.), *Certamen phonologicum*. Turin: Rosenberg and Sellier: 4–36.

——and EWEN, C. (1987). *Principles of Dependency Phonology*. Cambridge: Cambridge University Press.

——and JONES, C. (1974). 'Three theses concerning phonological representations'. *Journal of Linguistics*, 10: 1–36.

ANDERSON, S. R. (1981). 'Why phonology isn't "natural" '. *Linguistic Inquiry*, 12: 493–539.

——(1985). *Phonology in the Twentieth Century: Theories of Rules and Theories of Representations*. Chicago: University of Chicago Press.

ANGOUJARD, J.-P. (1997). *Théorie de la syllabe: rythme et qualité*. Paris: CNRS-editions.

ARCHANGELI, D. (1984). 'Underspecification in Yawelmani Phonology and Morphology'. Ph.D. dissertation, MIT.

——(1988). 'Aspects of underspecification theory'. *Phonology*, 5: 183–208.

——and LANGENDOEN, D. T. (eds.) (1997). *Optimality Theory: An Overview*. Oxford: Blackwell.

——and PULLEYBLANK, D. (1994). *Grounded Phonology*. Cambridge, Mass: MIT Press.

ARNAULD, A., and LANCELOT, C. (1660). *Grammaire générale et raisonnée*. Reprinted Paris: Republications Paulet, 1969.

ASLIN, R. N., SAFFRAN, J. R., and NEWPORT, E. L. (1998). 'Computation of conditional probability statistics by 8-month-old infants'. *Psychological Science*, 9: 321–4.

——(ed.) (1989). *Histoire des idées linguistiques*, i: *La Naissance des métalangages en orient et en occident*. Liège: Pierre Mardaga.

——(ed.) (1992). *Histoire des idées linguistiques*, ii: *Le Développement de la grammaire occidentale*. Liège: Pierre Mardaga.

AUROUX, S. (ed.) (2000). *Histoire des idées linguistiques*, iii: *L'Hégémonie du comparatisme*. Liège: Pierre Mardaga.

BADDELEY, A. D. (1986). *Working Memory*. Oxford: Oxford University Press.

BADIN, P., PERRIER, P., BOË, L.-J., and ABRY, C. (1991). 'Vocalic nomograms:

acoustic and articulatory considerations upon formant convergences'. *Journal of the Acoustical Society of America*, 87: 1290–300.

BAILLY, G. (1995). 'Recovering place of articulation for occlusives in VCV's'. *Proceedings of the XIIIth International Congress of Phonetic Sciences*, 2: 230–3.

——— LABOISSIÈRE, R., and SCHWARTZ, J.-L. (1991). 'Formant trajectories as audible gestures: an alternative for speech synthesis'. *Journal of Phonetics*, 19: 9–23.

——— BOË, L.-J., VALLÉE, N., and BADIN, P. (1995). 'Articulatory-acoustic vowel prototypes for speech production'. *Proceedings of Eurospeech 95*, Madrid, 3: 1913–16.

BAMBI, A. (1998). 'Préservation, minimalité et seuil de tolérance dans les emprunts français en lingala'. MA dissertation, Laval University, Quebec.

BAUDOIN DE COURTENAY, I. A. (1963). *Izbrannye trudy po obščemu jazykoznaniju 1899* (Selected works in General Linguistics). Moscow: Izdatel'stvo Akademii Nauk SSSR (1st edn. 1899).

BECHTEL, A., and ABRAHAMSEN, W. (1993). *Le Connexionnisme et l'esprit: introduction au traitement parallèle par réseaux*. Paris: La Découverte.

BECKMAN, M. E., and PIERREHUMBERT, J. (MS). 'Interpreting "phonetic interpretation" over the lexicon'. Paper presented at the Sixth Conference on Laboratory Phonology, University of York, July 1998. Submitted to *Papers in Laboratory Phonology*, vol. vi.

BÉLAND, R., and PARADIS, C. (1997). 'Principled syllabic dissolution in a primary progressive aphasia case: a comparison between paraphasias and loanword adaptation'. *Aphasiology*, 11/12: 1171–96.

BELL, A., and HOOPER, J. B. (1978). 'Issues and evidence on syllabic phonology'. In A. Bell and J. B. Hooper (eds.), *Syllables and Segments*. Amsterdam: North-Holland: 3–22.

BENEDICT, H. (1979). 'Early lexical development: comprehension and production'. *Journal of Child Language*, 6: 183–200.

BENOÎT, C., FUSTER-DURAN, A., and LEGOFF, B. (1996). 'An investigation of hypo- and hyper-speech in the visual modality'. *4th Speech Production Seminar, 1st ESCA Tutorial and Research Workshop on Speech Production Modeling: From Control Strategies to Acoustics*. 21–4 May 1996, Autrans: 237–40.

——— MOHAMADI, T., and KANDEL, S. D. (1994). 'Effects of phonetic context on audio-visual intelligibility of French'. *Journal of Speech and Hearing Research*, 37: 1195–203.

——— LALLOUACHE, T., MOHAMADI, T., and ABRY, C. (1992). 'A set of visual French visemes for visual speech synthesis'. In G. Bailly, C. Benoît, and T. R. Sawallis (eds.), *Talking Machines: Theories, Models and Designs*. Amsterdam: Elsevier Sc. Publications: 485–504.

BERENT, I., and PERFETTI, C. A. (1995). 'A rose is a REEZ: the two-cycles model of phonology assembly in reading English'. *Psychological Review*, 102: 146–84.

BERNSTEIN, L. E., DEMOREST, M. E., and TUCKER, P. E. (1998). 'What makes a good speechreader? First you have to find one'. In R. Campbell, B. Dodd, and

D. Burnham (eds.), *Hearing by Eye*, ii: *Perspectives and Directions in Research on Audiovisual Aspects of Language Processing*. Hove: Psychology Press: 211–28.

BEST, C. (1994). 'The emergence of native-language phonological influence in infants: a perceptual assimilation model'. In J. Goodman and H. Nusbaum (eds.), *The Development of Speech Perception: The Transition from Speech Sounds to Spoken Words*. Cambridge, Mass: MIT Press: 167–224.

—— MCROBERTS, G., and SITHOLE, N. (1988). 'Examination of perceptual reorganization for nonnative speech contrasts: Zulu click discrimination by English-speaking adults and infants'. *Journal of Experimental Psychology: Human Perception and Performance*, 14: 345–60.

—— et al. (in preparation). 'Native-language phonetic and phonological constraints on perception of non-native speech contrasts: A fMRI study'.

BINDER, J. R., FROST, J. A., HAMMEKE, T. A., COX, R. W., RAO, S. M., and PRIETO, T. (1997). 'Human brain language areas identified by functional magnetic resonance imaging'. *Journal of Neurosciences*, 17: 353–62.

BLADON, A. (1982). 'Arguments against formants in the auditory representation of speech'. In R. Carlson and B. Granström (eds.), *The Representation of Speech in the Peripheral Auditory System*. Amsterdam: Elsevier Biomedical: 95–102.

—— and FANT, G. (1978). 'A two-formant model and the cardinal vowels'. *Speech Transmission Laboratory, Quarterly Progress and Status Report*, 1:1–8.

—— and LINDBLOM, B. (1981). 'Modeling the judgment of vowel quality differences'. *Journal of the Acoustical Society of America*, 65: 1414–22.

BLAKE, B. (1979). 'Pitta-Pitta'. In R. Dixon and B. Blake (eds.), *Handbook of Australian Languages*, vol. i. Amsterdam: John Benjamins: 182–242.

BLANKEN, G. (1991). 'The functional basis of speech automatisms (recurring utterances)'. *Aphasiology* 5: 103–27.

—— and MARINI, V. (1997). 'Where do lexical speech automatisms come from?' *Journal of Neurolinguistics*, 10: 19–31.

—— WALLESH, C.-W., and PAPAGNO, C. (1990). 'Dissociations of language functions in aphasics with speech automatisms' (recurring utterances)'. *Cortex*, 26: 41–63.

BLOOMFIELD, L. (1914). *An Introduction to the Study of Language*. New York: Holt.

—— (1926). 'A set of postulates for the science of language'. *Language*, 2: 153–64. No. 5 of the Bobbs-Merrill reprint series in Language and Linguistics, Bloomington, Ind., 1948.

—— (1933). *Language*. New York: Holt.

—— (1939). 'Menomini morphophonemics'. *Travaux du Cercle Linguistique de Prague*, 8: 105–15.

BLUMSTEIN, S. E., and STEVENS, K. N. (1981). 'Phonetic features and acoustic invariance in speech'. *Cognition*, 10: 25–32.

BOAS, M. (1970). *The Scientific Renaissance 1540–1630*. London: Fontana Books (1st edn. 1962).

BOË, L.-J. (1997). 'Sciences phonétiques et relations forme/substance'. *Histoire épistémologie langage*, Partie i, 19/1: 5–41, Partie ii, 19/2: 5–25.

Boë, L.-J. and Abry, C. (1986). 'Nomogrammes et systèmes vocaliques'. *Actes des 15èmes journées d'étude sur la parole, Société Française d'Acoustique*: 303–6.

—— Vallée, N., Badin, P., Schwartz, J.-L., and Abry, C. (2000). 'Tendencies in phonological structures: the influence of substance on form'. *Bulletin de la communication parlée* 5/1. Grenoble: Institut de la Communication Parlée.

and Maeda, S. (1997). 'Modélisation de la croissance du conduit vocal: espaces vocaliques des nouveaux-nés et des adultes. Conséquences pour la phylogenèse et l'ontogenèse'. In *La Voyelle dans tous ses états*. Nantes: 98–105.

—— and Perrier, P. (1988). 'Comments on "Distinctive regions and modes: a new theory of speech production" by M. Mrayati, R. Carré and B. Guérin'. *Speech Communication*, 9: 217–30.

—— —— and Bailly, G. (1992). 'The geometric vocal tract variables controlled for vowel production: proposals for constraining acoustic-to-articulatory inversion'. *Journal of Phonetics*, 20: 27–38.

—— —— Guérin, B., and Schwartz, J. L. (1989). 'Maximal vowel space'. *Proceedings of Eurospeech 89*, 2: 281–4.

—— Schwartz, J. L., Laboissière, R., and Vallée, N. (1996). 'Integrating articulatory-acoustic constraints in the prediction of sound structures'. *4th Speech Production Seminar, 1st ESCA Tutorial and Research Workshop on Speech Production Modeling: From Control Strategies to Acoustics*, 21–4 May 1996, Autrans: 163–6.

—— Maeda, S., Abry, C., and Heim, J. L. (1998). '[i a u]? A la portée d'un conduit vocal de Neandertal'. *Actes des XXIIèmes journées d'étude sur la parole*, Martigny: 245–8.

Bohn, O. S., and Strange, W. (1995). 'Discrimination of coarticulated German vowels in the silent-center paradigm: 'target' spectral information non needed'. *Proceedings of the XIIIth International Congress of Phonetic Sciences*, Stockholm, 2: 270–3.

Booij, G. (1995). *The Phonology of Dutch*. Oxford: Clarendon Press.

Botinis, A. (to appear). *Intonation: Models and Applications*. Cambridge: Cambridge University Press.

Bouquet, S. (1997). *Introduction à la lecture de Saussure*. Paris: Payot.

Bradley, D. C., Sanchez-Casas, R. M., and Garcia-Albea, J. E. (1993). 'The status of the syllable in the perception of Spanish and English'. *Language and Cognitive Processes*, 8: 197–233.

Breeuwer, M., and Plomp, R. (1986). 'Speechreading supplemented with auditorily presented speech parameters'. *Journal of the Acoustical Society of America*, 79: 481–99.

Bregman, A. S. (1990). *Auditory Scene Analysis: The Perceptual Organization of Sound*. Cambridge, Mass.: MIT Press.

Brent, M. R., and Cartwright, T. A. (1996). 'Distributional regularity and phonotactic constraints are useful for segmentation'. *Cognition*, 61: 93–125.

Brickner, R. M. (1940). 'A human cortical area producing repetitive phenomena when stimulated'. *Journal of Neurophysiology*, 3: 128–30.

BROCA, P. (1861). 'Remarques sur le siège de la faculté du langage articulé, suivies d'une observation d'aphémie (perte de la parole)'. *Bulletin de la Société d'Anatomie de Paris*, 6: 330–57.

BROCKHAUS, W. G. (1995). 'Skeletal and suprasegmental structure within Government Phonology'. In Durand and Katamba (1995: 180–221).

—— INGLEBY, M., and CHALFONT, C. R. (1996). 'Acoustic signatures of phonological primes'. MS. Universities of Manchester and Huddersfield.

BROE, M., and PIERREHUMBERT, J. (2000). *Papers in Laboratory Phonology*, vol. v: *Acquisition and the Lexicon*. Cambridge: Cambridge University Press.

BROMBERGER, S., and HALLE, M. (1989). 'Why phonology is different'. *Linguistic Inquiry*, 20/1: 51–70.

————(1997). 'The contents of phonological signs: a comparison between their use in derivational theories and in optimality theory'. In I. Roca (ed.), *Derivations and Constraints in Phonology*. Oxford: Oxford University Press: 93–122.

————(2000). 'The ontology of phonology'. In Burton-Roberts, Carr, and Docherty (2000: 19–37).

BROWMAN, C. and GOLDSTEIN, L. (1986). 'Towards an articulatory phonology'. *Phonology*, 3: 219–52.

————(1989). 'Articulatory gestures as phonological units'. *Phonology*, 6: 201–52.

————(1992). 'Articulatory Phonology: an overview'. *Phonetica*, 49: 155–80.

BROWN, R., and HILDUM, D. (1956). 'Expectancy and the perception of syllables'. *Language*, 32: 411–19.

—— and LENNEBERG, E. H. (1954). 'A study in language and cognition'. *Journal of Abnormal and Social Psychology*, 49: 454–62.

BRUCK, A., FOX, R. A., and LAGALY, M. W. (1974). *Papers from the Parasession on Natural Phonology*. Chicago: Chicago Linguistic Society.

BRUCK, M., TREIMAN, R., and CARAVOLAS, M. (1995). 'The syllable's role in the processing of spoken English: evidence from a nonword comparison task'. *Journal of Experimental Psychology: Human Perception and Performance*, 21: 469–79.

BURNHAM, D. (1998). 'Harry McGurk and the McGurk effect'. *Proceedings of Audio-Visual Speech Processing 98*, Sydney: 1–2.

BURTON-ROBERTS, N. (2000). 'Where and what is phonology? A representational perspective'. In Burton-Roberts, Carr, and Docherty (2000: 39–66).

—— and CARR, P. (1996). 'On speech and natural language'. *Language Sciences*, 21/4: 371–406.

————(1997). 'Où se situe la phonologie? La linguistique et la conjecture représentationnelle'. *Histoire épistémologie langage*, 19/2: 73–103.

———— and DOCHERTY, G. (eds.) (2000). *Phonological Knowledge: Conceptual and Empirical Issues*. Oxford: Oxford University Press.

BYBEE, J. (1996). 'The phonology of the lexicon: evidence from lexical diffusion'. In M. Barlow and S. Kemmer (eds.), *Usage-Based Models of Language*. Stanford, Calif.: CSLI Publications.

BYBEE, J. (2000). 'Lexicalization of sound change and alternating environments'. In Broe and Pierrehumbert (2000: 250–68).

——CHAKRABORTI, P., JUNG, D., and SCHEIBMAN, J. (1998). 'Prosody and segmental effect: some paths of evolution for word stress'. *Studies in Language*, 22: 267–314.

CALVERT, G. A., BULLMORE, E. T., BRAMMER, M. J., CAMPBELL, R., WILLIAMS, S. C. R., MCGUIRE, P. K., WOODRUFF, P. W. R., IVERSON, S. D., and DAVID, A. S. (1997). 'Activation of auditory cortex during silent lip-reading'. *Science*, 276: 593–6.

CAMILLI, A. (1965). *Pronuncia e grafia dell'italiano*. Florence: Sansoni.

CAPLAN, D. (1987). *Neurolinguistics and Linguistic Aphasiology*. Cambridge: Cambridge University Press.

CAPPA, S. F., CAVALOTTI, G., and VIGNOLO, L. A. (1981). 'Phonemic and lexical errors in fluent aphasia: correlation with lesion site'. *Neuropsychologia*, 19: 171–7.

CARLSON, R., GRANSTRÖM, B., and FANT, C. G. M. (1970). 'Some studies concerning perception of isolated vowels'. *Speech Transmission Laboratory, Quarterly Progress and Status Report*, 2–3: 19–35.

————(1979). 'Vowel perception: the relative salience of selected acoustic manipulations'. *Speech Transmission Laboratory, Quarterly Progress and Status Report*, 34: 73–83.

CARR, P. (2000). 'Scientific Realism, sociophonetic variation and innate endowment in phonology'. In Burton-Roberts, Carr, and Docherty (2000: 67–104).

CARSTAIRS-MCCARTHY, A. (1999). *The Origins of Complex Language: An Inquiry into the Evolutionary Beginnings of Sentences, Syllables and Truth*. Oxford: Oxford University Press.

CARVALHO, J. BRANDÃO DE (1994). 'What are vowels made of? The "no-rule" approach and particle phonology'. *Studia linguistica*, 48: 1–27.

——(1998). 'From constraint-based theories to theory-based constraints'. Paper presented at the conference 'Current Trends in Phonology. Models and Methods 2', Royaumont, June 1998.

——and KLEIN, M. (1996). 'A subsymbolic approach to phonological primitives'. In B. Laks and J. Durand (eds.), *Current Trends in Phonology: Models and Methods*. Salford: ESRI: 99–123.

CASTAIGNE, P., LHERMITTE, F., SIGNORET, J. L., and ABELANET, R. (1980). 'Description et étude scannographique du cerveau de Leborgne: la découverte de Broca'. *Revue neurologique*, 136: 563–83.

CASTRO-CALDAS, A., PETERSSON, K. M., REIS, A., STONE-ELANDER, S., and INGVAR, M. (1998). 'The illiterate brain: learning to read and write during childhood influences the functional organization of the adult brain'. *Brain*, 121: 1053–63.

CATFORD, J. C. (1977). *Fundamental Problems in Phonetics*. Edinburgh: Edinburgh University Press.

CATHIARD, M.-A. (1988). 'Identification des voyelles et des consonnes dans le jeu de la protrusion-rétraction des lèvres en français'. Mémoire de Maîtrise de Psychologie, Université de Grenoble II.

—— (1998). 'Visual percepts of rounding in glides and vowels: static or dynamic?' *Fifth European Workshop on Ecological Psychology*, 7–10 July 1998, Pont-à-Mousson: 53–8.

——ABRY, C., and SCHWARTZ, J.-L. (1998). 'Visual perception of glides versus vowels: the effect of dynamic expectancy'. *Australian Workshop on Auditory-Visual Speech Processing*, Satellite of the International Conference on Spoken Language Processing (ICSLP 98), 4–7 Dec. 1998, Terrigal: 115–20.

—— and LALLOUACHE, M.-T. (1992). 'L'Apport de la cinématique dans la perception visuelle de l'anticipation et de la rétention labiales'. *Actes des 19èmes journées d'études sur la parole*, 19–22 May 1992, Brussels: 25–30.

—— —— and ABRY, C. (1996). 'Does movement on the lips mean movement in the mind?' In D. Stork and M. Hennecke (eds.), *Speechreading by Humans and Machines*, NATO ASI Series F. Computer and Systems Sciences 150. Springer-Verlag: 211–19.

——TIBERGHIEN, G., and ABRY, C. (1992). 'Face and profile identification skills for lip-rounding in normal-hearing French subjects'. *Bulletin de la communication parlée*, 2: 43–58.

—— ——TSEVA, A., LALLOUACHE, M.-T., and ESCUDIER, P. (1991). 'Visual perception of anticipatory rounding during acoustic pauses: a cross-language study'. *Proceedings of the XIIth International Congress of Phonetic Sciences*, 19–24 Aug. 1991, Aix-en-Provence, 4: 50–3.

——LALLOUACHE, M.-T., MOHAMADI, T., and ABRY, C. (1995). 'Configurational vs. temporal coherence in audiovisual speech perception'. *Proceedings of the XIIIth International Congress of Phonetic Sciences*, 13–19 Aug. 1995, Stockholm: iii. 218–21.

CATTS, H. W. (1997). 'Clinical exchange: the early identification of language-based reading disabilities'. *Language, Speech, and Hearing Services of Schools*, 28: 86–9.

CEDERGREN, H., and SANKOFF, D. (1974). 'Variable rules: performance as a statistical reflection of competence'. *Language*, 50: 333–55.

CHALFONT, C. R. (1997). 'Automatic Speech Recognition: A Government Phonology Perspective on the Extraction of Subsegmental Primes from Speech Data'. Ph.D. dissertation, University of Huddersfield.

CHALMERS, A. F. (1999). *What is this Thing Called Science?* 3rd edn. Buckingham: Open University Press.

CHAO, Y.-R. (1948). *Mandarin Primer*. Cambridge, Mass.: Harvard University Press.

CHAUVEL, P. C. (1976). 'Les Stimulations de l'aire motrice supplémentaire chez l'homme'. Ph.D. dissertation, Université de Rennes.

CHEVALIER, J.-C. (2000). 'Les Congrès internationaux et la linguistique'. In S. Auroux (ed.), *Histoire des idées linguistiques*, vol. iii, Sprimont: Pierre Mardaga: 517–28.

CHIBA, T., and KAJIYAMA, M. (1941). *The Vowel: Its Nature and Structure*. Tokyo: Tokyo-Kaseikan Pub. Co.

CHISTOVICH, L. A. (1976). *Physiology of Speech: Human Speech Perception.* Leningrad: Nauka (in Russian).

—— (1980). 'Auditory processing of speech'. *Language and Speech*, 23: 67–72.

—— and LUBLINSKAYA, V. V. (1979). 'The center of gravity effect in vowel spectra and critical distance between the formants'. *Hearing Research*, 1: 185–95.

—— SHEIKIN, R. L., and LUBLINSKAYA, V. V. (1979). ' "Centers of gravity" and the spectral peaks as the determinants of vowel quality'. In B. Lindblom and S. Ohman (eds.), *Frontiers of Speech Communication Research.* London: Academic Press: 143–58.

—— LUBLINSKAYA, V. V., MALLINIKOVA, T. G., OGORODNIKOVA, E. A., STOLJAROVA, E. I., and ZHUKOV, S. JA (1982). 'Temporal processing of peripheral auditory patterns of speech'. In R. Carlson and B. Granström (eds.), *The Representation of Speech in the Peripheral Auditory System.* Amsterdam: Elsevier Biomedical: 165–80.

CHOMSKY, N. (1957). *Syntactic Structures.* The Hague: Mouton.

—— (1964). *Current Issues in Linguistic Theory.* The Hague: Mouton & Co.

—— (1965). *Aspects of the Theory of Syntax.* Cambridge, Mass.: MIT Press.

—— (1968). *Language and Mind.* New York: Harcourt, Brace and World.

—— (1995). 'Language and Nature'. *Mind*, 104: 413–61.

—— (2000). *New Horizons in the Study of Language and Mind.* Cambridge: Cambridge University Press.

—— and HALLE, M. (1968). *The Sound Pattern of English.* New York: Harper and Row.

CHRISTOPHE, A., and DUPOUX, E. (1996). 'Bootstrapping lexical acquisition: the role of prosodic structure'. *Linguistic Review*, 13: 383–412.

CLEMENTS, G. N. (1979). 'The description of terraced-level tone languages'. *Language*, 55: 536–58.

—— (1985). 'The geometry of phonological features'. *Phonology Yearbook*, 2: 225–52.

—— and KEYSER, S. J. (1983). *CV Phonology: A Generative Theory of the Syllable.* Cambridge, Mass.: MIT Press.

COATES, R. (1979). 'Review of J. Foley 1977'. *Journal of Linguistics*, 15/1: 132–41.

CODE C. (1982*a*). 'Neurolinguistic analysis of recurrent utterance in aphasia'. *Cortex*, 18: 141–52.

—— (1982*b*). 'On the origins of recurrent utterances in aphasia'. *Cortex*, 18: 161–4.

—— (1983). 'On "Neurolinguistic analysis of recurrent utterances in aphasia": reply to De Bleser and Poeck'. *Cortex*, 19: 261–4.

—— (1987). *Language, Aphasia and the Right Hemisphere.* Chichester: John Wiley.

—— (1989). 'Speech automatisms and recurring utterances'. In C. Code (ed.), *The Characteristics of Aphasia.* London: Taylor and Francis.

—— (1994). 'Speech automatism production in aphasia'. *Journal of Neurolinguistics*, 8: 135–48.

COKER, C. H., CHURCH, K. W., and LIBERMAN, M. Y. (1990). 'Morphology and rhyming: two powerful alternatives to letter-to-sound rules for speech synthesis'. *Proceedings of the ESCA Workshop on Speech Synthesis*, 25–8 Sept. 1990, Autrans: 83–6.

COLEMAN, J. S. (1992). 'The phonetic interpretation of headed phonological structures containing overlapping constituents'. *Phonology*, 9: 1–44.

—— (1995). 'Declarative lexical phonology'. In J. Durand and F. Katamba (eds.) *Frontiers of Phonology: Atoms, Structures, Derivations*. Harlow: Longman: 333–82.

—— (1998a). *Phonological Representations: Their Names, Forms and Powers*. Cambridge: Cambridge University Press.

—— (1998b). 'Cognitive reality and the phonological lexicon: a review'. *Journal of Neurolinguistics*, 11: 295–320.

—— and PIERREHUMBERT, J. (1997). 'Stochastic phonological grammars and acceptability'. In *Computational Phonology. Third Meeting of the ACL Special Interest Group in Computational Phonology*. Somerset, NJ: Association for Computational Linguistics: 49–56.

—— (2000). 'Candidate selection'. *Linguistic Review*, 17: 167–79.

CONNELL, B., and ARVANITI, A. (1995). *Papers in Laboratory Phonology, iv: Phonology and Phonetic Evidence*. Cambridge: Cambridge University Press.

CORINA, D. P. (1992). 'Syllable priming and lexical representations: evidence from experiments and simulations'. In D. P. Corina (ed.), *Proceedings of the 14th Annual Conference of the Cognitive Science Society*. Hillsdale, NJ: Erlbaum: 779–84.

CORNETT, R. O. (1967). 'Cued speech'. *American Annals of the Deaf*, 112: 3–13.

COSTA, A. (1995). 'Suprasegmental structures in phonological encoding'. Paper presented at the European Summer School on 'Aspects of Speech Production', University of Birmingham, UK.

—— (1997). 'La codificación fonológica en la producción del lenguaje: unidades y procesos implicados' (Phonological encoding in speech production: units and processes). Doctoral dissertation, University of Barcelona.

—— and SEBASTIAN-GALLÉS, N. (1998). 'Abstract phonological structure in language production: evidence from Spanish'. *Journal of Experimental Psychology: Learning, Memory, and Cognition*, 24: 886–903.

CRUTTENDEN, A. (ed.) (1994). *Gimson's Pronunciation of English*. 5th edn. Cambridge: Cambridge University Press.

CUTLER, A. (1993). 'Language-specific processing: does the evidence converge?' In G. T. M. Altmann and R. Shillcock (eds.), *Cognitive Models of Speech Processing: The Second Sperlonga Meeting*. Hillsdale, NJ: Erlbaum: 115–23.

—— (1995). 'Spoken word recognition and production'. In J. Miller (ed.), *Speech, Language and Communication*. New York: Academic Press: 97–136.

—— (1997). 'The syllable's role in the segmentation of stress languages'. *Language and Cognitive Processes*, 12: 839–45.

—— and NORRIS, D. G. (1988). 'The role of strong syllables in segmentation for lexical access'. *Journal of Experimental Psychology: Human Perception and Performance*, 14: 113–21.

CUTLER, A., MEHLER, J., NORRIS, D. and SEGUI, J. (1983). 'A language specific comprehension strategy'. *Nature*, 304: 159–60.

—— —— —— ——(1986). 'The syllable's differing role in the segmentation of French and English'. *Journal of Memory and Language*, 25: 385–400.

DARWIN, C. J. (1989). 'The relationship between speech perception and the perception of other sounds'. In I. G. Mattingly and M. Studdert-Kennedy (eds.), *Modularity and the Motor Theory of Speech Perception*. Hillsdale, NJ: Lawrence Erlbaum Associates: 239–60.

DAVIS, C., and KIM, J. (1998). 'Repeating and remembering foreign language words: does seeing help?' *Proceedings of Audio-Visual Speech Processing 98*, Sydney: 121–5.

DE BLESER, R., and POECK, K. (1983). Comments on paper 'Neurolinguistic analysis of recurrent utterance in aphasia' by C. Code (*Cortex* 18 (1982): 141–52). *Cortex*, 19: 259–60.

DEDINA, M. J., and NUSBAUM, H. C. (1991). 'PRONOUNCE: a program for pronunciation by analogy'. *Computer Speech and Language*, 5: 55–64.

DEHAENE-LAMBERTZ, G., DUPOUX, E., and GOUT A. (in press). 'Electrophysiological correlates of phonological processing: a cross-linguistic study'. *Journal of Cognitive Neuroscience*.

DELGUTTE, B. (1984). 'Speech coding in the auditory nerve II: processing schemes for vowel-like sounds'. *Journal of the Acoustical Society of America*, 75: 879–86.

—— (1986). 'Analysis of French stop consonants using a model of the peripheral auditory system'. In J. S. Perkell and D. H. Klatt (eds.), *Invariance and Variability in Speech Processes*, Hillsdale, NJ: Erlbaum: 163–77.

DELL, F. (1973). *Les Règles et les sons*. Paris: Hermann.

—— (1984). 'L'Accentuation dans les phrases en français'. In F. Dell, D. Hirst, and J.-R. Vergnaud (eds,), *Forme sonore du langage*. Paris: Hermann: 65–122.

DELL, G. S. (1986). 'A spreading activation theory of retrieval in sentence production'. *Psychological Review*, 93: 283–321.

DÉMONET, J.-F. (1998). 'Tomographic brain imaging of language functions: prospects for a new brain/language model'. In B. Stemmer and H. A. Whitaker (eds.), *Handbook of Neurolinguistics*. San Diego: Academic Press: 132–42.

—— WISE, R., and FRACKOWIAK, R. S. J. (1993). 'Language functions explored in normal subjects by positron emission tomography: a critical review'. *Human Brain Mapping*, 1: 39–47.

—— CHOLLET, F., RAMSAY, S., CARDEBAT, D., NESPOULOUS, J. L., WISE, R., RASCOL, A., and FRACKOWIAK, R. S. J. (1992). 'The anatomy of phonological and semantic processing in normal subjects'. *Brain*, 115: 1753–68.

—— PRICE, C., WISE, R., and FRACKOWIAK, R. S. J. (1994a). 'Differential activation of right and left posterior sylvian regions by semantic and phonological tasks: a positron emission tomography study in normal human subjects'. *Neuroscience Letters*, 182: 25–8.

—— —— —— ——(1994b). 'A PET study of cognitive strategies in normal subjects during language tasks: influence of phonetic ambiguity and sequence processing on phoneme monitoring'. *Brain*, 117: 671–82.

—— Fiez, J. A., Paulesu, E., Petersen, S. E., and Zatorre, R. J. (1996). 'PET studies of phonological processing: a critical reply to Poeppel'. *Brain and Language*, 55: 352–79.

Derwing, B. L. (1992). 'A "pause-break" task for eliciting syllable boundary judgments from literate and illiterate speakers: preliminary results for five diverse languages'. *Language and Speech*, 35: 219–35.

Dick, J. P. R., Benecke, R., Rothwell, J. C., Day, B. L., and Marsden, C. D. (1986). 'Simple and complex movements in a patient with infarction of the right supplementary motor area'. *Movement Disorders*, 1: 255–66.

Dinner, D. S., and Luders, H. O. (1995). 'Human supplementary sensory motor area: electrical stimulation and movement-related potential studies'. In H. H. Jasper, S. Riggio, and P. S. Goldman-Rakic (eds.), *Epilepsy and the Functional Anatomy of the Frontal Lobe*. Raven Press.

Dinnsen, D. A. (ed.) (1980). *Current Approaches to Phonological Theory*. Bloomington: Indiana University Press.

Dixon, R. (1983). 'Nyawaygi'. In R. Dixon and B. Blake (eds), *Handbook of Australian Languages*, vol. iii. Amsterdam: John Benjamins: 430–531.

—— (1988). *A Grammar of Boumaa Fijian*. Chicago: University of Chicago Press.

Docherty, G., and Ladd, D. R. (eds.) (1992). *Papers in Laboratory Phonology II*. Cambridge: Cambridge University Press.

Dooling, R. J., Best, C. T., and Brown, S. D. (1995). 'Discrimination of synthetic full-formant and sinewave /ra-la/ continua by budgerigars (*Melopsittacus undulatus*) and zebra finches (*Taeniopygia guttata*)'. *Journal of the Acoustical Society of America*, 97: 1839–46.

—— Okanoya, K., and Brown, S. D. (1989). 'Speech perception by budgerigars (*Melopsittacus undulatus*): the voiced–voiceless distinction'. *Perception and Psychophysics*, 46: 65–71.

Dosse, F. (1991). *Histoire du structuralisme*, i: *Le Champ du signe, 1945–1966*. Paris: Éditions La Découverte.

—— (1993). *Histoire du structuralisme*, ii: *Le Chant du cygne, 1967 à nos jours*. Paris: Éditions La Découverte.

Dresher, B. E., and Kaye, J. D. (1990). 'A computational learning model for metrical phonology'. *Cognition*, 34: 137–95.

Dressler, W. U. (1981). 'Outlines of a Model of Morphonology'. In W. U. Dressler, O. E. Pfeiffer, and J. R. Rennison (eds.), *Phonologica 1980*. Innsbruck: Innsbrucker Beiträge zur Sprachwissenschaft: 113–22.

Dunn, L. M., Thériault-Whalen, C. M., and Dunn, L. M. (1993). *Échelle de vocabulaire en images peabody*. EVIP Psycan.

Dupoux, E. (1993). 'The time course of prelexical processing: the syllabic hypothesis revisited'. In G. T. M. Altmann and R. Shillock (eds.), *Cognitive Models of Speech Processing: The Second Sperlonga Meeting*. Hillsdale, NJ: Erlbaum: 81–114.

—— and Mehler, J. (1990). 'Monitoring the lexicon with normal and compressed speech: frequency effects and the prelexical code'. *Journal of Memory and Language*, 29: 316–35.

—— PALLIER, C., SEBASTIAN, N., and MEHLER, J. (1997). 'A destressing "deafness" in French?' *Journal of Memory and Language*, 36: 406–21.

—— KAKEHI, K., HIROSE, Y., PALLIER, C., and MEHLER, J. (1999). 'Epenthetic vowels in Japanese: a perceptual illusion?' *Journal of Experimental Psychology: Human Perception and Performance*, 25: 1568–78.

—— PEPERKAMP, S., and SEBASTIÁN-GALLÉS, N. (in press). 'A robust method to study stress "deafness" '. *Journal of the Acoustical Society of America*.

DURAND, J. (1982). 'Review of J. Foley 1979'. *Journal of Linguistics*, 18/2: 474–95.

—— (1990). *Generative and Non-linear Phonology*. London: Longman.

—— (1995). 'Universalism in phonology: atoms, structures, derivations'. In Durand and Katamba (1995: 267–88).

—— (2000*a*). 'Oral, écrit et faculté de langage'. In M.-M. Kenning and M.-N. Guillot (eds.), *Changing Landscapes in Language and Language Teaching: Text, Orality and Voice*. London: CiLT: 51–86.

—— (2000*b*). 'Les Traits phonologiques et le débat articulation/audition'. In P. Busuttil (ed.), *Points d'interrogation: phonétique et phonologie de l'anglais*. Pau: Publications de l'Université de Pau: 56–70.

—— and KATAMBA, F. (eds.) (1995). *Frontiers of Phonology: Atoms, Structures, Derivations*. London: Longman.

—— and LAKS, B. (eds.) (1996*a*). *Current Trends in Phonology: Models and Methods*. 2 vols. Salford: European Studies Research Institute.

—— —— (1996*b*). 'Why phonology is one'. In Durand and Laks (1996*a*: i. 1–15).

—— —— (2000). 'Relire les phonologues du français: Maurice Grammont et la loi des trois consonnes'. *Langue française*, 126: 29–38.

—— and LYCHE, C. (2000). 'La Phonologie: des phonèmes à la théorie de l'optimalité'. In P. Escudier and J.-L. Schwartz (eds.) (2000), *La Parole: des modèles cognitifs aux machines communicantes*. Paris: Hermès: 193–244.

DUVERNOY, H. M. (1999). *The Human Brain: Surface, Three-Dimensional Sectional Anatomy with MRI, and Vascularization*. New York: Springer.

EIMAS, P. D. (1999). 'Segmental and syllabic representations in the perception of speech by young infants'. *Journal of the Acoustical Society of America*, 105/3: 1901–11.

—— SIQUELAND, E. R., JUSCZYK, P., and VIGORITO, J. (1971). 'Speech perception in infants'. *Science*, 171: 303–6.

ELLIS, A. W., and YOUNG, A. W. (1988). *Human Cognitive Neuropsychology*. Hillsdale, NJ: Erlbaum.

ELMAN, G., BATES, E. A., JOHNSON, M. H., KARMILOFF-SMITH, A., PARISI, A., and PLUNKETT, K. (1996). *Rethinking Innateness: A Connectionist Perspective on Development*. Cambridge, Mass.: MIT Press.

ENCREVÉ, P. (2000) 'The old and the new: some remarks on phonology and its history'. In Goldsmith and Laks (2000*a*: 34–57).

ERBER, N. P. (1969). 'Interaction of audition and vision in the recognition of oral speech stimuli'. *Journal of Speech and Hearing Research*, 12: 423–5.

—— (1974). 'Effects of angle, distance and illumination on visual reception of speech by profoundly deaf children'. *Journal of Speech and Hearing Research*, 17: 99–112.

ERICKSON, T. C., and WOOLSEY, C. N. (1951). 'Observations on the supplementary area of Man'. *Transactions of the American Neurological Association*, 76: 50–2.

ERMENTROUT, B. (1994). 'An introduction to neural oscillators'. In F. Ventriglia (ed.), *Neural Modeling and Neural Networks*. Oxford: Pergamon Press: 79–110.

ESCUDIER, P., BENOÎT, C., and LALLOUACHE, T. (1990). 'Identification visuelle de stimuli associés à l'opposition /i/-/y/: étude statique'. *1er Congrès Français d'Acoustique*, 1: 541–4.

EVERITT, B. S. (1993). *Cluster Analysis*. 3rd edn. London: Arnold.

FALLOWS, D. (1981). 'Experimental evidence for English syllabification and syllable structure'. *Journal of Linguistics*, 17: 309–17.

FANT, C. G. M. (1960). *Acoustic Theory of Speech Production and Perception with Calculations Based on X-ray Studies of Russian Articulations*. The Hague: Mouton.

FEAR, B. D., CUTLER, A., and BUTTERFIELD, S. (1995). 'The strong/weak syllable distinction in English'. *Journal of the Acoustical Society of America*, 97/3: 1893–904.

FERRAND, L. (1995). 'Repeated prime-target presentations do not eliminate repetition and phonological priming in naming digits'. *Acta Psychologica*, 89: 217–27.

—— and GRAINGER, J. (1992). 'Phonology and orthography in visual word recognition: evidence from masked nonword priming'. *Quarterly Journal of Experimental Psychology*, 42A: 353–72.

—— —— (1993). 'The time-course of orthographic and phonological code activation in the early phases of visual word recognition'. *Bulletin of the Psychonomic Society*, 31: 119–22.

—— —— (1994). 'Effects of orthography are independent of phonology in masked form priming'. *Quarterly Journal of Experimental Psychology*, 47A: 365–82.

—— —— (1996). 'List context effects on masked phonological priming in the lexical decision task'. *Psychonomic Bulletin and Review*, 3: 515–19.

—— —— and SEGUI, J. (1994). 'A study of masked form priming in picture and word naming'. *Memory and Cognition*, 22: 431–41.

—— HUMPHREYS, G. W. and SEGUI, J. (1998). 'Masked repetition and phonological priming in picture naming'. *Perception and Psychophysics*, 60: 263–74.

—— and SEGUI, J. (1998). 'The syllable's role in speech production: are syllables chunks, schemas, or both?' *Psychonomic Bulletin and Review*, 5: 253–8.

—— —— and GRAINGER, J. (1995). 'Amorçage phonologique masqué et dénomination'. *L'Année psychologique*, 95: 645–59.

—— —— —— (1996). 'Masked priming of word and picture naming: the role of syllabic units'. *Journal of Memory and Language*, 35: 708–23.

FERRAND, L., SEGUI, J., and HUMPHREYS, G. W. (1997). 'The syllable's role in word naming'. *Memory and Cognition*, 25: 458–70.

FIEZ, J. A., RAICHLE, M. E., MIEZIN, F. M., PETERSEN, S. E., TALLAL, P., and KATZ, W. F. (1995). 'PET studies of auditory and phonological processing: effects of stimulus characteristics and task demands'. *Journal of Cognitive Neuroscience*, 7/3: 357–75.

FINNEY, S. A., PROTOPAPAS, A., and EIMAS, P. D. (1996). 'Attentional allocation to syllables in American English'. *Journal of Memory and Language*, 35: 893–909.

FIRTH, J. R. (1948). 'Sounds and prosodies'. *Transactions of the Philological Society*: 127–52. Reprinted in J. R. Firth, *Papers in Linguistics 1934–1951*. Oxford: Oxford University Press, 121–38, and F. R. Palmer (ed.), *Prosodic Analysis*. Oxford: Oxford University Press, 1970: 1–26.

FISCHER-JØRGENSEN, E. (1975). *Trends in Phonological Theory*. Copenhagen: Akademisk Forlag.

FLANAGAN, J. L. (1972). 'Voices of men and machines'. *Journal of the Acoustical Society of America*, 51: 1375–87.

—— and RABINER, L. R. (1973). *Speech Synthesis: Benchmark Papers on Acoustics*. Philadelphia: Dowden, Hutchinson and Ross Inc.

FODOR, J. (1975). *The Language of Thought*. Cambridge, Mass.: Harvard University Press.

—— and PYLYSHYN, Z. (1987). 'Connectionism and cognitive architecture: a critical analysis'. *Cognition*, 28: 3–73.

FOLEY, J. (1977). *Foundations of Theoretical Phonology*. Cambridge: Cambridge University Press.

—— (1979). *Theoretical Morphology of the French Verb*. Amsterdam: John Benjamins.

FORSTER, K. I. (1998). 'The pros and cons of masked priming'. *Journal of Psycholinguistic Research*, 27: 203–33.

FOWLER, C. (1986). 'An event approach to the study of speech perception from a direct-realist perspective'. *Journal of Phonetics*, 14: 3–28.

—— (1996). 'Listeners do hear sounds, not tongues'. *Journal of the Acoustical Society of America*, 99: 1730–41.

—— and DEKLE, D. J. (1991). 'Listening with eye and hand: crossmodal contributions to speech perception'. *Journal of Experimental Psychology: Human Perception and Performance*, 17: 816–28.

—— and ROSENBLUM, L. D. (1991). 'The perception of phonetic gestures'. In I. G. Mattingly and M. Studdert-Kennedy (eds.), *Modularity and the Motor Theory of Speech Perception*. Hillsdale, NJ: Erlbaum: 33–59.

FRACKOWIAK, R. S. J., and FRISTON, K. J. (1994). 'Functional neuroanatomy of the human brain: positron emission tomography—a new neuroanatomical technique'. *Journal of Anatomy*, 184: 211–25.

FRIEDERICI, A. (1985). 'Levels of processing and vocabulary types: evidence from on-line comprehension in normals and agrammatics'. *Cognition*, 19: 133–66.

——and WESSELS, J. (1993). 'Phonotactic knowledge of word boundaries and its use in infant speech perception'. *Perception and Psychophysics*, 54: 287–95.

FRISCH, S. (1996). 'Similarity and Frequency in Phonology'. Ph.D. dissertation, Northwestern University.

——LARGE, N. R., and PISONI, D. B. (2000). 'Perception of wordlikeness: effects of segment probability and length on the processing of nonwords'. *Journal of Memory and Language*, 42: 481–96.

FRITH, C. (1992). *The Cognitive Neuropsychology of Schizophrenia*. Hillsdale, NJ: Lawrence Erlbaum.

FROMKIN, V., and RODMAN, R. (1998). *An Introduction to Language*. 6th edn. New York: Harcourt, Brace Publishers.

FUDGE, E. C. (1969). 'Syllables'. *Journal of Linguistics*, 5: 253–86.

GARDNER, M. F. (1990). *Expressive One-Word Picture Vocabulary Test-Revised, EO-WPVT-R.* Novato, Calif.: Academic Therapy Publications.

GATHERCOLE, S., FRANKISH, C., PICKERING, S., and PEAKER, S. (1999). 'Phonotactic influences on short term memory'. *Journal of Experimental Psychology: Learning, Memory and Cognition*, 25: 84–95.

GERKEN, L. (1996). 'Phonological and distributional information in syntax acquisition'. In J. Morgan and K. Demuth (eds.), *Signal to Syntax: Bootstrapping from Speech to Grammar in Early Acquisition*. Mahwah, NJ: LEA: 411–25.

GIMSON, A. C. (1962). *An Introduction to the Pronunciation of English*. London: Edward Arnold.

GINNEKEN, J. VAN (1907). *Principes de linguistique psychologique*. Paris: Rivière.

GLASS, L., and MACKEY, M. C. (1988). *From Clocks to Chaos: The Rhythms of Life*. Princeton: Princeton University Press.

GOLDBERG, G. (1985). 'Supplementary motor area structure and function: review and hypotheses'. *Behavioral and Brain Sciences*, 8: 567–616.

GOLDINGER, S. D. (1997). 'Words and voices: perception and production in an episodic lexicon'. In Johnson and Mullenix (1997: 33–66).

GOLDSMITH, J. (1976). 'Autosegmental Phonology'. Ph.D. dissertation, MIT. Published New York: Garland Press, 1999.

——(1984a). 'Bantu -a-: the far past in the far past'. In R. Schuh (ed.), *Précis from the 1984 African Linguistics Conference*. Berkeley and Los Angeles: University of California.

——(1984b). 'Tone and accent in Tonga'. In G. N. Clements and J. Goldsmith (eds.), *Autosegmental Studies in Bantu Tone*. Dordrecht: Foris Publications.

——(1984c). 'Meeussen's Rule'. In M. Aronoff and R. Oehrle (eds.), *Language Sound Structure*. Cambridge: MIT Press.

——(1987). 'Stem tone patterns of the Lacustrine Bantu languages'. In David Odden (ed.), *Current Approaches to African Linguistics*, vol. iv. Dordrecht: Foris Publications.

——(1990). *Autosegmental and Metrical Phonology*. Oxford: Blackwell.

——(1991). 'Dynamic computational models'. In D. Andler, E. Beinstock, and

B. Laks (eds.), *Proceedings of the Interdisciplinary Workshop on Compositionality in Cognition and Neural Networks*, vol. i. Paris, École Polytechnique, CREA: 52–65.

—— (1992). 'Local modelling in phonology'. In S. Davis (ed.), *Connectionism: Theory and Practice*. Oxford: Oxford University Press: 229–46.

—— (1993*a*). 'Harmonic phonology'. In Goldsmith (1993*b*: 21–60).

—— (ed.) (1993*b*). *The Last Phonological Rule: Reflections on Constraints and Derivations*. Chicago: University of Chicago Press.

—— (1994). 'A dynamic computational theory of accent systems'. In Jennifer Cole and Charles Kisseberth (eds.), *Perspectives in Phonology*. Stanford, Calif.: Center for the Study of Language and Information: 1–28.

—— (ed.) (1995). *The Handbook of Phonological Theory*. Oxford: Blackwell.

—— (1998). 'Phonology with and without information theory'. *Current Trends in Phonology II*, 22–4 June 1998, Abbaye de Royaumont: Programme, 8 (A).

—— and HUCK, G. J. (1995). *Ideology and Linguistic Theory: Noam Chomsky and the Deep Structure Debate*. London: Routledge.

—— and LAKS, B. (eds.) (2000*a*). *The History of Phonology in the Twentieth Century*. *Folia linguistica* 34.

—— —— (2000*b*). 'Introduction'. *Folia linguistica*, 34: 1–10.

—— and LARSON, G. (1991). 'Constituency in phonology'. In D. Andler, E. Beinstock, and B. Laks (eds.), *Proceedings of the Interdisciplinary Workshop on Compositionality in Cognition and Neural Networks*, vol. i. Paris, École Polytechnique, CREA: 50–2.

GOPNIK, M., and CRAGO, M. B. (1991). 'Familial aggregation of a development language disorder'. *Cognition*, 39: 1–50.

GOTO, H. (1971). 'Auditory perception by normal Japanese adults of the sounds "l" and "r"'. *Neuropsychologia*, 9: 317–23.

GRACCO, V. L., and ABBS, J. H. (1985). 'Dynamic control of the perioral system during speech: kinematic analyses of autogenic and nonautogenic sensorimotor processes'. *Journal of Neurophysiology*, 54: 418–32.

GRAFTON, S. T., ARBIB, M., FADIGA, L., and RIZZOLATTI, G. (1996). 'Localisation of grasp representations in humans by Positron Emission Tomography: 2. Observation compared with imagination'. *Experimental Brain Research*, 112: 103–11.

GRAINGER, J. and FERRAND, L. (1994). 'Phonology and orthography in visual word recognition: effects of masked homophone primes'. *Journal of Memory and Language*, 33: 218–33.

—— —— (1996). 'Masked orthographic and phonological priming in visual word recognition and naming: cross-task comparisons'. *Journal of Memory and Language*, 35: 623–47.

GRAMMONT, M. (1965). *Traité de phonétique*. Paris: Delagrave.

GRANT, K. W., ARDELL, L. H., KUHL, P. K., and SPARKS, D. W. (1985). 'The contribution of fundamental frequency, amplitude envelope, and voicing duration cues to speechreading in normal-hearing subjects'. *Journal of the Acoustic Society of America*, 77: 671–7.

GREEN, K. P. (1996). 'Studies of the McGurk effect: implications for theories of speech perception'. *Proceedings of the International Conference on Spoken Language Processing 96*, Philadelphia: 1652–5.

—— (1998). 'The use of auditory and visual information during phonetic processing: implications for theories of speech perception'. In R. Campbell, B. Dodd, and D. Burnham (eds.), *Hearing by Eye*, ii: *Perspectives and Directions in Research on Audiovisual Aspects of Language Processing*. Hove: Psychology Press: 3–25.

—— and KUHL, P. K. (1989). 'The role of visual information in the processing of place and manner features in speech perception'. *Perception and Psychophysics*, 45: 34–42.

—— and MILLER, J. L. (1985). 'On the role of visual rate information in phonetic perception'. *Perception and Psychophysics*, 38/3: 269–76.

GREENBERG, J. (1978). *Universals of Language*, vol. ii: *Phonology*. Stanford, Calif.: Stanford University Press.

GREENBERG, S. (1995). 'The ears have it: the auditory basis of speech perception'. *Proceedings of the International Congress of Phonetic Sciences*, Stockholm, 3: 34–41.

GRIESER, D., and KUHL, P. K. (1989). 'Categorization of speech by infants: support for speech-sound prototypes'. *Developmental Psychology*, 25: 577–88.

GRODZINSKY, Y. (2000). 'The neurology of syntax: language use without Broca's area'. *Behavioral and Brain Sciences*, 23/1: 1–21.

GUSSENHOVEN, C. (1986). 'English plosive allophones and ambisyllabicity'. *Gramma*, 10: 119–41.

HAAG, E., HUBER, W., HÜNDGEN, R., STILLER, U., and WILLMES, K. (1985). 'Repetitives Sprachverhalten bei schwerer Aphasie'. *Nervenartz*, 56: 543–53.

HAAS, J.-C., BLANKEN, G., MEZGER, G., and WALLESH, C.-W. (1988). 'Is there an anatomical basis for the production of speech automatisms?' *Aphasiology*, 2/6: 557–65.

HABIB, M., and GALABURDA, A. M. (1994). 'Fondements neuroanatomiques et neurobiologiques du langage'. In X. Seron and M. Jeannerod (eds.), *Neuropsychologie humaine*. Sprimont: Mardaga: 320–35.

HAGÈGE, C. (1985). *L'homme de paroles*. Paris: Fayard.

HAKEN, H. (1987). *Synergetics: An Introduction*. 3rd edn. Berlin: Springer Verlag.

HALLE, M. (1983). 'On distinctive features and their articulatory implementation'. *Natural Language and Linguistic Theory*, 1: 91–105.

—— (1995). 'Feature geometry and feature spreading'. *Linguistic Inquiry*, 26: 1–46.

—— (1997a). 'Some consequences of the representation of words in memory'. *Lingua*, 100: 91–100.

—— (1997b). 'On stress and accent in Indo-European'. *Language*, 73/2: 275–313.

HALLÉ, P., and BOYSSON-BARDIES, B. DE (1994). 'Emergence of an early receptive lexicon: infants' recognition of words'. *Infant Behavior and Development*, 17: 119–29.

—— SEGUI, J., FRAUENFELDER, U., and MEUNIER, C. (1998). 'Processing of illegal consonant clusters: a case of perceptual assimilation?' *Journal of Experimental Psychology: Human Perception and Performance*, 24: 592–608.

HAMMOND, M. (1999). *The Phonology of English: A Prosodic Optimality-Theoretic Approach*. Oxford: Oxford University Press.

HARRIS, J. (1994). *English Sound Structure*. Oxford: Blackwell.

HARRIS, J., and LINDSEY, G. A. (1993). 'There is no level of systematic phonetic representation'. Paper presented at the Cognitive Phonology Workshop. Manchester, May 1993.

——— (1995). 'The elements of phonological representation'. In Durand and Katamba (1995: 33–79).

HARRIS, R.A. (1995). *The Linguistic Wars*. Oxford: Oxford University Press.

HATWELL, Y. (1993). 'Transferts intermodaux et intégration intermodale'. In M. Richelle, J. Reguin, and M. Robert (eds.), *Traité de psychologie expérimentale*. Paris: Presses Universitaires de France: 543–84.

HAUDRICOURT, A., and JUILLAND, A. (1970). *Essai pour une histoire structurale du phonétisme français*. 2nd edn. The Hague: Mouton.

HAYES, B. (1995). *Metrical Stress Theory*. Chicago: University of Chicago Press.

HEATH, J. (1989). *From Code-Switching to Borrowing: A Case Study of Moroccan Arabic*. London: Kegan Paul International Limited.

HÉCAEN, H., and ALBERT, M. L. (1978). *Human Neuropsychology*. Chichester, John Wiley.

HEIM, J. L. (1989). 'Une nouvelle reconstitution du crâne neandertalien de la Chapelle-aux-Saints'. *Comptes-Rendus de l'Académie des Sciences, Paris*, 308, sér. 2/6: 1187–92.

——— (1990). 'Une nouvelle reconstitution du crâne neandertalien de la Chapelle-aux-Saints: méthode et résultats'. *Bulletin et Mémoires de la Société D'Anthropologie de Paris 6*, 1–2: 94–117.

HELLWAG, C. F. (1781). *Dissertatio inauguralis physiologico medica de formatione loquelae*. University of Tübingen. Original text; introduction and translation into French by M.-P. Monin with a preface by Bernard Colombat, *Dissertation inaugurale physiologico-médicale sur la formation de la parole*, 1991. *Bulletin de la communication parlée*. Grenoble: Institut de la Communication Parlée.

HELMHOLTZ, H. L. F. VON (1867). *Die Lehre von den Tonempfindungen als physiologische Grundlage für die Theorie der Musik*. Braunschweig: Von Friedrich und Sohn. English translation, *On the Sensation of Tones*, New York: Dover.

HERMANSKY, H. (1998). 'Should recognizers have ears?' *Speech Communication*, 25: 3–28.

HJELMSLEV, L. (1953). *Prolegomena to a Theory of Language*, trans. F. Whitfield. Madison: University of Wisconsin Press.

HOCKETT, C. F. (1948). 'A note on "structure"'. *International Journal of American Linguistics*, 14: 269–71.

——— (1968). *The State of the Art*. The Hague: Mouton.

——— (1965). 'Language, mathematics, and linguistics'. In T. A. Sebeok (ed.), *Current Trends in Linguistics*, vol. iii: *Theoretical Foundations*. The Hague: Mouton & Co.

HOFFMAN, D. (1984). In C. Bonnet (ed.), *La Perception visuelle*. Bibliothèque Pour la Science. Paris: Diffusion Belin: 110–16.

HOLMES, J. N. (1988). *Speech Synthesis and Recognition*. Wokingham: Van Nostrand Reinhold.

HONDA, K., and TIEDE, M. (1998). 'An MRI study on the relationship between oral cavity shape and larynx position'. *Proceedings of the International Conference on Spoken Language Processing 98*, Sydney.

HOOPER, J. B. (1972). 'The syllable in phonological theory'. *Language*, 48: 525–40.

—— (1976*a*). 'Word frequency in lexical diffusion and the source of morphophonological change'. In W. Christie (ed.), *Current Progress in Historical Linguistics*. Amsterdam: North-Holland: 96–105.

—— (1976*b*). *An Introduction to Natural Generative Phonology*. New York: Academic Press.

—— (1981). 'The empirical determination of phonological representations'. In T. Myers, J. Laver, and J. Anderson (eds.), *The Cognitive Representation of Speech*. Amsterdam: North-Holland: 347–57.

HOWARD, M. A., VOLKOV, I. O., ABBAS, P. J., DAMASIO, H., OLLENDIECK, M. C., and GRANNER, M. A. (1996). 'A chronic microelectrode investigation of the tonotopic organization of human auditory cortex'. *Brain Research*, 724: 260–4.

HUBER, W., POECK, K., and WENIGER, D. (1989). In K. Poeck (ed.), *Klinische Neuropsychologie*, 2nd edn. New York: Thieme (1st edn. 1982).

HULST, H. VAN DER (1993). 'Units in the analysis of signs'. *Phonology* 10/2: 209–41.

—— and RITTER, N. (eds.) (1999). *The Syllable: Views and Facts*. Berlin: Mouton de Gruyter.

—— (2000). 'Modularity and modality in phonology'. In N. Burton-Roberts, P. Carr, and G. Docherty (eds.) *Phonological Knowledge: Conceptual and Empirical Issues*. Oxford: Oxford University Press: 207–43.

—— and SMITH, N. (eds.) (1982). *The Structure of Phonological Representations*. 2 vols. Dordrecht: Foris Publications.

—— —— (eds.) (1988). *Features, Segmental Structure and Harmony Processes*. 3 vols. Dordrecht: Foris.

HYMAN, L. M. (1977). 'On the nature of linguistic stress'. In L. M. Hyman (ed.), *Studies in Stress and Accent*. Los Angeles: Department of Linguistics, University of Southern California: 37–82.

—— and SCHUH, R. (1974). 'Universals of tone rules: evidence from West Africa'. *Linguistic Inquiry*, 5: 81–115.

HYMES, D., and FOUGHT, J. (1981). *American Structuralism*. The Hague: Mouton.

INGLEBY, M., and BROCKHAUS, W. G. (1998). 'A concurrent approach to the automatic extraction of subsegmental primes and phonological constituents from speech [with software demonstration]'. *Proceedings of the COLING-ACL '98 Conference*. Montreal: Université de Montréal: 578–83.

INTERNATIONAL PHONETIC ASSOCIATION (1999). *The Handbook of the International Phonetic Association*. Cambridge: Cambridge University Press.

JACKENDOFF, R. (1993). *Patterns in the Mind*. New York: Basic Books.

JACKSON, J. H. (1915). 'On the nature of the duality of the brain'. *Brain*, 38: 81–103 (1st pub. 1874).

JAKOBSON, R. (1971). *Studies on Child Language and Aphasia*. The Hague: Mouton and Co.

—— (1976). *Six leçons sur le son et le sens*. Paris: Éditions de Minuit.

—— FANT, C. G. M., and HALLE, M. (1952). *Preliminaries to Speech Analysis: The Distinctive Features and their Correlates*. Cambridge, Mass.: MIT Press.

—— and HALLE, M. (1956). *Fundamentals of Language*. The Hague: Mouton.

—— and WAUGH, L. R. (1979). *The Sound Shape of Language*. Brighton: Harvester Press.

JARDINE, N. and SIBSON, R. (1971). *Mathematical Taxonomy*. London: John Wiley and Sons.

JEANNEROD, M. (1996). *De la physiologie mentale: histoire des relations entre biologie et psychologie*. Paris: Éditions Odile Jacob.

JENSEN, S. (1994). 'Is ? an element? Towards a non-segmental phonology'. *SOAS Working Papers in Linguistics and Phonetics*, 4: 71–8.

JESPERSEN, O. (1904). *Phonetische Grundfragen*. Leipzig: Teubner.

JOHNSON, K., and MULLENIX, J. W. (eds.) (1997). *Talker Variability in Speech Processing*. San Diego: Academic Press.

JONAS, S. (1981). 'The supplementary motor region and speech emission'. *Journal of Communication Disorders*, 14: 349–73.

JONES, D. (1917). *English Pronouncing Dictionary*. London: J. M. Dent and Sons Ltd.

—— (1948). 'The London School of Phonetics'. *Zeitschrift für Phonetik und allgemeine Sprachwissenschaft*, 2/3–4: 127–35. Reprinted in Jones and Laver (1973): 180–6.

—— (1950). *The Phoneme: Its Nature and Use*. Cambridge: Heffer.

—— (1956). *An Outline of English Phonetics*. 8th edn. Cambridge: Heffer.

—— (1957). 'The history and meaning of the term "phoneme"'. Pamphlet published by the International Phonetic Association. Printed as an appendix to the 3rd (1957) edn. of Jones (1950). Reprinted in Jones and Laver (1973: 187–204).

JONES, W. E., and LAVER, J. (1973). *Phonetics in Linguistics: A Book of Readings*. London: Longman.

JOOS, M. (1963). *Readings in Linguistics*. Washington: American Council of Learned Societies (1st edn. 1957).

JÜRGENS, U. (1998). 'Speech evolved from vocalization, not mastication'. Commentary to P. MacNeilage, 'The frame/content theory of evolution of speech production'. *Behavioral and Brain Sciences*, 21/4: 519–20.

JUSCZYK, P. (1999). 'Dividing and conquering linguistic input'. In M. Gruber, K. Olson, and T. Wysocki (eds.), *Proceedings of the Chicago Linguistic Society*, 34, vol. ii: *The Panels*. Chicago: Chicago Linguistic Society.

—— and ASLIN, R. (1995). 'Infants' detection of sound patterns of words in fluent speech'. *Cognitive Psychology*, 29: 1–23.

—— CUTLER, A., and REDANTZ, N. (1993). 'Preference for the predominant stress pattern of English words'. *Child Development*, 64, 675–87.

—— LUCE, P. A., and CHARLES-LUCE, J. (1994). 'Infants' sensitivity to phonotactic patterns in the native language'. *Journal of Memory and Language*, 33: 630–45.

—— FRIEDERICI, A., WESSELS, J., SVENKERUD, V., and JUSCZYK, A. (1993). 'Infants' sensitivity to the sound pattern of native language words'. *Journal of Memory and Language*, 32: 402–20.

KAGER, R. (1999). *Optimality Theory*. Cambridge: Cambridge University Press.

KAHN, D. (1976). *Syllable-Based Generalizations in English Phonology*. Bloomington: Indiana University Linguistic Club.

KANDEL S. D., ORLIAGUET J. P., and BOË L.-J. (1994). 'Visual perception of motor anticipation in the time course of handwriting'. In G. Keuss, C. Faure, G. Lorette, and A. Vinter (eds.), *Advances in Handwriting and Drawing: A Multidisciplinary Approach*. Paris: France Télécom: 379–88.

KARBE, H., THIEL, A., WEBER-LUXENBURGER, G., HERHOLZ, K., KESSLER, J., and HEISS, W. D. (1998). 'Brain plasticity in poststroke aphasia: what is the contribution of the right hemisphere?' *Brain and Language*, 64/2: 215–30.

KARNICKAJA, E. G., MUCHNIKOV, V. N., SLEPOKUROVA, N. A., and ZHUKOV, S. (1975). 'Auditory processing of steady-state vowels'. In G. Fant and M. A. A. Tatham (eds.), *Auditory Analysis and Perception of Speech*. London: Academic: 37–53.

KAYE, J. (1989). *Phonology: A Cognitive View*. Hillsdale, NJ: Erlbaum.

—— LOWENSTAMM, J., and VERGNAUD, J.-R. (1985). 'The internal structure of phonological elements: a theory of charm and government'. *Phonology Yearbook*, 2: 305–28.

—— —— —— (1990). 'Constituent structure and government in phonology'. *Phonology*, 7: 193–231.

KEATING, P. (ed.) (1994). *Papers in Laboratory Phonology*, iii: *Phonological Structure and Phonetic Form*. Cambridge: Cambridge University Press.

—— and HUFFMAN, M. K. (1984). 'Vowel variation in Japanese'. *Phonetica*, 41: 191–207.

KELLY, J., and LOCAL, J. K. (1986). 'Long-domain resonance patterns in English'. In *International Conference on Speech Input/Output; Techniques and Applications*. Conference Publication No. 258. London: Institution of Electrical Engineers: 304–9.

KELSO, S. (1995). *Dynamic Patterns: The Self-Organization of Brain and Behavior*. Cambridge, Mass.: MIT Press.

KENSTOWICZ, M. (1994). *Phonology in Generative Grammar*. Oxford: Blackwell.

KENSTOWICZ, M. and PYLE, C. (1973). 'On the phonological integrity of geminate clusters'. In M. Kenstowicz and C. Kisseberth (eds.), *Issues in Phonological Theory*. The Hague: Mouton: 27–43.

KENT, R. D. (1997). *The Speech Sciences*. Singular Publishing Group.

KINGSTON, J., and BECKMAN, M. (eds.) (1990). *Papers in Laboratory Phonology*, i: *Between the Grammar and the Physics of Speech*. Cambridge: Cambridge University Press.

KIPARSKY, P. (1973). 'Phonological representations'. In O. Fujimura (ed.), *Three Dimensions of Linguistic Theory*. Tokyo: TEC: 5–56.

—— (1982). 'Lexical phonology and morphology'. In I. S. Yang (ed.), *Linguistics in the Morning Calm*. Seoul: Hanshin: 3–91.

KLATT, D. H. (1982). 'Prediction of perceived phonetic distance from critical-band spectra: a first step'. *Proceedings of the IEEE International Conference on Acoustics, Speech, and Signal Processing*: 1278–81.

KLEIN, M. (1993). 'La Syllabe comme interface de la relation entre production et réception phoniques'. In B. Laks and M. Plénat (eds.), *De natura sonorum*. Paris: Presses Universitaires de Vincennes: 101–41.

KLUENDER, K. R. (1991). 'Effects of first formant onset properties on voicing judgments result from processes not specific to humans'. *Journal of the Acoustical Society of America*, 90: 83–96.

—— DIEHL, R. L., and KILLEEN, P. R. (1987). 'Japanese quail can learn phonetic categories'. *Science*, 237: 1195–7.

—— and LOTTO, A. J. (1999). 'Virtues and perils of an empiricist approach to speech perception'. *Journal of the Acoustical Society of America*, 105: 503–11.

KOLINSKY, R., MORAIS, J. and CLUYTENS, M. (1995). 'Intermediate representations in spoken word recognition: evidence from word illusions'. *Journal of Memory and Language*, 34: 19–40.

KORNHUBER, H. H., BRUNNER, R. J., and WALLESH, C.-W. (1979). 'Basal ganglia participation in aphasia'. In O. Creutzfeldt, H. Scheich, and C. Schreiner (eds.), *Hearing Mechanisms and Speech*. New York: Springer: 183–8.

KOUTSOUDAS, A., SANDERS, G., and NOLL, C. (1974). 'On the application of phonological rules'. *Language*, 50: 1–28.

KOUWENBERG, S., and LACHARITÉ, D. (2000). 'The mysterious case of diminutive yala-yala'. In P. Christie (ed.), *Due Respect: Papers on English and English-Related Creoles in the Caribbean in Honour of Professor Robert LePage*. Barbados: University of the West Indies Press.

KUBOZONO, H. (1989). 'The mora and syllable structure in Japanese: evidence from speech errors'. *Language and Speech*, 32: 249–78.

KUHL, P. K. (1991). 'Human adults and human infants show a "perceptual magnet effect" for the prototypes of speech categories, monkeys do not'. *Perception and Psychophysics*, 50: 93–107.

—— (1992). 'Infants' perception and representation of speech: development of a new theory'. In J. J. Ohala, T. M. Nearey, B. L. Derwing, M. M. Hodge, and G. E. Weibe (eds.), *Proceedings of the International Conference on Spoken Language Processing*. Edmonton: University of Alberta: 449–56.

—— and MELTZOFF, A. N. (1982). 'The bimodal perception of speech in infancy'. *Science*, 218: 1138–41.

——— (1984). 'The intermodal representation of speech in infancy'. *Infant Behavior and Development*, 7: 361–81.

—— and MILLER, J. D. (1975). 'Speech perception by the chinchilla: voiced–voiceless distinction in alveolar plosive consonants'. *Science*, 190: 69–72.

——— (1978). 'Speech perception by the chinchilla: identification functions for synthetic VOT stimuli'. *Journal of the Acoustical Society of America* 63: 905–17.

—— and PADDEN, D. M. (1982a). 'Enhanced discrimination at the phonetic boundaries for the voicing feature in macaques'. *Perception and Psychophysics*, 32: 542–50.

——— (1982b). 'Enhanced discrimination at the phonetic boundaries for the place feature in macaques'. *Journal of the Acoustical Society of America*, 73: 1003–10.

—— WILLIAMS, K., LACERDA, F., STEVENS, K., and LINDBLOM, B. (1992). 'Linguistic experience alters phonetic perception in infants by six months of age'. *Science*, 255: 606–8.

—— ANDRUSKI, J., CHISTOVICH, I., CHISTOVICH, L., KOZHEVNIKOVA, E., RYSKINA, V., STOLYAROVA, E., SUNDBERG, U., and LACERDA, F. (1997). 'Cross-language analysis of phonetic units in language addressed to infants'. *Science*, 277: 684–6.

KURYŁOWICZ, J. (1948). 'Contribution à la théorie de la syllabe'. *Biuletyn Polskiego Towarzystwa Jezykoznawczego*, 8: 80–114.

LABOISSIÈRE R., OSTRY, D., and FELDMAN, A. (1996). 'The control of multi-muscle systems: human jaw and hyoid movements'. *Biological Cybernetics*, 74: 373–84.

LABOV, W. (1972). 'The study of language in its social context'. In W. Labov, *Sociolinguistic Patterns*. Oxford: Blackwell: 183–259.

LaCHARITÉ, D., and PARADIS, C. (1993). 'The emergence of constraints in generative phonology and a comparison of three current constraint-based models'. In C. Paradis and D. LaCharité (eds.), *Constraint-Based Theories in Multilinear Phonology: Canadian Journal of Linguistics*, 38/2: 127–53.

LADEFOGED, P. (1982). *A Course in Phonetics*. San Diego: Harcourt Brace Jovanovich.

—— (1988). 'A view of phonetics'. *UCLA Working Papers in Phonetics*, 70, also plenary address, International Congress of Phonetics Sciences XII, Tallin.

—— (1989). 'Representing Phonetic Structure'. *UCLA Working Papers in Phonetics* 73.

—— (1993). *A Course in Phonetics*. 3rd edn. Fort Worth: Harcourt Brace Jovanovich.

—— and MADDIESON, I. (1996). *The Sounds of the World's Languages*. Oxford: Blackwell.

LAITMAN, J. T. (1983). *The Evolution of Hominid under Respiratory System and Implication for the Origin of Speech*. Glossogenetics 63–90. London: Harwood Academic Publishers.

LAITMAN, J. T. et al. (1990). 'The Kebara hyoid: what can it tell us about the evolution of the hominid vocal-tract?' *American Journal of Physical Anthropology*, 81: 254.

LAKATOS, I. (1970). 'Falsification and the methodology of scientific research programmes'. In I. Lakatos and A. Musgrave (eds.), *Criticism and the Growth of Knowledge*. Cambridge: Cambridge University Press: 91–196.

LAKS, B. (1995). 'A connectionist account of French syllabification'. *Lingua*, 95: 56–75.

—— (1996a). *Langage et cognition: l'approche connexionniste*. Paris: Hermès.

—— (1996b). 'Réseaux de neurones et syllabation du français'. *Linx*, 34/35: 327–46.

—— (ed.) (1997a). *Nouvelles Phonologies*. Langages 125. Paris: Larousse.

—— (1997b). *Phonologie accentuelle: métrique, autosegmentalité et constituance*. Paris: Éditions du CNRS.

—— (to appear). 'Un siècle de phonologie'. *Modèles linguistiques*.

—— and PLÉNAT, M. (eds.) (1993). *De natura sonorum: essais de phonologie*. Vincennes: Presses Universitaires de Vincennes.

LAMB, S. (1998). *Pathways of the Brain: The Neurocognitive Basis of Language*. Amsterdam: John Benjamins.

LA METTRIE, J. O. DE (1751) *Œuvres philosophiques*, 2 vols. London.

LARSON, G. N. (1992). 'Dynamic Computational Networks and the Representation of Phonological Information'. Ph.D. dissertation, University of Chicago.

LAUTER, J. L., HERSCOVITCH, P., FORMBY, C., and RAICHLE, M. E. (1985). 'Tonotopic organization in human auditory cortex revealed by positron emission tomography'. *Hearing Research*, 20: 199–205.

LAVER, J. (1994). *Principles of Phonetics*. Cambridge: Cambridge University Press.

LEBRUN, Y. (1986). 'Aphasia with recurrent utterance: a review'. *British Journal of Disorders of Communication*, 21: 3–10.

LEE, S., BECKMAN, M., and JACKSON, M. (1994). 'Jaw targets for strident fricatives'. *International Conference on Spoken Language Processing*, Yokohama: 37–40.

LEHISTE, I. (1970). *Suprasegmentals*. Cambridge, Mass.: MIT Press.

LEVELT, W. J. M. (1989). *Speaking: From Intention to Articulation*. Cambridge, Mass.: MIT Press.

—— (1993). 'Timing in speech production with special reference to word form encoding'. *Annals of the New York Academy of Sciences*, 682: 283–95.

—— (1999). 'Models of word production'. *Trends in Cognitive Sciences*, 3/6: 223–32.

—— and SCHILLER, N. O. (1998). 'Is the syllable frame stored?' Commentary to P. MacNeilage, 'The frame/content theory of evolution of speech production'. *Behavioral and Brain Sciences*, 21/4: 520.

—— and WHEELDON, L. (1994). 'Do speakers have access to a mental syllabary?' *Cognition*, 50: 239–69.

LEVIN, J. (1985). 'A Metrical Theory of Syllabicity'. Ph.D. dissertation, MIT.

LEYBAERT, J., ALEGRIA, J., HAGE, C., and CHARLIER, B. (1998). 'The effect of exposure to phonetically augmented lipspeech in the prelingual deaf'. In

R. Campbell, B. Dodd, and D. Burnham (eds.), *Hearing by Eye*, ii: *Perspectives and Directions in Research on Audiovisual Aspects of Language Processing*. Hove: Psychology Press: 283–301.

LIBERMAN, A. M. (1966). *Speech: A Special Code*. Cambridge, Mass.: MIT Press.

—— ISENBERG, D., and RAKERD, B. (1981). 'Duplex perception of cues for stop consonants: evidence for a phonetic mode'. *Perception and Psychophysics*, 30: 133–43.

—— and MATTINGLY, I. G. (1985). 'The motor theory of speech perception revised'. *Cognition*, 21: 1–36.

—— COOPER, F. S., SHANKWEILER, D. P., and STUDDERT-KENNEDY, M. (1967). 'Perception of the speech code'. *Psychological Review*, 74: 431–61.

LIEBERMAN, P. (1972). *The Speech of Primates*. The Hague: Mouton.

—— (1991). *Uniquely Human: The Evolution of Speech, Thought, and Selfless Behaviour*. Cambridge, Mass.: Harvard University Press.

—— and CRELIN, E. S. (1971). 'On the speech of the Neandertal man'. *Linguistic Inquiry*, 2: 203–22.

LIGHTFOOT, D. (1999). *The Development of Language. Acquisition, Change, Evolution*. Oxford: Blackwell.

LILJENCRANTS, J., and LINDBLOM, B. (1972). 'Numerical simulations of vowel quality systems: the role of perceptual contrast'. *Language*, 48: 839–62.

LINDBLOM, B. (1986). 'Phonetic universals in vowel systems'. In J. J. Ohala and J. J. Jaeger (eds.), *Experimental Phonology*. New York: Academic Press: 13–44.

—— (1990). 'On the notion of possible speech sound'. *Journal of Phonetics*, 18: 135–52.

—— (1995). 'A view of the future of phonetics'. In K. Elenius and P. Brandrud (eds.), *Proceedings of the XIIIth International Congress of Phonetic Sciences*. Stockholm: University of Stockholm: 462–9.

—— (1996). 'Role of articulation in speech perception: clues from production'. *Journal of the Acoustical Society of America*, 99: 1683–92.

—— (forthcoming). 'A model of phonetic variation and selection and the evolution of vowel systems'. In S.-Y. Wang, (ed.), *Language Transmission and Change*. New York: Blackwell.

—— LUBKER, J., and GAY, T. (1979). 'Formant frequencies of some fixed-mandible vowels and a model of speech motor programming by predictive simulation'. *Journal of Phonetics*, 7: 147–61.

LINDSEY, G. A., and HARRIS, J. (1990). 'Phonetic interpretation in generative grammar'. *UCL Working Papers in Linguistics*, 2: 355–69.

LING, C. (1994). 'Learning the past tense of English verbs: the symbolic pattern associator vs. connectionist models'. *Journal of Artificial Intelligence Research*, 1: 208–29.

LISKER, L., and ROSSI, M. (1992). 'Auditory and visual cueing of the [± rounded] feature of vowels'. *Language and Speech*, 35: 391–417.

LŒVENBRUCK, H., and PERRIER, P. (1996). 'How could undershot vowel targets be recovered? A dynamical approach based on the equilibrium point hypothesis for the control of speech movements'. *4th Speech Production Seminar, 1st ESCA Tutorial and Research Workshop on Speech Production Modeling: From Control Strategies to Acoustics*, 21-4 May 1996, Autrans: 117–20.

——— (1997). 'Motor control information recovering from the dynamics with the EP hypothesis'. *Proceedings of Eurospeech 97*, Rhodes, 4: 2035–8.

LOTTO, A. J., KLUENDER, K. R., and HOLT, L. L. (1997). 'Perceptual compensation for coarticulation by Japanese quail (*Coturnix coturnix japonica*)'. *Journal of the Acoustical Society of America*, 102: 1134–40.

LOWENSTAMM, J. (1996). 'CV as the only syllable type'. In B. Laks and J. Durand (eds.), *Current Trends in Phonology: Models and Methods*. Salford: ESRI: 419–41.

LUKATELA, G., and TURVEY, M. T. (1994). 'Visual access is initially phonological: 1. Evidence from associate priming by words, homophones, and pseudohomophones'. *Journal of Experimental Psychology: General*, 123: 107–18.

LUND, J. P. (1998). 'Is speech just chewing the fat?' Commentary to P. MacNeilage, 'The frame/content theory of evolution of speech production'. *Behavioral and Brain Sciences*, 21/4: 522.

LYONS, J. (1991). *Natural Language and Universal Grammar: Essays in Linguistic Theory*, vol. i. Cambridge: Cambridge University Press.

McCARTHY, J. J. (1979). 'Formal Properties of Semitic Phonology and Morphology'. Ph.D. dissertation, MIT.

——— (1981). 'A prosodic theory of nonconcatenative morphology'. *Linguistic Inquiry*, 12: 373–418.

——— (1988). 'Feature geometry and dependency: a review'. *Phonetica*, 43: 84–108.

——— and PRINCE, A. (1993). 'Prosodic Morphology I: constraint interaction and satisfaction'. MS. University of Massachusetts, Amherst and Brandeis University.

McCAWLEY, J. D. (1967). 'Sapir's phonological representation'. *International Journal of American Linguistics*, 33: 106–11.

——— (1970). 'Some tonal systems that come close to being pitch accent systems but don't quite make it'. In *Papers from the Chicago Linguistic Society 6*. Chicago: Chicago Linguistic Society.

MACCHI, M. J. (1980). 'Identification of vowels spoken in isolation versus vowels spoken in consonantal context'. *Journal of the Acoustical Society of America*, 68: 1636–42.

McCLISH, I. (1999). 'Traitement de six contextes syllabiques marqués dans un cas d'aphasie progressive primaire'. MA dissertation, Laval University.

McCULLOCH, W., and PITTS, W. (1943). 'A logical calculus of ideas immanent in nervous activity'. *Bulletin of Mathematical Biophysics*, 5: 115–33.

McGURK, H., and MacDONALD, J. (1976). 'Hearing lips and seeing voices'. *Nature*, 264: 746–8.

MacKAY, D. (1987). *The Organization of Perception and Action: A Theory for Language and Other Cognitive Skills*. New York: Springer.

MacLeod, A., and Summerfield, Q. (1987). 'Quantifying the contribution of vision to speech perception in noise'. *British Journal of Audiology*, 21: 131–41.

MacNeilage, P. (1998). 'The frame/content theory of evolution of speech production'. *Behavioral and Brain Sciences*, 21/4: 499–546.

——and Davis, B. (1990). 'Acquisition of speech production: frames, then content'. In M. Jeannerod (ed.), *Motor Representation and Control*. Attention and Performance XIII. Hillsdale, NJ: Lawrence Erlbaum: 453–76.

Macoir, J. (1997). 'L'Interface entre les codes phonologique, morphologique et orthographique dans l'aphasie'. Ph.D. dissertation, University of Sherbrooke.

——and Béland, R. (1998). 'Acquired dyslexia affecting the processing of final consonant in French: a morphophonological account'. *Journal of Neurolinguistics*, 11/4: 355–76.

MacWhinney, B., and Leinbach, J. (1991). 'Implementations are not conceptualisations: revising the verb learning model'. *Cognition*, 29: 121–57.

————Taraban, R., and McDonald, J. (1989). 'Language learning: cues or rules?' *Journal of Memory and Language*, 28: 255–77.

Maddieson, I. (1984). *Patterns of Sounds*. Cambridge Studies in Speech Science and Communication. Cambridge: Cambridge University Press (2nd edn. 1986).

——and Precoda, K. (1989). 'Updating UPSID'. *UCLA WPP* 74: 104–11.

Mandel, D., Jusczyk, P., and Pisoni, D. (1995). 'Infants' recognition of the sound pattern of their own names'. *Psychological Science*, 6: 314–17.

Marchman, V. (1993). 'Constraints on plasticity in a connectionist model of English past tense'. *Journal of Cognitive Neuroscience*, 5: 215–24.

Marr, D. (1982). *Vision: A Computational Investigation into the Human Representation and Processing of Visual Information*. San Francisco: W. H. Freeman and Co.

Marslen-Wilson, W., and Tyler, L. K. (1980). 'The temporal structure of spoken language understanding'. *Cognition*, 8: 1–71.

Martinet, A. (1962). *Éléments de linguistique générale*. Paris: Armand Colin.

Massaro, D. W. (1989). 'Multiple book review of speech perception by ear and eye: a paradigm for psychological inquiry'. *Behavioral and Brain Sciences*, 12: 741–94.

——and Cohen, M. (1983). 'Phonological context in speech perception'. *Perception and Psychophysics*, 34: 338–48.

Matteson, E. (1965). *The Piro Arawakan Language*. Berkeley and Los Angeles: University of California Press.

Matthews, P. H. (1993). *Grammatical Theory in the United States from Bloomfield to Chomsky*. Cambridge: Cambridge University Press.

Mattingly, I. G. (1990). 'The global character of phonetic gestures'. *Journal of Phonetics*, 18: 445–52.

Mehler, J., Dupoux, E., and Segui, J. (1990). 'Constraining models of lexical access: the onset of word recognition'. In G. Altmann (ed.), *Cognitive Models of Speech Processing: Psycholinguistic and Computational Perspectives*. Cambridge, Mass.: MIT Press: 236–62.

——Dommergues, J., Frauenfelder, U., and Segui, J. (1981). 'The syllable's role in speech segmentation'. *Journal of Verbal Learning and Verbal Behavior*, 20: 298–305.

——Jusczyk, P., Lambertz, G., Halsted, N., Bertoncini, J., and Amiel-Tison, C. (1988). 'A precursor of language acquisition in young infants'. *Cognition*, 29: 144–78.

—— Bertoncini, J., Dupoux, E., and Pallier, C. (1996). 'The role of suprasegmentals in speech perception and acquisition'. In T. Otake and A. Cutler (eds.), *Phonological Structure and Language Processing: Cross-linguistic Studies*. Berlin: Mouton de Gruyter: 145–69.

Meijer, P. J. A. (1996). 'Suprasegmental structures in phonological encoding: the CV structure'. *Journal of Memory and Language*, 35: 840–53.

Meltzoff, A. N., and Moore, K. M. (1983). 'Newborn infants imitate facial gestures'. *Child Development*, 54: 702–9.

Meyer, A. S. (1990). 'The time course of phonological encoding in language production: the encoding of successive syllables of a word'. *Journal of Memory and Language*, 29: 524–45.

—— (1991). 'The time course of phonological encoding in language production: phonological encoding inside a syllable'. *Journal of Memory and Language*, 30: 69–89.

Miller, G. A., Heise, G. A., and Lichten, W. (1951). 'The intelligibility of speech as a function of the context of the test materials'. *Journal of Experimental Psychology*, 41: 329–35.

Mills, A. E. (1987). 'The development of phonology in the blind child'. In B. Dodd and R. Campbell (eds.), *Hearing by Eye: The Psychology of Lipreading*. London: Lawrence Erlbaum Associates: 145–61.

Milner, J.-C. (1982). *Ordres et raisons de la langue*. Paris: Éditions du Seuil.

Mitton, R. (1992). 'A computer-usable dictionary file based on the Oxford Advanced Learner's Dictionary of Current English'. File *text710.dat*, in the Oxford Text Archive, http://ota.ox.ac.uk/

Mohanan, K. P. (1986). *The Theory of Lexical Phonology*. Dordrecht: D. Reidel.

Moon, C., Cooper, R., and Fifer, W. (1993). 'Two-day-olds prefer their native language'. *Infant Behavior and Development*, 16: 495–500.

Morais, J. (1985). 'Literacy and awareness of the units of speech: implications for research on the units of perception'. *Linguistics*, 23: 707–21.

—— (1993). 'Phonemic awareness, language and literacy'. In R. M. Joshi and C. K. Leong (eds.), *Reading Disabilities: Diagnosis and Component Processes*. Dordrecht: Kluwer: 175–84.

—— Cary, L., Alegria, J., and Bertelson, P. (1979). 'Does awareness of speech as a sequence of phones arise spontaneously?' *Cognition*, 7: 323–31.

—— Content, A., Cary, L., Mehler, J., and Segui, J. (1989). 'Syllabic segmentation and literacy'. *Language and Cognitive Processes*, 4: 57–67.

Morgan, J., Shi, R., and Allopenna, P. (1996). 'Perceptual bases of rudimentary grammatical categories: toward a broader conceptualization of bootstrapping'. In

J. Morgan and K. Demuth (eds.), *Signal to Syntax: Bootstrapping from Speech to Grammar in Early Acquisition*. Mahwah, NJ: LEA: 263–83.

MOUNIN, G. (1968). *Saussure ou le structuraliste sans le savoir*. Paris: Seghers.

MULFORD, R. (1988). 'First words of the blind child'. In M. D. Smith and J. L. Locke (eds.), *The Emergent Lexicon: The Child's Development of a Linguistic Vocabulary*. New York: Academic Press: 293–338.

MUMMERY, C. J., PATTERSON, K., HODGES, J. R., and WISE, R. J. S. (1996). 'Generating "tiger" as an animal name or a word beginning with T: differences in brain activation'. *Proceedings of the Royal Society of London*, B 263: 989–95.

MUNHALL, K. G., and JONES, J. A. (1998). 'Articulatory evidence for syllabic structure'. Commentary to P. MacNeilage, 'The frame/content theory of evolution of speech production'. *Behavioral and Brain Sciences*, 21/4: 524–5.

MURPHY, K., CORFIELD, D. R., FINK, G. R., WISE, R. J. S., GUZ, A., and ADAMS, L. (1997). 'Neural mechanisms associated with the control of speech in man'. *NeuroImage*, 5/4: S 253.

NÄÄTÄNEN, R., LEHTOKOVSKI, A., LENNES, M., CHEOUR, M., HUOTILAINEN, M., IIVONEN, A., VAINIO, M., ALKU, P., ILMONIEMI, R., LUUK, A., ALLIK, J., SINKKONEN, J., and ALHO, K. (1997). 'Language-specific phoneme representations revealed by electric and magnetic brain responses'. *Nature*, 385: 432–4.

NAVARRO TOMAS, T. (1965). *Manual de pronunciación española*. Madrid: Consejo Superior de Investigaciones Científicas.

NAZZI, T., BERTONCINI, J., and MEHLER, J. (1998). 'Language discrimination by newborns: toward an understanding of the role of rhythm'. *Journal of Experimental Psychology: Human Perception and Performance*, 24: 756–66.

NEAREY, T. (1989). 'Static, dynamic and relational properties in vowel perception'. *Journal of the Acoustical Society of America*, 85: 2088–113.

——(1995). 'Evidence for the perceptual relevance of vowel-inherent spectral change for front vowels in Canadian English'. *Proceedings of the XIIIth International Congress of Phonetic Sciences*, Stockholm 2: 678–81.

——(1997). 'Speech perception as pattern recognition'. *Journal of the Acoustical Society of America*, 101: 3241–54.

NEELY, K. K. (1956). 'Effects of visual factors on the intelligibility of speech'. *Journal of the Acoustical Society of America*, 28: 1275–7.

NESPOR, M., and VOGEL, I. (1986). *Prosodic Phonology*. Dordrecht: Foris.

NEUMANN, J. VON (1992). *L'Ordinateur et le cerveau*. Paris: Éditions de la Découverte (1st edn. 1958).

NEVILLE, H., MILLS, D., and LAWSON, D. (1992). 'Fractionating language: different neural subsystems with different sensitive periods'. *Cerebral Cortex*, 2: 244–58.

NEWMEYER, F. J. (1986). *The Politics of Linguistics*. Chicago: University of Chicago Press.

NICOL, J. L. (1996). 'Syntactic priming'. *Language and Cognitive Processes*, 11: 675–9.

ODDEN, D. (1994). 'Adjacency parameters in phonology'. *Language*, 70: 289–330.

OGDEN, R. A. (1999). 'A declarative account of strong and weak auxiliaries in English'. *Phonology*, 16: 55–92.

OHALA, J. J. (1996). 'Speech perception is hearing sounds, not tongues'. *Journal of the Acoustical Society of America* 99: 1718–25.

OTAKE, T., HATANO, G., CUTLER, A., and MEHLER, J. (1993). 'Mora or syllable? Speech segmentation in Japanese'. *Journal of Memory and Language*, 32: 258–78.

PALLIER, C., BOSCH, L., and SEBASTIÁN-GALLÉS, N. (1997). 'A limit on behavioral plasticity in speech perception'. *Cognition*, 64: B9–B17.

—— SEBASTIÁN-GALLÉS, N., FELGUERA, T., CHRISTOPHE, A., and MEHLER, J. (1993). 'Attentional allocation within the syllabic structure of spoken words'. *Journal of Memory and Language*, 32: 373–89.

PARADIS, C. (1983). *Description phonologique du guéré*. Abidjan: Presses de l'Université d'Abidjan.

—— (1988*a*). 'On constraints and repair strategies'. *Linguistic Review*, 6/1: 71–97.

—— (1988*b*). 'Towards a theory of constraint violation'. *McGill Working Papers in Linguistics*, 5/1: 25–69.

—— (1995*a*). 'Native and loanword phonology as one: the role of constraints'. In C.M. Bellman and A. Strindberg (eds.), *Proceedings of the XIIIth International Congress of Phonetic Sciences*. Stockholm: Stockholm University Publications: 74–82.

—— (1995*b*). 'Derivational constraints in phonology: evidence from loanwords and implications'. In A. Dainora, R. Hemphill, B. Luka, B. Need, and S. Pargman (eds.), *Proceedings of the 31st Chicago Linguistic Society Meeting*. Chicago: Chicago Linguistic Society: 360–74.

—— (1996). 'The inadequacy of faithfulness and filters in loanword adaptation'. In J. Durand and B. Laks (eds.), *Current Trends in Phonology: Models and Methods*. Salford: Salford Press: 509–34.

—— and LACHARITÉ, D. (1997). 'Preservation and minimality in loanword adaptation'. *Journal of Linguistics*, 33/1: 379–430.

—— and PRUNET, J.-F. (2000). 'Nasal vowels as two segments: evidence from borrowings'. *Language*, 26: 324–57.

—— —— (1998). 'Unpacking nasal vowels: a cross-linguistic survey'. *Phonological Studies*, 1: 211–18.

—— McCLISH, I., MACOIR, J. and BÉLAND, R. (2001). 'Traitement syllabiques et prédictions dans un cas d'aphasie progressive primaire'. *Langues et Linguistique*, 27: 59–94.

PASCAL, B. (1663). *Traités de l'équilibre des liqueurs et de la pesanteur de la masse de l'air concernant l'explication des causes de divers effets de la nature qui n'avaient point été bien connus jusques ici et particulièrement de ceux que l'on avait attribués à l'horreur du vide*. Reprinted in B. Pascal, *Œuvres complètes*. Paris: Seuil, 1963: 233–64.

PASSINGHAM, R. E. (1993). *The Frontal Lobes and Voluntary Action*. Oxford: Oxford University Press.

PAULESU, E., FRITH C. D., and FRACKOWIAK, R. S. J. (1993). 'The neural correlates of the verbal component of working memory'. *Nature*, 362: 342–5.

PENFIELD, W., and WELCH, K. (1951). 'The supplementary motor area of the cerebral cortex: a clinical and experimental study'. *Archives of Neurology and Psychiatry*, 66: 289–317.

PENG, S.-H. (2000). 'Lexical versus "phonological" representations of Mandarin sandhi tones'. In Broe and Pierrehumbert (2000: 152–67).

PENTLAND, A. P. (1989). 'Shape information from shading'. In J. C. Simon (ed.), *From Pixels to Features*. Amsterdam: Elsevier Science Publishers: 103–13.

PEPERKAMP, S. (1997). *Prosodic Words*. The Hague: Holland Academic Graphics.

—— and DUPOUX, E. (in press *a*). 'On infants' acquisition of phonological alternations'. In I. Lasser (ed.), *Proceedings of GALA*. Berlin: Peter Lang Verlag.

———— (in press *b*). 'Coping with phonological variation in early lexical acquisition'. In I. Lasser (ed.), *The Process of Language Acquisition*. Berlin: Peter Lang Verlag.

PERETZ, I., LUSSIER, I., and BÉLAND, R. (1996). 'The roles of phonological and orthographic code in word stem completion'. In A. Cutler and K. Otake (eds.), *Phonological Structure and Language Processing: Cross-linguistic Studies*. Amsterdam: Mouton de Gruyter: 217–26.

———— (1998). 'The differential role of syllabic structure in stem completion for French and English'. *European Journal of Cognitive Psychology*, 10: 75–112.

PERFETTI, C. A., and BELL, L. C. (1991). 'Phonemic activation during the first 40 ms of word identification: evidence from backward masking and priming'. *Journal of Memory and Language*, 30: 473–85.

PETITOT-COCORDA, J. (1985). *Les Catastrophes de la parole*. Collection Recherches Interdisciplinaires. Paris: Maloine.

PHILLIPS, C., MARANTZ, A., McGINNIS, M., PESETSKY, D., WEXLER, K., YELLIN, E., POEPPEL, D., ROBERTS, T., and ROWLEY, H. (1995). 'Brain mechanisms of speech perception: a preliminary report'. MIT Working Papers in Linguistics 26.

—— GOVINDARAJAN, K., MARANTZ, A., POEPPEL, D., ROBERTS, T., ROWLEY, H., and YELLIN, E. (1997). 'MEG studies of vowel processing in auditory cortex'. Poster paper presented at the Cognitive Neuroscience Society Meeting, Boston, 24 March 1997. Downloadable from http://www.ling.udel.edu/colin

PICARD, N., and STRICK, P. I. (1996). 'Motor areas and the medial wall: a review of their location and functional activation'. *Cerebral Cortex*, 6: 342–53.

PIERREHUMBERT, J. (1994). 'Knowledge of variation'. *Chicago Linguistic Society 30: Papers from the Parasession on Variation*. Chicago: Chicago Linguistic Society: 232–56.

—— and BECKMAN, M. E. (1988). *Japanese Tone Structure*. Cambridge, Mass.: MIT Press.

———— and LADD, D. R. (1996). 'Laboratory phonology'. In B. Laks and J. Durand (eds). *Current Trends in Phonology: Models and Methods*. Salford: ESRI: 535–48.

—— —— (2000). 'Conceptual foundations of phonology as laboratory science'. In N. Burton-Roberts, P. Carr, and G. Docherty (eds.), *Phonological Knowledge: Conceptual and Empirical Issues*. Oxford: Oxford University Press: 273–303.

PIERREHUMBERT, J., HAY, J., and BECKMAN, M. (MS). 'Speech perception, well-formedness and lexical frequency'. Paper presented at the Sixth Conference on Laboratory Phonology, University of York, July 1998. Submitted to *Papers in Laboratory Phonology*, vol. vi.

—— and NAIR, R. (1995). 'Word games and syllable structure'. *Language and Speech*, 38/1: 77–114.

PIKE, K., and PIKE, E. (1947). 'Immediate constituents of Mazateco syllables'. *International Journal of American Linguistics*, 13: 78–91.

PINAULT, G.-J. (1989). 'Travaux à partir du corpus védique'. In S. Auroux (ed.), *Histoire des idées linguistiques*, vol. i. Paris: Pierre Mardaga.

PING, L., and MacWHINNEY, B. (1996). 'Cryptotype, overgeneralization and competition: a connectionist model of the learning of English reversive prefixes'. *Connection Science*, 8/1.

PIQUEMAL, M., SCHWARTZ, J. L., BERTHOMMIER, F., LALLOUACHE, T., and ESCUDIER, P. (1996). 'Détection et localisation auditive d'explosions consonantiques dans des séquences VCV bruitées'. *Actes des XXIèmes journées d'études sur la parole, Société Française d'Acoustique*: 143–6.

PITERMANN, M., and SCHOENTGEN, J. (1996). 'Dependence on speaking rate and contrastive stress of vowel formants and vowel formant targets'. *4th Speech Production Seminar, 1st ESCA Tutorial and Research Workshop on Speech Production Modeling: From Control Strategies to Acoustics*, 21–4 May 1996, Autrans: 17–20.

PITT, M. (1998). 'Phonological processes and the perception of phonotactically illegal consonant clusters'. *Perception and Psychophysics*, 60: 941–51.

—— SMITH, K. L., and KLEIN, J. M. (1998). 'Syllabic effects in word processing: evidence from the structural induction paradigm'. *Journal of Experimental Psychology: Human Perception and Performance*, 24: 1596–611.

PLOMP, R. (1970). 'Timbre as a multidimensional attribute of complex tones'. In R. Plomp and G. F. Smoorenburg (eds.), *Frequency Analysis and Periodicity Detection in Hearing*. Leiden: Sijthoff: 397–414.

POECK, K., DE BLESER, R., and GRAF VON KEYSERLINGK, D. (1984). 'Neurolinguistic status and localization of lesion in aphasic patients with exclusively consonant-vowel recurring utterances'. *Brain*, 107: 199–217.

POEPPEL, D. (1996a). 'A critical review of PET studies of phonological processing'. *Brain and Language*, 55: 317–51.

—— (1996b). 'Some remaining questions about studying phonological processing with PET: response to Demonet, Fiez, Paulesu, Petersen, and Zatorre (1996)'. *Brain and Language*, 55: 380–5.

POGGIO, T. (1984). 'Low-level vision as inverse optics'. *Symposium on Computational Model of Hearing and Vision (Tallinn, USSR)*: 123–7.

POLIVANOV, E. (1974). 'The subjective nature of the perceptions of language sounds'. In E. Polivanov, *Selected Works: Articles on General Linguistics*, compiled A. Leont'ev. The Hague: Mouton: 223–37.

POLKA, L. (1991). 'Cross-language speech perception in adults: phonemic, phonetic and acoustic contributions'. *Journal of the Acoustical Society of America*, 89: 2961–77.

—— and WERKER, J. (1994). 'Developmental changes in perception of non-native vowel contrasts'. *Journal of Experimental Psychology: Human Perception and Performance*, 20: 421–35.

POLS, L. C. W. (1975). 'Analysis and synthesis of speech using a broad-band spectral representation'. In G. Fant and M. A. A. Tatham (eds.), *Auditory Analysis and Perception of Speech*. London: Academic: 23–36.

POSNER, M. I., and RAICHLE, M. E. (1994). *Images of Mind*. New York: Scientific American Library.

POSTAL, P. (1968). *Aspects of Phonological Theory*. New York: Harper and Row.

PRASADA, S., and PINKER, S. (1993). 'Generalisation of regular and irregular morphological patterns'. *Language and Cognitive Processes*, 8: 1–56.

PRICE, C. J. (1998). 'The functional anatomy of word comprehension and production'. *Trends in Cognitive Sciences*, 2/8: 281–8.

PRIDGEN, S., COLLINS, J., and FOX, P. (1999). 'Chronometric characterization of the effects of TMS on SMA during cued movement'. *NeuroImage*, 9/6: poster no. 487.

PRINCE, A., and SMOLENSKY, P. (1993). *Optimality Theory: Constraint Interaction in Generative Grammar*. Technical Report No. 2, Rutgers University Center for Cognitive Science. Piscataway, NJ: Rutgers University.

—— —— (to appear). *Optimality Theory*. Cambridge: MIT Press.

PULGRAM, E. (1970). *Syllable, Word, Nexus, Cursus*. The Hague: Mouton.

PULLEYBLANK, D. (1986). *Tone in Lexical Phonology*. Dordrecht: D. Reidel.

RAHIM M. G. (1994). *Artificial Neural Nets for Speech Analysis/Synthesis*. London: Chapman and Hall.

RAND, D., and SANKOFF, D. (1988). *GoldVarb: A Variable Rule Application for the Macintosh*. Montreal: Centre des Recherches Mathématiques, Université de Montréal.

RÉE, J. (1999). *I See a Voice*. London: Harper and Collins.

REED, C. M., DURLACH, N. I., and BRAIDA, L. D. (1982). 'Research on tactile communication of speech: a review'. *American Speech, Language and Hearing Association (ASHA)*, Mono 20: 1–23.

—— DOHERTY, M. J., BRAIDA, L. D., and DURLACH, N. I. (1982a). 'Analytic study of the Tadoma method: further experiments with inexperienced observers'. *Journal of Speech and Hearing Research*, 25: 216–23.

—— DURLACH, N. I., BRAIDA, L. D., and SCHULTZ, M. C. (1982b). 'Analytic study of the Tadoma method: identification of consonants and vowels by an experienced Tadoma user'. *Journal of Speech and Hearing Research*, 25: 108–16.

—— RABINOWITZ, W. M., DURLACH, N. I., DELHORNE, L. A., BRAIDA, L. D.,

PEMBERTON, J. C., MULCAHEY, B. D., and WASHINGTON, D. L. (1992). 'Analytic study of the Tadoma method: improving performance through the use of supplementary tactual displays'. *Journal of Speech and Hearing Research*, 35: 450–65.

REED, L. J., BULLMORE, E. T., WEBSTER, P. M., WILLIAMS, S. C. R., SIMMONS, A., ANDREW, C., BRAMMER, M. J., CHECKLEY, S. A., and GRASBY, P. (1997). 'Dopaminergic modulation of supplementary motor area activation by two "willed action" tasks: a functional magnetic resonance imaging study'. *NeuroImage*, 9/6: poster no. 394.

REISBERG, D., McLEAN, J., and GOLDFIELD, A. (1987). 'Easy to hear but hard to understand: a lipreading advantage with intact auditory stimuli'. In B. Dodd and R. Campbell (eds.), *Hearing by Eye: The Psychology of Lipreading*. London: Lawrence Erlbaum Associates: 97–113.

REMEZ, R. E. (1996). 'Perceptual organization of speech in one and several modalities: common functions, common resources'. *Proceedings of the International Conference on Spoken Language Processing 96*, Philadelphia: 1660–3.

—— RUBIN, P. E., PISONI, D. P., and CARRELL, T. D. (1981). 'Speech perception without traditional speech cues'. *Science*, 212: 947–50.

RENNISON, J. R. (1995). 'Wann ist ein Merkmal kein Merkmal? Inhaltliche Aspekte phonologischer Strukturen in der Rektionsphonologie (Government Phonology)'. MS. University of Vienna.

REPP, B. H. (1983). 'Categorical perception: issues, methods, findings'. In N. J. Lass (ed.), *Speech and Language: Advances in Basic Research and Practice*, vol. x. New York: Academic Press: 243–335.

RICE, K. (1987). 'On defining the intonation phrase: evidence from Slave'. *Phonology Yearbook*, 4: 37–59.

RIETVELD, A. (1980). 'Word boundaries in the French language'. *Language and Speech*, 23: 289–96.

RIZZOLATTI, G., FADIGA, L., GALLESE, V., and FOGASSI, L. (1996a). 'Premotor cortex and the recognition of motor actions'. *Cognitive Brain Research*, 3: 131–41.

—— MATELLI, M., BETTINARDI, V., PAULESU, E., PERANI, D., and FAZIO, F. (1996b). 'Localisation of grasp representations in humans by PET: 1. Observation versus execution'. *Experimental Brain Research*, 111: 246–52.

ROACH, P. (2000). *English Phonetics and Phonology*. 3rd edn. Cambridge: Cambridge University Press.

—— and HARTMAN, J. (eds.) (1997). Daniel Jones' *English Pronouncing Dictionary*. 15th edn. Cambridge: Cambridge University Press.

ROBERT-RIBES, J. (1995). 'Modèles d'intégration audiovisuelle de signaux linguistiques: de la perception humaine à la reconnaissance automatique des voyelles'. Ph.D. dissertation, Institut National Polytechnique de Grenoble.

—— SCHWARTZ, J. L., and ESCUDIER, P. (1995). 'A comparison of models for fusion of the auditory and visual sensors in speech perception'. *Artificial Intelligence Review Journal*, 9: 323–46.

————— LALLOUACHE, T., and ESCUDIER, P. (1998). 'Complementarity and synergy in bimodal speech: auditory, visual and audiovisual identification of French oral vowels in noise'. *Journal of the Acoustical Society of America*, 103: 3677–89.

ROBINS, R. H. (1990). *A Short History of Linguistics*. 3rd edn. London: Longman.

ROCA, I. M. (1994). *Phonological Theory*. London: Routledge.

——— (ed.) (1997). *Derivations and Constraints in Phonology*. Oxford: Clarendon Press.

ROMANI, C. (1992). 'The representation of prosodic and syllabic structure in speech production.' Doctoral dissertation, Johns Hopkins University.

ROMANI, G. L., WILLIAMSON, S. J., KAUFMAN, L., and BRENNER, D. (1982). 'Characterization of the human auditory cortex by the neuromagnetic method'. *Experimental Brain Research*, 47: 38–393.

ROSEN, S., FOURCIN, A. J., and MOORE, B. (1981). 'Voice pitch as an aid to lipreading'. *Nature*, 291: 0–152.

ROSENBAUM, D. A., WEBER, R. J., HAZELETT, W. M., and VAN HINDORFF, V. (1986). 'The parameter remapping effect in human performance: evidence from tongue twisters and finger fumblers'. *Journal of Memory and Language*, 25: 710–25.

ROSENBLUM, L. D., and SALDANA, H. M. (1996). 'An audio-visual test of kinematic primitives for visual speech perception'. *Journal of Experimental Psychology: Human Perception and Performance*, 22: 8–331.

ROSENTHAL, D. F., and OKUNO, H. G. (eds.) (1998). *Computational Auditory Scene Analysis*. Mahwah, NJ: Lawrence Erlbaum Associates.

ROSH-HEIDER, E. (1972). 'Universals in color naming and memory'. *Journal of Experimental Psychology*, 93: 10–20.

RUMELHART, D., McCLELLAND, J., and the PDP Research Group (eds.) (1986). *Parallel Distributed Processing: Exploration in the Micro-Structure of Cognition*. 2 vols, Cambridge, Mass.: Bradford MIT Press.

SACKS, O. (1989). *Seeing Voices*. Berkeley and Los Angeles: University of California Press.

SAFFRAN, J. R., ASLIN, R. N., and NEWPORT, E. L. (1996). 'Statistical learning by 8-month-olds'. *Science*, 274: 1926–8.

SAGEY, E. (1986). 'The Representations of Features and Relations in Non-linear Phonology'. PhD. dissertation, MIT. (Published New York: Garland Publishing Co., 1990.)

SAGISAKA, Y., CAMPBELL, N., and HIGUCHI, N. (eds.) (1997). *Computing Prosody*. Berlin: Springer-Verlag.

SANGUINETI, V., LABOISSIÈRE, R., and OSTRY, D. J. (1998). 'A dynamic biomechanical model for neural control of speech production'. *Journal of the Acoustical Society of America*, 103/3: 1615–27.

SAPIR, E. (1921). *Language*. New York: Harcourt Brace Jovanovich.

——— (1933). 'La Réalité psychologique des phonèmes'. *Journal de psychologie normale et pathologique*, 30: 247–65. English translation 'The psychological reality of phonemes', in D. G. Mandelbaum, *Edward Sapir: Selected Writings in*

Language, Culture and Personality. Berkeley and Los Angeles: University of California Press, 1985: 46–60.

SAUSSURE, F. DE (1976). *Cours de linguistique générale* (1915), ed. T. de Mauro. Paris: Payot.

——(1993). *Troisième cours de linguistique générale* (1910–11), *d'après les cahiers d'Émile Constantin. Saussure's Third Course of General Lectures on General Linguistics* (1910–11). *From the notebooks of Émile Constantin,* ed. Eisuke Komatsu and Roy Harris. Oxford: Pergamon Press.

SAVARIAUX, C., PERRIER, P., and ORLIAGUET, J. P. (1995). 'Compensation strategies for the perturbation of the rounded vowel [u] using a lip-tube: a study of the control space in speech production'. *Journal of the Acoustical Society of America,* 98: 2428–42.

—— —— —— and SCHWARTZ, J. L. (1999). 'The effects of a lip-tube perturbation through perceptual analysis'. *Journal of the Acoustical Society of America,* 106: 381–93.

SCHANE, S. A. (1968). *French Phonology and Morphology.* Cambridge, Mass.: MIT Press.

—— ——(1971). 'The phoneme revisited'. *Language,* 47: 503–21.

——(1984). 'The fundamentals of particle phonology'. *Phonology Yearbook,* 1: 129–55.

SCHEER, T. (1998). 'La structure interne des consonnes'. In P. Sauzet (ed.), *Langues et grammaire II–III: phonologie.* Paris: Université Paris 8: 140–72.

SCHILLER, N. O. (1998*a*) *The Effect of Visually Masked Syllable Primes on Word Production in English.* Poster given at the 39th Annual Meeting of the Psychonomic Society, Dallas (Texas).

——(1998*b*). 'The effect of visually masked syllable primes on the naming latencies of words and pictures'. *Journal of Memory and Language,* 39: 484–507.

SCHÜTZ, A. (1985). *The Fijian Language.* Honolulu: University of Hawaii Press.

SCHWARTZ, J. L., and ESCUDIER, P. (1987). 'Does the human auditory system include large scale spectral integration?' In M. E. H. Schouten (ed.), *The Psychophysics of Speech Perception.* Nato Asi Series. Dordrecht: Martinus Nijhoff Publishers: 284–92.

—— ——(1989). 'A strong evidence for the existence of a large scale integrated spectral representation in vowel perception'. *Speech Communication,* 8: 235–59.

—— ROBERT-RIBES, J., and ESCUDIER, P. (1998). 'Ten years after Summerfield . . . a taxonomy of models for audiovisual fusion in speech perception'. In R. Campbell, B. Dodd, and D. Burnham (eds.), *Hearing by Eye,* ii: *Perspectives and Directions in Research on Audiovisual Aspects of Language Processing.* Hove: Psychology Press: 85–108.

—— ARROUAS, Y., BEAUTEMPS, D., and ESCUDIER, P. (1992). 'Auditory analysis of speech gestures'. In M. E. H. Schouten (ed.), *The Auditory Processing of Speech: From Sounds to Words.* Speech Research 10. Berlin: Mouton de Gruyter: 239–52.

—— BEAUTEMPS, D., ABRY, C., and ESCUDIER, P. (1993). 'Interindividual and cross-linguistic strategies for the production of the [i] vs [y] contrast'. *Journal of Phonetics*, 21: 411–25.

—— Boë, L.-J., Vallée, N., and Abry, C. (1997*a*). 'Major trends in vowel system inventories'. *Journal of Phonetics*, 25: 233–54.

—— —— —— —— (1997*b*). 'The dispersion-focalization theory of vowel systems'. *Journal of Phonetics*, 25: 255–86.

Scobbie, J. M., Coleman, J. S., and Bird, S. (1996). 'Key aspects of declarative phonology'. In Durand and Laks (1996*a*: 685–709).

Sebastian-Gallés, N., Dupoux, E., Segui, J., and Mehler, J. (1992). 'Contrasting syllabic effects in Catalan and Spanish'. *Journal of Memory and Language*, 31: 18–32.

Ségéral, P., and Scheer, T. (1999). 'The coda mirror'. Paper presented at the conference 'The Strong Position: Lenition and Fortition', Nice, June 1999.

Segui, J. (1984). 'The syllable: a basic perceptual unit in speech perception?' In H. Bouma and D. G. Bouwhuis (eds.), *Attention and Performance*, x: *Control of Language Processes*. Hillsdale, NJ: Erlbaum: 165–81.

—— Dupoux, E., and Mehler, J. (1990). 'The role of the syllable in speech segmentation, phoneme identification, and lexical access'. In G. T. M. Altmann (ed.), *Cognitive Models of Speech Processing: Psycholinguistic and Computational Perspectives*. Cambridge, Mass.: MIT Press.

—— Frauenfelder, U. H., and Mehler, J. (1981). 'Phoneme monitoring, syllable monitoring and lexical access'. *British Journal of Psychology*, 72: 471–7.

Selkirk, E. O. (1982). 'The syllable'. In H. van der Hulst and N. Smith (eds.), *The Structure of Phonological Representations*, part 2. Dordrecht: Foris: 337–464.

Sevald, C. A., and Dell, G. S. (1994). 'The sequential cueing effect in speech production'. *Cognition*, 53: 91–127.

—— —— and Cole, J. S. (1995). 'Syllable structure in speech production: are syllables chunks or schemas?' *Journal of Memory and Language*, 34: 807–20.

Shady, M., Jusczyk, P., and Gerken, L. (1998). 'Infants' sensitivity to function morphemes'. Paper presented at the 23rd Annual Boston University Conference on Language Development, Boston.

Shattuck-Huffnagel, S. (1987). 'The role of word-onset consonants in speech production planning: new evidence from speech error patterns'. In E. Keller and M. Gopnik (eds.), *Motor and Sensory Processes of Language*. Hillsdale, NJ: Erlbaum: 17–51.

Shi, R. (1995). 'Perceptual Correlates of Content Words and Function Words in Early Language Input'. Ph.D. dissertation, Brown University.

—— Morgan, J., and Allopenna, P. (1998). 'Phonological and acoustic bases for earliest grammatical category assignment: a cross-linguistic perspective'. *Journal of Child Language*, 25: 169–201.

Shillcock, R. (1990). 'Lexical hypotheses in continuous speech'. In G. T. M. Altmann (ed.), *Cognitive Models of Speech Processing*. Cambridge, Mass.: MIT Press: 24–49.

SLEDD, J. H. (1966). 'Breaking, umlaut and the southern drawl'. *Language*, 42: 18–41.

SMITH, B. L., BROWN-SWEENEY, S., and STOEL-GAMMON, C. (1989). 'A quantitative analysis of reduplicated and variegated babbling'. *First Language*, 9: 175–90.

SMITH, N., and TSIMPLI, I.-M. (1995). *The Mind of a Savant: Language Learning and Modularity*. Oxford: Basil Blackwell.

SMOLENSKY, P. (1988). 'On the proper treatment of connectionism'. *Brain and Behavioral Sciences*, 11: 1–74.

SNEATH, P. H. A., and SOKAL, R. R. (1973). *Numerical Taxonomy*. San Francisco: W. H. Freeman and Co.

STAMPE, D. (1973). 'A Dissertation on Natural Phonology'. Ph.D. dissertation, University of Chicago.

STAPPERS, L. (1973). *Esquisse de la langue mituku*. Tervuren: Musée Royal de l'Afrique Centrale.

STERIADE, D. (1987). 'Redundant values'. In A. Bosch, B. Need, and E. Schiller (eds.), *Papers from the Parasession on Autosegmental and Metrical Phonology*. Chicago: Chicago Linguistics Society: 339–62.

STERNBERG, S., MONSELL, S., KNOLL, R. L., and WRIGHT, C. E (1978). 'The latency and duration of rapid movement sequences: comparisons of speech and type-writing'. In G. E. Stelmach (ed.), *Information Processing in Motor Control and Learning*. London: Academic Press: 117–52.

STEVENS, K. N. (1972). 'The quantal nature of speech: evidence from articulatory-acoustic data'. In E. E. Davis, Jr., and P. B. Denes (eds.), *Human Communication: A Unified View*. New York: McGraw-Hill: 51–66.

—— (1989). 'On the quantal nature of speech'. *Journal of Phonetics*, 17: 3–45.

—— (1999). *Acoustic Phonetics*. Cambridge, Mass.: MIT Press.

STEVICK, E. (1969). 'Tone in Bantu'. *International Journal of American Linguistics*, 35: 330–41.

STOEL-GAMMON, C. (1988). 'Prelinguistic vocalizations of hearing-impaired and normally hearing subjects: a comparison of consonantal inventories'. *Journal of Speech and Hearing Disorders*, 53: 302–15.

STRANGE, W. (1989). 'Dynamic aspects of coarticulated vowels spoken in sentence context'. *Journal of the Acoustical Society of America*, 85: 2135–53.

—— VERBRUGGE, R. R., SHANKWEILER, D. P., and EDMAN, T. R. (1976). 'Consonant environment specifies vowel identity'. *Journal of the Acoustical Society of America*, 60: 213–22.

SUMBY, W. H., and POLLACK, I. (1954). 'Visual contribution to speech intelligibility in noise'. *Journal of the Acoustical Society of America*, 26: 212–15.

SUMMERFIELD, Q. (1987). 'Some preliminaries to a comprehensive account of audio-visual speech perception'. In B. Dodd and R. Campbell (eds.), *Hearing by Eye: the Psychology of Lipreading*. London: Lawrence Erlbaum Associates: 3–51.

—— and MCGRATH, M. (1984). 'Detection and resolution of audio-visual incompatibility in the perception of vowels'. *Quarterly Journal of Experimental Psychology: Human Experimental Psychology*, 36: 51–74.

SUPPES, P. (1972). 'Probabilistic grammars for natural languages'. In D. Davidson and G. Harman (eds.), *Semantics of Natural Language*. Dordrecht: D. Reidel: 741–62.

SUSSMAN, H. M., HOEMECKE, K., and AHMED, F. (1993). 'A cross-linguistic investigation of locus equations as a relationally invariant descriptor for place of articulation'. *Journal of the Acoustical Society of America*, 94: 1256–68.

—— McCAFFREY, H. A., and MATTHEWS, S. A. (1991). 'An investigation of locus equations as a source of relational invariance for stop place categorization'. *Journal of the Acoustical Society of America*, 90: 1309–25.

SZIGETVÁRI, P. (1994). 'The Special Nature of Coronal Consonants'. University degree dissertation, Eötvös Loránd University.

TALAIRACH, J., and TOURNOUX, P. (1988). *Co-planar Stereotaxic Atlas of the Human Brain*. New York: Thieme Medical Publications.

TANJI, J. (1996). 'New concepts of the supplementary motor area'. *Current Opinion in Neurobiology*, 6: 782–7.

TEISSIER, P., ROBERT-RIBES, J., SCHWARTZ, J. L., and GUÉRIN-DUGUÉ, A. (1999). 'Comparing models for audiovisual fusion in a noisy-vowel recognition task'. *IEEE Transactions Speech and Audio Processing* (in press).

TERRELL, T. (1986). 'La desaparición de /s/ postnuclear a nivel léxico en el habla dominicana'. In R. A. Núñez Cedeño, I. P. Urdaneta, and J. Guitart (eds.), *Estudios sobre la fonología del español del Caribe*. Ediciones La Casa de Bello: 117–34.

THIERRY, G., DOYON, B., and DÉMONET, J.-F. (1998). 'ERP mapping in phonological and lexical semantic monitoring tasks: a study complementing previous PET results'. *NeuroImage*, 8: 391–408.

TREIMAN, R. (1983). 'The structure of spoken syllables: evidence from novel word games'. *Cognition*, 15: 49–74.

—— and DANIS, C. (1988). 'Syllabification of intervocalic consonants'. *Journal of Memory and Language*, 27: 87–104.

—— STRAUB, K., and LAVERY, P. (1994). 'Syllabification of bisyllabic nonwords: evidence from short-term memory errors'. *Language and Speech*, 37: 45–60.

—— and ZUKOWSKI, A. (1990). 'Toward an understanding of English syllabification'. *Journal of Memory and Language*, 29: 66–85.

—— FOWLER, C. A., GROSS, J., BERCH, D., and WEATHERSTON, S. (1995). 'Syllable structure or word structure? Evidence for onset and rime units with disyllabic and trisyllabic stimuli'. *Journal of Memory and Language*, 34: 132–55.

TRUBETZKOY, N. S. (1939). *Grundzüge der phonologie*. Travaux du Cercle Linguistique de Prague 7. Prague: Cercle Linguistique de Prague. French translation, *Principes de phonologie*. Paris: Klincksiek, 1964.

TYLER, L. K., and MARSLEN-WILSON, W. (1977). 'The on-line effects of semantic context on syntactic processing'. *Journal of Verbal Learning and Verbal Behavior*, 16: 683–92.

References

321

ULLMAN, S. (1979). *The Interpretation of Visual Motion*. Cambridge, Mass.: MIT Press.

ULRICH, C. H. (1998). 'Loanword adaptation in Lama: testing the TCSR model'. *Journal of Linguistics*, 42/4: 415–63. To appear.

VAGO, R. (1980). *The Sound Pattern of Hungarian*. Washington: Georgetown University Press.

VALLÉE, N., SCHWARTZ, J. L., and ESCUDIER, P. (1999). 'Phase spaces of vowel systems: a typology in the light of the Dispersion-Focalisation Theory (DFT)'. *Proceedings of the XIVth International Congress of Phonetic Sciences*, 1: 333–6.

VANDEBERGHE, R., PRICE, C., WISE, R., JOSEPHS, O., and FRACKOWIAK, R. S. J. (1996). 'Functional anatomy of common semantic systems for words and pictures'. *Nature*, 383: 254–6.

VAN LANCKER, D. (1987). 'Nonpropositional speech: neurolinguistic studies'. In A. W. Ellis (ed.), *Progress in the Psychology of Language*, vol. iii. Hillsdale, NJ: Lawrence Erlbaum.

VAN SON, R. J. J. H. (1993). 'Vowel perception: a closer look at the literature'. *Proceedings of the Institute of Phonetic Sciences*. Amsterdam: University of Amsterdam, 17: 33–64.

VENNEMANN, T. (1972). 'On the theory of syllabic phonology'. *Linguistische Berichte*, 18: 1–18.

—— (1973). 'Phonological concreteness in natural generative phonology'. In R. Shuy and C. J. Bailey (eds.), *Toward Tomorrow's Linguistics*. Washington: Georgetown University Press.

VIHMAN, M. M. (1992). 'Early syllables and the construction of phonology'. In C. A. Ferguson, L. Menn, and C. Stoel-Gammon (eds.), *Phonological Development: Models, Research, Implications*. Toronto: York Press: 393–422.

—— MACKEN, M. A., MILLER, R., SIMMONS, H., and MILLER, J. (1985). 'From babbling to speech: a re-assessment of the continuity issue'. *Language*, 61: 397–445.

VILAIN, A., ABRY, C., BADIN, P., and BROSDA, S. (1999). 'From idiosyncratic pure frames to variegated babbling: evidence from articulatory modelling'. *International Congress of Phonetic Sciences*. San Francisco: 2497–500.

VITEVICH, M. S., and LUCE, P. A. (1998). 'When words compete: levels of processing in perception of spoken words'. *Psychological Science*, 9/4: 325–9.

—— —— CHARLES-LUCE, J., and KEMMERER, D. (1997). 'Phonotactics and syllable stress: implications for the processing of spoken nonsense words'. *Language and Speech*, 40: 47–62.

VIVIANI, P., and SCHNEIDER, R. (1991). 'A developmental study of the relation between geometry and kinematics in drawing movements'. *Journal of Experimental Psychology: Human Perception and Performance*, 17: 198–218.

—— and STUCCHI, N. (1992). 'Biological movements look uniform: evidence of motor-perceptual interactions'. *Journal of Experimental Psychology: Human Perception and Performance*, 18: 603–23.

VOGEL, I. (1982). *La sillaba come unità fonologica*. Bologna: Zanichelli.

——(1988). 'Prosodic constituents in Hungarian'. In P. M. Bertinetto and M. Loporcaro (eds.), *Certamen phonologicum: Papers from the 1987 Cortona Phonology Meeting*. Tornino: Rosenberg and Sellier: 231–50.

WALLESH, C.-W. (1990). 'Repetitive verbal behaviour: functional and neurological considerations'. *Aphasiology*, 4: 133–54.

WARBURTON, E., PRICE, C. J., SWINBURN, K., and WISE, R. J. S. (1999). 'Mechanisms of recovery from aphasia: evidence from positron emission tomography studies'. *Journal of Neurology, Neurosurgery and Psychiatry*, 66: 155–61.

WELLS, J. C. (1990). *Longman Pronunciation Dictionary*. Harlow: Longman.

WERKER, J., and TEES, R. (1984*a*). 'Cross language speech perception: evidence for perceptual reorganization during the first year of life'. *Infant Behavior and Development*, 7: 49–63.

—— ——(1984*b*). 'Phonemic and phonetic factors in adult cross-language speech perception'. *Journal of the Acoustical Society of America*, 75: 1866–78.

WEST, P. (1997). 'Perception of distributed co-articulatory properties of English /l/ and /ɹ/'. *Journal of Phonetics*, 27: 405–26.

WHEELDON, L. R., and LEVELT, W. J. M. (1995). 'Monitoring the time course of phonological encoding'. *Journal of Memory and Language*, 34: 311–34.

WIESE, R. (1996). *The Phonology of German*. Oxford: Oxford University Press.

WILLIAMS, B. (1982). 'The problem of stress in Welsh'. *Cambridge Papers in Phonetics and Experimental Linguistics* 1. Department of Linguistics, University of Cambridge.

WILLIAMS, G. (1998). 'The Phonological Basis of Speech Recognition'. Ph.D. dissertation, SOAS, University of London.

WOLPERT, D. M., MIALL, R. C., and KAWATO, M. (1998). 'Internal models in the cerebellum'. *Trends in Cognitive Sciences*, 2/9: 338–47.

WOZNIAK, V. D., and JACKSON, P. L. (1979). 'Visual vowel and diphthong perception from two horizontal viewing angles'. *Journal of Speech and Hearing Research*, 22: 355–65.

WRIGHT, C. (1979). 'Duration differences between rare and common words and their implications for the interpretation of word frequency effects'. *Memory and Cognition*, 7: 411–19.

WRIGHT, R. (MS). 'Factors of lexical competition in vowel articulation'. Paper presented at the Sixth Conference on Laboratory Phonology, University of York, July 1998. Submitted to *Papers in Laboratory Phonology*, vol. vi.

WU, Z. L., SCHWARTZ, J. L., and ESCUDIER, P. (1996). 'Physiologically plausible modules for the detection of articulatory-acoustic events'. In B. Ainsworth (ed.), *Advances in Speech, Hearing and Language Processing*, iii: Cochlear Nucleus. JAI Press: 479–95.

WYNN, K. (1990). 'Children's understanding of counting'. *Cognition*, 36: 155–93.

YAMADA, J. (1990). *Laura: A Case for the Modularity of Language*. Cambridge, Mass.: MIT Press.

YIP, M. (1993). 'Cantonese loanword phonology and Optimality Theory'. *Journal of East Asian Linguistics*, 2: 261–91.

YOUNG, S. J. (1996). 'A review of large-vocabulary continuous speech recognition'. *IEEE Signal Processing Magazine*, Sept.: 45–57.

ZATORRE, R. J., MEYER, E., GJEDDE, A., and EVANS, A. C. (1996). 'PET studies of phonetic processing of speech: review, replication, and reanalysis'. *Cerebral Cortex*, 6 (Jan./Feb.): 21–30.

ZIEGLER, W., KILIAN, B., and DEGER, K. (1997). 'The role of the left mesial frontal cortex in fluent speech: evidence from a case of left supplementary motor area hemorrhage'. *Neuropsychologia*, 35/9: 1197–208.

ZWITSERLOOD, P., SCHRIEFERS, H., LAHIRI, A., and VAN DONSELAAR, W. (1993). 'The role of syllables in the perception of spoken Dutch'. *Journal of Experimental Psychology: Learning, Memory and Cognition*, 19: 260–71.

Subject Index

distinctive feature 22–5, 115–18,
  131–4
distributed 42
dominant recoding (DR) 266–7
downstep 82, 88
Dynamic Linear Model (DLM) 41

ElectroEncephaloGraphic (EEG)
  recording 228, 247
elements (in Government Phonology)
  4, 54, 132
empty-headed expression 135–6
Event Related Potentials (ERPs) 7,
  247, 251–3

feet 97, 105–8
focal points 276–7
focalization 277
formal neurone 41–2
formant 133, 141, 144, 145, 257,
  259, 273–7
frame/content theory 7, 79, 230–2,
  236, 241–2, 254
function-based model 245
functional Magnetic Resonance
  Imaging (fMRI) 246

generative phonology 23–36, 126,
  131
gesture recovery 262–5, 276
gesture shaping 258–9
global aphasia 230, 237
glossematics 16
government phonology 27, 31, 132

harmonic phonology 27
head(edness) 135–6, 147
headed expression 136
headless expression 135–6
Hidden Markov Models (HMM)
  143–4, 147

insertion 192, 198, 210–25
Interactive Bootstrapping 169, 177,
  184–90
International Phonetic Association
  (IPA) 13–45
invariance 139, 272

laboratory phonology 27, 38–40
language engineering 139
langue 16
legality principle 156
length 52–3, 78
level 25, 83–4, 89, 93, 152
lexical phonology 27, 93
linear predictive coding (LCR) 141
loanword 191–225
localization 227–8, 237–8, 246
log probability 107–8

MagnetoEncephaloGraphic (MEG)
  recording 247
Mahalanobis distance 148–9
Marked(ness) 29, 64–70, 192, 196,
  203–5, 208, 210–25
Marker:
  Object 83
  Subject 83
  Tense 83
masked priming technique 153, 163
mathematical taxonomy 145
Meeussen's rule 89, 91
metrical constraint 200, 204, 210,
  219
metrical phonology 27, 29, 94
minimal combination (of elements)
  135
modeller 255
mora 80, 94, 102, 109–10, 166
moraic theory 27
motor recoding (MR) 266–7
motor theory 112–13, 134, 255–6,
  258, 271
multimodal fusion 265–7

natural generative phonology 27–8
natural phonology 27–9
network (neural) 40–4, 94, 126–30,
  175, 227
neuroimaging 245–53
neurone 41–4
neurophysiology 43, 246, 256–7
No Line Crossing 62–3, 77, 94
no motion manifold 229
non-linear phonology 27
N-tier 3, 63

Index of Names